SPOTLIGHT ACT

25 LESSONS ILLUMINATE THE MOST FREQUENTLY TESTED TOPICS

Laneshia Thomas
Mary Wink

KAPLAN)

PUBLISHING

New York

Vice President and Publisher: Maureen McMahon
Editorial Director: Jennifer Farthing
Development Editors: Anne Kemper and Sheryl Gordon
Production Editor: Julio Espin
Production Designer: Ivelisse Robles and Carly Schnur
Cover Designer: Carly Schnur

Published by Kaplan Publishing, a division of Kaplan, Inc.
1 Liberty Plaza, 24th Floor
New York, NY 10006

Printed in the United States of America

September 2007
07 08 09 10 9 8 7 6 5 4 3 2 1

ISBN-13: 978-1-4277-5223-9

TABLE OF CONTENTS

HOW TO
USE THIS BOOK

There's no one single way to use this book. We've designed it specifically to satisfy various learning styles and to address different concerns about the ACT. You'll notice the special ranking system in the Table of Contents and at the beginning of each lesson that rates the relative importance of three factors: Frequency, Difficulty, and the "Surprise Factor," or the chance that a relatively easy topic may catch you off guard with one or two surprisingly difficult questions. Using this ranking system, you can target your study plan to cover those topics that concern you the most.

You'll also notice a special set of colorful stickers at the back of the book that you can use to tag topics with different levels of importance. Use them to help you remember which topics to revisit (Learn Your Lines), or to call out topics you've mastered and never need to look at again (Bravo!!). The four sticker choices are:

1. Learn your lines
2. Understudy
3. Audition again
4. Bravo!!

Be creative and feel free to clutter up the book with these colorful sticker "notes." They are intended to give you a sense of direction and progress and to make studying a little less boring and a little more interactive.

LESSON CONTENT

In each lesson, you'll find a thorough explanation of the topic, tips on how to avoid common answer traps, rules and formulas for mastering the topic, sample questions with walk-through explanations, and a 10-item self-test quiz or sample essay topic.

Start with any section or any lesson—how you choose to organize your study plan is up to you. Start with the most difficult topics, or the most frequent, or the trickiest. It's important, though, to read the "ACT Basics" introductions before you begin the lesson content. This will give you the bird's-eye view of both the exam and each section within the exam and will be a useful foundation for mastering the most important content for each unique section of the ACT.

DON'T FORGET ABOUT MOBILE PREP
AND EXTRA PRACTICE ONLINE!

Practice doesn't end with the book. Spotlight ACT has a robust online companion that offers a diagnostic quiz, a practice test, sample essay prompts, and more. Since you're constantly on the move, this material is designed to let you practice almost anytime and anywhere. Access the online practice materials through kaptest.com/booksonline; make sure to have your book handy the first time you log on, because a prompt will ask you a password question that is answered only in the text.

Have fun formulating your ACT plan of attack and enjoy the creative freedom this book allows. We're confident that Spotlight ACT will give you the flexibility and the expertise you need to perform your very best on test day.

Ready?

Lights…camera…action!

KAPLAN

ACT BASICS

Before you begin the lessons, there are a few ACT basics you should know.

The ACT is a three-hour exam (three and a half hours if you take the optional Writing test) taken by high school juniors and seniors for admission to college. It is not an IQ test; it is a test of problem-solving skills—which means you can improve with practice and preparation. The exam is mostly multiple-choice, and it's divided into four subject tests: English, Math, Reading, and Science, as well as an optional Writing test.

The ACT sections are broken down like this:

Section	Length	Content	Type
1. English	45 minutes, 75 questions	grammar, punctuation, writing style	Multiple-choice
2. Math	60 minutes, 60 questions	pre-algebra, algebra, plane geometry, coordinate geometry, trigonometry	Multiple-choice
3. Reading	35 minutes, 40 questions	four reading passages—social studies, natural sciences, humanities, prose fiction	Multiple-choice
4. Science	35 minutes, 40 questions	figure interpretation, pattern analysis, scientific reasoning	Multiple-choice
5. Writing (optional)	30 minutes	One essay prompt	Student-written essay

ACT SCORING

When configuring your score, the test makers add up all of your correct answers on the ACT to get what they call a "raw score." They then, by way of their own formula, convert this raw score to a "scaled score."

The ACT scaled scores range from 1 to 36. Your score report for the ACT will contain many separate numbers—you will receive your main scaled score, technically called the "composite score." The composite score is the most important number—it is the average of your four major subject scores. You will also receive seven or eight subscores.

Here's the full battery of ACT scores you'll receive. Few people (except maybe you and your parents) will care about anything other than your composite score for college admissions, though some schools use subscores for course placement.

English Score (1–36)	Usage/Mechanics subscore (1–18); Rhetorical Skills subscore (1–18); (optional) Writing subscore (2–12)
Math Score (1–36)	Pre-algebra/Elementary Algebra subscore (1–18); Algebra/ Coordinate Geometry subscore (1–18); Plane Geometry/ Trigonometry subscore (1–18)
Reading Score (1–36)	Social Sciences/Sciences subscore (1–18); Arts/Literature subscore (1–18)
Science Score (1–36)	There are no subscores in Science.
(Optional) Combined English-Writing Score	Does not count towards your composite score

You should note that ACT scores are based only on your number of correct answers. This means that questions you leave blank and questions you answer incorrectly don't count. Unlike some standardized tests, the ACT has no "wrong answer penalty." That's why you should always guess on every ACT question you can't answer, even if you don't have time to read it. Though the questions vary enormously in difficulty, harder questions are worth exactly the same as easier ones. Therefore, it pays to guess on the really hard ones that might take a lot of your time and to spend your time answering as many easy questions correctly as you can.

IMPORTANT GROUND RULES

These are ACT rules you can use to your advantage. Knowing these rules will keep you from asking questions and wasting precious time and from committing minor errors that result in serious penalties.

- You are NOT allowed to jump back and forth between sections.
- You are NOT allowed to return to earlier sections to change answers.
- You are NOT allowed to spend more than the allotted time on any section.
- You CAN move around within a section.
- You CAN flip through your section at the beginning to see what types of questions are coming up.

That covers the ACT basics! Make sure to read about the details of each individual section—English, Math, Reading, Science, and Writing—in the section introductions.

ENGLISH

ENGLISH BASICS

The English test lasts 45 minutes and includes 75 questions. That works out to about 30 seconds per question. When it comes down to it, though, you should spend less time on easier questions and more on harder questions.

Almost all of the English questions follow a standard format. A word, phrase, or sentence in a passage is underlined. You're given four choices: to leave the underlined portion alone (NO CHANGE, which is always the first choice) or to replace it with one of three alternatives.

...Pike's Peak in southwestern Colorado is named <u>before</u> 37 <u>Zebulon Pike, an early explorer.</u> 37 He traveled through the area, exploring...	37. **A.** NO CHANGE **B.** before Zebulon Pike became an explorer. **C.** after Zebulon Pike, when **D.** after Zebulon Pike.

The best answer for Question 37 above is D. The other choices all have various problems: grammatical, stylistic, and logical. Only D makes the sentence sensible and correct. That's why it's the answer.

Note: You're not tested on spelling or vocabulary here, or even the rules of grammar. Rather, the ACT is designed to test your understanding of the conventions of English—punctuation, grammar, sentence structure—and of rhetorical skills. Rhetorical skills are strategic things like organizing the text and making sure it's styled clearly.

ACT ENGLISH QUESTION
BREAKDOWN

18 sentence structure questions
12 grammar and usage questions
12 strategy questions
12 style questions
11 organization questions
10 punctuation questions

● TO OMIT OR NOT TO OMIT

Some English questions offer, as one of the alternatives, the chance to omit the underlined portion completely, usually as the last of the four choices.

Later, Pike fell while valiantly

defending America in the War

of 1812. It goes without saying
      <u>   </u>
                32
that this took place after he
<u>   </u>
                32
discovered Pike's Peak. He
<u>   </u>
                32
actually died near York (now

called Toronto)...

32. F. NO CHANGE
    G. Clearly, this must have occurred subsequent to his discovering Pike's Peak.
    H. This was after he found Pike's Peak.
    J. OMIT the underlined portion.

In this case, J is correct. The idea really does "go without saying." For that reason, it shouldn't be stated. On recent ACTs, when OMIT has appeared as an answer choice, it's been correct more than half the time. (As you can see, the ACT makers aren't the only ones with a department of little statistician elves.) This doesn't mean you should always automatically select OMIT, however, because it's also been wrong almost half of the time.

● NONSTANDARD FORMAT QUESTIONS

Finally, some ACT English questions—usually about 10 per exam—don't follow this standard format. These items pose a question and offer four possible responses. In many cases, the responses are either YES or NO, with an explanation. Pay attention to the reasoning. Question 40 could have appeared in a nonstandard format as follows:

Later, Pike fell while valiantly defending America in the War of 1812. He actually died near York (now called Toronto)...

40. Suppose the author considered adding the following sentence at this point: "It goes without saying that this occurred after he discovered Pike's Peak." Given the overall purpose of the passage, would this sentence be appropriate?

F. No, because the sentence adds nothing to the meaning of the passage.

G. No, because the passage is not concerned with Pike's achievements.

H. Yes, because otherwise the sequence of events would be unclear.

J. Yes; though the sentence is not needed, the author recognizes this fact by using the phrase *it goes without saying*.

The correct answer for this question is F. Though G correctly states that the sentence doesn't belong in the passage, it offers a pretty inappropriate reason; the passage is concerned with Pike's achievements. Choices H and J are wrong because they recommend including a sentence that is clearly redundant.

Now that you're familiar with the ACT English question format, turn the page to learn about the types of questions you will see on Test Day.

Sentence Sense

DIFFICULTY: ★ ★

FREQUENCY: ★ ★ ★ ★

SURPRISE FACTOR: ★ ★ ★

• INTRODUCTION TO SENTENCE SENSE QUESTIONS

Sentence Sense questions test your understanding of how words are combined to form clear and correct sentences. You probably remember learning the definition: a sentence is a group of words that contains a subject and a verb and forms a complete thought. In this lesson, you'll refine your understanding of the definition so that you can easily recognize complete sentences. Many of the concepts in this lesson are essential to understanding the rules for punctuation, which you can find in Lesson 2.

Characteristics of Sentence Sense Questions

Before we look at ACT questions, let's consider some sentence structure errors and go over some terminology that will help you identify these errors. A clause is a group of words that contains both a subject and a verb. There are two kinds of clauses: dependent and independent. A dependent clause, even though it has a subject and a verb, cannot stand alone as a sentence. A dependent clause doesn't express a complete thought, so you can think of it as "depending" on additional information to be part of a complete sentence. An independent clause is defined as one that can stand alone as a complete sentence. Here's an example in ACT format:

> Many sports and extracurricular activities are offered at the high school. Toni enjoys running, she hopes to join the cross-country team.

In this example, "Toni enjoys running" forms an independent clause. What follows it, "she hopes to join the cross-country team," is also an independent clause. Two independent clauses can't be joined simply by a comma. In Performance Techniques, you'll learn several ways to combine independent clauses correctly.

Most Common Types of Sentence Sense Questions

Sentence Sense questions fall into three categories:

1) **Sentence structure** questions test your ability to recognize whether a sentence expresses a complete thought or whether too many thoughts are strung together incorrectly.

2) **Consistency** questions require you to understand how non-underlined verbs and pronouns may dictate the appropriate form of an underlined verb or pronoun.

3) **Word order** questions test your ability to recognize problematic phrase combinations that lead to illogical statements.

Sentence structure questions test fragments and run-ons. A fragment is group of words that can't stand alone as a sentence, either because it is a dependent clause or because it contains a verb ending in –*ing* as the main verb. Here are some examples of fragments, along with additions that transform the fragments into complete sentences:

FRAGMENT: Although rain is predicted for tonight.

SENTENCE: Although rain is predicted for tonight, **we still plan to go camping.**

FRAGMENT: Lucinda and I **going** to the same college.

SENTENCE: Lucinda and I **will be going** to the same college.

Whenever an underlined sentence contains more than one clause, that is, more than one subject-verb combination, you need to make sure that the clauses are combined in a way that forms a correct and complete sentence. A **run-on sentence** occurs when two independent clauses are joined in a way that doesn't follow the rules for sentence structure and punctuation. Here's an example:

DeWane planned his time carefully, he finished his term paper a day early.

With only a comma joining two independent clauses, this sentence is not punctuated correctly. In Performance Techniques, you will learn about several ways to correct this problem.

Here's an example of inconsistent pronoun usage:

> WRONG: **A politician** should do everything **they** can to improve the lives of **their** constituents.

Here, because "politician" is singular, it's incorrect to use the plural pronouns "they" and "their." The simplest way to correct this error is to make "politician" plural:

> RIGHT: **Politicians** should do everything **they** can to improve the lives of **their** constituents.

Sentence Sense questions that test word order usually hinge on the placement of modifiers. A modifier is a word or group of words that provides information about another word in the sentence. Word order questions require you to rearrange the word order so that a modifying word, phrase, or clause is placed close to the word it modifies. In this example, the modifying phrase, printed in bold, is not next to the word it modifies:

> **Practicing diligently over the course of several months,** the audience was stunned by the excellent quality of the school musical.

In Performance Techniques, you'll learn an easy way to correct word order errors like this one.

• THE TRAP DOOR: STEERING CLEAR OF ANSWER TRAPS

As you read through an ACT English passage, keep in mind the three types of Sentence Sense issues—sentence structure, consistency, and word order—and look for clues that a particular question may be testing Sentence Sense. Being alert for these clues will help you eliminate wrong answer choices. The test maker doesn't set traps per se for Sentence Sense questions. Instead, answer traps are the wrong answers that may seem tempting when you fail to recognize that a particular question tests sentence sense.

Types of Sentence Sense Answer Traps

This section presents tips to help you notice typical traps.

DEPENDENT CLAUSES

Watch for words that introduce dependent clauses. A list of some of these words is provided. If you see one of these words, either in the underlined part of the sentence or elsewhere in the sentence, make sure that the sentence contains an independent clause.

WORDS THAT CAN INTRODUCE DEPENDENT CLAUSES		
after	since	which
although	that	while
because	though	who
before	unless	whoever
if	whereas	

VERBS ENDING IN *–ING*

Notice when the underlined part of the sentence contains a verb ending in *–ing*. Sometimes the test maker uses this verb form without a helping verb as the main verb in a clause. When you see this, a revision is always needed.

UNDERLINED SENTENCES

Notice when an entire sentence is underlined. In this case, occasionally, the NO CHANGE choice will be correct. Usually, however, when a whole sentence is underlined, either you should choose OMIT, because the sentence is off-topic for the paragraph, or the question is testing sentence sense by offering three answer choices that are unclear or confusing because the word order is incorrect. Something about each of the wrong answer choices won't make sense.

Techniques for Avoiding Sentence Sense Question Answer Traps

Avoid the Sentence Sense traps by using the tips above. For sentence structure, look for words that introduce dependent clauses. For pronoun and verb consistency, refer to the nonunderlined parts of the passage for clues about which form of the pronoun or verb is correct. For modifier placement in word order questions, think about whether a sentence easily makes sense to a reader. In all cases, you need to find the answer choice that gives the most logical phrasing and follows the principles of correct sentence structure.

• PERFORMANCE TECHNIQUES: KEY RULES

SENTENCE STRUCTURE RULE

A sentence must contain at least one independent clause. The *–ing* form of the verb cannot be used alone (without a helping verb such as *is* or *has*) as the main verb of a clause.

Here's an example of a sentence that violates the sentence structure rule:

WRONG: **That** Samantha will play goalie.

The word *that* always introduces a dependent clause. The sentence structure rule tells you that a sentence must contain at least one independent clause. Depending on the context, you could correct this sentence by either deleting "that" or adding words to make the clause independent, for example, "The coach said that Samantha will play goalie."

Here's another example that violates the sentence structure rule:

WRONG: Deborah **playing** in the band concert tonight.

The verb form "playing" must have a helping verb. Depending on the context, *is*, *was*, or *will be* could be used.

Recall the run-on sentence presented earlier: "DeWane planned his time carefully, he finished his term paper a day early." Here are several options for correctly revising this sentence structure error.

Option #1. Separate the independent clauses into two sentences:

DeWane planned his time carefully. He finished his term paper a day early.

Option #2. Join the two independent clauses with a semicolon:

DeWane planned his time carefully; he finished his term paper a day early.

Option #3. Use a transition word that shows the relationship between the clauses:

Because DeWane planned his time carefully, he finished his term paper a day early.

Option #4. Use a comma followed by a FANBOYS word (*for, and, nor, but, or, yet, so*) to join the two clauses:

DeWane planned his time carefully, **so** he finished his term paper a day early.

While there may be several ways to combine two independent clauses into a correctly formed complete sentence, remember that only one correct way will be offered among the choices on an ACT question.

VERB TENSE CONSISTENCY RULE

The verb tense used in the underlined part of the sentence must relate logically to any nonunderlined verb in the sentence. The verb tense must also be consistent with other nonunderlined verb tenses used in the passage. Here's an example in ACT format:

Before I can pack my suitcase, I still <u>needed</u> to do some shopping.

Because the nonunderlined verb "can pack" is in the present tense, the past tense verb "needed" must be changed to the present tense, *need*, to establish consistency between verb tenses.

PRONOUN CONSISTENCY RULE

Whenever an underlined segment includes a pronoun, make sure the nonunderlined part of the passage contains a noun or pronoun to which the underlined pronoun clearly refers. Within a passage, do not shift unnecessarily between the pronouns one, you, and they.

In general, whenever you see that an underlined segment includes a pronoun or a verb, check for consistency with other words in the nonunderlined context. Below is a short sample passage with some verbs and pronouns underlined because they're used inconsistently. To give you a little help in correcting these, the verbs and pronouns that serve as clues are printed in boldface. See if you can tell how the underlined words should be revised:

Quite a bit of preparation **is** needed for a camping trip. **You** must make sure that all **your** equipment—tent, sleeping bags, lanterns, and cookware—**is** in good condition. Someone **has** to plan the menu and <u>decided</u> when to do the shopping. Will **you** shop in advance to buy everything **you** need before <u>one leaves</u> home, packing the meat and dairy products in a cooler? Or will <u>one</u> drive to the campground first and purchase all the food locally? Time **is** another thing to think about. It <u>was</u> easier to choose a spot and set up tents in daylight than it **is** in the dark.

Notice that the predominant tense in the passage is the present tense. You know this because of the present tense verbs "is" and "has." Therefore, "decided" is wrong because it's in the past tense. It should be changed to the present tense, decide. Do not move between past and present tense within a sentence or passage unless there is a logical reason to do so.

Now consider the pronouns. This passage uses "you," so the writer is directly addressing the reader. Therefore, it's wrong to start using the noun "one." The phrase "one leaves" should be changed to *you leave*. The other underlined pronoun, "one," should be changed to *you*.

WORD ORDER RULE

A modifying phrase should be placed next to the word it describes.

A sentence that violates the word order rule usually sounds confusing. You can think of it as a scrambled sentence. Your task is to rearrange the various parts of the sentence so that the whole thing makes sense. Here's an example:

> WRONG: Suddenly, when the baseball, holding the expensive crystal glassware, was knocked to the floor, the high shelf came crashing through the window.

To unscramble a sentence like this, you need to think about the meaning of the words and apply some logic. Think about the modifying phrase "holding the expensive crystal glassware." Because of its placement in this sentence, it appears to modify the noun "baseball." Logic, however, tells us that this phrase modifies, and therefore should be placed next to, the noun "shelf." The adverb "suddenly" modifies the verb "came crashing." Here is a more logical wording of the sentence that places modifying words and phrases near the parts of the sentence they modify:

> RIGHT: The high shelf holding the expensive crystal glassware was knocked to the floor when the baseball suddenly came crashing through the window.

While you'll often be able to recognize a Sentence Sense question like this one because the entire sentence is underlined, you may also see Sentence Sense questions that test modifier placement when only part of the sentence is underlined.

● DRESS REHEARSAL: SAMPLE QUESTIONS AND DETAILED EXPLANATIONS

Dependent Clause

1. <u>Umbrellas, which people often forget in public places,</u> other portable items such as cameras and cell phones.

   A. NO CHANGE
   B. Umbrellas, people often forget them in public places, and in addition
   C. People, who often forget umbrellas in public places, along with
   D. People often forget umbrellas in public places, along with

Notice that the sentence contains the word "which" and recall that this word is used to introduce a dependent clause. Therefore, check the sentence to make sure that it includes an independent clause. As written, it doesn't, because there is no verb to go with the noun "umbrellas." **Choice D, the correct answer, appropriately revises the underlined part so that it forms an independent clause,** "People often forget umbrellas in public places." Choice B does include the independent clause "people often forget them in public places," but the rest of the sentence doesn't make sense with it. Choice C is incorrect because it uses the noun "People" without a verb to go with it, creating a sentence that lacks an independent clause.

Verb Ending in -*ing*

2. As they prepared the dinner, Cyndi and <u>Lauren finding,</u> to their dismay, that they had forgotten to purchase two key ingredients.

   F. NO CHANGE
   G. Lauren, they found,
   H. Lauren found,
   J. Lauren, who found,

When you see a verb ending in –*ing* underlined, make sure it's not used as the only verb in a clause. In this sentence as written, there is no appropriate verb to go with the subject "Cyndi and Lauren." **Choice H corrects this error and follows the rules of sentence structure.** Choice G is wrong because it's incorrect to use the pronoun "they," which unnecessarily repeats the meaning of the subject words, "Cyndi and Lauren." Choice J, in using "who found," establishes a dependent clause, and this sentence needs the formation of an independent clause.

Pronoun Agreement

3. While the librarian taught us some important research skills that go into preparing a term paper, very few <u>students actually applied it</u>.

   A. NO CHANGE
   B. students actually applied them
   C. of the students, in fact, actually applied it
   D. students actually applied what it was they had learned

When you notice a pronoun in the underlined segment, check to make sure that this pronoun refers to a word in the nonunderlined sentence in a way that's both logically and grammatically correct. In choice A, the pronoun "it" is singular. The sentence does contain two singular nouns, "librarian" and "paper," but neither is logically referred to by "it" in this sentence. Ask yourself here, what is it that the students applied? The answer is "skills." **The plural pronoun "them" correctly refers to skills, so choice B is the best answer.** Choice C, which retains the pronoun "it," fails to correct the error contained in choice A. Choice D is not grammatically incorrect, but it reflects a style problem: this version is wordy. If two choices are both grammatically correct, the more concise one must be considered the "best" answer. (You can read more about the issue of wordiness in Lesson 4.)

Verb Agreement

4. Before he moved to Boston, the Alabama native hardly <u>imagines</u> how cold a New England winter actually could be.

   F. NO CHANGE
   G. could have been imagining
   H. could have imagined
   J. will imagine

If the underlined part of the sentence includes a verb, make sure that it is logically consistent with any other verbs that appear in the sentence. Because the nonunderlined part of this sentence uses the past tense verb "moved" in a clause that starts with "before," the present tense verb "imagines" in choice F isn't logically consistent here. Likewise, choice G, which uses a past tense "could have been imagining," is illogical. **Choice J is incorrect because it uses the future tense.** Choice H is the correct answer because its use of the past tense is consistent with the verb tense in the nonunderlined part of the sentence.

Word Order

5. Exhausted after a stressful day at work, <u>the fender bender during the evening rush hour only added to Susan's frustration.</u>

    A. NO CHANGE
    B. frustration only increased for Susan as a result of the fender bender during the evening rush hour
    C. the evening rush hour led to a fender bender that only increased Susan's frustration
    D. Susan became even more frustrated after the fender bender during the evening rush hour

The presence of a verb ending in *–ing* or *–ed* at the beginning of a sentence is often a clue that a modifying phrase is present. You should get in the habit of noticing such modifying phrases—even when they aren't underlined. Here, ask yourself, *who* or *what* is "exhausted after a stressful day at work"? Logically, the answer to this question is "Susan." Therefore, "Susan" is the noun that must immediately follow the modifying phrase. **Choice D is the correct answer because it's the only one that corrects this word order problem.** Choices A, B, and C are all incorrect because they follow the introductory modifying phrase with a noun other than the noun the phrase modifies.

● THE FINAL ACT: PRACTICE QUIZ

Directions: In the passage that follows, certain words and phrases are underlined and numbered. In the right-hand column, you will find alternatives for the underlined part. In most cases, you are to choose the one that best expresses the idea, makes the statement appropriate for standard written English, or is worded most consistently with the style and tone of the passage as a whole. If you think the original version is best, choose NO CHANGE. For each question, choose the alternative you consider best.

Crew: The Sport of Rowing

More than 2,000 years ago, the Greeks discovered that fixing an oar to the side of a boat is more effective than using an unattached paddle. After this discovery, <u>rowing was used</u> to transport both goods
1
and armies. By the 13th century, Venetian festivals included some boat racing as entertainment. Rowing for sport <u>gets</u>
2
<u>its start</u> in England with the watermen,
2
or professional river taxi drivers, on the Thames River in the early 1700s. One of the first modern races, the Doggett's Coat and Badge, <u>was established</u> in
3
1716 in London and is still held today. Later, amateurs as well as professionals <u>beginning to take part in</u> rowing races.
4
In 1829, a competition (called the Boat Race) between Oxford and Cambridge Universities took place in England. Intercollegiate rowing in the United States got its start in 1852 with the

1. A. NO CHANGE
   B. it was rowing that was used
   C. rowing being used
   D. the use for rowing was

2. F. NO CHANGE
   G. gets their start
   H. got its start
   J. got their start

3. A. NO CHANGE
   B. which was established
   C. establishing
   D. it was

4. F. NO CHANGE
   G. began to take part in
   H. began the taking part of
   J. who began to take part in

Harvard-Yale Regatta. Rowing has been part of the modern Olympics since 1900.

There are several variables in rowing <u>races, the</u> number of rowers in a boat,
₅ also known as a "crew," can be 1, 2, 4, or 8. Sometimes the team includes a coxswain, that is, a person who does not row but who calls out commands regarding steering and race tactics <u>in the guiding of their teammates.</u>
₆ Another variable is the number of oars handled by each rower. In *sweep* rowing, the rower uses a single oar, holding it with both <u>hands, in *sculling,*</u> each rower uses
₇ two oars, holding one oar in each hand.

A boat without a coxswain is known as a coxless or "straight" boat. While boats of two or four rowers may be either coxed or coxless, a boat of eight rowers, because of its size and speed, always <u>required</u> a coxswain. The rower in the
₈ first seat is called the "stroke" because this rower's movements establish the timing of the stroke for the other rowers.

5. A. NO CHANGE
   B. races, for example, the
   C. races. The
   D. races; and the

6. F. NO CHANGE
   G. to guide their teammates
   H. to guide their rowers
   J. to guide the rowers

7. A. NO CHANGE
   B. hands; whereas in *sculling,*
   C. hands. In *sculling,*
   D. hands, by contrast, in *sculling,*

8. F. NO CHANGE
   G. requires
   H. was requiring
   J. had required

As opposed to the stroke, the "bowman," ⁹ sitting opposite at the end, is in charge of ⁹ setting, or stabilizing, the boat. ⁹

Rowing demands endurance, skill, concentration, and teamwork. The sport attracts people of all ages, from teens

9. A. NO CHANGE
   B. Sitting at the opposite end from the stroke, the "bowman" is responsible for setting, or stabilizing, the boat.
   C. Sitting at the opposite end from the stroke, the boat is stabilized by the "bowman," who has the responsibility for setting, or stabilizing, the boat.
   D. The responsibility for setting, or stabilizing, the boat, sitting at the opposite end from the stroke, belongs to the "bowman."

to senior citizens. Rowers who find that ¹⁰ competitive racing is a challenging and exhilarating sport.

10. F. NO CHANGE
    G. finding
    H. who happen to find
    J. find

• THE FINAL ACT: ANSWERS AND EXPLANATIONS FOR SENTENCE SENSE QUESTIONS

1. A. Choice A correctly uses the past tense to be consistent with the other tenses used in this paragraph. Choice B is wordy. The use of "it was" in choice B is indirect wording. In choice C, "being" is wrong. Remember that the –*ing* verb form must always be used with a helping verb if it is the main verb in a clause. Choice D is a wordy and less direct expression than choice A.

2. H. Choice H correctly uses the past tense "got" to be consistent with the predominant tense of the essay and the singular possessive pronoun "its" to refer to the singular noun "rowing." Choice F is incorrect because it uses the present tense "gets," Choice G is incorrect because it uses the present tense "gets" and it uses the plural possessive pronoun "their" to refer to a singular noun. Choice J is wrong because it uses the plural pronoun "their."

3. A. Choice A maintains correct sentence structure and uses the past tense verb "was established" to be consistent with the other past tense verbs in the passage. Choice B, by introducing "which," makes the expression a fragment instead of a complete sentence. Choice C is incorrect because it uses the *–ing* verb form without a helping verb as the main verb of a clause. Choice D introduces the pronoun "it," which incorrectly restates the subject, "one."

4. G. Choice G maintains correct sentence structure and uses the past tense "began" to be consistent with the other past tense verbs in the passage. Choice F is incorrect because it uses the *–ing* verb form, "beginning," as the main verb of a clause. Choice H uses the correct verb form, "began," but the expression "the taking part of" is wordy and indirect. Choice J, by introducing "who," creates a fragment instead of a complete sentence.

5. C. Choice C correctly uses a period to separate two independent clauses. Choices A and B create run-on sentences by using a comma without a FANBOYS word to join two independent clauses. Choice D is incorrect because it uses a semicolon to join two independent clauses when a FANBOYS word is present. (See pages 24–25 for FANBOYS.)

6. J. Choice J correctly eliminates the plural pronoun "their." In this sentence, there is no plural noun for "their" to logically refer to. The word apparently refers to "person," which is singular. Choices F, G, and H are all incorrect because they use a plural pronoun to refer to a singular noun.

7. C. Choice C uses correct sentence structure by separating two independent clauses into two sentences. Choice A creates a run-on sentence by using a comma to join two independent clauses without a FANBOYS word. Choice B, by introducing the word "whereas," makes the words after the semicolon a fragment rather than an independent clause. Choice D creates a run-on by using a comma rather than a semicolon after "hands" to join two independent clauses.

8. G.   Choice G uses the present tense "requires," which is consistent with the other verbs in this part of the passage. The first paragraph of the passage starts out in the past tense, using the verbs such as "discovered" and "was used." However, the local context of this later paragraph uses the present tense verbs "is" and "may be." Therefore, this sentence needs a present tense verb, which only choice G provides. Note that the subject of this sentence is "boat," not "rowers," so the singular verb "requires" maintains correct subject-verb agreement.

9. B.   When an entire sentence is underlined, either the sentence is not relevant in context and should be omitted, or the question is asking for the most appropriate word order. Word order is being tested here. Choice A is confusing. The phrase "sitting at the opposite end" refers to the "end" of the "boat," but those two words are separated. Also, the use of both "opposite" and "opposing" is repetitive. Choice B correctly places the modifying phrase "sitting at the opposite end from the stroke" immediately before the noun it modifies, "the bowman." Choice C incorrectly opens with a modifying phrase that is not next to the word it describes. The word order in choice D incorrectly suggests that the phrase "sitting at the opposite end from the stroke," describes the noun "boat." Logic tells you that this phrase describes the noun "bowman." Remember that a modifying phrase should be placed next to the word it describes.

10. J.   Choice J is correct because it uses the correct verb form, "find." Choice F is wrong because the word "who" introduces a dependent clause, and the sentence as it stands contains no independent clause. Choice G is wrong because the –*ing* verb form, "finding," cannot be used without a helping verb as the main verb in a clause. Choice H is wrong because the introduction of the word "who" means the sentence doesn't contain an independent clause.

Punctuation

DIFFICULTY: ★ ★

FREQUENCY: ★ ★ ★

SURPRISE FACTOR: ★ ★

● INTRODUCTION TO PUNCTUATION QUESTIONS

Punctuation is tested heavily on the ACT. More than half of the punctuation questions involve commas, while some also test semicolon and colon usage. To do well on these questions, you must have a good understanding of correct sentence formation. Therefore, if punctuation is an area of difficulty for you, make sure that you are thoroughly comfortable with the material in Lesson 1, "Sentence Structure," as you work on making sense of the rules for commas, semicolons, and colons in this lesson.

Punctuation may seem difficult because you need to be able to apply some specific rules to do well on punctuation questions. However, not every aspect of punctuation is tested on the ACT. For example, you don't need to be concerned with how to use commas and quotation marks correctly to punctuate a direct quotation. The rules you need for the ACT are limited in number, and you will find all of them here in this lesson.

Make sure you're thoroughly comfortable with the rules and examples presented here. Paying special attention to the traps described in this lesson will help you understand exactly how the ACT tests punctuation and will help you avoid being confused and caught off guard.

Characteristics of Punctuation Questions

Questions that test punctuation are easy to recognize on the ACT. Look at this example and notice the differences among the four answer choices:

1. Many doctors have had more than 20 years of formal education by the time they begin practicing medicine. Not all <u>doctors, however,</u> attend medical school immediately after finishing college.

   A. NO CHANGE
   B. doctors; however,
   C. doctors, however
   D. doctors however,

In each of the four answer choices above, the words are identical; the choices differ only in the kinds of punctuation marks and their placement. This feature is typical of ACT punctuation questions. The words in all four choices either will be identical, as in the example above, or vary only slightly. In addition, whenever you see an answer choice that includes a semicolon, consider it a signal that punctuation and sentence structure are being tested together. With punctuation, as with most other topics, examining the answer choices can provide a clue about what English topic is being tested and, therefore, which rules you need to apply.

Most Common Types of Punctuation Questions

Because the comma is the most heavily tested punctuation mark on the ACT, this lesson emphasizes comma usage. Rules for semicolons and colons are also discussed here. Although fewer questions test semicolons and colons, understanding how to use these punctuation marks correctly can help you eliminate incorrect answer choices on many questions.

Like commas, semicolons, and colons, the dash is also related to sentence structure. You will see only one or two questions on dashes. Understanding how the test maker uses dashes on the ACT can help you eliminate incorrect answer choices.

The ACT also includes a few questions that test the apostrophe. Apostrophes are used both in contractions (for example, *it's*, *who's*, *there's*) and in possessives (for example, *the children's choir*).

● THE TRAP DOOR: STEERING CLEAR OF ANSWER TRAPS

When you know which punctuation marks are tested on the ACT and how you can recognize when a question is asking you to determine the correct punctuation, there's only one trap you need to be aware of. It's not really a trap the test maker deliberately sets for you; it's more of a trap you create for yourself by losing focus. Familiarizing yourself with this trap will help you keep your eye on the big picture and not get bogged down by a list of rules.

Types of Punctuation Answer Traps

The main trap for punctuation is the comma trap. Because the comma is the most heavily tested punctuation mark on the ACT, it's easy to get carried away with commas. You know that commas are used frequently, you're trying to remember all the situations they're used in, and you see lots of commas in the various answer choices. You're highly focused on commas, so it's tempting to think, "Commas are important, and this answer choice has the most commas, so it must be the right answer." This is a trap!

Techniques for Avoiding the Punctuation Question Answer Trap

You can steer clear of the ACT comma trap by remembering one important guideline: Avoid unnecessary commas! As you read through the rules in Performance Techniques, you'll be focusing on which situations call for using commas. On many ACT comma questions, your task is not actually to use a comma but, rather, to determine when a comma has been inserted unnecessarily. In other words, the correct answer to a comma question may be the answer choice that deletes one, or sometimes even two, commas that are present in the three other answer choices.

Let's look at an example:

2. All of the <u>people, in the theater, quickly got up</u> from their seats when the fire alarm sounded.

   F. NO CHANGE

   G. people in the theater quickly, got up,

   H. people in the theater, quickly, got up

   J. people in the theater quickly got up

After reading through the Performance Techniques below, you'll be able to recognize that none of the commas used in this example performs a necessary function. Even at this point, however, you may be able to see intuitively why some of these commas are unnecessary. In choice F, the commas after "people" and "theater" incorrectly separate the prepositional phrase from the rest of the sentence. In choice G, the comma after "quickly" incorrectly separates the subject of the sentence, "All of the people in the theater," from the verb, "got up." In addition, the comma after "up" separates the verb, "got up," from the prepositional phrase that modifies it. Choice H uses commas to set off the adverb "quickly," which is incorrect. Choice J is the correct answer because it does not use any unnecessary commas. The unnecessary commas in each of the three wrong answer choices break the logic and flow of the sentence.

Sometimes, thinking of how you would speak a sentence aloud can help you avoid the comma trap. When you're reading aloud and you see a comma, you pause briefly. On the ACT, if you have trouble deciding whether a comma is necessary or not, read the sentence with the answer choice you're considering. **Try to hear the words in your head** as you would hear them if they were spoken aloud. Pause slightly when you come to a comma. If the pause sounds artificial or unnecessary to you, there's a good chance the comma should be deleted. Let's look at an example of an incorrectly used comma:

WRONG: The fourth-grade teacher created a geography unit, based on her trip to Asia.

In this sentence, the comma after "unit" breaks up the flow of the sentence. The phrase "based on her trip to Asia" modifies, or describes, "unit." The comma here is wrong because a modifier should not be separated by a comma from the word it modifies. Here's another example of an incorrectly used comma in the same sentence:

WRONG: The fourth-grade teacher created a geography unit based on, her trip to Asia.

Here, a comma separates the preposition "on" from its object, "her trip." Using a comma between a preposition and its object is incorrect because it disturbs the flow of the sentence.

When a sentence contains a **compound subject or verb**, that is, two words joined by *and* that serve the same function in the sentence, there should be no commas separating the two parts of the compound. See if you can spot the errors here:

> **WRONG:** Jonah, and his best friend, decided to go camping, and
> backpacking together.

All three of the commas in this sentence are used incorrectly. The two parts of the compound subject, "Jonah and his best friend," should not be separated by a comma. The comma after "friend" incorrectly separates the subject and verb. The comma after "camping" incorrectly separates the two verbs "camping" and "backpacking."

Make sure you understand these examples, remembering that a comma indicates a pause in the sentence and that some parts of a sentence should not be broken up by a pause. If you do this, you will easily be able to recognize the incorrect use of commas on the ACT.

• PERFORMANCE TECHNIQUES: KEY RULES

While this section presents rules for the semicolon, colon, dash, and apostrophe as well as the comma, remember that the ACT tests the comma much more than the other punctuation marks.

RULES FOR COMMAS

Four correct uses of the comma are tested on the ACT. They are described here in a single rule.

Comma Rule. Use a comma to do the following:

- Separate introductory words from the main part of the sentence.
- Set off words or phrases that aren't essential to the sentence.
- Separate two independent clauses that are joined by a FANBOYS word (*for, and, nor, but, or, yet, so*).
- Separate items in a list or series.

Below are some correctly written examples that use commas to separate introductory material from the main point of the sentence. Read through these examples and notice that the introductory phrases are never an essential part of the sentence:

> **RIGHT: Over the course of the year,** I will get better at note taking.

> **RIGHT: In the summer,** Marla enjoys swimming and reading novels.

RIGHT: **After his next birthday,** Stephen will be able to vote.

RIGHT: **At school,** Tonya often skips lunch.

Theses examples should give you an idea of what we mean by "introductory." Introductory phrases are not an integral part of a sentence. They provide useful information, but they don't contain the subject or verb. Deleting an introductory phrase would not compromise the sentence structure because the subject and verb are not part of the introductory phrase.

Now let's look at some examples of commas that are used to set off **nonessential information:**

RIGHT: My grandmother, **even though she is 85,** still enjoys traveling frequently.

RIGHT: Jonathan, **who has been playing soccer since he was eight,** is our best goalie.

RIGHT: The rose bushes, **which were nearly killed by insects last year,** are healthy now.

RIGHT: Mr. Hernandez, **my history teacher,** often assigns group projects.

Notice that the phrases designated as "nonessential" do contain valuable descriptive information. When we're talking about commas, the word nonessential doesn't mean "not relevant" or "not important." Rather, part of a sentence is considered nonessential if deleting it would not destroy the integrity of the sentence. In other words, a nonessential phrase doesn't contain any words that are part of the subject or verb. In each example above, if you deleted the nonessential phrase, the remaining words would still make up a complete, grammatically correct sentence.

Punctuation and sentence structure are also tightly connected when **joining two independent clauses with a comma and a FANBOYS word.** There are several grammatically correct ways to express more than one idea in a sentence. One of these ways is to use a comma after an independent clause, then follow the comma with a FANBOYS word and a second independent clause. FANBOYS is simply an acronym for these words: *for, and, nor, but, or, yet,* and *so.* Here are some examples that each use a comma and a FANBOYS word to correctly join two independent clauses:

RIGHT: I'm hoping to jog outdoors today, **but** the ice storm may prevent me.

RIGHT: Julia may go to the party tonight, **or** she may stay at home.

RIGHT: My brother is a dedicated student, **and** I'm trying to be more like him.

RIGHT: I was cold, **so** I decided to adjust the thermostat.

The key pattern in the above examples is that whatever appears on either side of the comma-FANBOYS word combination is a group of words that could stand alone as a sentence. Sentences that are joined by a comma and a FANBOYS word must have two parts, each capable of forming a grammatically correct sentence by itself. Thus, you need to use your understanding of sentence structure, that is, be able to distinguish between dependent and independent clauses, to use commas correctly near a FANBOYS word.

The typical example of a **series** is a shopping list. Commas are used correctly in this sentence:

RIGHT: When I'm out today, I need to buy **shampoo, gym socks, and a set of markers**.

This example is a straightforward list in which each item in the series is a noun. The kind of list you're more likely to see on the ACT, however, will be made up of something other than nouns. Look at this example of a series in which each item of the series is a verb phrase:

RIGHT: I can't believe that she would **do** such a thing, **lie** about it, and then **blame** her best friend.

Remember that a series can include grammatical units other than nouns, and commas must be used to separate parts of a series that includes three or more items.

RULE FOR SEMICOLONS

People are often intimidated by semicolons, but you needn't be. Here's why: essentially only one use of the semicolon is tested on the ACT. If you can tell the difference between a dependent and an independent clause, you can always answer the semicolon questions correctly.

Semicolon Rule. A semicolon is used to join two closely related independent clauses without a FANBOYS word.

Here's an example:

> RIGHT: We don't get many snowstorms in late March; **[note: there is no FANBOYS word here]** by April, I'm usually able to use my bike for local errands.

On the ACT, you don't need to be concerned with whether or not two independent clauses are "closely related." You need only be aware of whether a group of words forms a dependent or independent clause. The above sentence could also be written with a FANBOYS word:

> RIGHT: We don't get many snowstorms in late March, **[note comma here]** so, I'm usually able to use my bike for local errands by April.

This version is correct because a comma is used with a FANBOYS word to join two independent clauses. You would not see both of the above sentences offered as answer choices for an ACT question. You won't need to decide which of two correct ways to punctuate a sentence is preferable; you will only have to recognize the one correct answer choice that's offered.

The semicolon rule has two parts: the semicolon is correct when (1) the sentence contains two independent clauses and (2) no FANBOYS words are used with the semicolon. You should be aware that certain non-FANBOYS words are often used after a semicolon. Some examples are listed in the box below. Recognizing that these words are acceptable after an independent clause followed by a semicolon, but *not* after an independent clause followed by a comma, will help you rule out wrong answer choices on punctuation questions.

EXAMPLES OF CONNECTING WORDS THAT CAN FOLLOW A SEMICOLON

furthermore	nevertheless
however	therefore
moreover	thus

RULE FOR COLONS

There are several uses for the colon, but they are all similar. The colon isn't tested nearly as frequently as the comma. However, being able to recognize the correct use of the colon will help you eliminate wrong answer choices.

Colon Rule. Use a colon after an independent clause to introduce an example, an explanation, a short phrase, a quotation, or a list or to show emphasis. The words following the colon need not constitute an independent clause.

The second part of the colon rule is important in helping you determine the best answer for questions that offer both the semicolon and the colon in the answer choices. A semicolon can be correct only if what follows it is an independent clause. Here's an example of a colon used to show emphasis. Note that the colon can be acceptable when what follows it does not form a sentence on its own:

RIGHT: Yolanda is moving to a city known for its rainy weather: Seattle.

In this example, the colon emphasizes the word "Seattle" by separating it from the rest of the sentence.

Never use a colon after any form of the verb *to be (am, are, is, was, were)*, and never use a colon between a verb and its object. The following two examples violate this rule:

WRONG: Sarah and Kevin are: the leading actors in the fall musical.

WRONG: Lonnie will set up: tents for the junior high campers.

To understand why the above examples are wrong, it helps to think of the colon as a punctuation mark that breaks up a sentence to some extent. Breaking up a sentence after the verb *to be* or between a verb and its object disturbs the logical flow of the sentence and so is incorrect. Using a colon for the purposes described in the rule does not interfere with the flow of the sentence.

RULE FOR DASHES

The dash isn't tested frequently on the ACT, but understanding when to use it in a sentence will help you get the most possible points.

Dash Rule. Use a dash to indicate a hesitation or a break in thought. If the break comes in the middle of the main part of the sentence, use a dash both before and after the interruption to set it off from the rest of the sentence.

Here's an example in which the break comes in the middle of the sentence:

RIGHT: Dashes—a single dash or a pair of dashes—are used to indicate a break in thought.

The main thing you need to know about dashes for the ACT is that you can't pair a dash with a comma in the middle of a sentence. Consider this question:

3. This year's prices at the amusement <u>park—I know because I come here every year,</u> are much higher than last year's.

A. NO CHANGE
B. park, I know because I come here every year—
C. park—I know because I come here every year—
D. park—I know because I come here every year;

The correct answer is C. Choice C correctly uses two dashes to set off the interruption, "I know because I come here every year." Choice A starts well by using the dash after "park," but it is incorrect because the comma after "year" should be a dash. Choice B is incorrect because the comma after "park" should be a dash. Choice D is incorrect because a second dash is needed after "year" to set off the interruption. In addition, you can tell that choice D is incorrect because a semicolon can not be used when the words that follow it do not make up an independent clause.

In the example above, two dashes are used together to set off a mid-sentence interruption. A single dash can be used to set off information at the beginning or end of a sentence. Here's an example:

I couldn't believe it—we won the game after all!

This use of the dash appears infrequently on the ACT.

RULES FOR APOSTROPHES

Apostrophes are used for two purposes: to show possession and to indicate that one or more letters is omitted in a contraction. Neither of these situations is complicated, but to handle them, you need to slow down and pay attention to detail.

Apostrophe Rules:
- To indicate a contraction, use an apostrophe to show where letters are left out.
- To show the possessive case of a singular noun or of a plural noun that does not end with s, add an apostrophe and the letter s.
- To show the possessive case of a plural noun that does end with s, simply add an apostrophe. Do not use an apostrophe in a plural noun that does not show possession.

The apostrophe rules sound more complicated than they are. Read through the correct examples here and make sure you recognize how each one applies the rules.

Here are some examples that correctly use apostrophes to indicate possession:

RIGHT: **Roma's** mother is a doctor. [**Roma is a singular noun.**]

RIGHT: Both my **grandparents'** families are from France.
[**Grandparents, it can be determined from the context, is a plural here.**]

RIGHT: The **women's** room is being renovated.
[**Women's is a plural noun not ending in s.**]

Notice that in the following examples, the plural noun is not possessive and so does not take an apostrophe:

RIGHT: The **babies** enjoy the infant aquatics class.

RIGHT: The **students** are working diligently.

On the ACT, part of using the apostrophe correctly involves knowing when not to use one.

In addition to recognizing the correct use of the apostrophe to show possession, you should also remember that **possessive pronouns** are possessive by definition and do *not* use an apostrophe to indicate possession. Train your eye to recognize the correct use of the possessive pronouns in these examples:

RIGHT: The fault is not **yours;** clearly the fault is **ours.**

RIGHT: Melinda affirmed that the coat is **hers.**

RIGHT: The book is missing **its** jacket.

RIGHT: The family could not believe the new house was finally **theirs.**

RIGHT: Does anyone know **whose** car we can use?

Very few contractions are tested on the ACT. Refer to the box below to familiarize yourself with them.

CONTRACTIONS COMMONLY TESTED ON THE ACT

it's—it is	they're—they are
there's—there is, there has	who's—who is, who has

• DRESS REHEARSAL: SAMPLE QUESTIONS AND DETAILED EXPLANATIONS

Joining Two Independent Clauses with a Semicolon

1. My boss could not believe that I ignored her <u>instructions; and</u> she threatened to fire me for this lapse.

   A. NO CHANGE
   B. instructions and
   C. instructions; moreover,
   D. instructions, moreover

This is a typical punctuation question. Only two words are under-lined, and the second one is a FANBOYS conjunction, "and." Your task here is to figure out how to correctly punctuate this sentence. Look at the whole sentence and notice that it starts with an independent clause: "My boss could not believe that I ignored her instructions." Now look at the second nonunderlined part of the sentence: "she threatened to fire me for this lapse." This is also an independent clause. Recall that the punctuation rules offer two correct ways to combine independent clauses in a sentence. If a FANBOYS word is used, it must be preceded by a comma. Thus, choice A is incorrect because it uses a semicolon. Choice B is incorrect because there is no comma before "and." If two independent clauses are joined without using a FANBOYS word, then a semicolon must separate the two clauses. **For this reason, choice C is correct.** Choice D is incorrect because it uses a comma and "moreover" is not a FANBOYS word.

Joining Two Independent Clauses with Comma and FANBOYS Word

2. Matthew admitted he had been nervous when he first walked on <u>stage: yet he</u> appeared perfectly calm to those of us in the audience.

   F. NO CHANGE
   G. stage, he
   H. stage; yet he
   J. stage, yet he

You can see from the underlined part of the sentence and the answer choices that this question is testing how to punctuate correctly in the middle of a sentence. Notice that the sentence contains two independent clauses. The first is "Matthew admitted that he had been nervous when he first walked on stage." The second is "he appeared perfectly calm to those of us in the audience." Remember the rules for combining two independent clauses: if a FANBOYS word is present, it must be followed by a comma; if no FANBOYS word is present, the two clauses must be separated by a semicolon. **Choice J correctly uses the comma with the FANBOYS word "yet."** Choice F is wrong because it uses a colon where the comma should be. Choice G is incorrect because it uses a comma without a FANBOYS word. Choice H is wrong because you can't follow a semicolon with a FANBOYS word.

Avoiding Unnecessary Commas

3. Wanda claims that she can effectively do <u>homework, and instant-message</u> her friends at the same time.

   A. NO CHANGE
   B. homework and, instant-message,
   C. homework and, instant-message
   D. homework and instant-message

With a quick glance through the answer choices here, you can see that this question is testing commas. All the choices use identical wording; the only difference is where the commas appear. Read through the sentence and think about how it's constructed. Does the sentence contain any nonessential information that must be set off with commas? Does it contain a list whose parts must be separated with commas? Is it made up of two independent clauses joined by a FANBOYS word? If you can't answer yes to one of these questions, chances are that this sentence doesn't need commas. Remember the comma trap: On the ACT, you're sometimes asked to delete unnecessary commas. The trap applies in this situation. **Choice D is correct.** All the commas used in the answer choices for this question are unnecessary and disrupt the flow of the sentence. Notice that the sentence contains a dependent clause, "that she can...do homework and instant-message...." This dependent clause has two verbs, but they aren't separated by any nonessential information. Therefore, there is no reason to include commas, and all the answer choices that use commas here are incorrect.

Using the Apostrophe in Contractions

4. Let me consider the arguments overnight; right now, <u>its' not clear to me whose</u> position I want to support.

F. NO CHANGE
G. it's not clear to me whose
H. its not clear to me who's
J. it's not clear to me who's

When the underlined part of the sentence includes one or more words that contain apostrophes, there's a good chance the question is testing apostrophe usage. Remember that the ACT tests a few words that use apostrophes in contractions, and it also tests apostrophes used to show possession. This particular question tests both uses of apostrophes. Remember that *its'* is never correct in any context. Knowing this, you can eliminate choice F. Next, determine whether "it is" would be correct in the sentence. If so, then "it's" is correct. That is indeed the case here, so you can rule out choice H. To choose between choices G and J, you need to determine whether "whose" or "who's" is correct here. Remember that who's can only be correct when "who is" or "who has" would make sense. Because you wouldn't say "it's not clear to me who is position," you can rule out choice J here. **Choice G is correct** because "whose" is the possessive pronoun that goes with "position" in this sentence.

Using the Apostrophe to Show Possession

5. The <u>teenager's summer job at the childrens'</u> hospital inspired him to pursue research in pediatric endocrinology.

A. NO CHANGE
B. teenagers' summer job at the children's
C. teenager's summer job at the children's
D. teenagers' summer job at the childrens'

Because "teenager" is singular (you know this because "teenager" is replaced by the singular pronoun "him" in the nonunderlined part of the sentence), the correct possessive form is "teenager's." Knowing this, you can eliminate choices B and D. Because "children" is a plural noun that does not end in *s*, its possessive is formed by adding an apostrophe before adding *s*. Choices A and D violate this rule. **The correct answer is C.**

● THE FINAL ACT: PRACTICE QUIZ

Directions: In the passage that follows, certain words and phrases are underlined and numbered. In the right-hand column, you will find alternatives for the underlined part. In most cases, you are to choose the one that best expresses the idea, makes the statement appropriate for standard written English, or is worded most consistently with the style and tone of the passage as a whole. If you think the original version is best, choose NO CHANGE. For each question, choose the alternative you consider best.

Why Bake Bread?

A few generations ago, the only way

to have bread was to bake it at home.

Now, <u>however many alternatives</u> are
            1

available. In most areas, bakeries sell

a wide variety of freshly baked breads.

Grocery stores sell products ranging

1. A. NO CHANGE
   B. however, many alternatives,
   C. however, many alternatives
   D. however many alternatives,

<u>from mixes for quick breads,</u> and muffins,
           2

to frozen garlic bread to canned dough

from the refrigerated section.

2. F. NO CHANGE
   G. from mixes, for quick breads
   H. from mixes for quick breads
   J. from mixes for quick, breads

The automatic bread maker offers

consumers yet another option. <u>With this</u>
                  3

<u>machine its</u> possible to enjoy not only
  3

the taste but also the aroma of freshly

3. A. NO CHANGE
   B. With this machine, it's
   C. With this machine it's
   D. With this machine, its

baked bread at home. <u>This appliance's</u>
4
<u>convenience:</u> is widely appreciated. The
4
bread maker, controlled by its own little

computer, does everything from mixing

to baking.

    <u>Why, when fresh bread can be</u>
5
<u>obtained so easily</u> would anyone bother
5
to make bread in the old-fashioned way?

Baking enthusiasts offer various reasons.

Some say they prefer the quality of their

own homemade bread. <u>Others however,</u>
6
<u>report that</u> the process of making the
6
bread is part of the pleasure they find

in it. With the fast pace of modern life,

they reason, baking bread from scratch

is one thing that allows them to slow

down and enjoy the process as well

as the product. Baking <u>bread, they say</u>
7
changes their perception of time and lets

them experience life more fully.

    People who regularly bake their

own bread generally appreciate that the

process does, in fact, take time. Devoted

4. F. NO CHANGE
   G. This appliances'
      convenience:
   H. This appliances
      convenience:
   J. This appliance's
      convenience

5. A. NO CHANGE
   B. Why, when fresh bread,
      can be obtained so
      easily,
   C. Why when fresh bread
      can be obtained so
      easily,
   D. Why, when fresh bread
      can be obtained so
      easily,

6. F. NO CHANGE
   G. Others, however, report
      that
   H. Others, however, report
      that,
   J. Others, however report,
      that

7. A. NO CHANGE
   B. bread: they say,
   C. bread; they say,
   D. bread, they say,

bakers view the multiple <u>steps, mixing,</u>
₈
<u>kneading, waiting for the rises, and</u>
₈
<u>baking</u>—as part of a rhythmic dance,
₈
and they work these steps in around

other activities. They might converse with

family members or listen to music while

mixing and <u>kneading; they</u> might walk
₉
the dog or work on the computer during

the rising and baking time. They see their

bread making as harmonizing with other

activities. They bake bread from scratch

because the <u>process and not simply the</u>
₁₀
<u>product,</u> is meaningful to them.
₁₀

8. F. NO CHANGE
   G. steps—mixing, kneading, waiting for the rises, and baking—
   H. steps—mixing— kneading, waiting for the rises, and baking,
   J. steps—mixing, kneading, waiting for the rises, and baking,

9. A. NO CHANGE
   B. kneading; or they
   C. kneading, they
   D. kneading they

10. F. NO CHANGE
    G. process; and not simply the product
    H. process and not simply, the product
    J. process, and not simply the product,

• THE FINAL ACT: ANSWERS AND EXPLANATIONS FOR PUNCTUATION QUESTIONS

1. C. In this sentence, "however" is a nonessential word that needs to be set off by commas. Choice C correctly adds the comma after "however." Choice A lacks the necessary comma after "however." Choice B adds a comma after "alternatives," incorrectly separating the subject from the verb, "are." Choice D doesn't use a comma after "however" and also incorrectly adds a comma after "alternatives."

2. H. No commas are needed here. The comma in choice F incorrectly breaks up the prepositional phrase "for quick breads and muffins." The comma in choice G incorrectly separates "mixes" from the prepositional phrase, "for quick breads," that describes it. The comma in choice J incorrectly separates the adjective "quick" from the noun it describes, "breads."

3. B. This question tests both comma and apostrophe usage. Choice B is the only choice that handles both correctly. Choice A fails to use a comma after "machine" to set off an introductory phrase, and it uses the possessive "its" where the contraction "it's" is required. Choice C correctly uses the contraction for "it is" but does not include the necessary comma after "machine." Choice D places the comma after "machine" but doesn't use the apostrophe as needed in "its."

4. J. This question tests both apostrophe and colon usage. Choice J correctly uses the apostrophe to show possession in "appliances" and deletes the incorrectly used colon. Choice F uses the apostrophe correctly in "appliance's" but incorrectly uses a colon to separate the subject, "convenience," from the verb, "is." Choice G places the apostrophe incorrectly in "appliances'." This would be the correct usage if the sentence were talking about more than one appliance; however, the singular "this" tells us that "appliance" is singular in this context. Choice G also incorrectly uses the colon to separate the subject and verb. Choice H correctly uses the apostrophe in "appliance's" but doesn't delete the incorrectly used colon.

5. D. Choice D correctly uses commas after "why" and after "easily" to set off the nonessential information, "when fresh bread can be obtained so easily." Choice A correctly places the comma after "why" but does not include a comma after "easily." Choice B correctly uses commas after "why" and "easily," but it incorrectly adds a comma after "bread," thus separating it from the verb, "can be obtained." Choice C leaves out the necessary comma after "why."

6. G. Choice G adds the comma after "others" correctly to set off the nonessential word "however." Choice F is wrong because there is no comma after "others." Choice H correctly uses commas to set off "however," but it incorrectly adds a comma after "that," thus breaking up the flow of the clause "that the process...is part of the pleasure...." Choice J doesn't use the necessary comma after "however" and incorrectly adds a comma after "report," thus separating a noun from the dependent clause that follows it.

7. D. Here "they say" is parenthetical to the main part of the sentence. Choice D correctly uses commas to separate this parenthetical information from the main part of the sentence. Choice B incorrectly uses a colon after "bread." Remember that the colon should be used to introduce or emphasize an explanation or a short phrase. There is no need for the colon here, and it incorrectly breaks up the sentence. Choice C incorrectly uses the semicolon after "baking bread," which is not an independent clause.

8. G. Choice G correctly uses two dashes to set off an interruption in the middle of the sentence. Here the interruption is "mixing, kneading, waiting for the rises, and baking." The interruption is an explanation of the "steps." Because it's not necessary to the meaning of the sentence, it should be set off. Choice F is incorrect because the comma after "steps" does not match the dash used after "baking." Choice H is incorrect because the dash after "mixing" occurs too soon; the other steps after the "mixing" need to be stated before the dash. Choice J is incorrect because the dash after "steps" is not paired with a dash after "baking."

9. A. Choice A correctly uses a semicolon to join two independent clauses without a FANBOYS word. Choice B is wrong because it uses a semicolon with the FANBOYS word "or" to join two independent clauses. Choice C is incorrect because the use of a comma without a FANBOYS word between the two independent clauses creates a run-on sentence. Choice D is incorrect because no punctuation is used between two independent clauses, creating a run-on sentence.

10. J. Choice J correctly uses commas to set off the nonessential information "and not simply the product." Choice F is incorrect because it needs a comma after the word "process" to set off the nonessential phrase. Choice G is wrong because the words before the semicolon do not form an independent clause. Choice H is wrong because there is no comma after the word "process," and the comma used after "simply" incorrectly disturbs the flow of the sentence.

Word Choice

DIFFICULTY: ★ ★ ★

FREQUENCY: ★ ★ ★

SURPRISE FACTOR: ★ ★ ★ ★

● INTRODUCTION TO WORD CHOICE QUESTIONS

Word Choice questions ask you to choose the word or phrasing that follows the conventions of standard written English. Thus, these questions are fairly straightforward. The challenge here is learning which rules the ACT tests and being able to recognize when a question violates one of the rules. The one exception is idiom questions, which don't follow predictable rules.

Characteristics of Word Choice Questions

Word Choice questions usually involve one of four parts of speech. Verb usage is tested most frequently. Pronouns are also tested fairly often. Adjectives (which are sometimes used erroneously in place of adverbs) and prepositions also appear in word choice questions. Most types of word choice questions below are described in terms of the parts of speech they test. Another, less common type of Word Choice question asks you to determine the best word in context based on meaning. (See Question 5 in Dress Rehearsal for an example.)

Most Common Types of Word Choice Questions

VERB USAGE

A verb usage question may ask you to choose either the correct subject-verb agreement or the correct form of a particular verb. Here's an example of an ACT question that tests both:

1. The managers of the finance department <u>has went</u> to the conference.

   A. NO CHANGE
   B. has gone
   C. have went
   D. have gone

The correct answer here is D. The subject is "managers," so it's incorrect to use "has." The verb form *went* is never correct with a helping verb like *has* or *had*, so "have gone" is the correct usage here. When answer choices include two forms of the same verb, such as "has" and "have" here, that's a clue that subject-verb agreement is being tested. Other combinations appearing in answer choices for questions that test subject-verb agreement might be *is* and *are* or *walks* and *walk*.

PRONOUNS

A Word Choice question involving pronouns may test either agreement, case, or form. Let's look at what's behind each. You remember that a pronoun is a word that substitutes for or refers to a noun or another pronoun. It must agree with, that is match, the word or words it takes the place of or refers to. See if you can determine what the pronoun "her" refers to in this sentence:

> WRONG: Would you believe that Mindy and Lucretia both lost **her** history books?

Here, "her" refers to "Mindy and Lucretia." Because two people are referred to, correct agreement requires a plural, not singular, pronoun. Therefore, "their" must be used here.

> RIGHT: Would you believe that **Mindy and Lucretia** both lost **their** history books?

If answer choices include both plural and singular pronouns, such as *his* and *their*, this characteristic indicates that the question is testing pronoun agreement.

While the pronoun agreement tested on the ACT revolves around the distinction between singular and plural, pronoun **case** concerns how a pronoun is used within the sentence. The **subject** of a sentence is usually the person or thing that does the action expressed by the verb. In the following examples, the subject is printed in bold:

> RIGHT: **He** is my brother.

RIGHT: **They** are hosting the party.

RIGHT: **She** attends my school.

The object in the sentence is either the object of a verb or the object of a preposition. Here pronouns used as objects are shown in bold:

RIGHT: After taking her nephew to the park, Sharon returned **him** to his parents.

RIGHT: Please pass **me** the salt.

RIGHT: The teacher instructed **us** to return the exam booklets to **him**.

If a pronoun is used as the subject, a subjective case pronoun (*I, we, he, she, they, who*) must be used. If a pronoun is used as an object, an objective case pronoun (*me, us, him, her, them, whom*) is called for. In the following sentence, "I" is the subject, and the pronoun "him" is the object of the verb "hand":

RIGHT: I don't mind holding the baby, but if he cries, I'll hand **him** back to his mother. [Not "I'll hand **he** back to his mother."]

A sentence that contains a preposition will also contain the object of the preposition. The object is always the next noun or pronoun that comes after the preposition. Note the correct use of the objective pronoun as the object of the preposition "to" in this sentence:

RIGHT: Trish gave the book to **me**. [Not "Trish gave the book to **I**."]

Any question that combines answer choices containing *me, us, him, her, them,* or *whom* with answer choices containing *I, we, he, she, they,* or *who* is testing pronoun case.

POSSESSION

The third type of pronoun question involves choosing the appropriate form (the correct spelling) of pronouns that show possession, such as *its, their,* and *theirs.* Try your hand at this ACT question that tests both form and case:

2. When Jill and her cousin came here on vacation, <u>them and my mother visited there</u> old neighborhood.

   F. NO CHANGE

   G. they and my mother visited their

   H. them and my mother visited their

   J. they and my mother visited there

The correct answer is B. Because "them" is an objective case pronoun, it can't be used as the subject of "visited." The correct case is "they visited." The correct spelling of the possessive pronoun is "their," not "there." Refer to the Performance Techniques section, where the box "Commonly Confused Words" provides additional clarification for *their*, *there*, and *they're*. Know these words; they are tested on the ACT.

ADJECTIVES

Questions that include an adjective in the underlined part of the sentence may be testing either adjective-adverb confusion or the use of the comparative and superlative forms. The comparative form of an adjective is used when only two things are being compared. The words *better* and *worse* are the comparative forms of *good* and *bad*. Generally the comparative form ends in *–er*, as in *taller*, *larger*, and *younger*. The superlative form of an adjective is used when three or more things are being compared. The words *best* and *worst* are the superlative forms of good and bad. Typically the superlative form ends in *–est*, as in *tallest*, *largest*, and *youngest*. Here's an ACT question that tests both adjective-adverb confusion and superlative-comparative confusion:

3. Because I got tired and ran so <u>slow, my afternoon race results were worser</u> than my morning race results.

   A. NO CHANGE
   B. slowly, my afternoon race results were worse
   C. slowly, my afternoon race results were worst
   D. slow, my afternoon race results were the more badder

The answer is B. The adverb "slowly," not the adjective "slow," is needed to modify the verb "ran." The comparative form "worse," not the superlative form "worst," is used when only two things, here the morning and afternoon races, are being compared. The form "more badder" is never correct.

IDIOMS

The fourth part of speech that's important to notice for word choice questions is the preposition. A preposition is a word that shows the relationship between two nouns. Some examples are *above, for, from, in, into, on, over,* and *with*. Prepositions are important in idioms. An idiom is formed by two or more words that are used together to express a certain meaning (e.g., *astounded by, borrow from,* and *impressed with.*) In these examples, the prepositions *by, from,* and *with* form idiomatically correct expressions with the words *astounded, borrow,* and *impressed* respectively. Here's an ACT question that tests idiomatic expression:

4. When I got to the exit of the megastore, I was stopped <u>from the security guard, who insisted on checking</u> my receipt.

   F. NO CHANGE
   G. by the security guard, who insisted to check
   H. by the security guard, who insisted on checking
   J. from the security guard, who insisted on checking

The answer is H. The correct idiomatic expressions here are "stopped by [a person]" and "insisted on checking."

● THE TRAP DOOR: STEERING CLEAR OF ANSWER TRAPS

Many types of Word Choice answer traps exist, and these traps appear frequently. As you read through the English section, be alert for these traps. The traps make recognizing Word Choice errors a bit tricky, but if you know what to look for, you won't be caught off guard.

Types of Word Choice Answer Traps

PRONOUN CASE TRAP

Conjunctions such as *and, or,* and *nor* are used near pronouns. You would never say "Him went to the store," so don't say "Him and Sue went to the store."

SUBJECT-VERB AGREEMENT TRAP

The subject and verb are separated from each other by intervening words, such as a prepositional phrase or two or a descriptive clause. In the following example, notice that it is the subject that agrees with the verb, not a noun that's part of the descriptive clause:

> RIGHT: The **salads** that were made with mayonnaise **have** spoiled.
> [Correct subject-verb agreement is "salads have" not "mayonnaise have."]

WORD CHOICE DISTRACTER TRAP

Answer choices for a particular question offer different wordings, each of which is acceptable. Considering those differences distracts you from thinking about whatever issue the question is actually testing, such as pronoun or verb usage.

Techniques for Avoiding Word Choice Question Answer Traps

The key to avoiding the word choice traps is to know what to look for, usually in the underlined part of the sentence but sometimes in a non-underlined part of the passage. Therefore, techniques for avoiding the traps give you specific things to look for. Think of these techniques as prompts that offer you clues about possible errors.

PRONOUN CASE TRAP

In the underlined part of the sentence, watch for pronouns that are used near the words *and*, *or*, and *nor*.

These conjunctions are used by the test maker to make it a little trickier for you to recognize a pronoun case error. You would never say "*Me* ran a mile," but because you need to work quickly on the ACT, you might miss the error in "*Me* and Tiffany ran a mile." Be on the alert any time you see a pronoun and a conjunction that appear together. This situation is a clue that you should slow down and think carefully about pronoun case.

SUBJECT-VERB AGREEMENT TRAP

When a verb is underlined, don't assume that whatever noun comes just before the verb is the subject. The test maker often places words between the subject and the verb to make it trickier for you to notice an error in subject-verb agreement. Sometimes the intervening words constitute a prepositional phrase; other times, a descriptive clause comes between the subject and verb.

In this sentence, see if you can determine the subject of the verb "contain":

WRONG: The basket at the bottom of the stairs **contain** books.

The subject, that is, the thing doing the containing, is "the basket," not "the stairs." The sentence includes two prepositional phrases, "at the bottom" and "of the stairs," between the subject and the verb. Therefore, this sentence should be revised:

RIGHT: The **basket** at the bottom of the stairs **contains** books.

Remember, the verb must agree with its subject, not with the object of a preposition.

WORD CHOICE DISTRACTER TRAP

Watch for answer choices that offer alternative wordings of a phrase that isn't wrong. Verbs and pronouns are the most heavily tested parts of speech in word choice question, so focus on underlined verbs and pronouns.

Notice how the different phrasings offered for the word "generally" can distract you from the real issue in this question:

5. Advertising pages for the theater program is generally sold up until a week before the play.

   A. NO CHANGE

   B. are generally

   C. is, in general,

   D. is usually

The correct answer is B. This question is testing subject-verb agreement, but two traps are present: the subject-verb agreement trap and the distracter trap. You should notice the subject-verb agreement trap created by the prepositional phrase "for the theater program." The subject of this sentence is "pages," so the correct verb is "are." If you don't notice the prepositional phrase, you can easily be distracted by the phrasing differences in the answer choices. It makes no difference whether you use the use the wording "generally," "in general," or "usually." Any of those three phrasings is acceptable.

• PERFORMANCE TECHNIQUES: KEY RULES

Remember that you don't need to memorize every rule in the grammar book to do well on the ACT. Instead, you need to know which rules are tested and how to recognize which rule to apply in a given situation. In addition to the rules, this section includes a short list of frequently confused words.

PRONOUN CASE

Whenever you see the pronouns *I, me, he, she, him, her, we, us, they,* or *them* underlined, check for an error in pronoun case. If the pronoun functions as the subject in the sentence, it should be *I, he, she, we,* or *they.* If it functions as an object of a verb or preposition, it should be *me, him, her, us,* or *them.* You and *it* take the same form whether used as a subject or an object, so case is never an issue for these pronouns.

COMMONLY MISUSED WORDS

accept—to receive: *I am happy to accept your gift.*

except—leaving out: *Everyone except Caitlyn will perform.*

affect—to influence: *The weather may affect our plans.*

effect—an influence: *The wind had a negative effect on my race results.*

fewer [use with things that can be counted]: *Jackie has fewer toys.*

less [use with things that aren't countable]: *I now have less respect for him.*

its [use only as a possessive pronoun]: *The house needs its roof repaired.*

it's—it is, it was: *It's time for dinner.*

of [is not interchangeable with have, as in *might have, could have,* etc.]

their [use only as possessive pronoun]: *John and Mary are walking their dogs.*

theirs [use only as possessive pronoun]: *The Smiths claimed the land was theirs.*

there [use only with a verb such as *is* or *were*]: *There were two people waiting.*

there's—there is, there was: *There's enough for everybody.*

they're—they are: *They're going to Alaska.*

which [use only to refer to things, not people]

who [use to refer to people]: *the friend who cares*

IRREGULAR VERBS

Learn to recognize incorrect forms of irregular past tenses. Refer to the box for a list of verbs that appear frequently on the ACT and are never correct.

PAST TENSE VERB FORMS

ALWAYS WRONG	CORRECT FORM
begun	began, had begun
had took	took, had taken
had went	went, had gone

COMPARATIVES AND SUPERLATIVES

Whenever you see an underlined adjective that ends in –*er* or –*est*, follow the rules for comparatives and superlatives. The comparative form usually ends in –*er* and is used when only two things are being compared. For example:

RIGHT: Of my *two* sisters, Tillie is the **older.**

The superlative usually ends in –*est* and is used when three or more things are being compared. For example:

RIGHT: Of *all* Kevin's oil paintings, the seascape is the **largest.**

Never use the word *least* or the word *most* with a superlative adjective that ends in –*est*. For example:

WRONG: The blue fabric has the **most shiniest** surface of all.

RIGHT: The blue fabric has the **shiniest** surface of all.

IDIOMATIC USAGE

Whenever you see an underlined preposition, ask yourself whether the expression it appears in is clear and correct. The question may be testing idiomatic usage. The English language contains a lot of idiomatic expressions, and it would be impossible to list all that might appear on the ACT. You have to rely on your ear, that is, your sense of what "sounds" correct to you, to handle idiom questions. You don't need to be overly concerned about idioms, however, because they appear in only a small fraction of the questions.

ADJECTIVES AND ADVERBS

Whenever you see an underlined adjective, make sure it modifies a noun or pronoun. If you notice that any answer choices include words ending in –*ly*, think about what the word modifies. Remember that an adjective can modify only a noun or pronoun. An adverb (many of which end in –*ly*) must be used to modify a verb.

• DRESS REHEARSAL: SAMPLE QUESTIONS AND DETAILED EXPLANATIONS

Subject-Verb Agreement with Distracter Trap

1. The main library's collection of anatomy books <u>are being moved to the medical library, which is next door.</u>

    A. NO CHANGE
    B. is being moved to the adjacent medical library
    C. are being moved next door to the medical library
    D. are moving to the medical library, which is next door

The underlined part of this sentence is fairly long. The first thing you should notice is the verb "are." Whenever a verb form like that is underlined, look for the subject and check for subject-verb agreement. It's tempting to think that "books," the plural noun immediately preceding the plural verb "are," is the subject, but it's not. The noun "books" is the object of the preposition "of," so it can't possibly be the subject. The singular noun "collection" is the subject, and correct subject-verb agreement is "collection is" (singular verb), not "collection are." Therefore, **choice B is the only one that can be correct**. Notice that the different phrasings using "adjacent" and "next door" are distracters.

Pronoun Case (*Who/Whom*) and Subject-Verb Agreement Errors

2. My teachers, <u>whom are very caring and incredibly dedicated, plans</u> to email me all the class notes so I can stay caught up while I'm recovering from my surgery.

    F. NO CHANGE
    G. whom are very caring and incredibly dedicated, plans
    H. who are very caring and incredibly dedicated, plan
    J. who couldn't be more caring and dedicated, plans

Whenever the underlined part of the sentence contains *who* or *whom*, determine how the pronoun functions in the sentence. You need to ask yourself whether the pronoun is the subject of a verb or the object of a verb or a preposition. In this question, the pronoun functions as the subject of the verb "are." Therefore, the pronoun "who" is necessary here, and you can eliminate choices F and G. Now consider the differences between choices H and J. Two different forms of the verb "plan" appear. Because the subject, "teachers," is plural, the verb form here should be "plan." **Choice H is correct** because it uses the correct subject-verb agreement, "teachers...plan."

Idiom

3. My boss is consistent in demanding that her employees exhibit respect <u>for</u> one another at all times.

   A. NO CHANGE

   B. with

   C. in

   D. at

All the answer choices are prepositions, so idiomatic usage is the tested issue here. **The correct answer is A.** Your ear should tell you that the correct idiom is "respect for." If you're not sure about this, make your best guess and move on to the next question. Remember, you can't predict which idiomatic expressions will be tested on the ACT. Focus your attention on the rule-based issues that you know you'll see, such as verb and pronoun usage, adjective-adverb confusion, and superlative-comparative errors.

Comparative/Superlative Error

4. While touring the country, I visited <u>one of the most oldest</u> churches I have ever seen.

   F. NO CHANGE

   G. one of the oldest

   H. the most old, by far,

   J. one of the more older

Because one of the underlined words here is an adjective ending in –*est*, you have a clue to check that the rules for superlatives and comparatives are being followed. From the context of the sentence, "ever," you can infer that more than two "churches" are being compared. Therefore, the superlative form "oldest" is called for here, and you can eliminate choice J. Choice H, "most old," is not the correct superlative form for the adjective "old," so you can eliminate it. Choice F is incorrect because the adjective "oldest" is a superlative, so it shouldn't be preceded by "most." **The correct answer is G.**

Choosing the Most Appropriate Meaning in Context

5. Health professionals hold many <u>conflicting</u> opinions about the best dietary choices for the average person.

   A. NO CHANGE
   B. contesting
   C. inflicting
   D. rivaling

The correct answer is A. The answer choices offer four different words, all of which end in the same form, *–ing*. Because the form is the same, it should be clear that this question is asking you to differentiate subtle shades of meaning. The meaning of three of the words, in choices A, B, and D, is related to a tension between two opposites. Choice C, "inflicting," doesn't have a similar meaning, but it has a similar sound to the word in choice A. **The best choice is choice A.** The words "contesting" and "rivaling" are generally used with people, not with "opinions."

● THE FINAL ACT: PRACTICE QUIZ

Directions: In the passage that follows, certain words and phrases are underlined and numbered. In the right-hand column, you will find alternatives for the underlined part. In most cases, you are to choose the one that best expresses the idea, makes the statement appropriate for standard written English, or is worded most consistently with the style and tone of the passage as a whole. If you think the original version is best, choose NO CHANGE. For each question, choose the alternative you consider best.

Great Grandma and
the Great Depression

It's one thing to read about history

from a textbook, but it's quite a different

thing to hear about it firsthand. When

I interviewed my great-grandmother

about her experience of growing up in

the 1930s, I was <u>amazed for hearing</u>
¹
about the extreme poverty she had lived

1. A. NO CHANGE
   B. surprised for hearing
   C. amazed to hear
   D. surprised upon the
      hearing

through. Until I listened <u>careful as she</u>
²
<u>answered</u> my questions, the terms "Great
²
Depression" and "Stock Market Crash"

2. F. NO CHANGE
   G. careful for her answering
   H. carefully as she answered
   J. for her careful answering
      of

<u>was just</u> something to memorize for a
³
history test. When Great Grandma told

3. A. NO CHANGE
   B. were just
   C. were justly
   D. was in justice

me that <u>her and her siblings</u> sometimes
⁴

4. F. NO CHANGE
   G. her and her sisters and
      brothers
   H. she and her siblings
   J. her, along with her
      siblings,

didn't know where <u>there next meal</u> would
⁵
come from, the words in my history book

5. A. NO CHANGE
   B. there next lunch or supper
   C. their next meal
   D. their subsequent meal

took on a whole new <u>meaning.</u>
⁶
   In addition to making history come

alive, the stories Great Grandma told

6. F. NO CHANGE
   G. definition
   H. vocabulary
   J. type of meaning

me <u>also gave me some insight on</u> her
⁷
personality. I had always wondered why

7. A. NO CHANGE
   B. gave me some insight into
   C. gave me an insight within
   D. also provided an insight
      on

a woman as <u>financial comfortable</u> as
                        8
she currently is would be so obsessed

with not wasting food. As she explained,

growing up in poverty had <u>ingrained in</u>
                                    9
<u>her</u> the habit of using wisely everything
9
she had. In a week, Great Grandma told

me, she wouldn't have <u>threw away the</u>
                                10
<u>amount of food</u> that my parents and I
        10
discard after only one meal.

8. **F.** NO CHANGE
   G. financially comfortable
   H. in comfort financially
   J. comfortably financial

9. **A.** NO CHANGE
   B. imprinted onto her
   C. impressed within her
   D. ingrained onto her

10. **F.** NO CHANGE
    G. wasted away the
       amount of food
    H. threw away the amount
       of leftovers
    J. thrown away the amount
       of food

● THE FINAL ACT: ANSWERS AND EXPLANATIONS FOR WORD CHOICE QUESTIONS

1. C. This question is testing whether you know that the best form for the verb *to hear*. Don't get distracted trying to choose between "surprised" and "amazed." Either is acceptable, but the verb/preposition combinations in choices A, B, and D are not idiomatic.

2. H. This question tests adjective-adverb confusion. Choices F and G incorrectly use the adjective "careful" to modify the verb "listened." Choice H is the best choice because it correctly uses the adverb "carefully" to modify "listened." Choice J distorts the meaning by using "careful" to modify "answering" when the context of the sentence suggests that "careful" is meant to modify "listened."

3. B. When you see a verb underlined, always make sure it agrees with its subject. The subject here is plural, "terms." Therefore "were" (not "was") is the correct verb. This question is complicated by the different word choices offered to replace "just." In this context, just is used to mean "only." The other offerings, "justly" and "in all justice" relate to a different meaning of "just."

4. H. This question tests pronoun case. Only choice H can be correct because it's the only choice that correctly uses "she" as the subject of the verb "know." Don't get distracted by the alternative wording for "siblings" in choice G.

5. C. Whenever you see "there" underlined, check to see if it should be the possessive pronoun *their* instead. That's the case here. In addition to the correct pronoun form, another word choice issue is tested in this question. Though "next" and "subsequent" are related in meaning, "subsequent" (choice D) is incorrect in the context of this sentence.

6. F. When a question has only a single word underlined and the answer choices are all similar in meaning, think carefully about subtle differences. The words "definition" and "vocabulary" don't fit the context of this sentence, and "type of meaning" is wordy.

7. B. This question is testing idiomatic expression. You need to know that "into" is the correct preposition to be used after the word "insight." Don't be distracted by choice D's use of "provided." While "provided" is acceptable, "also" is redundant because the nonunderlined part of the sentence includes "in addition to," and "on" is not idiomatically correct.

8. G. When you see an adjective underlined, check to see if it's used correctly, modifying a noun or pronoun. Here an adjective, "financial," incorrectly modifies another adjective, "comfortable." Choice H is incorrect because it creates the nonidiomatic expression "as in comfort." Choice J does use an adverb to modify an adjective, but it distorts the intended meaning of the sentence.

9. A. This question tests whether you can recognize the subtle distinctions among three related but distinct words, "imprinted," "impressed," and "ingrained." Because the nonunderlined part of the sentence includes the word "habit," the appropriate word in this context is "ingrained." Correct idiomatic usage requires the preposition "in," not "onto," following the word "ingrained."

10. J. This question tests the correct past tense verb form. The word *threw* is the correct simple past tense, that is, the past tense without a helping verb, but *threw* is never correct with a helping verb. The form *thrown* must be used after *have*. Choice G's expression "wasted away" refers to illness, not discarding things. Choice H can't be correct because "have threw" is incorrect, so don't get distracted by the substitution of "leftovers" for "food."

Lesson 4: Wordiness

DIFFICULTY: ★ ★

FREQUENCY: ★

SURPRISE FACTOR: ★ ★

● INTRODUCTION TO WORDINESS QUESTIONS

The ACT values economy in writing. In finance, economy means not spending more money than necessary. In writing, economy means not using more words than necessary. Therefore, on the ACT English section, the shortest answer choice is often the best. A relatively small number of questions test wordiness as the main issue. However, even on questions that test other issues, such as Sentence Sense and Style, you can use the principle of economy to rule out wrong answer choices because they're wordy.

Characteristics of Wordiness Questions

Many Wordiness questions are easy to recognize. If you skim through the English section of a sample ACT, ignoring the text of the English passages and looking only at the answer choices, you'll notice that a few questions contain answer choices that say the same thing in different phrasings. Look at this example:

1. The Historical Society of Prospect Hill <u>began and started</u> in the early 1800s.

    A. NO CHANGE (began and started)

    B. was established when it began

    C. was founded

    D. got its start when it originated

You should notice here that many of the words have the same meaning: "began," "started," "established," "founded," "originated." Be on the lookout for questions such as this one in which the answer choices all express the same meaning but use different words. This feature is a characteristic of Wordiness questions. On these questions, you can often guess—correctly!—that the shortest answer is best without even referring to the context of the passage. Unless you're pressed for time, however, you should still take a moment to read your answer back into the sentence in the passage.

You can read the shortest answer—**choice C**—back into in this sentence and verify that the shortest answer choice is indeed best here: "The Historical Society of Prospect Hill [was founded] in the early 1800s." The other three answer choices all use unnecessary words to convey the same meaning.

Most Common Types of Wordiness Questions

Most Wordiness questions on the ACT use phrasings that are redundant. Redundancy means unnecessary repetition. Here's an example:

> WORDY: When I **repeat myself and say the same thing twice,** I'm being redundant.

> CONCISE: When I **repeat myself,** I'm being redundant.

Here, the idea of "saying the same thing twice" is already expressed by the word "repeat."

REDUNDANCY WITHIN THE UNDERLINED PASSAGE

In the easiest type of Wordiness question, repetition is contained within the underlined part of the sentence. See if you can identify why this sentence is redundant:

> I'm looking forward to going back and returning to the site of our adventures.

This sentence is redundant because "going back" and "returning" mean the same thing. To avoid wordiness, you need to use one or the other, not both. Because you naturally focus on the differences among the answer choices, it probably won't be too difficult to find and correct wordiness in questions like this one.

REDUNDANCY OUTSIDE THE UNDERLINED PASSAGE

The second type of Wordiness question, however, is a little trickier. When an underlined part of the sentence repeats an idea that's contained in the nonunderlined part of the passage, you need to pay careful attention to the context of the passage, not just to the underlined words. See if you can spot the wordiness here:

> The hikers, on the way up the mountain, found the terrain to be much more difficult to navigate than they had expected. They found, <u>as they ascended,</u> many fallen trees across the trail.

Here, the words "as they ascended" are unnecessary because they repeat the meaning expressed by "on the way up the mountain" in the previous sentence. In this case, the underlined phrase should be omitted. In fact, you should consider the presence of OMIT among the answer choices as clue that a question may be testing wordiness.

TOO MANY WORDS

A third type of Wordiness question uses phrasings that aren't necessarily repetitive but contain unnecessary words. Eliminating the unnecessary words altogether or choosing a shorter phrasing, depending on the situation, makes the sentence stronger and more direct. Notice the wordiness in these examples:

WORDY: The chattering in the back row lasted **throughout the duration of the** movie.

CONCISE: The chattering in the back row lasted **throughout** the movie. [Unnecessary words are eliminated.]

WORDY: The dog **displayed feelings of anxiety** during the thunderstorm.

CONCISE: The dog **appeared anxious** during the thunderstorm. [A shorter phrasing is used.]

Correcting this kind of wordiness demands that you choose the shortest, most direct wording. These question types are a bit harder, because there's no repetition to recognize and eliminate.

● THE TRAP DOOR: STEERING CLEAR OF ANSWER TRAPS

The test maker doesn't really set traps to throw you off with Wordiness questions. The only trap here involves your own awareness. First, you have to be aware that economy is valued in writing on the ACT. Sometimes, the only difference between the best answer and the wrong answers is simply that the best answer is shorter.

It's one thing to know that wordiness errors will show up on the ACT, but it's quite another to be able to recognize these errors when you're working quickly through the English section. Identifying wordiness is complicated by the fact that **wordy sentences often don't sound wrong.** Questions that test grammar, usage, and mechanics may be easier because some of the answer choices will sound incorrect to your ear. To recognize wordiness, you need to pay attention to the meanings of individual words. Remember that some Wordiness questions contain redundancy within the answer choices themselves, while others demand that you pay attention to nonunderlined words in the passage to recognize the redundancy. Still others test whether you can revise a statement using the most direct wording.

Types of Wordiness Answer Traps

With Wordiness questions, it's easy to get distracted by choices in the answers that are grammatically correct but redundant. If you're rushing through the English section, not thinking much about whether an underlined segment is concise or wordy, you are likely to fall into a trap. Don't choose the first "right" answer you see—there might be a better, more concise answer. Wordiness questions offer different phrasings that mean pretty much the same thing. In a Wordiness question, the issue is not choosing between, for example, *started* and *originated*. The issue is recognizing that the word *started* is a more concise way of saying *had its origin*.

Techniques for Avoiding Wordiness Question Answer Traps

Don't focus on slight differences in the meanings of words and phrases that mean essentially the same thing; these are distractions. You can avoid traps by remembering that economy of phrasing is valued on the ACT, so the best answer is often the shortest and most direct statement.

Here are some hints for distinguishing Wordiness questions from other types of questions.

If a question is testing, say, verb usage, you'll notice that the answer choices involve **different forms of the same word**. Look at this example:

2. On the night before I take a big test, I had tried to go to bed early.

   F. NO CHANGE

   G. tried

   H. had been trying

   J. try

The four answer choices use different forms of a single verb: "had tried," "tried," "had been trying," and "try." (In case you're wondering, the correct answer is J.)

Similarly, in a question that tests pronoun usage, you'll see different pronouns offered as answer choices, for example, *his, its, it's,* and *theirs.* Though the words are different, all the choices use the same part of speech, the pronoun.

In Wordiness questions, on the other hand, you'll see different several phrasings that convey **the same meaning but use different vocabulary.** Notice the differences in these answer choices for this question:

3. The village has spent 10 years trying to build and construct a new fire station.

   A. NO CHANGE

   B. in the attempt to construct

   C. trying to build

   D. in the effort to build

Don't fall into the trap of trying to decide whether "attempt," "trying," or "effort" sounds better here. Likewise, don't bother debating the relative merits of "construct" and "build." In a Wordiness question, usually one particular word is no better than any other. Rather, what matters is how concise and direct the whole expression is. Choice C is correct because it's the most concise.

● PERFORMANCE TECHNIQUES: KEY RULES

WORDINESS RULE: ELIMINATE UNNECESSARY WORDS.

The best answer choice forms a direct, concise statement. This is the basic rule to remember when faced with Wordiness questions on the ACT. Here are some tips that can help you recognize wordiness in specific questions:

- Notice if OMIT is the answer choice for choice D or J. If so, it's possible that the question tests wordiness. (Another possibility when you see the choice OMIT is that the question tests relevance, which you can read about in Lesson 6, Organization.)
- Notice whether the answer choices use a variety of words that have the same meaning, for example, *taught* and *instructed*.
- Trust your gut if you sense that an answer choice seems too long. Watch for indirect phrasing. Here's an example of indirect phrasing:

WORDY: The student council **held a meeting for the purpose of planning** the upcoming dance.

CONCISE: The student council **met to plan** the upcoming dance.

In this example, the phrase "held a meeting" is wordy, while the single verb "met" is direct. Likewise, "for the purpose of planning" unnecessarily includes the word "purpose," which is implicitly expressed by "to plan." Using a strong specific verb ("met") conveys meaning more directly than pairing a less specific verb with a noun ("held a meeting").

● DRESS REHEARSAL: SAMPLE QUESTIONS AND DETAILED EXPLANATIONS

Repetitive Words

1. The concerned parents chose Emma as their babysitter because <u>she had a maternal, motherly way of interacting</u> with their toddler.

    A. NO CHANGE

    B. of her motherly way of interacting maternally

    C. she had a maternal way of interacting

    D. she acted like a mother in her style, which was maternal, of interacting

The shortest answer is the best one here. Note that on a quick reading, choice A doesn't sound bad. As you consider the answer choices, you should notice that choice B includes both the words "motherly" and "maternally," and choice D includes both "mother" and "maternal." Remember, when you notice several answer choices that contain two words closely related in meaning, you should suspect that these choices are incorrect because they're wordy. **The correct answer is C.** If you read the shortest answer choice back into the sentence and it sounds acceptable, go with it!

Too Many Words

2. Many yoga classes are structured so that <u>the last ten minutes of the class</u> are devoted to practicing relaxation techniques.

   F. NO CHANGE
   G. a 10-minute period at the end of the class
   H. the class's last 10 minutes
   J. the final 10 minutes

If you're thinking about wordiness when you come to a question like this one, you'll notice right away that choice J is the shortest answer. If, on the other hand, you're reading quickly and the issue of wordiness doesn't strike you right away, you're likely to get distracted by the differences in the answer choices. You may think this question is asking whether "last," "final," or "at the end" is the best wording. Choosing the best way to describe the end of the class is not the issue here, however. The issue is that the nonunderlined part of the sentence includes the words "yoga classes." Therefore, it's unnecessary to repeat the word "class," which all the answer choices except choice J do. **The correct answer is choice J.**

String of Prepositional Phrases

3. The senatorial candidate attracted many supporters <u>by the focus she gave to education during the process of her campaigning</u>.

   A. NO CHANGE
   B. by her focus on education during the time she spent campaigning
   C. because she focused on education during her campaign
   D. through the focus she put on education while she was in the process of campaigning

Notice that all the answer choices say pretty much the same thing. Remember that this is a characteristic of Wordiness questions. **Choice C is correct** because it is the most concise and directly worded statement. In choice A, "by the focus she gave to" is less direct than choice C's wording, "because she focused." In choice B, "during the time she spent campaigning" can be expressed more concisely as "during her campaign." Choice D is wordy in using "the focus she put on education" in place of "she focused on education." In addition, "while she was in the process of campaigning" is a cumbersome way of saying "during her campaign."

Repetition from Nonunderlined Part

4. The corporation president, inspired by the teen's moving speech, decided to give <u>and make a donation of</u> a significant sum to the memorial fund.

    F. NO CHANGE

    G. and donate

    H. a large donation of

    J. OMIT

Whenever choice J is OMIT, your first step should be to read the sentence carefully and ask yourself whether the underlined part is necessary. If you consider choices G and H first, then you waste time thinking about how to word a phrase that doesn't even belong in the sentence. OMIT will not be the correct answer every time it's offered, but frequently it is. This time, **the correct answer is choice J**. Read choice F and notice whether the nonunderlined part of the sentence includes any words or phrases that mean the same thing as the underlined part. Notice that "give" in the nonunderlined part of this sentence repeats the meaning of "make a donation of." Therefore, the underlined segment should be omitted. A quick glance at choices G and H confirms that this question is testing redundancy in the context of the sentence.

Wordiness and Sentence Structure

5. During October, a selection of books about fire <u>prevention that</u> is lined up on the "Featured Reading" section at the entrance of the library.

    A. NO CHANGE

    B. prevention

    C. prevention, it

    D. prevention and

This question doesn't test wordiness in the sense of redundancy. Rather, all of the wrong answer choices create problems with sentence structure. In choice A, all the words after "prevention" are part of a descriptive clause. The sentence doesn't contain a verb to go with the apparent subject "selection." In choice C, the word "it" repeats the subject "selection." In choice D, the word "and" used immediately before the verb "is lined" suggests that something is missing: "a selection of books about fire prevention and [what other topic?]" Notice that choice B, the answer choice that corrects the sentence structure problem, happens to be the shortest answer, if only by one word. **The correct answer is choice B.** Even when wordiness is not the main issue tested, knowing that the shortest answer is often the best can help you zero in on the correct answer quickly.

● THE FINAL ACT: PRACTICE QUIZ

Directions: In the passage that follows, certain words and phrases are underlined and numbered. In the right-hand column, you will find alternatives for the underlined part. In most cases, you are to choose the one that best expresses the idea, makes the statement appropriate for standard written English, or is worded most consistently with the style and tone of the passage as a whole. If you think the original version is best, choose NO CHANGE. For each question, choose the alternative you consider best.

Emergency at the Playground!

All my skills and strengths as a babysitter were tested when I was looking after the O'Hare twins, five-year-old Kitty and Michael. Their parents left <u>and went out</u>[1] for dinner, and I fed the children sandwiches at home before taking them out to the nearby playground.

1. A. NO CHANGE
   B. and were going out
   C. the house and went
   D. OMIT

I agreed to kick around Kitty's soccer

ball with her while Michael played and
                                    2
amused himself on the slides and climb-
    2
ing toys. I felt secure knowing that

Michael is a very cautious child who

doesn't go near the taller platforms and

slide unless I'm standing quite close to
                              3
where he presently is. However, I was in
    3
for a surprise.

Kitty, a pretty good soccer player

for a five-year-old, kept me busy. Every

minute or so, I glanced over to check

on Michael. He was enjoying himself,

staying, as is his usual habit, on all the
                4
low climbing equipment.

Then, all of a sudden, I heard a

scream. Looking in Michael's direction,

I was amazed to see him on the ground at
        5
the base of the tall slide. He was holding

up his arm, which was dripping blood.

As I ran to him, I heard him screaming

something about a "sharp thing." Sure

enough, next to Michael was a broken

bottle with a long jagged edge. It had

2. F. NO CHANGE
   G. played and occupied himself
   H. played, quite capable of amusing himself
   J. played

3. A. NO CHANGE
   B. near him
   C. right there close to where he is
   D. very close to his vicinity

4. F. NO CHANGE
   G. as he typically does,
   H. as usual,
   J. in the way that is typical for him,

5. A. NO CHANGE
   B. amazed and astonished
   C. truly in a state of surprise
   D. surprisingly amazed
   C. was conscious of the fact
   D. could see the truth

caused a wound of tremendous
                6
magnitude in Michael's arm. His face
  6
was pale, his lips were turning blue,

6. F. NO CHANGE
   G. been the cause of gigantic wound
   H. caused a huge wound
   J. caused a sizeable wound to occur

and I became aware that he was losing
       7
blood quickly.

7. A. NO CHANGE
   B. realized
   C. was conscious of the fact
   D. could see the truth

    My first aid training told me this
was a serious situation. I got Michael to
     8
lie down and tried to soothe him while I
grabbed my cell phone to call 911. Then
I reached the O'Hares, who said they'd
meet us at the hospital.

8. F. NO CHANGE
   G. a situation of the most dire sort
   H. indeed a gravely serious situation
   J. a situation that was serious

    Have you ever ridden in an ambu-
lance with a bleeding, screaming five-
year-old and his terrified twin sister?
Trust me, it's not fun. The five-minute
ambulance ride seemed to last five
hours. By the time we reached our
                 9
destination, which was the hospital,
       9
I think Kitty was screaming louder than
her brother. Fortunately, Mr. and Mrs.
O'Hare were waiting for us. They went

9. A. NO CHANGE
   B. got to the hospital, our destination
   C. reached our destination, the hospital
   D. arrived at the hospital

into the triage room with Michael, trusting

me to soothe Kitty in the waiting room.

Things turned out well for Michael,

and Mr. and Mrs. O'Hare were <u>grateful</u>
₁₀
<u>I'd gotten him</u> to the hospital in time.
₁₀
The next few times I babysit Kitty and

Kevin, I think we'll stay inside and play

board games.

10. F. NO CHANGE
     G. filled with gratitude that I'd gotten him
     H. thankful I'd been able to get him
     J. grateful that I'd seen to it that he'd gotten

● THE FINAL ACT: ANSWERS AND EXPLANATIONS FOR WORDINESS QUESTIONS

1. D. In this question, the underlined words duplicate a meaning that is conveyed elsewhere. Whenever you notice that OMIT is offered as an answer choice, consider that wordiness may be an issue. (OMIT is always the shortest answer choice!) In choices A and C, the word "went" repeats the idea expressed by "left" in the nonunderlined part of the sentence. In choice B, it's not necessary to use "the house," because that idea is conveyed implicitly in the passage.

2. J. In this question, the underlined segment contains redundancy. The phrase "amused himself" is similar to the meaning of the word "played." Choices G and H also contain words that duplicate the meaning of "played." Choice J eliminates the redundancy.

3. B. Choice A is the longest answer. In addition to being wordy, it uses the word "presently," which sounds formal and doesn't match the conversational tone of the passage. Choices C and D are unnecessarily long; each takes several words to the express the meaning of the word "near." Choice B eliminates the wordiness.

4. H. When one answer choice is shorter than the others, it may be a clue that wordiness is an issue. Choice F, in addition to being wordy, sounds too formal to suit the tone of this passage. Choice G uses the clause "he typically does" when the single word "usual" would work.

Choice J uses the general phrase "in the way that," which doesn't contribute to the sentence's meaning. Don't be distracted by trying to decide whether the word "typical" or "usual" is more appropriate here. Both mean the same thing. The issue is wordiness.

5. A. Choice A is the shortest and best answer. The words in choice B, "amazed and astonished," mean the same thing. Choice C unnecessarily introduces the phrase "truly in a state of." Choice D inappropriately pairs the adverb "surprisingly" with the adjective "amazed," creating redundancy.

6. H. Don't get distracted trying to figure out whether "magnitude," "gigantic," "huge," or "sizeable" is the best way to say "large" here. The issue isn't the particular word choice; it's wordiness. Choice H has the shortest and best wording. Notice that "caused" is more concise than "had been the cause of," the wording used in choice G.

7. B. Don't use a phrase when a single word will do. Choice B's wording, "realized," means the same as choice A's "became aware." In choices C and D, "the fact" and "the truth" do not need to be stated explicitly. Choice B is best because it's the shortest and most direct.

8. F. Choice F is the shortest answer and the only one that isn't wordy. In choice G, the prepositional phrase "of the most dire sort" can be shortened to simply "dire," placed before the word "situation." Choice H uses an adverb, "gravely," which repeats the meaning of the following adjective, "serious." Choice J unnecessarily uses the words "that was."

9. D. All choices except choice D include redundancy because the meaning of "destination" is already expressed by the verbs "got to," "reached," and "arrived." Don't be distracted by trying to choose among these three words, which mean the same thing. Notice that one answer is shorter and realize that wordiness, not word choice, is the issue here.

10. F. The incorrect answers here all use different ways to say the same thing. The question tests whether you can recognize wordiness, not whether "grateful" is preferable to "thankful." In choice G, "filled with gratitude" is less concise than choice F's wording, "grateful." In choice H, "I'd been able to get" is wordier than "I'd gotten." In choice J, "I'd seen to it that he'd gotten" is longer than "I'd gotten him."

LESSON 5

Writing Strategy and Style

DIFFICULTY: ★ ★ ★ ★

FREQUENCY: ★ ★ ★

SURPRISE FACTOR: ★ ★

● INTRODUCTION TO WRITING STRATEGY AND STYLE QUESTIONS

Writing Strategy questions ask you explicitly to consider specific choices an author makes in the writing process. Some center on the best phrasing to express a particular meaning, while others ask whether a passage fulfills a specified goal. Style questions require you to match the style and tone of the passage. Instead of asking you to apply the rules of grammar and principles of good writing (as with most English questions), these question types focus on the author's goals and methods.

Most Writing Strategy questions and Style questions require you to have a good sense of the passage as a whole. You can think of them as similar to questions in the Reading section. As you work through a Reading passage, you think about the main idea of the passage, the writer's purpose, and the writer's tone, or attitude, toward the topic. Focusing on these aspects of a passage will also help you to answer Writing Strategy and Style questions in the English section.

You have to think carefully about Writing Strategy and Style questions, and they may take you a little longer to answer than other English questions. However, once you learn to recognize these question types and understand that they require a special approach, you'll feel more confident.

Characteristics of Writing Strategy and Style Questions

Writing Strategy questions always include a question stem. Most other English questions appear with the question number immediately followed by the answer choices. Here's an example:

1. A. NO CHANGE
    B. went
    C. had gone
    D. were going

This question asks you to determine the most appropriate verb form in context. It provides answer choices only, with no question stem.

Here, on the other hand, is a typical Writing Strategy question, with a question stem preceding the answer choices:

2. Given that all of the answer choices are true, which one would most effectively tie the ending of this essay back to the beginning?
    F. NO CHANGE
    G. such as William Shakespeare and Queen Elizabeth.
    H. other writers of the Elizabethan age.
    J. other playwrights working in England at the time.

To answer a Writing Strategy question, you have to read the question stem carefully and determine what it's asking. The key phrase in the question above is "most effectively tie the ending of this essay back to the beginning."

Unlike Writing Strategy questions, Style questions don't always include a question stem. Instead, you may see four answer choices, each expressing the same meaning in a different way. You need to choose the answer that best fits the overall style of the passage, whether formal or informal, humorous or serious, personal or detached. Here's an example:

3. A. NO CHANGE [The internal workings of the characters' minds are subtly expressed by the careful cinematography.]
    B. The viewer is certain to be moved by the stunning cinematography that lends insight into the characters' emotions.
    C. You'll be awed by how great the director is at making the characters come alive!
    D. The camera angles offer a sensitive portrayal of the characters' inner lives.

There's no question stem to alert you that this question is testing style. Reading each choice carefully, you should see that each conveys the same information, but only in choice C does the writer take an informal tone and address the reader personally. The other three choices use a more serious and detached tone.

Most Common Types of Writing Strategy Questions

Writing Strategy questions can be grouped into four categories. All are written from the perspective of the writer who is making revisions. These questions ask

1) whether or not a particular sentence should be added to the passage,

2) the effect of deleting a particular phrase or sentence,

3) whether or not the passage fulfills a given purpose or assignment, or

4) the most effective wording to accomplish a specified purpose.

Here's an example of the format of a question that involves adding material to the passage:

4. At this point, the writer is considering adding the following TRUE statement:

    The xxx of the yyy is certainly aaa and achieves bbb.

    Should the writer make this addition here?

    F. Yes, because...

    G. Yes, because...

    H. No, because...

    J. No, because...

Note that the answer choices above don't offer words you would add to the passage. Rather, these choices address the question stem. Answering a question about adding a sentence has two parts: deciding between yes and no and choosing the appropriate reason for your decision.

Now let's look at a typical format for a question that asks about **deleting material**: [The number 5 would appear in a box at the end of the paragraph that's referred to here.]

5. Upon reviewing this paragraph, the writer considers deleting the preceding sentence. If the writer were to delete the sentence, the paragraph would primarily lose:

   A. an insight into...
   B. an exaggeration that...
   C. an explanation of the...
   D. an example of...

The answer choices are not words that would be deleted. Instead, they describe the rhetorical function of the words the author might delete. You have to think about what the words do. Typical answer choices might include words such as examples, an illustration, an opinion, or specific details about.

Here's a typical format for a question that asks you to determine whether the passage **meets a specified goal**:

6. Suppose the writer's goal had been to write an essay that describes xxx in yyy way. Would this essay fulfill that goal?

   F. Yes, because...
   G. Yes, because...
   H. No, because...
   J. No, because...

As with questions about whether or not a sentence should be added to the passage, you have to decide between yes and no and choose the appropriate reason to justify your decision.

Answer choices for the first three Writing Strategy question types are statements that say something about the writer's strategy, rather than phrasings to be used in the passage. For the fourth question type, however, whichever answer you choose becomes part of the text of the passage. This question type asks you to **determine the best phrasing to accomplish a particular purpose.** The purpose is stated in the question stem, as in this example:

7. Given that all the choices are true, which one would most effectively express the narrator's initial reservations about participating in the program?

   A. NO CHANGE [The program offered many benefits, including the chance to travel abroad.]

B. I had heard many positive reports from students who had participated in the program over the last several years.

C. When I first heard about length of the program, I wasn't sure it was right for me.

D. The minute I read the brochure, I knew I had to participate in the program.

The key words that help you determine what the question is asking are the words that follow the phrase "most effectively express."

● THE TRAP DOOR: STEERING CLEAR OF ANSWER TRAPS

The traps for Writing Strategy questions aren't set for you by the test maker. You create them for yourself by not working carefully enough. You need to be certain of what a Writing Strategy question stem is asking before you look at the answer choices.

Some questions that test your understanding of style don't appear with a question stem. You may not immediately see that the answer you're looking for is the one that matches the overall style of the passage.

Types of Writing Strategy and Style Answer Traps

Writing Strategy Trap: Reading the Question. You look at the answer choices before you've taken the time to determine exactly what the question stem is asking.

Writing Strategy Trap: Distracter Answers. You choose an answer because it contains words you remember seeing in the passage, not because it addresses the issue in the question stem.

Style Trap: Recognizing the Question Type. You don't recognize that a question with answer choices only (no question stem) is testing style instead of an issue that is rule based, such as sentence structure, punctuation, or word choice.

Techniques for Avoiding Writing Strategy and Style Question Answer Traps

You can avoid the Writing Strategy traps by making sure you know what the question stem is asking. Read carefully. The question stem will include some words that could appear in a question about any passage on any topic. The words you need to focus on are the words that are specific to this particular question. Using your pencil to under-line those words in the test booklet can help you stay focused on the question and avoid distracter answers. Here are some sample question stems with the passage-specific words underlined:

Given that all the choices are true, which would most effectively...

- illustrate the term *plan* as is it used in this sentence?
- communicate the mother's positive attitude toward the narrator's behavior?
- provide a specific description of the painting? [Note that a statement *about* the painting, such as, "The artist completed this work in 1898," does not provide a specific description.]

Homing in on what the question is asking virtually guarantees that you'll spot the correct answer. Just determine what the question asks before you read through the answer choices so that you won't fall for tempting distracters.

You can avoid the Style trap by developing your awareness of style. Notice the style and the author's tone as you work through each Eng-lish passage. Some passages use a formal style, similar to that of a textbook. Other passages will be less formal and written from the point of view of an engaged narrator. A conversational style could be appro-priate in a less formal passage but would not be appropriate in a more formal passage in which the writer is more removed from the topic.

Writing Style

INFORMAL

- May focus on a topic involving personal experience.
- May have a first-person narrator (uses *I*).
- May address the reader directly (uses *you*).
- Uses easily understandable vocabulary and fairly simple sentence structure.
- May have a conversational tone (writer uses words as though talking).
- May be written to inform in an entertaining way.
- May appeal to the reader's emotions.

FORMAL

- May focus on a topic you might study in school.
- Is written in the third person (the writer does not use *I*).
- Does not address the reader directly (does not use *you*).
- May introduce technical vocabulary specific to the topic.
- May use paragraph and sentence structure that are more complicated than in an informal speech or conversation.
- Is written to illustrate, explain, or educate in a serious manner.
- Appeals more to reason than emotion.

These descriptions of formal and informal style don't provide clear-cut rules for determining style. However, any passage that includes a Style question will have a recognizable style. Style questions don't ask you to label a particular style but to infer the overall style of the passage and harmonize with it.

● PERFORMANCE TECHNIQUES: KEY RULES

UNDERSTANDING THE QUESTION

Don't try to answer a Writing Strategy question until you understand what it is asking. The English section presents a lot of questions to answer in a limited amount of time. It's easy to feel rushed and fall for tempting distractions. Writing Strategy questions may take a little more time than other question types. However, when you take the time to determine exactly what the question asks, the correct answer often jumps out at you.

SKIPPING A QUESTION

Know when to skip a question and come back to it after reading the entire passage. If a Writing Strategy or Style question requires an overall sense of the passage, skip it and return after you've read further on. For example, if a question in the middle of the passage asks you to choose a wording that accomplishes a specified purpose "and is consistent with the focus of the passage as a whole," you should read to the end so that you're clear on what the whole passage's focus is.

USING THE PASSAGE TITLE

The title of the passage is usually a phrase that conveys the focus of the passage. Therefore, to answer a question about whether or not the passage fulfills a specified goal, you should refer to the title. Your own reading of the passage, knowing the main idea of each paragraph and how the paragraphs work together, is the ultimate guide to answering such a question. Very often, though, the title sums up the passage's topic.

● DRESS REHEARSAL: SAMPLE QUESTIONS AND DETAILED EXPLANATIONS

All five sample questions refer to the following passage:

Stress is an inevitable part of life. Over the past decade, significant attention has been given to the role of stress management in a healthy lifestyle. Though Americans have long thought of health in terms of their physical well-being, many are becoming increasingly aware of the connections between psychological well-being and physical health. As a result, many people are turning to various stress-relief techniques, both to manage specific conditions and to improve their overall sense of well-being.

Cardiac patients, for example, <u>in addition to participating in nutrition</u>
<u>workshops and exercise programs</u>, are now likely to receive education
1
about the negative effects of stress on health. [2] Conscious relaxation methods—such as meditation, yoga, visualization, deep breathing, even journaling and prayer—are promoted as adjuncts to traditional medical treatments. [3] Few doctors would recommend these stress-management practices as substitutes for, say, a blood-pressure-lowering drug for a high-risk patient, but many physicians advocate <u>some kind of deliberate relaxation</u>
4
<u>technique</u> as part of an as part of an overall approach to health.
4

Which Phrase Best Accomplishes a Specified Purpose?

1. Which of the following best conveys that cardiac patients are not relying solely on stress management techniques to treat their conditions?

   A. NO CHANGE

   B. hoping to benefit from the mind-body connection

   C. eager to explore a new approach

   D. having given up on traditional medicine

The key words in this question stem are "cardiac patients are not relying solely on stress management techniques to treat their conditions." If patients aren't relying only on stress-management techniques, they are using other methods as well. **The correct answer is A.** Choice A addresses the style issue by using the phrase "in addition" and by stating other methods patients use, "nutrition workshops and exercise programs." Once you identify what the question asks for, you will see that three of the choices don't come close to answering it. While choice B mentions a main point of the passage, "the mind-body connection," it does not address the question in the stem.

Should a Sentence Be Added?

2. At this point, the writer is considering adding the following sentence:

   It's well-known that inadequate medical insurance has a negative effect on overall health.

   Should the writer make this addition?

   F. Yes, because this detail describes an obstacle to good health.

   G. Yes, because it costs money to learn relaxation methods and most people need insurance coverage to pay for classes.

   H. No, because smoking is a more serious obstacle to good health than lack of insurance coverage.

   J. No, because bringing up a second obstacle to good health distracts from the essay's focus on stress management.

When you're asked about adding a sentence, you must first determine whether or not it relates to the topic of the paragraph. The sentence just before the proposed addition mentions "the negative effects of stress on health." You should read further ahead in the paragraph to figure out that the focus is not on negative influences on health in general. Rather, the paragraph focuses on the benefits of stress-management techniques. This tells you that the proposed addition would not be appropriate, so the correct answer must be either choice H or J. Now you need to identify the correct reason. The reason given in choice H doesn't mention any topic present in the passage. **The correct answer is J.**

What Would Be Lost If a Phrase Were Deleted?

3. The writer is considering deleting the following phrase from the preceding sentence:

    —such as meditation, yoga, visualization, deep breathing, even journaling and prayer—

    If the writer were to make this deletion, the essay would primarily lose:

    A. explicit directions for managing stress
    B. a fact that supports the thesis of the essay
    C. examples of specific stress-management techniques
    D. a detail that provides information about stress management studies

Remember that a question about deleting a phrase asks you to think about the function of the phrase. Don't consider whether the phrase uses correct grammar or sentence structure. Instead, ask yourself how the phrase helps the writer express an idea. To do this, you need to focus on the given phrase and its context. Think about the possible answers before you read the answer choices. In this particular phrase, the words "such as" indicate that the phrase provides examples. The context of the passage tells you that the examples are of "conscious relaxation methods," which is another way of describing the "stress-management techniques" mentioned in choice C. **The correct answer is C.**

Using Consistent Style and Tone (No Question Stem)

4. F. NO CHANGE
    G. chilling out
    H. learning to be less uptight
    J. de-stressing because it is majorly important

If you notice that choice G is a lot shorter than the other choices, you might think that the tested issue is wordiness and that the shortest answer is best. Don't go for that without first thinking about the style and tone of the passage. The tone is formal and detached; the writer is treating a serious topic in a serious manner. Therefore, no phrasing that sounds too relaxed or informal will be appropriate. The shortest answer, choice G's "chilling out," is considered slang and doesn't fit the tone of the passage. Choice H is a little better, but it still sounds somewhat conversational. While the word "majorly" (choice J) might be used in conversation, it is not appropriate in a formal written essay. **Choice F best matches the formal, serious tone used in the passage.**

Does the Essay Fulfill a Given Purpose?

> **Question 5 asks about the preceding passage as a whole.**

5. Suppose the writer had chosen to write a brief essay giving specific advice about how to relax. Would this essay fulfill the writer's goal?

   A. No, because not everyone relaxes in the same way, so specific advice would not be useful.

   B. No, because the essay does not describe in detail any of the relaxation methods that are mentioned.

   C. Yes, because several different methods of conscious relaxation are mentioned.

   D. Yes, because the essay makes a good case for the crucial importance of relaxation.

The key words in the question stem are "specific advice about how to relax." If an essay contains specific advice, then it gives directions you could follow to achieve a goal. This essay describes some examples of relaxation techniques and discusses the importance of relaxation for health, but it doesn't actually provide specific advice. Eliminate choices C and D. Now examine the reason given in choice A. Although the reason uses the words "relaxes" and "specific advice," it doesn't address the issue in the question stem. Choice A attempts to answer the question, "Would specific advice about how to relax be useful?" This isn't the question to address, though. Make sure you answer only the question posed by the question stem! **The correct answer is B.**

● THE FINAL ACT: PRACTICE QUIZ

Directions: In the passage that follows, certain words and phrases are underlined and numbered. In the right-hand column, you will find alternatives for the underlined part. In most cases, you are to choose the one that best expresses the idea, makes the statement appropriate for standard written English, or is worded most consistently with the style and tone of the passage as a whole. If you think the original version is best, choose NO CHANGE. For each question, choose the alternative you consider best.

Nathaniel Hawthorne,
American Romantic

Nathaniel Hawthorne was born in

1804 in Salem, Massachusetts, <u>where</u>
1
<u>some of his ancestors participated in</u>
1
<u>the witch trials during the late 1600s.</u>
1
Hawthorne's birthplace and family

history had a profound effect on his

writing. His short stories and novels

1. The writer is considering deleting the underlined portion. If the writer were to make this deletion, the essay would primarily lose:

   A. a relevant historical fact
   B. an introduction to the main topic of the essay
   C. a detail that explains the reference to "family history"
   D. an explanation for Hawthorne's choice of writing as a career

<u>are based on</u> sin, guilt, and judgment.
2

2. F. NO CHANGE
   G. are about
   H. show that he was really into
   J. explore the themes of

Hawthorne associated himself with the Transcendentalists, including Ralph Waldo Emerson and Henry David Thoreau. [3] Transcendentalism was an American expression of the Romantic ideals that had been popular in Europe.

3. At this point, the writer is considering adding the following sentence:

> Thoreau is known for his writings on civil disobedience.

Would this be a relevant addition?

A. Yes, because the statement provides additional detail about Henry David Thoreau.

B. Yes, because the detail about civil disobedience is important to the reader's understanding of Hawthorne.

C. No, because Thoreau has nothing to do with Hawthorne.

D. No, because the detail about Thoreau adds nothing to the discussion of Hawthorne.

Hawthorne shared the Romantic view that intuition is a higher value than scientific rationalism and external authority.
4

4. F. NO CHANGE

G. was pretty much into the Romantic thing

H. held the view, which the Romantics were also big fans of,

J. was really keen on the idea of the Romantics

Hawthorne joined the Transcendentalists' <u>experimental commune, Brook Farm</u>, in the hope of allowing
₅
₅

himself more time to write. <u>Though he found communal living pretty awful, he</u>
₆
₆
used the experience as the basis for a novel, *The Blithedale Romance.* Hawthorne left Brook Farm and eventually returned to Salem, where he worked at the Customs House. After losing the job for political reasons, he began to work in earnest on *The Scarlet Letter.* The publication of this novel brought Hawthorne <u>fame and fortune.</u>
₇
Puritan New England, which he described with symbolism and allegory in *The Scarlet Letter,* provided Hawthorne

5. Which of the following choices most effectively conveys that Brook Farm existed only for a short time?

A. NO CHANGE
B. utopian community, Brook Farm
C. Brook Farm, a commune with many famous members,
D. famous commune, Brook Farm

6. Which of the following phrases best describes Hawthorne's negative opinion of living at Brook Farm and maintains the overall tone of the essay?

F. NO CHANGE
G. While he found communal living unattractive, he
H. Because life at Brook Farm appealed greatly to Hawthorne, he
J. Though it turned out he couldn't stand life on the commune, he

7. Given that all of the choices are true, which one most effectively conveys that Hawthorne had concerns about money?

A. NO CHANGE
B. the admiration of many young writers
C. tremendous literary recognition and many social invitations
D. fame and financial independence

with artistic inspiration

he found lacking in the
8
contemporary world. He
8
did, however, use his own

experience as the basis for a

sketch called "The Customs

House," which appeared as

a preface to the novel. This
9
popular novel was followed
9
by many others, as well as
9
numerous short stories.
9

8. The writer is considering deleting the underlined portion. If this deletion were made, the paragraph would primarily lose:

F. an indication of the writer's opinion

G. a contrast that clarifies the source of Hawthorne's inspiration

H. a detail that helps the modern reader relate to the subject of the essay

J. an element of surprise

9. Given that all are true, which sentence most effectively maintains the essay's focus and concludes the essay?

A. NO CHANGE

B. The novel is nonetheless grounded in the romantic tradition, using symbolism and improbable elements in the story.

C. The novel is read by thousands of high school students every year.

D. Many film adaptations testify to the popularity of the novel.

Question 10 asks about the preceding passage as a whole.

10. Suppose the writer had been assigned to write an essay that describes Transcendentalism in America. Would this essay fulfill that assignment?

F. No, because the writer focuses more on Hawthorne than on Transcendentalism.

G. No, because the writer focuses more on the Romantic movement in Europe.

H. Yes, because the writer mentions several prominent Transcendentalists.

J. Yes, because Transcendentalism is described as important in Hawthorne's life.

THE FINAL ACT: ANSWERS AND EXPLANATIONS FOR WRITING STRATEGY AND STYLE QUESTIONS

1. C. The phrase mentions the activities of Hawthorne's "ancestors" and describes what is meant by "family history" in the next sentence. Choice A is not as specific and relevant to the essay as choice C. Choice B is wrong because the main topic of the passage is Hawthorne himself, not his ancestors. Choice D is wrong because while Hawthorne's family history is described as having an effect on Hawthorne's writing, it isn't described as influencing his choice of writing as a career.

2. J. Because no stem appears with this question, it may be hard to recognize as a style question. On first glance, choice F sounds like a reasonable answer. Choice G is a little vague. Choice H uses language, "was really into," that is informal and doesn't match the style of the passage, which is formal and serious. Choice J is more precise than choices G and H. The style and tone used in choice J is appropriate to the passage.

3. D. In the first sentence of the paragraph, Thoreau is mentioned only to provide a context for understanding Hawthorne. Because the essay focuses on Hawthorne, the sentence about Thoreau's writings would be distracting.

4. F. This is a style question without a question stem. Remember to keep the overall style of the passage in mind when you evaluate answer choices. Choices G, H, and J all include wordings that are too informal and conversational to be appropriate for this passage: "pretty much into," "big fans of,"and "really keen."

5. A. The key words here are "Brook Farm existed only for a short time." Details offered by the other choices, "utopian," "many famous members," and "famous," have nothing to do with duration. In choice A, "experimental" suggests that the commune may have been short-lived. The question asks which choice "most effectively conveys" the short duration, and only choice A comes close.

6. G. This question stem has two key phrases: "describe Hawthorne's negative opinion of living at Brook Farm" and "maintain the overall tone of the essay." The essay uses a detached and formal tone. Two choices, G and H, use a formal tone, but choice H doesn't describe a negative opinion. Choices F and J present a negative opinion but use an informal, conversational tone.

7. D.   They key phrase in this question stem is "Hawthorne had concerns about money." Only choices A, which uses "fortune," and D, which uses "financial independence," have to do with money. Choice D suggests that Hawthorne did not have financial independence prior to the publication of the novel.

8. G.   The sentence in question begins with "Puritan New England." This contrasts with "the contemporary world" in the phrase under consideration. The contrast is carried further by the words "provided with" and "found lacking in." Choice F is wrong because the phrase is not presented as the writer's opinion. Choice H is tempting because it uses the word "modern," and "contemporary" in the proposed deletion means the same thing. However, the word "contemporary" refers to Hawthorne's contemporaries and isn't meant to help the "modern reader" relate to the passage.

9. B.   To answer this question, you need to identify the focus of the essay. Remember that the title of an English passage is almost always helpful in identifying the topic. The title here reminds you that essay, though written as a biography, focuses on Hawthorne primarily as a writer in the Romantic tradition. Choice B describes how *The Scarlet Letter* fits into that tradition. Choices A, C, and D all maintain the paragraph's focus on *The Scarlet Letter* but do not connect the novel to Hawthorne's identity as a Romantic.

10. F.   A question asking whether or not the essay fulfills a given purpose will appear only at the end of the question set. By that point, you know the essay's focus. Make sure you also know what the question asks. The key phrase here is "describes Transcendentalism in America." The passage describes Transcendentalism briefly. Because the essay doesn't focus on Transcendentalism, the answer is no. Although the essay mentions the Romantic movement in Europe, it is not the focus of the essay.

LESSON 6

Organization

DIFFICULTY: ★ ★

FREQUENCY: ★ ★ ★

SURPRISE FACTOR: ★ ★ ★

INTRODUCTION TO ORGANIZATION QUESTIONS

Organization questions ask you to think about how a passage is put together and how ideas are related. You need to keep three issues in mind: sequence, focus, and logical relationships. Sequence refers to ordering elements of the passage, either sentences or paragraphs, most effectively. Focus relates to deleting phrases or sentences that distract from the main point of a paragraph. Logical relationships, such as contrast or cause-and-effect, are expressed by connecting words and phrases.

Like Writing Strategy and Style questions, Organization questions demand that you take a big-picture view of the passage. You usually can't answer these questions correctly by looking at a single sentence. You may have to consider an entire paragraph or even the passage as a whole to answer an Organization question.

Characteristics of Organization Questions

SEQUENCE QUESTIONS

Some Organization questions include question stems that refer to paragraph or sentence numbers. The numbers are clues alerting you to consider organizational issues. Anytime you see a passage that includes bracketed numbers before each paragraph, you can expect to find some type of organization question. If paragraphs are numbered, it's possible that they're presented in an incorrect order; you may be asked to reorder them, as in this question:

1. For the sake of logic and coherence, Paragraph 5 should be placed
   A. where it is now.
   B. after Paragraph 1.
   C. after Paragraph 2.
   D. after Paragraph 3.

A question stem may present a new sentence and ask you where it should be placed. The answer choices refer to the paragraph numbers. Here's an example of an organization question that asks you where to add new material:

2. In reviewing the essay, the writer realizes that some information has been left out and composes the following sentence to add:

   The process is complicated because the leaves of the tea plant must be harvested within 24 hours.

   The most logical and effective place to add this sentence would be after the third sentence of Paragraph:
   F. 2
   G. 3
   H. 4
   J. 5

To answer this question, you would have to determine which paragraph has a focus that encompasses the additional detail about harvesting.

LOGICAL RELATIONSHIP QUESTIONS

Not all Organization questions, however, appear in the context of numbered sentences or numbered paragraphs. Some Organization questions may not even include question stems. In format and appearance, those that don't include stems seem similar to questions that test word choice and wordiness. Here's an Organization question dealing with logical relationships that looks similar to a Word Choice question:

As recently as 20 years ago, the only items circulated by public libraries

were print materials—books and periodicals—and some musical

recordings. Gradually, <u>therefore</u>, with the proliferation of electronic
                        3
media, the range of materials loaned by libraries has increased.

3. A. NO CHANGE
    B. in fact
    C. however
    D. as a consequence

While this question does ask you to make a choice about wording, it doesn't test one of the issues covered in the Word Choice lesson. This is an Organization question, because each of the answer choices is a word that expresses a particular logical relationship between ideas. In this case, the underlined word, "therefore," expresses cause and effect. To answer this question, you need to think about the sentence in which the word appears and the preceding sentence. Because the relationship between the two sentences is one of contrast, the correct answer is choice C.

RELEVANCE QUESTIONS

The logical relationship question isn't the only type of Organization question that can masquerade as a different type. The relevance question, because it always includes OMIT as an answer choice, can look like a Wordiness question. There's a key difference though: when an entire sentence is underlined and OMIT is offered as an answer choice, the question is often testing whether or not the sentence is relevant to the topic of the passage. Here's an example:

(For context, suppose the following sentence appears in a passage that focuses specifically on the game of tennis.)

Like tennis, badminton is a sport in which players use racquets to volley an object over a net.

4. F. NO CHANGE
    G. In badminton, as in tennis, players use racquets as they volley an object over a net.
    H. Players use racquets to volley an object over a net, making badminton similar to tennis.
    J. OMIT

Noticing that OMIT is a choice, you might think this is a Wordiness question. However, the sentence on badminton is not relevant to a passage that focuses on tennis. Even though OMIT is an answer choice, the other three choices are not wordy. Choice D is the correct answer because the underlined sentence distracts from the focus of the passage.

Most Common Types of Organization Questions

Organization questions fall into three categories. The first has to do with **sequence**. You must determine the correct ordering of paragraphs, as in Question 1 above, or the correct ordering of sentences within a single paragraph.

The second type deals with **focus**, the main topic of either a paragraph or a whole passage. Question 2 above, which asks you to determine where to add a given sentence, is an example. Another type of focus question asks you to choose an appropriate sentence to serve as a transition between two paragraphs. To do this, you need to identify the topics of both paragraphs. Questions that hinge on relevance to the topic, such as Question 4 above, are also focus questions, because the answer depends on the main topic of the paragraph.

The third type deals with a specific set of words that you can think of as **connections** questions. Question 3 above is an example. These questions include connecting or transition words and phrases in the answer choices. They focus on relationships and the logical flow of ideas. (You can read more about connections and transition words in Lesson 25, "Idea Development.")

● THE TRAP DOOR: STEERING CLEAR OF ANSWER TRAPS

Of the three organization traps described below, only the first is a function of how the test is written. The other two traps occur when you fail to recognize that organization is the tested issue.

Types of Organization Answer Traps

ORGANIZATION TRAP 1: **Sequence.** You might get confused about what the boxed and bracketed numbers refer to.

ORGANIZATION TRAP 2: **Focus.** You might waste time by considering answers in light of grammar and usage issues instead of thinking about paragraph topics and the logical flow of ideas.

ORGANIZATION TRAP 3: **Connections.** You might not immediately recognize that the answer choices are connecting words and phrases.

Techniques for Avoiding Organization Question Answer Traps

SEQUENCE TRAP

You can avoid the sequence trap by doing enough practice so that you become comfortable with the ACT numbering system. Here's a guide to help you follow it.

Underlined Words: Most English questions refer to a group of underlined words in the passage. The question number for these questions is centered under the underlining in the text. If the underlined text spans more than one line, the question number is repeated under each line.

Boxed Numbers: Some organization questions do not refer to underlined text; you need to read the question stem to know what the question is asking. In this case, the question number appears within a box at the end of the paragraph it refers to. For an illustration, refer to Question 1 in the Dress Rehearsal.

Sequential Numbers: Some passages include sequential numbers that label either paragraphs or sentences. If paragraphs are labeled to facilitate an organization question, the paragraph number appears in square brackets, centered just above the first line of the paragraph. If sentences within a particular paragraph are numbered, the sentence number appears in square brackets before the first word of the sentence. The passage in the Dress Rehearsal includes paragraph numbers, and two of the paragraphs also include numbered sentences.

FOCUS TRAP

You can avoid the focus trap by understanding that when a question relates to focus, the incorrect answer choices don't usually contain any errors in usage or mechanics. If you don't immediately recognize that a question hinges on focus, you can become distracted by looking for errors in the answer choices. When a question tests focus, the right answer hinges on the ideas that are expressed. If you don't see any obvious mistake, or if OMIT is included as an answer choice, consider the possibility that the question is testing focus. (See Questions 6 and 8 in the Final Practice for examples.)

CONNECTIONS TRAP

You can avoid the connections trap by learning to recognize the most commonly used connecting words and phrases and being able to identify the logical relationship that each one expresses. Study the list in the Performance Techniques section and think about the relationships between ideas in the passage when you notice connecting words and phrases in the answer choices. (Questions 3 and 4 in the Final Practice test connections.)

● PERFORMANCE TECHNIQUES: KEY RULES

ORDERING PARAGRAPHS

For a sequence question that asks you to unscramble the order of paragraphs, look for a paragraph that sounds like an introduction or one that sounds like a conclusion. You can often use elimination strategies. For example, if you can identify that the second paragraph should actually be the introduction, then any sequence that doesn't start with Paragraph 2 is automatically wrong.

ORDERING SENTENCES

For sentence sequence questions, look for an organizing principle in the paragraph. Some paragraphs follow a linear sequence. Words like *first*, *then*, *next*, and *after the completion of* indicate that the paragraph describes steps in a process. Some passages include biographical information, which should usually be presented chronologically.

RECOGNIZING FOCUS QUESTIONS

Remember to pay attention to the main topic of paragraphs when a question asks you to do any of the following:

- Determine where to add a new sentence.
- Provide a sentence that serves as a transition between paragraphs or as an introductory or concluding sentence for the passage.
- Determine whether an entire sentence should be omitted.

RECOGNIZING IRRELEVANT SENTENCES

Whenever an entire sentence is underlined and OMIT is offered as an answer choice, ask yourself if the sentence relates to the main topic of the paragraph. If the sentence isn't relevant, it should be omitted. If so, you don't need to spend time considering the second and third answer choices.

RECOGNIZING CONNECTIONS

Learn to recognize the most commonly used connecting words and phrases and know the logical relationship that each one expresses. Connecting words and phrases are crucial. They appear in passages of all kinds, no matter what the topic. In the box below, connecting words are grouped into three broad categories: (1) cause and effect, (2) contrast, and (3) examples, emphasis, similarity, or continuation.

CONNECTING WORDS AND PHRASES

Cause and effect: as a result, because, consequently, so, therefore, thus

Contrast: although, but, despite, however, on the other hand, though, while, yet

Examples, emphasis, similarity, continuation: for example, for instance, in addition, in fact, likewise, moreover, similarly

---

● DRESS REHEARSAL: SAMPLE QUESTIONS AND DETAILED EXPLANATIONS

[1]

[1] Gustav Stickley, the famous American furniture maker, enjoyed tremendous success but was not able to maintain it throughout his lifetime. [2] Stickley was born in 1858 and went to work while still a child. [3] By the age of 12, he was already a journeyman stone mason. [4] In 1884, Stickley and his brothers founded the Stickley Furniture Company, which did both wholesale and retail trade. [5] He found his true calling, however, when he began working in his uncle's chair factory in 1875. ☐1

[2]

In 1901, Gustav Stickley started publishing a magazine, *The Craftsman.*
2

Then in 1888, Gustav Stickley left the family business and started his own company. Stickley created furniture in what came to be known as the Craftsman style. At a time when most furniture was highly ornamented and machine made, Stickley produced pieces that were simply designed with clean lines and natural materials; <u>however</u>, all
3
his furniture was handmade.

[3]

[1] The Stickley style, also known as "Mission Oak," was highly profitable during the early years of the 20th century. [2] Stickley was a better artisan than businessman; in addition, popular taste was turning away from the simple Craftsman style and back toward older, more elaborate designs. [3] Tastes change, <u>therefore</u>, and today, new
4
furniture in Stickley's Mission Oak style is once again popular. ⊡5⊡

Correcting Sentence Sequence

1. For the sake of the logic and coherence of this paragraph, Sentence 5 should be placed

   A. where it is now.
   B. after Sentence 1.
   C. after Sentence 2.
   D. after Sentence 3.

First, note that Question 1 is associated with the boxed numeral printed at the end of the first paragraph. When you're reading through an English passage and you come to a boxed numeral, you should refer to the list of questions; you'll find an organization question with a question stem that refers to the paragraph you've just read.

Next, read Sentence 5 carefully. Notice that it, along with other sentences in the paragraph, includes a date. The paragraph is organized chronologically, so the dates serve as clues to help you determine the correct ordering of sentences. Sentence 5, describing an occurrence in 1875, should be placed between Sentence 3 and Sentence 4, which refers to 1884. Sentence 2 contains an indirect date reference in the phrase "by the time he was 12." You can infer that this was some time around 1860, making Sentence 5 fit most logically between Sentences 3 and 4. **The correct answer is D.**

Identifying an Appropriate Transitional Sentence

2. Given that all the choices are true, which one would most effectively introduce Paragraph 2?

F. NO CHANGE

G. Gustav Stickley's brothers did not become as famous as he did.

H. The furniture designed by Stickley shared some features with Shaker-style furniture.

J. Two years later, the Stickley brothers expanded their enterprise by opening a chair factory.

The phrase "introduce the paragraph" in the question stem suggests that this question hinges on focus. Don't try to answer a question about a paragraph transition until you have a good understanding of the topic of both paragraphs. The first paragraph gives a chronology of events in Stickley's early life, and the second paragraph focuses on Stickley's career as a furniture maker. **Choice J is the best choice** because it leads into the discussion of Stickley's role in the furniture business; in addition, the date reference "two years later" works well with the chronological flow of the passage.

Choice F is incorrect because starting a magazine doesn't relate directly to Stickley's career in the furniture business; in addition, the date reference, "1901," disrupts the chronological flow because it is followed by "Then in 1888." Choice G is incorrect because the paragraph focuses on Gustav Stickley, not his brothers. Choice H is incorrect because, although the paragraph does discuss the style of Stickley's furniture, choice H doesn't contain a date reference that would connect the sentence to the second sentence in the paragraph, which begins "Then in 1881."

Using a Connecting Word That Expresses Continuation

3. A. NO CHANGE

B. similarly

C. furthermore

D. likewise

The correct answer is C. Notice that all the words in the answer choices are connecting words. This is a clue that you need to think about relationships between ideas. Carefully read the sentence in which this question appears and think about its meaning. It expresses a contrast between the typical furniture of the time (it was "highly ornamented and machine made") and Stickley's furniture (which was "simply designed" and "handmade"). The connecting word we're looking for relates the two aspects of Stickley's furniture. The design is different, and the way the furniture is produced is different. The continuation word "furthermore" expresses the second way in which the differences are evident, **the correct answer is C.**

Using a Connecting Word That Expresses Contrast

4. F. NO CHANGE
   G. however
   H. moreover
   J. consequently

Notice that all the answer choices are connecting words, so think about the relationships between ideas. In this case, you need to pay attention to the ideas expressed in the sentence that contains the underlined word and also the sentence before it. Sentence 2 states that changing taste led to a decline in the popularity of Stickley's furniture. Sentence 3 states that eventually changing taste led to a renewal in the popularity of Stickley's furniture. The contrast between the two shifts in the public's taste for furniture is expressed by the word "however." **The correct answer is G.** Choices F and J are incorrect because they both express cause and effect. Choice H is incorrect because it expresses emphasis.

Determining Where to Add a New Sentence

5. Upon reviewing Paragraph 3 and realizing that information has been left out, the writer composes the following sentence:

   > Though Stickley's financial success peaked in 1913, in 1916 his furniture-building enterprise dissolved.

   The most logical placement of this sentence would be

   A. before Sentence 1.
   B. after Sentence 1.
   C. after Sentence 2.
   D. after Sentence 3.

This is a sequence question, so determine the organizing principle of the paragraph. The paragraph traces the end of Stickley's career and the eventual resurgence of appreciation for his style. The sentence we're asked to add relates only to Stickley's furniture business, so it makes sense to place it before Sentence 2, which brings up the idea of shifting taste. **The correct answer is B.**

● THE FINAL ACT: PRACTICE QUIZ

The Use of House Plants to Purify Indoor Air

[1]

[1] Wolverton's research showed that house plants are very effective in absorbing all three of the toxic gases he studied. [2] Certain plants are more effective at targeting individual pollutants, but the flowering chrysanthemum proved to be effective in controlling all three. [3] Still other common plants, the philodendron, spider plant, and golden pothos, were most effective at lowering formaldehyde levels. $\boxed{1}$

[2]

[1] House plants are more than decorative. [2] According to a NASA study conducted by Dr. Bill Wolverton, plants can serve as natural air purifiers, filtering toxins that may accumulate in closed spaces. [3] Wolverton's study examined the effects of common house plants on three major chemicals, formaldehyde, benzene, and trichloroethylene. [4] <u>While</u> it's obvious that NASA must be concerned with air quality
$\underset{2}{}$
in vehicles designed for space travel, it may be less apparent that even earthbound citizens should be concerned with the air quality in their home environments. [5] However, because newer housing uses insulation and airtight doors and windows to control energy costs, indoor air quality

is a concern for everyone. [6] <u>Thus,</u> the very same chemicals involved in Wolverton's NASA study are also ⃞3⃞ present in buildings. ⃞4⃞

[3]

Formaldehyde gas may be emitted from a building itself as well as from household items. Foam insulation and adhesive binders in floor coverings can give off formaldehyde. <u>On the other hand</u>, furniture,
5
anything containing plywood or pressed wood, is another contributor. Even products such as grocery bags and waxed paper are sources of formaldehyde. The other two chemicals Wolverton studied, benzene and tricholorethylene, are given off by inks, paints, and varnishes. <u>Wolverton</u>
6
<u>has also done studies on the benefits of using plants in the purification of</u>
6
<u>water in sewage treatment systems.</u>
6

[4]

These, along with many of the other plants proved helpful by Wolverton's study, are easily obtained and easy to grow. <u>Therefore,</u>
7
more people are becoming interested in the benefits of houseplants. <u>In addition, the use of natural products in cleaning solutions is gaining</u>
8
<u>popularity.</u> A single large plant per 100 square feet of space is an effective
8
air purifier—one that adds visual interest to a room and doesn't make any noise. ⃞9⃞

1. Upon reviewing Paragraph 1 and realizing that some information has been left out, the writer composes the following sentence:
    Another flowering plant, the Gerbera daisy, was shown to be efficient in reducing air concentrations of both benzene and trichloroethylene.

The most logical placement of this sentence would be

A. before Sentence 1.

B. after Sentence 1.

C. after Sentence 2.

D. after Sentence 3.

2. F. NO CHANGE

G. Apparently

H. However

J. Conversely

3. A. NO CHANGE

B. In fact

C. By way of contrast

D. Surprisingly

4. Upon reviewing Paragraph 2 and realizing that some information has been left out, the writer composes the following sentence:

They can also be beneficial to human health.

They most logical placement of this sentence would be

F. before Sentence 1.

G. after Sentence 1.

H. after Sentence 5.

J. after Sentence 6.

5. A. NO CHANGE

B. In addition

C. However

D. In contrast

6. F. NO CHANGE

G. Water purification is another area of Wolverton's research.

H. Wolverton has also investigated the use of plants to purify water in sewage treatment systems.

J. OMIT

7. Which of the following would NOT be an acceptable alternative to the underlined portion?

    A. As a result

    B. Nonetheless

    C. For this reason

    D. Consequently

8. F. NO CHANGE

    G. The use of natural products in cleaning solutions is also gaining popularity.

    H. Many people are interested in cleaning solutions that use natural ingredients as well.

    J. OMIT

9. Which of the following sentences, if added here, would provide the best conclusion to the paragraph and be most consistent with the main focus of the essay?

    A. It almost makes you wonder if Dr. Wolverton runs a horticulture business as a side venture.

    B. Of course, displaying artwork is another way to add visual interest to a room.

    C. Wolverton's study suggests that house plants may be a viable alternative to mechanical air purifiers.

    D. One can't help wondering what researchers will discover next.

Question 10 asks about the preceding passage as a whole.

---

10. For the sake of logic and coherence, the best ordering of paragraphs in this passage is

    F. as they are now.

    G. 2, 3, 1, 4.

    H. 4, 2, 1, 3.

    J. 4, 1, 3, 2.

● THE FINAL ACT: ANSWERS AND EXPLANATIONS FOR ORGANIZATION QUESTIONS

1. C.   Sentence 2 mentions a specific plant, "the flowering chrysanthemum," and Sentence 3 uses the phrase "Still other common plants." The new sentence, opening with "Another flowering plant," fits most logically between Sentences 2 and 3.

2. F.   Because the answer choices are all connecting words, think about the relationship between ideas in the sentence. This sentence contains the contrast between air quality concerns in "vehicles designed for space travel" and similar concerns for "earthbound citizens." Choice F is the appropriate contrast word here. Choice G is not a contrast word. Choices H and J are contrast words, but they don't work with the structure of this particular sentence.

3. B.   Choice A is wrong because a sentence introduced by "Thus" must follow logically from the previous sentence, and that is not the case here. A connecting word that shows emphasis is needed here, so only choice B works. Choices C and D both express contrast.

4. G.   Because the sentence to be added starts with "They," the sentence it follows must contain an appropriate plural noun for "They" to refer to. It logically refers to "houseplants" and, therefore, must follow Sentence 1.

5. B.   This sentence expands on the previous sentence, describing "another contributor of formaldehyde gas" in buildings. The appropriate connecting word must express continuation; only choice B does so. Choices A, C, and D express contrast.

6. J.   When you notice that a complete sentence is underlined, see if OMIT is one of the answer choices. If so, the sentence often isn't relevant to the paragraph, as is the case here. Because this paragraph focuses on sources of chemicals in indoor air, a sentence about the use of houseplants in sewage treatment is irrelevant.

7. B.   Be careful: notice the word NOT in the question stem here. This means that three of the answer choices work well in the context of the passage, and one does not. The correct answer to the question is actually the choice that makes the least sense logically. Because the answer choices are connecting words, determine the logical relationship between this sentence and the previous one. It is one of cause and effect: Because houseplants are "easily obtained and easy to grow," it follows that "many people are becoming interested" in them. Choices A, C, and D all offer acceptable ways of expressing cause and effect. Choice B is not an acceptable alternative because it expresses contrast.

8. J.   As in Question 6 above, when OMIT is one of the answer choices, consider the issue of relevance. The introduction of "natural cleaning products" constitutes a digression in this paragraph, whose focus is houseplants.

9. C.   When a question asks about the best sentence to conclude a paragraph (and in this case the whole essay as well), make sure you know the focus of the paragraph. This paragraph focuses on the ease of using houseplants to purify indoor air. Only choice C matches this focus.

10. G.   When a question asks about the best ordering of paragraphs, a good approach is to determine which paragraph sounds like an introduction to the topic. It should be obvious that Paragraph 1 needs something before it, so you can eliminate choice F. Consider paragraphs 2 and 4. Paragraph 2 sounds more like an introductory paragraph than Paragraph 4, and this is all the information you need to select choice G as the best answer.

Challenging English Questions

DIFFICULTY: ★ ★ ★

FREQUENCY: ★

SURPRISE FACTOR: ★ ★ ★ ★

● INTRODUCTION TO CHALLENGING QUESTIONS

Some English questions present special challenges. The form of the question, rather than its content, is what makes a challenging question tricky. The questions discussed in this lesson test issues covered in the other lessons.

Characteristics of Challenging Questions

You can easily recognize the first kind of challenging question because its question stem includes a word that's printed in all capital letters. You can think of this as the NOT-LEAST-EXCEPT question. Here's an example:

1. Silvia is considering pursuing a career in <u>law; she</u> is exploring the field through a part-time job in a law firm.

    Which of the following alternatives to the underlined portion would NOT be acceptable?

    A. law. She
    B. law, so she
    C. law, she
    D. law; therefore,

This question tests the principles of sentence structure and punctuation. The correct answer is C.

In addition to the NOT-LEAST-EXCEPT phrasing of a question, another challenging question format occurs when one sentence includes two different test questions. Such sentences contain **two different underlined parts.** Here's an example of this situation:

In contrast at our cousins whom have been living in Japan for the
      2   3
past three years, my brother and I have never traveled outside of the United States.

2. F. NO CHANGE
   G. Unlike
   H. Similarly to
   J. Differently than

3. A. NO CHANGE
   B. which
   C. that
   D. who

Both questions test word choice. Question 2 tests whether you can recognize a correctly worded idiomatic expression. The correct answer is G. Question 3 asks you to determine the correct pronoun in context. The correct answer is D.

Most Common Types of Challenging Questions

The formats of the two challenging question types are described above. For the NOT-LEAST-EXCEPT question type, think about what kinds of language issues (that is, topics covered in the other English lessons) lend themselves to the negatively worded format. They must be issues that can be correctly handled in more than one way, because three of the answer choices are acceptable. Sentence structure is more likely than other topics to be tested in this way because two independent clauses can be combined in several grammatically correct ways. (See Example 1 above.) Word choice is another topic that might be tested in the NOT-LEAST-EXCEPT format. There are often multiple ways of expressing the same meaning correctly, using different words or different idiomatic expressions.

Another question that will pose special difficulties is any question contained in a sentence that **spans two pages** of the test booklet. You need to work quickly, so it can be tempting to take shortcuts. Remember, though, that the correct answer for an English question is determined by its context in the sentence, and sometimes even the sentence before or after that. Remember to refer to the context of the passage even for questions that appear at the top of a new page in your text booklet.

● THE TRAP DOOR: STEERING CLEAR OF ANSWER TRAPS

NOT-LEAST-EXCEPT questions pose a definite trap: they turn the logic you typically use on its head. Usually as you work through each English question, you check the answer choices looking for errors. You're looking for the one answer choice that is correct. However, NOT-LEAST-EXCEPT questions offer three answer choices that are acceptable in the context of the sentence. For a question like this, the answer choice you're looking for is the one that does not correctly apply the rules of grammar and the principles of good writing.

Types of Challenging Question Answer Traps

The logic of the NOT-LEAST-EXCEPT question is easy enough to understand: you need to choose the answer that sounds worst in context, not best. Because there are so few questions like this, however, it can be challenging to switch out of your usual habit of looking for the answer that sounds best. You're actually battling two traps here, the test maker's deliberate trap in phrasing the question negatively with the word "not" or "least" or "except" and your own habit of looking for a single acceptable answer.

Techniques for Avoiding Challenging Question Answer Traps

You can more easily avoid the NOT-LEAST-ACCEPT trap if you know which kinds of language issues are likely to be tested in one of these questions. If you think about it, you'll realize that many issues tested on the ACT can have only one correct answer, so you would never see them tested in a NOT-LEAST-ACCEPT question. Some topics that can't have multiple correct answers are subject-verb agreement, adjective-adverb confusion, and pronoun usage.

Now, think about what kinds of writing issues can be correctly handled in more than one way. **Combining two independent clauses**, for example, can be done in several ways. Sometimes **modifiers** and **prepositional phrases** can be correctly placed in more than one location. These issues are likely to be tested in a NOT-LEAST-EXCEPT question.

• PERFORMANCE TECHNIQUES: KEY RULES

DON'T RUSH WHEN READING QUESTION STEMS.

It's surprisingly easy to miss a negative word in a question stem, even though it's printed in capital letters. For NOT-LEAST-EXCEPT questions, when you first read the question stem, circle the word that appears in all capital letters. The physical act of circling the word may help you remember that the usual logic for test questions—picking the one answer that is correct—is turned around here.

TWO QUESTIONS: ANSWER THE EASIER ONE FIRST.

For sentences that contain underlined parts that relate to two different test questions, read through the whole sentence and answer the easier question first. For any English question, you should always read to the end of the sentence that contains the question. The context of the sentence, that is, the words that aren't underlined, almost always contains clues that help you determine the correct answer. When two questions appear in a single sentence, reading for clues can be trickier. Answering the easier question first is more likely to ensure that you're thinking about the appropriate context when you try to answer the second question. Note that which question is "easier" will be different for different people. If the first question feels tricky for you, don't guess immediately. Go ahead and try the second question. If you get that correct and you read your answer choice back into the sentence, you might find that the first question has become easier. In the following sentence, it makes sense to answer the second question before you try to answer the first question:

> Because he <u>hopes for being</u> at the top of his class in U.S. history,
> 4
> Alex <u>studying</u> several binders full of class notes for the last week.
> 5

4. F. NO CHANGE
   G. hopes at being
   H. is hoping to be
   J. will be hoping to place

5. A. NO CHANGE
    B. have been studying
    C. were studying
    D. has been studying

Let's think through the two questions in this sentence. Question 4 tests verb tense and idiom at the same time. The sentence contains two clauses, so the verbs in each clause must make sense in relation to each other. Skip Question 4, then, and look at the verb in the second clause. Notice that the verb in the second clause is also underlined. However, it shouldn't be too difficult to get the correct answer to Question 5, especially if you remember the rule that a verb ending in *–ing* can never be used as the main verb in a clause. (Even if you don't explicitly remember this rule, you'll probably notice the error anyway because it will "sound" funny as you read the words.) Choices B and C don't work because "Alex" is singular, so it would never be correct to say "Alex have" or "Alex were." Thus, you should be able to tell, without too much difficulty, that choice D is the correct answer here.

You can use that information when you go back to consider Question 4. Because the second clause in the sentence uses "Alex has been studying," you can at least eliminate choice J because it uses the future tense verb "will be hoping." In terms of verb tenses, the correct answer could be either "hopes," used in choices F and G, or "is hoping," used in choice H. You still have the idiom issue to deal with, that is, choosing between "for being" in choice F, "at being" in choice G, and "to be" in choice H, but at least you've eliminated choice J. (Choice H is correct here.) Even if you get stuck on the idiom aspect of Question 4, you'll still have a better chance of guessing correctly because you answered Question 5 first.

● DRESS REHEARSAL: SAMPLE QUESTIONS AND DETAILED EXPLANATIONS

Remember that challenging questions are challenging only because of their format, not the particular issues they test. All the issues tested in the questions below are addressed in previous lessons. Therefore, you can think of this Dress Rehearsal as a minireview of several tested issues.

Challenging Question: NOT

1. The salesman <u>took us smoothly</u> from a presentation about the car's features to a description of the new low rates for financing.

   Which of the following alternatives to the underlined portion would NOT be acceptable?

   A. took us effortlessly
   B. progressed in a smooth manner
   C. took us smooth
   D. moved his presentation seamlessly

This question is testing word choice. If you don't immediately recognize that choice C incorrectly uses the adjective "smooth" to modify the verb "took," you may get distracted by the differences in phrasing among the other answer choices. In that case, think about what's similar and what's different about the phrasings. Notice that the adverbs "effortlessly" in choice A and "seamlessly" in choice D are each used correctly in context, modifying a verb. It may be less obvious at first, but choice B contains a phrase, "in a smooth manner," that functions as an adverb to modify the verb. Remember, for a NOT-LEAST-EXCEPT question, you're looking for the one answer that violates a rule of grammar or usage. Because choice C uses the adjective "smooth" to modify the verb "took," it is not acceptable. **Thus, the correct answer is choice C.**

Challenging Question: LEAST

2. You certainly <u>have as good a chance of winning</u> the contest as anyone else.

   Which of the following alternatives to the underlined portion would be LEAST acceptable?

   F. are as likely to win
   G. have as good a chance at winning
   H. could win
   J. are as likely to be the winner of

Because the nonunderlined part of the sentence finishes a comparison using the word "as," the word "as" also needs to appear earlier in the sentence ("as" is part of the coordinating expression "as... [adjective]...as"). In this question, the three acceptable answer choices,

F, G, and J, all include the word "as." **The correct answer is H.** The problem with choice H is that it is doesn't include the word "as."

Challenging Question: EXCEPT

3. The candidate knew he needed to temper his hard-nosed, authoritarian <u>image, so he began</u> appearing more frequently at community functions and mingling with voters.

   All of the following alternatives to the underlined portion are correct EXCEPT:

   A. image; for this reason, he began
   B. image, on the other hand, he began
   C. image. Therefore, he began
   D. image. He began, therefore,

This sentence is made up of two independent clauses. Three of the answer choices use correct sentence structure and punctuation to join the two clauses. Three of the choices use a connecting word or phrase. Because the underlined portion in this NOT-LEAST-EXCEPT question is not itself incorrect, any connecting word or phrase it contains determines the logical relationship. Here, the underlined word "so" tells you that cause and effect, not contrast, is the relationship between the two clauses. Three choices, choice A ("for this reason") and choices C and D ("therefore") also express cause and effect. Furthermore, each of those answer choices follows punctuation rules. Choice B is incorrect (and, therefore, the right answer) in two ways. The comma after "image" creates a run-on, and the connecting phrase "on the other hand" expresses contrast, which is the wrong relationship in this context. Thus, **choice B is the correct answer.**

Challenging Question: EXCEPT

4. During the 1920s, because of Prohibition laws, the manufacture and sale of alcoholic beverages <u>in the United States</u> was forbidden.

   All of the following would be acceptable placements for the underlined portion EXCEPT:

   F. where it is now
   G. at the beginning of the sentence (revising the capitalization accordingly)

H. after the word *because*

J. after the word *forbidden* (ending the sentence with a period)

Because this question asks where a phrase can be correctly placed, ask yourself how the phrase functions in the sentence. The words "in the United States" form a prepositional phrase that tells where something took place. This modifying phrase would make sense describing either of two things: where Prohibition laws were in effect and where "the manufacture and sale of alcoholic beverages was forbidden." From the logic of the sentence, it's apparent that both of these actions occurred in the same location, so it doesn't matter which one you place the modifying phrase near. Thus, the phrase would be acceptable at the beginning of the sentence (choice B), before the verb "was forbidden" (choice A), or after the verb "was forbidden" (choice D). The phrase "because of Prohibition laws" describes cause and effect, and placing the modifier "in the United States" in the middle incorrectly separates the cause from the connecting word "because." Thus, **the correct answer is choice H.**

Challenging Questions: Two Underlined Portions of One Sentence

As they proceed through the exhibition, the <u>visitors encounters</u>
5
many volunteer guides <u>who were</u> quite capable of answering their
6
questions.

5. A. NO CHANGE
   B. visitor encounters
   C. visitors will encounter
   D. visitors encountered

6. F. NO CHANGE
   G. which are
   H. which were
   J. who are

Question 5 contains an error in subject-verb agreement. If you try to correct that, you see that the answer choices include verbs in three different tenses. Question 6 also includes an underlined verb. You need to find a clue in the nonunderlined part of the sentence that lets you determine the correct tense. This clue comes from the opening of the sentence, "As they proceed." Because "proceed" is not underlined, the other verbs used in the sentence must fit well with that. If you try to correct the subject-verb agreement error in question 5, choice B, with the verb in the present tense, may seem at first to work well. However, the singular "visitor" in choice B doesn't work with the nonunderlined plural pronoun, "they." Rule out choice D because the past tense doesn't work with the nonunderlined "As they proceed." **The correct answer is choice C**, which uses the future tense verb, because the noun "visitors" must be plural to agree with "they" in the nonunderlined part of the sentence.

Question 6 also poses choices that involve both verb tense and noun-pronoun agreement. Having determined that you need a verb tense that works with the present tense "proceed" and the future tense "will encounter," you can rule out choices F and H. Then you have to decide between "which" (choice G) and "who" (choice J). Ask yourself what this pronoun refers to: "they...the visitors." Because only "who" and not "which" can refer to people, **choice J is correct.** Though it may not make a difference which of these questions you answer first, it helps to notice that two issues, verb tense and noun-pronoun agreement, are tested in both questions. Remember that Question 5 also tests subject-verb agreement.

For questions paired in one sentence, it can be more important than for other questions to tease out which specific grammatical issues are being tested. When a sentence contains only one question, often your ear alone will help you choose the correct answer.

● THE FINAL ACT: PRACTICE QUIZ

Directions: In the passage that follows, certain words and phrases are underlined and numbered. In the right-hand column, you will find alternatives for the underlined part. In most cases, you are to choose the one that best expresses the idea, makes the statement appropriate for standard written English, or is worded most consistently with the style and tone of the passage as a whole. If you think the original version is best, choose NO CHANGE. For each question, choose the alternative you consider best.

Paperless Society
Starts with the Young

It seems that the paperless society is becoming a reality, especially for younger people. Older people tend to be less comfortable when it comes to letting go of paper. Young adults, <u>growing up surrounded by</u> technology, have less fear
₁
than their grandparents that important data will vanish into the unseen innards of the computer. Most recent college

graduates <u>have no memory of living</u>
₂
without at least one computer at home.

It seems quite natural for them, <u>therefore,</u> to conduct transactions electronically
₃

that could <u>once</u> be done only on paper.
₄
Young adults form a perfect market for corporations looking to save money on printing and postage.

1. Which of the following alternatives to the underlined portion would NOT be acceptable?

   A. NO CHANGE
   B. having grown up with
   C. who were raised to be comfortable with
   D. grown up around

2. Which of the following alternatives to the underlined portion is LEAST acceptable?

   F. NO CHANGE
   G. do not even remember their life being
   H. cannot recall living
   J. have never experienced living

3. A. NO CHANGE
   B. on the other hand
   C. despite this
   D. however

4. Which of the following alternatives to the underlined portion is LEAST appropriate?

   F. NO CHANGE
   G. in the future
   H. formerly
   J. at one time

The shift away from paper has been gradual, as the banking industry illustrates. Today's generation of grand- parents remembers going to the bank with a passbook, which the teller would roll into a typewriter to record deposits, withdrawals, and interest payments.

5. All of the following alter- natives to the underlined portion would be acceptable EXCEPT:

  A. The grandparents of today remember

  B. Today's grandparents remember

  C. Grandparents of today's young adult remembers

  D. Modern grandparents still remember

Their grandchildren, on the other hand, may never even have heard of a passbook.

When the ATM card was introduced, the passbook became unnecessary.

6. Which of the following alter- natives to the underlined portion is LEAST acceptable?

  F. NO CHANGE

  G. in contrast

  H. thus

  J. however

Paper, however, was still involved in every transaction and in subsequent record keeping. There was the receipt immediately spit out by the teller machine and, then, a paper statement that would arrive monthly by snail mail.

Now, the ATM machine lets you choose not to print a paper record of your transaction, and banks offer small

7. All of the following alter- natives to the underlined portion would be correct EXCEPT:

  A. NO CHANGE

  B. still had a part

  C. still involving

  D. continued to play a part

rewards for customers <u>who agree to</u>
<u>forgo</u> the monthly paper statements
8
and instead manage their accounts

completely electronically. It's now

8. Which of the following alternatives to the underlined
portion is NOT acceptable?

F. NO CHANGE

G. agreed to give up

H. who are willing to forgo

J. who will give up

possible <u>receiving</u> nearly all of your
9

9. A. NO CHANGE

B. to receive

C. the receiving of

D. for receiving

monthly bills <u>online and pay them via</u>
10
<u>paper while not handling any email.</u>
10
While the younger generation appreciates

the convenience, more than a few senior

citizens resent that corporations are

simply trying to extract our money from

us without our even thinking about it.

10. F. NO CHANGE

G. via email and pay them
online without handling
any paper

H. on paper and pay them
online without handling
any email

J. without handling any
paper online and to pay
them via email

• THE FINAL ACT: ANSWERS AND EXPLANATIONS FOR CHALLENGING ENGLISH QUESTIONS

1. D. Choice D doesn't work in this context because a helping verb (such as "having," which Choice B uses) is needed to go with the verb form "grown" here.

2. G. Choice G is least desirable for two reasons. First and maybe most obviously, it's wordy. Second, "their life" isn't the best wording. The plural pronoun "their" correctly refers to "graduates," but because they all have individual lives, it doesn't make sense to use the singular noun "life."

3. A. When you see connecting words in the answer choices, look for a logical relationship between ideas. The previous sentence states that young people are familiar with computers. This sentence states that young people are comfortable with electronic transactions. The relationship is one of cause and effect. Only choice A expresses cause and effect. Choices B, C, and D all express contrast.

4. G. This is a Word Choice question. Think about the meaning of the sentence. The phrase "in the future" doesn't make sense here. Choices F, H, and J all express similar meanings by referring to the past, so any of them would work well here.

5. C. This question tests word choice, specifically subject-verb agreement. In choice C, the subject is the singular noun "generation." Remember that the noun that comes right before the verb is not always the subject. In choice C, "adult" is not the subject but the object of the preposition "of," and "grandparents...remembers" is incorrect subject-verb agreement.

6. H. When you see connecting words in the answer choices, focus on logical relationships. The previous sentence mentions that grandparents used a passbook; this sentence mentions that grandchildren haven't heard of a passbook. The relationship is one of contrast. All the answer choices except choice H correctly convey contrast. Choice H is wrong (and, therefore, the correct answer) because it expresses cause and effect.

7. C. The underlined part of the sentence here functions grammatically as the main verb in an independent clause. Remember that the *–ing* verb form can't be used by itself as the main verb of a clause. Choice C is wrong (the right answer) for this reason.

8. G. Choice G is wrong because it uses the past tense verb "agreed." Choices F and H use a present tense verb, and Choice J uses a future tense verb. Both present and future tenses work here, but the past tense in choice G is incorrect because it's inconsistent with the other verbs in this paragraph, which are in the present tense.

9. B. This question tests word choice, specifically idiomatic usage. The verb form "to receive" is the only one that works after the expression "it's possible."

10. G. This is a Sentence Sense question. You need to choose the clearest and most logical way to express the meaning. Choice G correctly places "and pay them online" immediately following the mention of receiving bills "via email." This choice uses the most logical placement of modifiers and makes the sentence easy to understand. The other three choices cause confusion because the word order is mixed up.

MATH BASICS

The ACT Math section is 60 minutes long and includes 60 questions. This works out to one minute per question, but you'll want to spend less time on the easier questions and more on the hard ones.

All of the Math questions have the same basic multiple-choice format. The test poses questions on a full range of math topics—from pre-algebra and elementary algebra through intermediate algebra and coordinate geometry to plane geometry and trigonometry—and each question offers five possible choices. Having five choices is unique to the Math section—all other sections only have four answer choices.

MATH QUESTION BREAKDOWN

24 pre-algebra and elementary algebra questions
14 plane geometry questions
10 intermediate algebra questions
8 coordinate geometry questions
4 trigonometry questions

The questions in the Math section, like those in other sections, aren't ordered in terms of difficulty. We've noticed that questions from elementary school or junior high tend to come earlier in the section, while those from high school math curricula tend to come later. However, this doesn't mean that the easier questions come first and the harder questions come later. We've found that high school subjects tend to be fresher in most students' minds than things they were taught years ago, so you may actually find the later questions easier. Remember, each question is worth the same number of points—answer those you know you can get right first!

● USING YOUR CALCULATOR (OR NOT)

You are allowed to use a calculator on the ACT Math section. How-ever, you never need a calculator to solve an ACT problem. No Math question requires messy or tedious calculations. Yes, you can do compu-tations faster, but you may be tempted to waste time using a calculator on questions that shouldn't involve lengthy computation. If you ever find yourself doing extensive calculations—elaborate division or long drawn-out multiplication—stop. You probably missed a shortcut.

Should I Just Leave My Calculator at Home?

No. Bring it. By zeroing in on the parts of problems that need calcula-tion, you can save yourself time and increase your score on the ACT by using your calculator.

What Kind of Calculator Should I Bring?

One that you're comfortable with. If you don't have a calculator now, buy one right away and practice using it between now and Test Day. You can use just about any small calculator; however, you must abide by a few restrictions. You may not bring the following:

- Calculators that print out your calculations
- Handheld minicomputers or laptop computers
- Any calculators with a typewriter keypad
- Calculators with an angled readout screen
- Calculators that require a wall outlet
- Calculators that make noise

When Should I Use My Calculator?

Remember, a calculator can be useful when used selectively and stra-tegically. Not all parts of a problem will necessarily be easier with a calculator.

Consider this problem:

1. $\sin 495° =$

   A. $-\dfrac{\sqrt{2}}{2}$ C. $\dfrac{1}{2}$ E. $3\dfrac{\sqrt{2}}{2}$

   B. $-\dfrac{1}{2}$ D. $\dfrac{\sqrt{2}}{2}$

Without a calculator, this is a very difficult problem. To find a trigonometric function of an angle greater than or equal to 90°, sketch a circle of radius 1 and centered at the origin of the coordinate grid. Start from the point (1,0) and rotate the appropriate number of degrees counterclockwise. When you rotate counterclockwise 495°, you rotate 360° (which brings you back to where you started), and then an additional 135°. That puts you midway into the second quadrant. Now you need to know whether sine is positive or negative in the second quadrant. Pretty scary, huh?

With a calculator this problem becomes simple. Just punch in "sin 495°," and you get 0.7071067811865. Choices A and B are negative, so they're out, and 0.7071067811865 is clearly not equal to $\frac{1}{2}$, so C is also wrong. That leaves only D or E. Now, with respect to choice E: $\sqrt{2}$ is greater than 1, so if you multiply it by another number greater than 1 (namely $\frac{3}{2}$), the result is obviously greater than 1. So you can eliminate E, **leaving D as the correct answer.** With a calculator, you can get this question right without really understanding it.

The key to effective calculator use is practice, so don't run out the night before the test to buy a fancy new calculator. If you don't already have a calculator (and intend to use one on the test), buy one now. Unless you're studying math or science in college, you won't need anything more complex than trig functions. You're better off bringing a straightforward model you're familiar with than an esoteric model you don't know how to use.

When Should I Avoid My Calculator?

You may be tempted to use your calculator on every problem, but many questions will be easier without it. Look at this example:

2. The sum of all the integers from 1 to 44, inclusive, is subtracted from the sum of all the integers from 7 to 50, inclusive. What is the result?

    F.   6
    G.   44
    H.   50
    J.   264
    K.   300

You could…add all the integers from 1 through 44, and then all the integers from 7 through 50, and then subtract the first sum from the second, punching in all the numbers into the calculator. And hoping you didn't hit any wrong buttons.

But that's the long way…and the wrong way. That way involves hitting over 250 keys on your calculator. It'll take too long, and you're too likely to make a mistake. The amount of computation involved in solving this problem tells you that there must be an easier way. Remember, no ACT problem absolutely requires the use of a calculator.

Look at the problem again: A calculator can help you on this question, but you have to think first. Both sums contain the same number of consecutive integers, and each integer in the first sum has a corresponding integer 6 greater than it in the second sum. Here's the scratch work:

$$
\begin{array}{cc}
1 & 7 \\
+2 & +8 \\
+3 & +9 \\
\cdot & \cdot \\
\cdot & \cdot \\
\cdot & \cdot \\
+42 & +48 \\
+43 & +49 \\
+44 & +50 \\
\end{array}
$$

This means there are 44 pairs of integers which are each 6 apart. So the total difference between the two sums will be the difference between each pair of integers, times the number of pairs. Now you can pull out your calculator, punch "6 × 44 =" and get the correct answer of 264 with little or no time wasted. Mark J in your test booklet and move on.

The main rule to remember is always to **look for the quickest way to solve problems.** This sometimes requires creative thinking. However, taking the time to asses what is in front of you means solving more problems correctly, which leads to more points and a higher score!

Percents

DIFFICULTY: ★ ★

FREQUENCY: ★ ★

SURPRISE FACTOR: ★

● INTRODUCTION TO PERCENTS QUESTIONS

Percents questions are common on the ACT Math Test. The simplest Percents problems will be written out in basic algebraic form, and the most complicated problems will most likely be Percents problems disguised as word problems. Percents problems can range in difficulty from questions that simply ask you to find what percent one number is of another to questions that include multiple percents in one problem. However, most Percents problems can be solved using a specific three-part formula.

Most Common Types of Percents Questions

PERCENT TAKEN OFF

The most common Percents questions deal with a percent taken off. They either give you a whole and ask you to find a new value when a percent is taken off or give you a new value after a percent is taken off and ask you to find the original value. Here's an example:

1. A jacket regularly priced at $135 is discounted by 10%. What is the discounted price of the jacket?

These questions are relatively easy and straightforward. They require a simple three-step process:

Step 1: Subtract the percent from 100.

Step 2: Convert the percent to a decimal.

Step 3: Multiply the decimal by the original whole. (The answer is $121.50.)

PERCENT CHANGE

The next type of Percents problem involves percent increase or decrease. These question types will typically present you with an original value and a new value and ask you to find the percent increase or decrease. Alternatively, they will give you the original value and the percent change and ask you to find the new value or give you the new value and the percent change and ask you to find the old value. Here's an example:

2. A sweater that originally cost $100 is discounted to $70. What percent discount was applied to the sweater?

Again, these questions should not be too involved. There is a simple three-part formula that deals with these problems:

$$\text{percent} = \frac{\text{actual change}}{\text{original whole}} * 100.$$

(The answer to the above question is 30%.)

COMBINED PERCENTS

The final type of Percents problem that you may encounter on the ACT is a combined percents problem. These problems will usually give you an original whole, then take a percent off of the original twice, consecutively. Here's an example:

3. A television set originally costs $250. It is discounted 20% one day and another 15% the next. What is the total percent discount applied to the television set?

This is a more difficult problem because it involves more steps and more manipulation. Combined percents problems will ask you to find a new whole, find the original whole, or find the missing percent. These questions usually involve both of the question types listed above. There is no formula to apply directly to solve multiple percents problems; however, you can break these problems into parts to make them easier to solve. (The answer to the above example is 32%.)

THE TRAP DOOR: STEERING CLEAR OF ANSWER TRAPS

Students commonly encounter several pitfalls with Percents questions.

PERCENT CHANGE

Many students get confused between percent increase and decrease. If the problem asks you to find the percent increase or decrease, it is asking you to find the percent change between the old and new price. The initial thought may be just to divide the new price by the old one to find the percent increase or decrease, but this would be incorrect. Let's take Question 2 from above:

2. A sweater that originally cost $100 is discounted to $70. What percent discount was applied to the sweater?

The percent discount applied to the sweater is not simply $\frac{\$70}{\$100} \times 100$. It is important to remember that percent increase or decrease problems involve using the percent change formula:

$$\text{percent change} = \frac{\text{actual change}}{\text{original}} \times 100$$

Percent increase or decrease questions often appear as percent discount or sale questions. Whenever you see *discount* or *sale*, you should think "percent increase or decrease" and be ready to use the percent change formula.

MULTIPLE PERCENTS

Multiple Percents questions cause the most difficulty for students. The golden rule of combining percents: NEVER JUST ADD THE PERCENTS! This will lead you to a wrong answer every time—one that will most likely be among the answer choices. Why can't you just add the percents? Once you take the first percent, you have a second whole, one that is smaller than the original whole. The second percent will be applied to this second whole, not the original whole. Take, for instance, Question 3 from above:

3. A television set originally costs $250. It is discounted 20% one day and another 15% the next. What is the total percent discount applied to the television set?

This combined percents problem is asking for the total discount or, in other words, the total percent taken off the original price of the television. It is not simply 35%. To attack a problem like this, you need to break it down into simpler parts. The first is taking 20% off $250. Once you get that answer ($250 × 0.80 = $200), you can move on to the second part. Using your answer from part one as the new whole, take 15% off of that. This final answer is the final cost of the television set ($200 * 0.85 = $170). Now you have the original cost of the television set ($250) and the final cost of the television set ($170). The last step is to use the percent change formula to find the percent discount. Remember for percent change, you want to use the actual change ($250 − $170 = $80). We will walk through all the steps when we revisit this problem in the example below.

• PERFORMANCE TECHNIQUES: KEY FORMULAS AND RULES

So how do you avoid the pitfalls of Percents questions? First, you must be sure you understand exactly what the question is asking, and second, you must choose the appropriate formula to solve the problem.

THE BASICS

Percent simply means 100th. A percent is 1/100th of something. Using this relationship, you can change a percentage into a decimal or fraction.

To change a **percent into a decimal,** just move the decimal point to the left two places and drop the percent sign.

75% = 0.75

To change a percent into a fraction, simply divide the percent by 100 and reduce the fraction to its lowest terms if necessary.

$75\% = \dfrac{75}{100}$; divide numerator and denominator by 25 to get $\dfrac{3}{4}$.

These relationships can be used to transform the percent into whatever form is easiest for you to work with.

THE PERCENT FORMULA

Most of the Percents problems you encounter will be solvable using the simple three-part percent formula:

$$\text{percent} = \frac{\text{part}}{\text{whole}} * 100$$

When working with a Percents problem, always be sure to identify which value goes with which part of the formula. Unless it is the missing part of the formula, the percent will usually be the most obvious part to pick out of the question. The whole is a little harder to identify, but it is usually associated with the words of or off. Let's look at an example:

4. What is the new price when 25% is taken off a $40 sweater?

In this example, the percent is taken off the whole, and the whole is $40.

The part can usually be found after or associated with the word *is*, as in the following example:

5. 7 is 30% of what number?

In this example, the percent is obviously 30%. By remembering that the whole is usually preceded by of or off, we can deduce that the whole here is just "a number." That leaves 7 to be the part. Notice that seven is followed by the word is. A helpful way to remember what goes with which part of the formula is to reword the formula:

$$\text{percent} = \frac{\text{part}}{\text{whole}} \times 100 = \frac{\text{is}}{\text{of}} \times 100$$

This will help you to remember which part of the formula is associated with which word.

PERCENT INCREASE AND DECREASE

When dealing with a percent increase or decrease in which the percent and the original whole are both given, using a simple three-step solution simplifies things immensely. For percent increase:

Step 1: Add the percent to 100.

Step 2: Convert the percent to a decimal.

Step 3: Multiply the decimal by the original whole.

For percent decrease, the only difference is in Step 1, in which the percent is subtracted from 100 instead of being added.

When you are given the percent change and the new price but not the original whole, the same steps should be followed. However, when you get to Step 3, because you do not know the whole, you must assign it a variable and set up an equation. Here's an example:

6. A jacket is discounted by 30% to $129.50. What was its original price?

First, recognize that this is a percent decrease problem without the original whole. Applying our three-step formula we have:

Step 1: $100 - 30\% = 70\%$

Step 2: $\dfrac{70}{100} = 0.7$

Step 3: This is where we have to assign the original whole a variable and set up an equation. Let's call the original price of the jacket j. Remember that in Step 3, we multiply the original whole by the decimal from Step 2 to get the new price. Our equation would then be:

$0.7j = \$129.50$

Solving this equation for j, we get $j = \$185$, so the jacket originally cost $185.

PERCENT CHANGE FORMULA

The percent change formula comes into play when you are dealing with a percent increase or decrease in which the percent is not given, as in Question 2 above:

A sweater that originally cost $100 is discounted to $70.
What percent discount was applied to the sweater?

In this case, you are given the original whole and the new price and asked to find the percent increase or decrease. The simple formula is:

$$\text{percent} = \frac{\text{actual change}}{\text{original whole}} \times 100$$

Here you must be careful to divide the change by the old price, not the new price by the old price. The question asks for the percent discount so you need to know how much is taken off the original price. To find how much was taken off the original price, subtract the new price from the original price: $100 - \$70 = \$30$. This is the actual change in value.

Once you have identified the parts of the formula, it is a simple matter to solve for what you do not have. As long as you have any two of the three parts of the formula, you can solve for the third. We found that the actual change is $30 and we know that the original whole is $100. Now all we have to do is plug these into the formula to find the percent change.

$$\text{percent change} = \frac{\$30}{\$100} \times 100 = 30\%$$

COMBINING PERCENTS

Combined Percents questions can best be handled by breaking the problem down into parts and applying the relevant three-part formula or process to the individual parts one at a time. In the case of a multiple percent decrease problem, the three-step process for percent decrease should be used on the first percent to find the second whole. Once you have the second whole, go through the three-step process using the second whole as the original and the second percent to get the final part. Once you have the final part, you can plug it into the percent change equation along with the original and solve for the total percent discount. Let's look at Question 3 again:

3. A television set originally costs $250. It is discounted 20% one day and another 15% the next. What is the total percent discount applied to the television set?

This is a two-part percent decrease problem. For the first part, the percent is 20% and the whole is $250. To get the new whole, apply the three-step process for percent decrease.

Step 1: $100 - 20\% = 80\%$

Step 2: $\frac{80\%}{100\%} = 0.8$

Step 3: $0.8 \times \$250 = \$200$

The value you get in Step 3 will then be your new whole in the second part of this problem, and 15% will be your new percent.

Step 1: $100 - 15\% = 85\%$

Step 2: $\frac{85\%}{100\%} = 0.85$

Step 3: $0.85 \times \$200 = \$170$

So $170 is the final price of the television set. Now we must be careful. The problem asks for the total percent discount. This final step is a percent change problem. The original is $250 and the new price is $170, so the actual change is $250 - $170 = $80, and the percent change is $\frac{\$80}{\$250} \times 100 = 32\%$.

Had we just combined the percents (20% + 15%), we would have gotten 35%.

● DRESS REHEARSAL: SAMPLE QUESTIONS AND DETAILED EXPLANATIONS

Now that you know how to tackle those tricky Percents questions, let's practice with a few problems.

1. Emily has $350 in a savings account. If she increases the amount in her savings account by 25% and then withdraws 40%, how much money does she have left in her savings account?

   A. $140.00
   B. $157.50
   C. $192.50
   D. $262.50
   E. $297.50

This is a combined percents problem. Don't just add the percents!

Let's separate this problem into its parts. The first part is a percent increase question. The whole is $350 and the percent increase (Emily's deposit) is 25%.

Step 1: $100 + 25 = 125$

Step 2: $\dfrac{125}{100} = 1.25$

Step 3: $1.25 \times \$350 = \$437.50$

The result, $437.50, is the new whole for part two of the problem, and 40% is the percent. Part two of the problem is a percent decrease problem so our three-step process is

Step 1: $100 - 40 = 60\%$

Step 2: $\dfrac{60\%}{100} = 0.6$

Step 3: $0.6 \times \$437.50 = \$262.50$

The final amount Emily has in her savings account is $262.50. **So the answer is D.**

Let's look at the other answer choices. If you had just combined the percents, you would have gotten a 25% increase and a 40% decrease for a net 15% decrease ($-40\% + 25\% = -15\%$). Plugging this percent decrease into the formula would have given you an answer of $297.50, which is E. This illustrates the importance of not just adding the percent.

2. In a class, 25% of the students are seniors. If 72 of the students in the class are not seniors, how many students are in the class?

   F. 90
   G. 96
   H. 97
   J. 180
   K. 288

This is a simple Percents question. The first thing to do is to identify what the question is asking. It is asking you to find the total number of students in the class, so you need to find the whole. The question says that 25% of the students are seniors and 72 are not seniors. What does this mean? If 25% of the students are seniors, then 75% are not seniors. Now we have our percent and our part: 75% are not seniors and 72 students are not seniors, so 72 is 75% of the total number of students. Plugging this part and whole into the percent formula you get:

$$75\% = \frac{72}{\text{whole}} \times 100$$

Rearrange this formula to solve for the whole:

$$\text{whole} = \frac{72}{0.75} = 96$$

So there are 96 students total in the class, and **the correct answer is G.**

3. The cost of attendance at a private university increases 4% to $43,004.00. What was the original cost of attendance?

   A. $44,724.16
   B. $41,283.84
   C. $41,350.00
   D. $39,696.00
   E. $42,000.39

This is a percent increase question. A big clue is given in the question stem, namely the fact that it asks for the original cost of attendance. This should indicate that you are looking for the original whole. So let's follow the steps for dealing with percent increase.

Step 1: Add the percent to 100: $100 + 4 = 104\%$

Step 2: Convert the percent to a decimal: $\frac{104}{100} = 1.04$.

Step 3: Multiply by the original whole to find the new price.

In this case, the original whole is what we are trying to find. We must set up an equation, designating the original whole as a variable x. The equation should look like this:

$1.04x = 43,004$

To solve this equation, divide both sides by 1.04 to isolate x. When that is done, we get $x = \$41,350.00$. **So the correct answer is C.**

4. The regular price for a bike is $125.00. If the bike is discounted by 20%, what is the new price?

    F. $100.00

    G. $105.00

    H. $112.50

    J. $120.00

    K. $122.50

This is a simple percent discount question. Let's follow the three-step process for percent discount questions.

Step 1: Subtract the percent from 100: $100 - 20 = 80\%$

Step 2: Convert the percent to a decimal: $\dfrac{80}{100} = 0.8$

Step 3: Multiply the decimal by the original whole: $0.8 \times \$125.00 = \$100$

So the correct answer is F.

5. If 110% of a number is 528, what is 75% of that number?

    A. 360

    B. 396

    C. 480

    D. 528

    E. 581

This problem has two percents, but it is not the typical multiple percents problem. These two percents are not applied to a known whole. What you have to do here is find the whole and then take a percent of it. This problem can be solved be applying the percent formula twice. First, we have 110% of "a number" is 528. The is should alert you to the fact that 528 is the part. The of indicates the whole, in this case just "a number" that we are trying to find. Plug this into the percent formula:

$$\text{percent} = \frac{\text{part}}{\text{whole}} \times 100$$

$$110\% = \frac{528}{\text{whole}} \times 100$$

Solve this equation for the whole:

$$\text{whole} = \frac{528}{1.10} = 480$$

So this is the new whole. Now the problem asks for 75% of this whole. Plug these new numbers into the percents formula:

$$75\% = \frac{\text{part}}{480} \times 100$$

Solve this problem for the part:

$$\text{part} = 0.75 \times 480 = 360$$

The correct answer is A.

Now that you've had an introduction to percents and walked through some problems, try a few on your own. Take the Practice Quiz on the next page.

● THE FINAL ACT: PRACTICE QUIZ

1. After a football team won its first game, the attendance at its second game rose 15% to 17,250 fans. What was the attendance at the first game?

   A. 2,600
   B. 15,000
   C. 12,750
   D. 14,600
   E. 15,525

2. The price of a concert ticket is $45 if purchased in advance. If purchased at the door, the price is 30% more. Elena wants to purchase a ticket at the door, and she has a coupon for 10% off the door price. How much does she pay for her ticket?

F. $28.35

G. $36.00

H. $52.65

J. $54.00

K. $58.50

3. One store has a coat priced at $135. Another store has the same coat priced at $150 but also offers a 15% discount. What is the difference between the prices of the coat at the two stores?

A. $7.50

B. $15.00

C. $20.25

D. $22.50

E. $35.25

4. A new car costs $23,860.76. The car depreciates (decreases in value) at a rate of 5% per year. How much is the car worth after four years? (Round to the nearest cent.)

F. $19,088.61

G. $19,434.73

H. $20,457.62

J. $21,534.34

K. $22,667.72

5. If 135% of a number is 405, what is 80% of the number?

A. 205

B. 240

C. 270

D. 300

E. 324

6. Liz saves 15% of every paycheck. If she saved $37.50 of her last paycheck, how much was her last paycheck?

   F. $25.00
   G. $56.25
   H. $112.50
   J. $225.00
   K. $250.00

7. Ten students in a chemistry class received an A on the final exam. If 20% of the students got As, how many students are in the class total?

   A. 12
   B. 15
   C. 18
   D. 20
   E. 50

8. There are 230 student athletes at a high school. Of these, 69 play basketball, and 138 play football. No students play more than one sport. What percentage of student athletes play a sport other than basketball and football?

   F. 10%
   G. 30%
   H. 60%
   J. 70%
   K. 90%

9. Alex signed up for cable, telephone, and Internet services. As a package deal, he got all three for $115.00 per month. If he had bought them individually, he would have paid $71.25 per month for the cable, $31.50 per month for the telephone, and $41.00 per month for Internet. What percent did he save by getting the package deal?

   A. 20%
   B. 22%
   C. 29%
   D. 50%
   E. 80%

10. During the premier of a weekly television drama, 32 million people tuned in. During the second episode of the drama, there was an awards show on another channel, and only 12 million watched the second episode. If all of the viewers of the premier who didn't watch the second episode of the drama watched the awards show instead, what percentage of people who watched the premier the first week watched the awards show the second week?

F. 25.0%

G. 37.5%

H. 60.0%

J. 62.5%

K. 80.0%

● THE FINAL ACT: ANSWERS AND EXPLANATIONS FOR PERCENTS QUESTIONS

1. B. This is a percent increase question in which we do not know the original value, so we know right away that we will have to assign the number of fans at the first game to a variable. Let's call this value x. Now let's follow our steps for percent increase problems.

Step 1: Add the percent to 100: $100 + 15 = 115$

Step 2: Convert the percent to a decimal: $\frac{115\%}{100\%} = 1.15$

Step 3: Multiply by the original whole: $1.15x = 17,250$

In this case we want to know the original whole (x) and we know the final number, so we set up an equation that looks like this: $1.15x = 17,250$. Solving this equation for x, we get $x = 15,000$.

2. H. This is a combined Percents question. The first step is a percent increase question. The price at the door is increased by 30%. So let's apply our percent increase steps to this part of the problem first.

Step 1: Add the percent to 100: $100 + 30 = 130\%$

Step 2: Convert the percent to a decimal: $\frac{130\%}{100\%} = 1.30$

Step 3: Multiply by the original whole: $1.30 \times 45 = \$58.50$

So $58.50 (answer choice K) is the cost of the ticket at the door. Now let's move on to the second part of the problem. Elena is buying the ticket at the door, but she is getting 10% off the door price. This second part is a percent decrease, with the door price being the new whole. Let's apply our process for percent decrease.

Step 1: Subtract the percent from 100: $100 - 10 = 90\%$

Step 2: Convert the percent to a decimal: $\dfrac{90\%}{100\%} = 0.9$

Step 3: Multiply by the new whole: $\$58.50 \times 0.9 = \$52.65$.

Elena pays $52.65 for her ticket.

3. A. At first glance, this might seem like a combined Percents problem, but there is only one percent. The second store has the coat priced at $150, but it is giving a 15% discount. This is a percent decrease problem. Applying the steps for percent decrease, you get:

Step 1: Subtract the percent from 100: $100 - 15 = 85\%$

Step 2: Convert the percent to a decimal: $\dfrac{85\%}{100\%} = 0.85$

Step 3: Multiply by the original whole: $0.85 \times \$150 = \$127.50$

The price of the coat at the second store is $127.50. Now the question asks for the difference between the two prices. So the difference between the two prices is $135.00 - \$127.50 = \$7.50$.

4. G. Don't be fooled by the fact that only one percent is present. There is only one percent, but it is applied once each year for four years. This is a multiple percent decrease problem. Following the procedure for percent decrease problems:

Step 1: Subtract the percent from 100: $100\% - 5\% = 95\%$

Step 2: Convert the percent to a decimal: $95\% / 100\% = 0.95$

Step 3: Multiply by the whole: $\$23,860.76 \times 0.95 = \$22,667.72$

So the value of the car after one year is $22,667.72. The percent decrease is the same each year for the remaining three years as well, so just do Step 3 for each successive year using the price from the year before.

Year 2: $\$22,667.72 \times 0.95 = \$21,534.33$

Year 3: $\$21,534.33 \times 0.95 = \$20,457.61$

Year 4: $\$20,457.61 \times 0.95 = \$19,434.73$

So after four years, the value of the car is $19,434.73.

5. B. This question has two percents, but it is not the standard combined percents problem. It can be treated as two separate simple Percents problems. For the first part, the percent is 135%. Notice the word *is* before 405. This should be a clue that 405 is the part. The only piece of the formula left to find is the whole. So applying the formula:

$$\text{percent} = \frac{\text{part}}{\text{whole}} \times 100$$

$$135\% = \frac{405}{\text{whole}} \times 100$$

Solve the equation for the whole:

$$\text{whole} = 405 \times 1.35 = 300$$

This is not the end of the problem, but notice that 300 is answer choice A. It is important that you don't stop before you have completed all steps in the problem.

Now on to Step 2. The whole is 300. The new percent is 80%. Plug this new information into the percent formula:

$$80\% = \frac{\text{part}}{300} \times 100$$

Solve this equation for the part:

$$\text{part} = 0.8 \times 300 = 240$$

6. K. This is a very simple percents question. The question asks for the total of Liz's last paycheck. You are told that she saved 15%, which was $37.50. So 15% is obviously the percent in this problem, and $37.50 is the part. You want to find the whole. All you have to do is plug the numbers into the formula:

$$\text{percent} = \frac{\text{part}}{\text{whole}} \times 100$$

$$15\% = \frac{\$37.50}{\text{whole}} \times 100$$

Rearranging this to solve for the whole you get:

$$\text{whole} = \frac{\$37.50}{0.15} = \$250.00$$

So Liz's last paycheck was $250.00.

7. E. This is a very simple question. The percent is given to you: 20%. You are also told that 20% is 10 students. The word *is* should alert you that 10 is the part. Now all you have to do is plug these numbers into the percent formula:

$$\text{percent} = \frac{\text{part}}{\text{whole}} \times 100$$

$$20\% = \frac{10}{\text{whole}} \times 100$$

Rearrange this to solve for the whole:

$$\text{whole} = \frac{10}{0.2} = 50$$

So the total number of students in the class is 50.

8. F. First figure out what the question is asking for. You want to find the students who play a sport that is *not* basketball or football. The total number of students who play sports is 230, so that is the whole. Now you have to figure out the part. If 69 play basketball and 138 play football, a total of 207 play either basketball or football. So out of the 230 athletes, if 207 play either basketball or football, 23 play *neither* basketball nor football. The part that you want to use is 23. Now plug the part and the whole into the percent formula:

$$\text{percent} = \frac{\text{part}}{\text{whole}} \times 100 = \frac{23}{230} \times 100 = 10\%$$

9. A. This problem is asking for the percent difference between the package deal price and the total of the individual prices. First, find the total of the individual prices: $71.25 + $31.50 + $41.00 = $143.75. Now you have the two prices and you want to know the percent saved by getting the package deal. This has become a percent change problem. The amount $143.75 can be thought of as the original price and $115.00 as the new price. The percent change formula is:

$$\text{percent change} = \frac{\text{actual change}}{\text{original}} \times 100$$

The actual change is the difference between the old and new prices:

$$\text{actual change} = \$143.75 - \$115.00 = \$28.75$$

Plug the actual change and the original amount into the percent change formula:

$$\text{percent change} = \frac{\$28.75}{\$143.75} \times 100 = 20\%$$

10. J. Don't let the words confuse you. Also, don't worry about the "million" in the question stem. This is a Percents problem, but before you apply the formula, you must first figure out the parts. The problem asks for the percentage of viewers who watched the awards show instead of the second episode of the drama. The number of viewers who watched the awards show is the same as the number who did not watch the second episode. You can find this number by subtracting the number of people who watched the second episode of the drama from the number who watched the first episode: 32 − 12 = 20, so 20 million people watched the awards show instead of the drama. The part is 20 million, and the whole is 32 million. Plug these values into the percent formula to find the percent of people who switched to the awards show the second week:

$$\text{percent} = \frac{20}{32} \times 100 = 62.5\%$$

Notice that if you had used 12 as the part in the equation, you would have gotten answer G. This is incorrect because the question asks for the number of people who did not watch the television show the second week. Again, make sure to read the question carefully and understand what it is asking you before you attack the problem.

Proportions and Probability

DIFFICULTY: ★ ★ ★ ★

FREQUENCY: ★ ★ ★

SURPRISE FACTOR: ★

● INTRODUCTION TO PROPORTIONS AND PROBABILITY QUESTIONS

Proportions and Probability questions are very common on the ACT Math test. They appear in many forms, including questions about algebraic expressions or fractions as well as word problems. Proportions and Probability questions range in difficulty from very simple ratio problems to more complex word problems and problems including permutations or combinations. Although proportions and probability are tested in many different ways, some basic formulas will help to solve these types of problems.

Proportions and Probability problems include ratios, proportions, rates, averages, probability, permutations, and combinations. This may sound like a lot, but these different problem types are all closely related.

Ratios

Ratios are comparisons of two quantities by division. They may be written in fraction form $\left(\frac{x}{y}\right)$, with a colon ($x{:}y$), or in English (ratio of x to y). For example, the ratio of dogs d to cats c can also be expressed as $d{:}c$ or $\frac{d}{c}$. The dog-to-cat ratio is an example of a part-to-part ratio. Ratios can also be part-to-whole, as in the ratio of dogs to animals.

Common ratio problems will give a part-to-part ratio and ask for the part-to-whole ratio. Here's an example of a ratio problem:

1. If all pets in an animal shelter are either dogs or cats and the ratio of dogs to cats is 4:7, then what is the ratio of dogs to pets?

When questions ask for a part-to-whole ratio, they give you the part and expect you to find the whole. In this problem, the part is the number of dogs in the ratio, which is 4. To find the whole, simply add the parts of the ratio. In this case, the whole is the number of dogs + the number of cats, which is 4 + 7, so the whole is 11. This means that the ratio of dogs to pets is 4:11.

Other problems will give a ratio and the number of one of the parts and ask for either the other part or the whole. For example:

2. The ratio of dogs to cats is 4:7. If there are 12 dogs, how many cats are there?

This question gives a ratio and one number. It is important to remember here that ratios are written in lowest terms. They don't tell you what the numbers are, only what they must be a multiple of. In this case the ratio of dogs to cats is 4:7. There are 12 dogs, which is 4 × 3, so to get the actual number, the ratio must be multiplied by 3. To find the number of cats, multiply 7 by 3. There are 21 cats.

Ratios containing more than two terms can be more difficult. Common problems involving more than two terms include those that give the ratio of two separate quantities to a third quantity and ask for the ratio of the two original quantities. Here is an example:

3. The ratio of dogs to cats is 4:7, and the ratio of cats to hamsters is 1:2. What is the ratio of dogs to hamsters?

Problems like these require that the common term, in this case the number of cats, be equal in both ratios. To do this problem, you must find the least common multiple of the common term in both ratios. The number of cats is 7 in one ratio and 1 in the other, so the least common multiple is 7. The first ratio is fine as it is, but the second ratio must be multiplied by 7 so that the number of cats can be the same in both ratios. This makes the new ratio of cats to hamsters 7:14 (1 × 7 : 2 × 7). Now we have the ratio of dogs to cats to hamsters, which is 4:7:14, and the ratio of dogs to hamsters is 4:14.

Proportions

Proportions are simply two equal ratios and are usually written as two fractions set equal to each other. Generally in proportion problems, one term is missing, and you must find that missing term. When proportions are written as fractions, the simplest way to solve them is to cross multiply. For example:

4. $\dfrac{3}{12} = \dfrac{x}{36}$

To solve this problem, simply cross multiply: $12x = 3 \times 36$. Dividing both sides by 12 yields $x = 9$. Most proportion problems are relatively simple.

Averages

Average problems involve a simple three-part formula: average = sum of terms/number of terms. Common average problems will give two parts of the formula and ask for the third. For example, you might be given a group of numbers and be asked to find the average. Other types of average problems might give the average, the number of terms, and some of the terms and ask for the missing term. You can solve most average problems easily using the three-part formula. Let's look at an example:

5. Julie drove 15 miles on Monday, 23 miles on Tuesday, and 13 miles on Wednesday. What was the average number of miles Julie drove per day?

This is a simple problem. There are three terms and their sum is $15 + 23 + 13 = 51$. Therefore, the average number of miles Julie drove over the three days is $\dfrac{51}{3} = 17$.

Rates

A rate is any something per something, but the most common rate is distance/time, as in miles per hour or feet per second. As with averages, rate problems will often give two of the three terms and ask for the third. For example, they may give the distance and time and ask for the rate, or give the rate and time and ask for the distance. Here's an example:

6. Fred needed to drive 250 miles to get back to his college. For the first 225 miles, he drove 60 miles/hour, and for the last 25 miles, he drove 50miles/hour. What was his average speed during this trip?

To solve this problem, you need the total distance and the total time. The problem tells you that the total distance is 250 miles. Now, to find the total time, you need to find the times for each leg of the trip. The first leg was 60 miles/hr for 225 miles. The total time here would be $\frac{225}{60}$ = 3.75 hours. For the last 25 miles, he drove 50 miles/hour for a total time of $\frac{25}{50}$ = 0.5 hours. So the total time is 4.25. Therefore, the average speed is $\frac{250 \text{ miles}}{4.25 \text{ hours}}$ = 58.8 miles/hr.

Notice that to find the average speed for the *entire* trip, you must take the *total* distance and divide it by the *total* time, not just average the two parts of the trip.

Probability

Probability problems also appear frequently on the ACT. You can solve simple probabilities using another three-part formula:

$$\text{probability} = \frac{\text{\# of desired outcomes}}{\text{\# of possible outcomes}}$$

The most common probability questions will ask you to find the probability of something happening. Probability problems may also ask you to find the probability of multiple events happening together. To find the probability of multiple events coinciding, simply find their individual probabilities and then multiply those together. Probabilities, like ratios, can be written in three ways: as fractions, with a colon, or as a word problem. Here's an example of a probability problem:

7. There are 35 eighth-grade students, 22 seventh-grade students, and 43 sixth-grade students. If a student is randomly chosen to be principle for a day, what is the probability the chosen student will be in eighth grade?

There are 35 eighth-grade students, so the number of desired outcomes is 35. There is a total of 35 + 22 + 43 = 100 students, so the total number of outcomes is 100. Therefore, the probability that the chosen student will be in eighth grade is $\frac{35}{100}$, which reduces (divide each side by 5) to $\frac{7}{20}$.

• THE TRAP DOOR: STEERING CLEAR OF ANSWER TRAPS

Some Proportions and Probability problems are relatively straightforward, but others are a little more complex. Here are some common mistakes that students make on these problems.

RATIO PROBLEM TRAPS

Some students get confused with ratio problems. The most important thing to remember about ratios is that ratios are always written in lowest terms. They do not tell you the number of things or people, only what that number must be a multiple of. Also, before working on a ratio problem, you must identify whether it is a part-to-part or a part-to-whole ratio. A part-to-part ratio may be written in fraction form $\left(\frac{x}{y}\right)$, but it is not a fraction. On the other hand, a part-to-whole ratio is a fraction.

RATE PROBLEM TRAPS

With rate problems, the most common mistake is made in problems that involve average speed $= \frac{\text{total distance}}{\text{total time}}$ when multiple speeds are involved. Let's consider an example:

8. A car traveled 50 miles/hr for 2 hours and then traveled 70 miles/hr for 3 hours. What was the car's average speed for the entire trip?

The common mistake made here is to average the two legs of the trip to find the average speed. So the average of the two legs would be $\frac{(50 + 70)}{2} = 60$ miles/hr. That would be wrong. Average speed for the whole trip is not simply the average speed of the two separate legs of the trip. It is the total distance divided by the total time. To solve this problem, you must first find the total distance and the total time separately, then divide the total distance by the total time. The total time is simply 2 + 3, or 5 hours. The total distance is a little trickier. For the first leg of the trip, the car traveled 50 miles/hr for 2 hours. This is a simple rate problem where we have the rate and the time and want the distance. Remembering that rate $= \frac{\text{distance}}{\text{time}}$, we simply rearrange the formula to distance = rate × time to find the distance. So the distance for the first leg of the trip is 50 miles/hr × 2 hours = 100 miles. For the second leg of the trip, you get distance = 70 miles/hr × 3 hours = 210 miles. So the total distance for the trip is 100 miles + 210 miles, which is 310 miles. Divide that by the total time of 5 hours to get the average speed. Average speed $= \frac{310 \text{ miles}}{5 \text{ hrs}} = 62$ miles/hr.

PROBABILITY QUESTION TRAPS

Probability questions also sometimes give students trouble. The most important thing that students must do in probability questions is to determine what event is considered an outcome. Here's an example of a probability question:

9. If there are 3 green marbles, 8 red marbles, and 13 blue marbles in a jar, what is the probability that a red marble will be pulled out of the jar?

The event that is considered an outcome is pulling a marble out of the jar. The desired outcome is pulling a red marble, which can happen 8 times. The total number of outcomes is the total number of marbles that can be pulled out of the jar, which is 24 (3 + 8 + 13). So the probability that a red marble will be pulled out of the jar is $\frac{8}{24}$ or $\frac{1}{3}$. It is important to note that, when possible, probabilities are always expressed in simplified form.

You must also the remember that the probability formula is

$$\frac{\text{number of desired outcomes}}{\text{number of possible outcomes}}, \textit{not } \frac{\text{number of desired outcomes}}{\text{number of undesired outcomes}}.$$

● PERFORMANCE TECHNIQUES: KEY FORMULAS AND RULES

There are certain formulas and rules to follow for each type of Proportions and Probability problem to ensure you do not fall into an answer trap.

Ratios and Proportions

Ratios are relatively simple. If a question gives you a ratio only, you can only rearrange that ratio. For example, with a part:part ratio, you can rearrange it into a ratio of either of the two parts to the whole. Remember that to find the whole, you simply add the parts. Part-to-whole ratios are simply fractions. Part-to-part ratios are not fractions, even though they may be written in fraction form. To solve ratio problems, you must follow these steps:

Step 1: Identify the type of ratio the question gives you (part:part or part:whole).

Step 2: Identify what type of ratio you need to solve the question (again, part:part or part:whole).

Step 3: Identify what you need to solve for.

Step 4: Set up a proportion to solve the problem.

If the question gives you a ratio only, you cannot find any actual numbers or the actual whole, you can only find what it must be a multiple of. If a question gives you a part:part ratio and an actual part, you can find the other part and the whole. Solving a ratio problem that gives you a ratio and a value involves setting up a proportion, as in this example:

10.   The ratio of boys to girls in a class is 4:3. If there are 28 students in the class, how many girls are in the class?

This problem gives you a part-to-part ratio and the whole and asks you to find a part. To find the part from the whole, you need to convert the part-to-part ratio into the appropriate part-to-whole ratio. In this case, you need to convert the ratio of boys to girls to a ratio of girls to students. Remember, to find the whole in a ratio, simply add the parts, so the whole is 7 students (4 boys + 3 girls). Now the ratio of girls to the whole is 3 girls to 7 students. You know the actual number of students is 28, and you want to find the actual number of girls. The final step is to set up and solve a proportion. Your proportion should look like this: $\frac{3}{7} = \frac{x}{28}$, where x is the actual number of girls in the class. Solving this proportion for x by cross multiplying yields $7x = 84$. Divide both sides by 7, and your final answer is $x = 12$. So there are 12 girls in the class.

Averages

Average problems on the ACT are usually straightforward. All average problems can be solved with the three-part average formula: average = sum of terms/# of terms.

Some average problems might give you the average, the number of terms, and all the terms but one and ask you to find the missing term. For example:

11.   If Josh scored an 83, a 92, and an 87 on his first three tests, what score must he get on his last test to have an average of 90?

You want to find the fourth term; let's call that x.

Step 1:   Add all the terms: $83 + 92 + 87 + x = 262 + x$

Step 2:   Find the number of terms: 4

Step 3:   Set up the equation and solve for x:

$$262 + \frac{x}{4} = 90$$
$$262 + x = 360$$
$$x = 98$$

So Josh has to get a 98 on the fourth test to have an average score of 90.

Rates

Rates are solved using a three-part formula: rate $= \frac{x}{y}$. The most common rate you will see on the ACT is rate = distance/time, but all other rates follow the same principles. Rate problems usually give you two parts and ask for a third, or they give you the rate and one of the parts and ask you to find the other part. Here's an example of a rate problem:

12.   A train going from one city to another that is 350 miles away travels at a speed of 40 miles/hr. How many hours will it take the train to reach the other city?

Simply plug what you are given into the three-part formula: rate = distance/time. You know that the rate is 40 miles/hr and the distance is 350 miles, and you want to know the time. First set up the rate equation to solve for time:

$$\text{rate} = \frac{\text{distance}}{\text{time}}$$
$$\text{rate} \times \text{time} = \text{distance}$$
$$\text{time} = \frac{\text{distance}}{\text{rate}}$$

Now plug in the numbers: time $= \dfrac{350}{40} = 8.75$.

So it takes **8.75 hours** to reach the second city.

In rate problems, it is also important to **note the units.** Here the units of the answer were the same as they were in the question. A rate question might sometimes give you units in hours and ask for the answer in minutes or vice versa.

Probability

Probability problems may also be solved with a three-part formula: probability = # of desired outcomes/# of possible outcomes. The most important step in probability problems is determining what is considered an outcome. An outcome may be a single event, as in picking a marble out of a hat, or it may contain multiple events, as in flipping a coin and rolling a die or flipping three coins. Before you can determine the probability, you must first determine what outcome you are measuring. When you want the probability of two separate events, you must find their individual probabilities first and then multiply them together. Here's an example of a question that asks you to find the probability of two events:

13. What is the probability of getting heads in a coin flip and getting an odd number on the roll of a die?

This question asks for the probability of two separate events occurring together. First you must find the probability of the two events separately. The probability of getting heads is $\frac{1}{2}$. The one desired outcome is getting heads, and the two possible outcomes are getting heads or getting tails. The probability of getting an odd number on a die is a little more complicated. When rolling a die, there are six possible outcomes, any of the numbers 1 to 6. The desired outcomes are the odd numbers—1, 3, and 5—so there are three desired outcomes. So the probability of getting an odd number is $\frac{3}{6}$ or $\frac{1}{2}$. Now to find the probability of both events occurring at the same time, multiply their individual probabilities. The probability of both events occurring is $\frac{1}{2} \times \frac{1}{2} = \frac{1}{4}$.

● DRESS REHEARSAL: SAMPLE QUESTIONS AND DETAILED EXPLANATIONS

Now that you have gone through the rules for dealing with Proportions and Probability problems, let's do a few practice problems.

1. Alice is mixing punch for her party. The recipe says to use 3 gallons of fruit juice per 2 gallons of ginger ale. If she wants to make 15 gallons of punch, how many gallons of ginger ale will she need?

   A. 2
   B. 6
   C. 8
   D. 10
   E. 15

This problem gives you a part-to-part ratio and asks you to find a part-to-whole ratio and solve it. The first step is to convert the part-to-part ratio to a part-to-whole ratio. The ratio of fruit juice to ginger ale is 3:2, so the ratio of ginger ale to the whole is 2:5. Remember, to find the whole, simply add the parts. Now the problem says that the actual whole is 15 and asks you to find the actual gallons of ginger ale to be used. This involves setting up a ratio: $\frac{2}{5} = \frac{x}{15}$, where x is the gallons of ginger ale needed. Solving this proportion by cross multiplying gives $5x = 30$. Divide both sides by 5 to get $x = 6$. **The answer is B.**

2. The ratio of men to women in a yoga class is 2:9. If there are 27 women, how many men are there?

   F.   2

   G.   3

   H.   6

   J.   11

   K.   16

This is a part-to-part ratio that gives you one of the actual parts and asks you to find the other. It is a straightforward proportion problem involving the ratio of men to women. Set up the proportion $\frac{2}{9} = \frac{x}{27}$, where x is the actual number of men in the class. Solving this proportion by cross multiplying gives $9x = 54$. Divide both sides of the equation by 9 to get $x = 6$. **The answer is H.**

3. Regina's average score after 6 tests is 83. If she earns a 97 on the 7th test, what is Regina's new average?

   A. 85

   B. 86

   C. 87

   D. 88

   E. 90

This is a simple average problem. You can use the three-part average formula:

Step 1: Find the sum of the terms. You don't know the first 6 terms, but you do know that their average is 83, so you can treat the first 6 terms as if they were each 83. You know the 7th term is 97, so the sum of the terms is $83 + 83 + 83 + 83 + 83 + 97 = 595$.

Step 2: Find the number of terms: You are told that the number of terms is 7.

Step 3: Find the average: $\frac{595}{7} = 85$.

So Regina's new average is 85 and the answer is A.

4. A car travels 288 miles in 6 hours. At that rate, how many miles will it travel in 8 hours?

   F. 216
   G. 360
   H. 368
   J. 376
   K. 384

This is a two-step rate problem. The first step is to find the rate. You are told that the car travels 288 miles in 6 hours, so its rate is 288 miles/6 hrs or 48 miles/hr. Now you are asked to find the distance it will travel in 8 hours. Use the rate formula, rate = distance/time, and rearrange it to solve for distance: distance = rate × time. Next, plug in the rate and the time that are given: distance = 48 miles/hr × 8 hrs.

That is equal to a distance of 384 miles. **The answer is K.**

5. James has packed 10 white socks in a suitcase. He wants to add enough black socks so that the probability of randomly selecting a white sock from the suitcase is $\frac{1}{5}$. How many black socks should he add to the suitcase?

   A. 30
   B. 35
   C. 40
   D. 45
   E. 50

This is a probability question. You are given the probability and the number of desired outcomes. Now you must find the number of total possible outcomes. Use the three-part probability formula.

$$\text{Probability} = \frac{\text{\# of desired outcomes}}{\text{\# of possible outcomes}}.$$

Solving this formula for the number of possible outcomes gives:

$$\text{\# of possible outcomes} = \frac{\text{\# of desired outcomes}}{\text{probability}}.$$

Given that your probability is $\frac{1}{5}$ and the number of desired outcomes, pulling out a white sock, is 10, plug these in and solve for the number of possible outcomes:

$$\text{\# of possible outcomes} = \frac{10}{\frac{1}{5}} = 50.$$

If the number of possible outcomes is 50 and the number of desired outcomes is 10, then that means the number of undesired outcomes, black socks, must be the difference between the two, or 40. So James must add 40 black socks to the suitcase. The answer is C.

Now that you have had an introduction to Proportions and Probability problems and walked through a few practice problems, try some problems on your own. Take the practice quiz on the next page.

● THE FINAL ACT: PRACTICE QUIZ

1. A magazine pays writers for articles at a rate of $0.35 per word for the first 500 words and $0.25 per word for each word over 500 words. If the magazine paid $1,050 for three articles, each of which had exactly the same number of words, how many words was each article?

    A. 1,000
    B. 1,200
    C. 2,400
    D. 3,600
    E. 4,000

2. Carmen is playing a game in which she draws marbles from a box. There are 50 marbles, numbered 01 to 50. Carmen draws one marble from the box and sets it aside, then draws another marble. If both marbles have the same units digit, then Carmen wins. If the first marble she draws is numbered 25, what is the probability that Carmen will win on her next draw?

F. $\frac{1}{50}$

G. $\frac{1}{25}$

H. $\frac{2}{25}$

J. $\frac{4}{49}$

K. $\frac{1}{10}$

3. Janice types at an average rate of 12 pages per hour. At that rate, how long will it take Janice to type 100 pages?

   A. 8 hours and 3 minutes
   B. 8 hours and 15 minutes
   C. 8 hours and 20 minutes
   D. 8 hours and 30 minutes
   E. 8 hours and $33\frac{1}{3}$ minutes

4. In 3 fair coin tosses, what is the probability of obtaining exactly 1 head?

   F. $\frac{1}{8}$

   G. $\frac{1}{3}$

   H. $\frac{3}{8}$

   J. $\frac{1}{2}$

   K. $\frac{2}{3}$

5. Randall scored 150, 195, and 160 in 3 bowling games. What does he need to score on his next game if he wants to have an average score of exactly 175 for the 4 games?

   A. 165
   B. 175
   C. 185
   D. 195
   E. 205

6. Train A travels 50 miles/hr for 3 hours; Train B travels 70 miles/hr for 2.5 hours. What is the difference between the number of miles traveled by Train A and the number of miles traveled by Train B?

   F.   0
   G.   25
   H.   150
   J.   175
   K.   325

7. The ratio of girls to boys in a class is 3:5. If the total number of students is 32, how many more boys are there than girls?

   A.   3
   B.   5
   C.   8
   D.   12
   E.   20

8. The average of four integers is 14. When a fifth number is added to the four integers, the new average is 16. What is the fifth number?

   F.   16
   G.   18
   H.   21
   J.   24
   K.   26

9. At the end of the season, a basketball team's ratio of wins to losses was 3:7. If there were no ties, what percentage of its games did the team win?

   A.   30%
   B.   33%
   C.   37.5%
   D.   43%
   E.   60%

10. Mr. Coleman leaves his office and drives east at a constant rate. At the same time, Mr. Johnson leaves the same office and drives west at a rate 15 miles/hr faster than Mr. Coleman. At the end of five hours, the two cars are 475 miles apart. How many miles were traveled by the faster car?

    F. 200
    G. 250
    H. 275
    J. 300
    K. 350

● THE FINAL ACT: ANSWERS AND EXPLANATIONS FOR PROPORTION AND PROBABILITY QUESTIONS

1. B.   This is a rate problem. The first step is to simplify the problem and figure out what it is asking. The problem says the magazine pays by the word. If it then paid $1,050 for three articles of equal length, then it paid the same for each article: $1,050/3, or $350. Now, the magazine paid $0.35 per word for the first 500 words and $0.25 per word for every word after that. Let the number of words in each article be equal to x.

$$\$350 = \$0.35(500) + \$0.25(x - 500)$$

Simplifying this equation yields

$$\$0.25x = \$300$$

Solving this equation for x yields

$$x = 1,200$$

Each article had 1,200 words.

2. J.   Remember that the probability of something happening is the number of desired outcomes over the number of possible outcomes. Once Carmen has drawn a marble, 49 marbles are left, so there are 49 possible outcomes. Now of those 49, how many are desired outcomes? Carmen must draw a marble with a 5 in the units digit. How many of the remaining marbles will have a 5 in the units digit: 05, 15, 35, and 45. (Remember that Carmen has already drawn the 25.) So there are 4 desired outcomes. Therefore, the probability that Carmen will win is $\frac{4}{49}$.

3. C. This is a very simple proportions problem. If she types 12 pages/hour, then she types 100 pages/x hours. Set up the proportion:

$$\frac{12 \text{ pages}}{1 \text{ hour}} \times \frac{100 \text{ pages}}{x \text{ hours}}$$

Cross multiplying yields $12x = 100$. Divide both sides by 12 and you get $x = 8\frac{1}{3}$ hours. The answer choices are in hours and minutes, so you must convert the $\frac{1}{3}$ hours to minutes. $\frac{1}{3}$ of an hour is 20 minutes. Therefore, the answer is 8 hours and 20 minutes.

4. H. The first step here is to determine what event is considered an outcome. The three coin tosses together constitute one event. Of those three coin tosses, a single head can be gotten on the first one, the second one, or the third one (i.e., HTT, THT, TTH), so this is the number of desired outcomes. The number of possible outcomes is $2 \times 2 \times 2 = 8$. So the probability of getting exactly one head during three fair coin tosses is $\frac{3}{8}$.

5. D. We have the average and the number of games that Randall bowled, and we know all of the terms except for the one we are trying to find. This problem is as simple as plugging what we know into the three-part average formula. If we call the score of the fourth game x, then the average equation looks like this:

$$\frac{150 + 195 + 160 + x}{4} = 175$$

Simplifying this expression yields:

$$\frac{505 + x}{4} = 175$$

The final step is to solve this problem for x. When you do that, you get $x = 195$.

6. G. This again is a rate problem. If the rate is 50 miles/hr and the time is 3 hours, then by rearranging the rate equation you get: distance $= 50 \times 3 = 150$ miles traveled by Train A. If Train B travels 70 miles/hr for 2.5 hours, distance $= 70 \times 2.5 = 175$. Now you have to be careful; the problem asks for the difference between the distances the two trains traveled. The difference between the two distances is $175 - 150 = 25$.

7. C. This ratio problem gives you a part-to-part ratio and the whole and asks you to find the parts. The first step is to turn the part-to-part ratio into a part-to-whole ratio. It doesn't matter which part you choose to use for the ratio. Starting with the girls, the ratio of girls to the whole is 3:8. Now we have the ratio of girls to the whole, and we have the actual whole, so we can set up a proportion to figure out the actual number of girls:

$$\frac{3}{8} = \frac{x}{32}$$

Cross multiplying gives you $8x = 96$, and solving for x gives you $x = 12$. If there are 12 girls and 32 students, then there are 20 boys and there are $20 - 12 = 8$ more boys than girls.

8. J. This is a simple average problem. We know the average and the number of terms, and we know all of the terms but one. If the average of the four integers is 14, then we can say that each of the four integers is 14. Now you have to set up an equation to find the fifth integer:

$$\frac{14 + 14 + 14 + 14 + x}{5} = 16$$

Simplifying this equation gives $\frac{56 + x}{5} = 16$. Solving this equation for x gives $x = 24$.

9. A. This problem again gives you a part-to-part ratio and asks you about a part-to-whole ratio. If the ratio of wins to losses is 3:7, then the ratio of wins to games is 3:10. This is a part-to-whole ratio and so can be treated like a fraction. Convert the fraction into a percent to find the percentage of games the team won:

$$\frac{3}{10} \times 100 = 30\%$$

Notice that if you had tried to treat the part-to-part ratio as a fraction, you would have calculated 43% D., which would have been incorrect. Remember in ratio questions, only part-to-whole ratios can be considered fractions.

10. H. This question seems complicated, but remember that distance = rate × time. If you know any two numbers, you can find the third. To find the total distance traveled, you must first find the distance traveled by each man individually. Let's call Mr. Coleman's rate r. Then if Mr. Coleman drove at a rate of r for 5 hours, the total distance he covered is 5*r*. Mr. Johnson drove at a rate of $r + 15$ for 5 hours. So the total distance Mr. Johnson drove is $5(r + 15) = 5r + 75$. The combined distance traveled by both men was 475 miles, so the sum of their individual distances must add up to 475: $475 = 5r + 5r + 75$.

Solving this equation for *r* to find the rate yields $r = 40$.

$$475 = 10r + 75$$
$$400 = 10r$$
$$40 = r$$

Remember that r is the rate of Mr. Coleman, who was going slower. The question asks for the distance traveled by the faster car, so you need the rate of Mr. Johnson. His rate is equal to Mr. Coleman's rate plus 15, so his rate is $40 + 15 = 55$. Now we know both his rate and the time, so we can find the distance. Distance = rate × time = $55 \times 5 = 275$. Mr. Coleman traveled 275 miles in the faster car.

Variable Manipulation

DIFFICULTY: ★ ★

FREQUENCY: ★ ★ ★ ★

SURPRISE FACTOR: ★

• INTRODUCTION TO VARIABLE MANIPULATION PROBLEMS

Variable Manipulation problems are everywhere on the ACT. Some Variable Manipulation problems are straightforward, asking you to solve for a variable. (This is the type of work you have already seen in the previous chapters dealing with percents, proportions, and probabilities.) Others are more complicated. These problems come in all forms—word problems, algebraic sentences, even inequalities—and they can deal with many topics, from percents to geometry. Whatever the topic, there are certain ways to approach specific types of Variable Manipulation questions.

Simplifying an Expression

The first type of Variable Manipulation problem might ask you to simplify an expression. For example:

1. $\dfrac{(3x^2y^5)^2}{x^6y^7}$

The most important thing to remember about Variable Manipulation problems is that variables follow the same rules and order of operations as numbers. So in solving this problem, you would first get rid of the parentheses by squaring everything inside. Your new expression would be $\dfrac{9x^4y^{10}}{x^6y^7}$. Now remember the rules of exponents. When dividing by exponents with the same base, subtract the exponents. Since the x exponent on the bottom is bigger, the x will remain on the bottom of the expression while the y will go to the top of the expression. Simplifying like terms gives the final expression: $\frac{9y^3}{x^2}$.

Solving an Equation or Inequality

Another common Variable Manipulation problem will ask you to solve an equation. It can be as simple as solving for x in the equation $3x + 8 = 17$ or as difficult for finding values for x in the quadratic equation $x^2 - 6x + 12 = 3$.

You might have to solve an inequality as well, such as $8 - 3x \geq 17$.

Solving Equation Systems

More advanced Variable Manipulation problems include those that give you a system of equations, two equations with two variables, and asks you to solve for both the variables:

$$3x + 4y = 31$$
$$3x - 4y = -1$$

These types of problems can be solved using substitution or combination. Substitution involves solving for one variable in one equation, then plugging that back into the other equation. Combination involves adding or subtracting the equations. You will see an example of how to work with system of equations problems below.

Working with Quadratic Equations

Finally, Variable Manipulation questions involving quadratic equations may ask you to factor or expand and simplify a quadratic equation. These types of problems usually involve the FOIL method, which will be discussed later in this lesson. Here's an example of a quadratic equation problem:

2. Simplify the expression $(x - 4)(x + 3)$.

● THE TRAP DOOR: STEERING CLEAR OF ANSWER TRAPS

The most common answer traps in Variable Manipulation questions involve details, such as a negative sign. It is important to always be extra careful with the signs of numbers, especially when working with complex quadratic equations or inequalities. Negative signs are very easy to drop, and doing so will completely change your final answer.

Many inequality answer traps involve a **reversal of the inequality sign.** It is important to remember that when working with inequalities, multiplying or dividing by a negative number flips the inequality sign. This is *only* for multiplying and dividing; it does not apply to adding and subtracting.

When simplifying expressions, it is absolutely important to **remember the order of operations and the rules of exponents.** This is especially important for more complex expressions that may include multiple exponents and parentheses. Simplifying the parts of an expression in an incorrect order will lead you to a wrong answer. The order of operations can be remembered using the mnemonic device **PEMDAS**, which stands for Parentheses, Exponents, Multiplication, Division, Addition, Subtraction. You must follow this order of operations when dealing with equations and expressions.

The most important thing to remember when working with these equations is that you must **do the same thing to both sides**! If you subtract 8 from one side of the equation, you must also subtract it from the other side.

• PERFORMANCE TECHNIQUES: KEY FORMULAS AND RULES

As with all other types of problems in the ACT Math test, certain rules and formulas make many of the Variable Manipulation problems a lot easier.

Simplifying Expressions

These problems may include simple variable expressions or quadratic expressions. The first and most important thing to remember for simplifying variable expressions is to follow the order of operations. For example:

3. Simplify the following expression:

$$\frac{(4x^3y^2)^2}{x^4y^3}$$

Following the order of operations, the first thing to look at would be what's inside the parentheses. Because the expression inside the parentheses is already simplified, the next step is to look at the exponents.

One exponent is outside of the parentheses, so it must be distributed to everything inside the parentheses. Squaring everything inside the parentheses gives

$$\frac{8x^6y^4}{x^4y^3}$$

The next step is to deal with the exponents. Remember the rules for exponents: when dividing exponents with the same base, subtract the exponent on the bottom from the one on top. The final simplified expression would be $8x^2y$.

Solving Equations and Inequalities

When solving equations and inequalities, you should follow the same rules of exponents and the order of operations. There is one additional thing to remember: In an inequality, when multiplying or dividing by a negative number, you must flip the inequality sign. Let's look at this example:

4. What is the value of x if $12 - 5x \leq 47$?

This inequality can be solved the same way as an equation. The first step is to subtract 12 from both sides. The new inequality is $-5x \leq 35$. The next step is to divide both sides by -5. Because you are dividing by a negative number, you must flip the inequality sign from less than to greater than. Your final answer will be $x \geq -7$.

Solving Systems of Equations

A system of equations is a group of two or more equations that includes an equal number of variables. The most common type of system of equation problem on the ACT consists of two equations that contain two unknowns. Systems of equations can be solved in two ways: substitution or combination.

When solving a system of equations by **substitution**, solve the first equation for one of the variables, then plug that value into the second equation. When solving a system of equations by **combination**, you will either add or subtract one equation from the other. Using combination when adding or subtracting an equation will get rid of one of the variables.

Usually, one of these methods is easier to do than the other. Which method you choose to use will depend on the problem. Let's look at an example where we'll use the combination method, then the substitution method:

5. Solve the system of equations:

$$3x + 4y = 31$$
$$3x - 4y = -1$$

Here, both the x and y coefficients are the same, so this problem should be solved using combination. Either adding or subtracting will work. Let's add the equations. The y's cancel out, and the resulting equation is $6x = 30$. Solving this equation for x gives $x = 5$. Now that you have the value for x, plug it back into one of the equations to find the value for y. Simplifying the first equation, $3(5) + 4y = 31$, yields $15 + 4y = 31$. Solving the equation for y, you must first subtract 15 from both sides. This will give you the new equation, $4y = 16$. Next, divide both sides of the equation by 4: $y = 4$.

Before solving any Variable Manipulation problem, be sure you have read the question carefully and that you understand what it is asking you to do. Some questions may ask you to solve a system of equations, some may ask you to find a particular variable, and still others may ask you to just simplify or factor an equation. Factoring an equation comes into play when dealing with quadratic equations.

Working with Quadratic Equations

Quadratic equations are those of the form $ax^2 + bx + c$, where x is a variable and a, b, and c are constants. Remembering some classic quadratic equations might save you some time when taking the ACT:

$$(x + y)^2 = x^2 + 2xy + y^2$$
$$(x - y)^2 = x^2 - 2xy + y^2$$
$$(x + y)(x - y) = x^2 - y^2$$

These are some common quadratics that you might see on Test Day. Knowing these beforehand could save you some time. Quadratic equations problems will either give you a quadratic and ask you to factor it or give you factors and ask you to find the quadratic equation. When you are given factors and asked to find the quadratic equation, you must use the FOIL method. FOIL stands for First, Outside, Inside, Last, and it is the order in which you multiply the terms of quadratic factors together. Let's take a look at an example:

6. For all t, $(t + 4)(t + 5) =$

This is a simple quadratic equation. Use the FOIL method to solve it.

First: $t \times t = t^2$
Outside: $t \times 5 = 5t$
Inside: $4 \times t = 4t$
Last: $4 \times 5 = 20$

The last step is to add all of the terms together, combining like terms. The final answer to this problem is $t^2 + 9t + 20$.

When given a quadratic equation and asked to factor it, you must find two numbers that add up to b in the quadratic equation and multiply to produce c. Remember that a quadratic equation is in the form $ax^2 + bx + c$. Here's an example of factoring:

7. Factor the following quadratic equation: $x^2 - 11x + 24$.

Here b is -11 and c is 24. To factor this equation, you must find two factors of 24 whose sum is -11. These two factors are -8 and -3. Therefore, the factored form of this quadratic equation is $(x - 8)(x - 3)$.

● DRESS REHEARSAL: SAMPLE QUESTIONS AND DETAILED EXPLANATIONS

1. For all r, $(r + 4)(r - 4) + (2r + 2)(r - 2) =$
   A. $r^2 - 2r - 20$
   B. $3r^2 - 12$
   C. $3r^2 - 2r - 20$
   D. $3r^2 + 2r - 20$
   E. $5r^2 - 2r - 20$

This is a simple quadratic problem. You are given two factored quadratics and asked to simplify them. To solve this problem, use the FOIL method for each set of factors, and then add the two together. Let's start with the first one. Following the FOIL method:

First: r^2
Outside: $-4r$
Inside: $4r$
Last: -16

Adding all the terms and combining like terms gives $r^2 - 16$.

Now let's move on to the second one.

First: $2r^2$
Outside: $-4r$
Inside: $2r$
Last: -4

Adding all the terms and combining like terms gives $2r^2 - 2r - 4$. Now, adding the first and second expressions gives $r^2 - 16 + 2r^2 - 2r - 4$. Combining like terms gives $3r^2 - 2r - 20$. **The answer is C.**

2. The fee to rent a movie is a flat rate of $1.50. The late fee for a movie is $1.75 per day. If Josh spent $8.50 on the movie, how many days late was he in returning it?

    F. 0
    G. 1
    H. 3
    J. 4
    K. 5

This is a Variable Manipulation word problem. The first thing to do is determine what you are trying to find. The question asks how many days late Josh returned the movie. We can call the number of days late d. We know that Josh paid a flat fee of $1.50, a fee of $1.75 for each day he was late, and $8.50 total. Setting up an equation, we have $8.50 = $1.50 + $1.75d$. Next, we have to solve for d. The first step is to subtract $1.50 from both sides. This gives the new equation: $7.00 = $1.75d$. Solve this equation for d by dividing both sides by $1.75. This will give you $d = 4$. So Josh was four days late returning the movie, **and the answer is J.**

3. In the schools in a certain city, each ninth-grade gym class is to have 27 girls and each tenth-grade gym class is to have 18 girls. If there are x ninth-grade gym classes and y tenth-grade gym classes, what is an expression for the total number of ninth- and tenth-grade girls taking gym?

    A. $\left(\dfrac{18}{y}\right) + \left(\dfrac{27}{x}\right)$
    B. $27x + 18y$

C. $\dfrac{45}{(x+y)}$

D. $\dfrac{45}{xy}$

E. $\dfrac{(x+y)}{45}$

This problem asks you to find an expression for the total number of girls in ninth and tenth grade taking a gym class. Let's start with the ninth-grade girls. If each class holds 27 girls and there are x classes, then the total number of ninth-grade girls taking a gym class is $27x$. With the tenth-grade girls, each class holds 18 girls and there are a total of y classes, so a total of $18y$ tenth-grade girls are taking gym classes. The total number of girls taking gym classes is equal to $27x + 18y$. **The answer is B.**

4. If $-3x + 7 \le 4$, which of the following statements is true?

    F. $x \le 0$

    G. $x \le 1$

    H. $x \ge 0$

    J. $x \ge 1$

    K. $x \le -1$

The tricky part of this inequality is the negative sign in front of the $3x$. The first step is to subtract 7 from both sides. This leaves $-3x \le -3$. The next step is to divide both sides by the -3. Remember that the inequality sign has to flip when you divide by a negative number. The final answer is $x \ge 1$. **The answer is J.** Notice that if you had not flipped the sign, you would have chosen the incorrect answer G.

5. If $x^2 - 4x - 6 = 6$, what are the possible values for x?

    A.   4, 12

    B.   −6, 2

    C.   −6, −2

    D.   6, 2

    E.   6, −2

This is a quadratic equation. Before you can solve a quadratic equation, you must set it equal to zero. That is our first step, done here by subtracting 6 from both sides. Now we have $x^2 - 4x - 12 = 0$, which we can factor.

To factor this equation, we need two numbers whose sum is -4 and multiply together to give -12. Because the two numbers give a negative number when multiplied, they must have different signs. Secondly, because their sum is a negative number, the negative number must be bigger than the positive number. Now knowing this, what are two factors of -12 that would add to give -4? The answer is -6 and 2. So factored, this quadratic equation is $(x - 6)(x + 2) = 0$.

However, we are not finished yet. The question does not ask for the factors of the quadratic equation but for the possible values of x. Because the factors multiply to equal 0, one of the factors must equal 0. This means that either $x - 6 = 0$ or $x + 2 = 0$. To find the possible values of x, you must solve both of these equations for x. When you do this, you find that x can equal either 6 or -2. **The correct answer is E.** Notice that if you had stopped too early, at the factorization, you would have incorrectly chosen B. It is important always to read and understand a problem completely before attempting to solve it.

Now that you've had some practice with Variable Manipulation, put yourself to the test. Take the Practice Quiz on the next page.

● THE FINAL ACT: PRACTICE QUIZ

1. For a college football game, student tickets costs $5, and adult tickets cost $8. If 500 tickets were sold at the football game for a total of $3,475, how many adult tickets were sold?

    A. 125
    B. 200
    C. 325
    D. 400
    E. 450

2. If the factorization of the expression $x^2 + kx + 15$ is $(x - 3)(x - 5)$, what is the value of k?

    F. -15
    G. -8

    H.   0

    J.   8

    K.   15

3. If $ax + y = 23$, $3x - y = 9$, and $x = 8$, what is the value of a?

    A.   1

    B.   3

    C.   5

    D.   8

    E. 15

4. At a recent knowledge bowl competition, there were easy questions, worth 3 points each, and hard questions, worth 5 points each. If Daniel answered 21 questions correctly and had a total of 79 points, how many hard questions did he answer?

    F.   7

    G.   8

    H. 12

    J. 13

    K. 15

5. Which of the following is a factored form of $3xy^4 + 3x^4y$?

    A. $3x^4y^4(x + y)$

    B. $3xy(xy^3 + x^3)$

    C. $6xy(y^3 + xy^3)$

    D. $3x^4y^4$

    E. $5x^5y^5$

6. If $p - q = -4$ and $p + q = -3$, then $p^2 - q^2 =$

    F.   25

    G.   12

    H.   7

    J.   −7

    K. −12

7. If there is only one solution for the equation $x^2 - 6x + k$, what is the value of k?

    A. 0

    B. 3

    C. 6

    D. 9

    E. 12

8. Which of the following is a value of b for which $(b - 3)(b + 4) = 0$?

    F. 3

    G. 4

    H. 7

    J. 10

    K. 12

9. If $2x + 3 = -5$, what is the value of $x^2 + 7x$?

    A. −44

    B. −12

    C. −4

    D. 12

    E. 44

10. If $x = \frac{1}{3}t + 2$ and $y = 4 - t$, which of the following expresses y in terms of x?

    F. $y = 2 - \frac{1}{3}x$

    G. $y = 4 - x$

    H. $y = 10 - 3x$

    J. $y = -2 - 3x$

    K. $y = 6 - 3x$

• THE FINAL ACT: ANSWERS AND EXPLANATIONS FOR VARIABLE MANIPULATION QUESTIONS

1. C. The first step is to translate this problem into math. Let's call the number of adult tickets a and the number of student tickets s. If each adult ticket costs $8 and each student ticket costs $5, then the total amount of money earned from all the tickets sold was $8a + 5s = \$3,475$. Next, because you know 500 tickets were sold, the total number of adult and student tickets sold must add up to 500, that is, $a + s = 500$. What you have now is a system of equations including two equations and two unknowns. Because neither of the variables has the same coefficient in both equations, the quickest way to solve this problem is through substitution. Solve the second equation for s. That gives you $s = 500 - a$. Now plug this value into the first equation:

$$8a + 5(500 - a) = 3,475$$

Now get rid of the parentheses and combine the common terms:

$$8a + 2,500 - 5a = 3,475$$
$$3a = 975$$

Finally, solve the equation for a: $a = 325$.

2. G. Remember that when factoring quadratic equations, you need two numbers that add up to b and multiply to equal c (quadratic equations take the form $ax^2 + bx + c$). In this case, k equals b, so the two factors must add to equal k. The two factors are -3 and -5, so k is equal to $-3 + -5 = -8$.

3. A. There are three equations and three unknowns, so it is possible to solve this problem. Remember that to solve a variable problem, you must have as many equations as you have variables. The first step is to plug x into the second equation to find a value for y. You know that $x = 8$. Plugging that into the second equation gives you $3(8) - y = 9$, or $24 - y = 9$. Next, solve this equation for y: $y = 15$. The final step is to plug these values into the first equation and solve it for a.

$$8a + 15 = 23$$
$$8a = 8$$
$$a = 1$$

4. G. This problem involves two variables, the number of easy questions e. and the number of hard questions h. that Daniel got right. Two variables means you need two equations. You know that Daniel answered 21 questions correctly, so the first equation is simply $h + e = 21$.

Next, you know that Daniel got 79 points and that easy questions are worth 3 points while hard questions are worth 5. So the second equation is $5h + 3e = 79$. Again, because neither variable has the same coefficient, the quickest way to solve this problem is by substitution. Solve the first equation for e: $e = 21 - h$. Next, plug this value into the second equation:

$$5h + 3(21 - h) = 79$$

Combine like terms and simplify the equation:

$$63 + 2h = 79$$

Solve this equation for h:

$$2h = 16$$
$$h = 8$$

So Daniel answered 8 hard questions.

5. B. To factor this problem, you must find the greatest common factor between the two expressions. Both expressions contain the number 3. The greatest x exponent common to both expressions is simply 1. The greatest y exponent common to both is also 1. So the greatest common factor is $3xy$. Now to factor this problem, divide out $3xy$ from each expression. That leaves $3xy(x^3 + y^3)$.

6. G. At first look, you may think that this is a system of equations problem, and in fact this problem may be solved that way. However, if you recognize that $p^2 - q^2$ is one of the classic quadratic equations, you would save yourself a lot of time. Factored, this classic quadratic is $(p + q)(p - q)$. The problem itself gives you the value of both these factors. To find the answer, simply multiply them together: $(-4)(-3) = 12$. See how being aware of the classic quadratic equations can be helpful?

7. D. Quadratic equations always have two factors. If there is only one solution for this equation, both of the factors are the same. Remember that the factors must multiply to add up to c, which is k in this case. Because both factors are the same, this means k must be a perfect square. Of the answer choices given, only 9 is a perfect square.

8. F. This is a factored form of a quadratic equation. Because it is set equal to zero, one of the factors must be zero. This means that either $b - 3 = 0$ or $b + 4 = 0$. So $b = 3$ or $b = -4$. Of these two choices, only 3 is one of the answer choices.

9. E. To solve the second equation, you must first find the value of x using the first equation. Solving the first equation for x gives you:

$$2x + 3 = -5$$
$$2x = -8$$
$$x = -4$$

Now plug this value into the second equation:

$$(-4)^2 + 7(-4) = 16 + 28 = 44.$$

10. H. This problem asks for y in terms of x. You know both x and y in terms of t. This is a system of equations question. You can solve the first equation to get t in terms of x. When you solve the first equation for t in terms of x, you get $t = 3x - 6$. Now plug this into the second equation to eliminate t and get y in terms of x.

$$y = 4 - (3x - 6)$$
$$y = 4 - 3x + 6$$
$$y = 10 - 3x$$

Translating Word Problems

DIFFICULTY: ★ ★ ★ ★

FREQUENCY: ★ ★ ★ ★

SURPRISE FACTOR: ★

● INTRODUCTION TO WORD PROBLEMS

Word problems are everywhere on the ACT Math test, and they cover just about every topic: percents, proportions, probability, variable manipulation, and even geometry. Because Word problems encompass such a wide range of material, many students have difficulty with them. The hardest part of any Word problem is expressing what it is saying in terms of algebra. Once that is figured out, you will be able to solve the problem using the appropriate strategy for that type of problem (e.g., percents, variable manipulation, etc.). This lesson demonstrates how to translate those tricky word problems from English into mathematical terms.

● THE TRAP DOOR: STEERING CLEAR OF ANSWER TRAPS

Most students dislike Word problems because you have to go through the step of translating the problem before you can begin to work on solving it. The good news is that once you get through the translating phase, you stand a good chance of being able to solve the problem because (1) you will have a good understanding of it and (2) the concepts and ideas are nothing new—you already know them. There are a few traps involved in Word problems that you will want to avoid on Test Day.

THE ORDER OF TERMS

When you have to translate a word problem into an equation, be careful of the order in which you translate the terms. For example:

1. 8 less than 5x is equal to 9.

This translates into $5x - 8 = 9$, not $8 - 5x = 9$. We will go over other common translations later in the chapter.

VARIABLES

Remember that variables stand for missing numbers, so they follow the same rules as numbers. Don't get confused because there is an x in the problem instead of a number.

VARIABLE NAMES

If a word problem requires you to make up your own variables, use the same variable for the same quantity throughout the problem. It helps to name the variables in ways that will make it clear what they stand for, so you don't confuse them.

● PERFORMANCE TECHNIQUES: KEY FORMULAS AND RULES

When dealing with Word problems, it is important to understand what the problem is actually saying. Here are the steps for dealing with word problems:

Step 1: Read through the entire problem first. Do this to get an idea of what it is saying, what type of problem it is, and what you are looking for.

Step 2: Identify what type of problem it is (e.g., Percents, Proportion, Variable Manipulation, etc.).

Let's look at Step 2 in action:

2. The price of a car decreased by 15%.

This is a Percents question. Here's another look:

3. z is x less than y.

This is a Variable Manipulation problem.

Step 3: Look for key words or phrases. These signify what operations you need to perform to get to the answer. The translation table below lists some of the common words and phrases that you will encounter in word problems and their meanings.

Translation Table	
Equals, is, was, will be, costs, adds up to, is the same as, gets	=
Times, of, multiplied by, product of, twice, double, half, triple	* or ×
Divided by, per, out of, each, ratio of ___ to ___	÷
Plus, added to, sum, combined, and, more than, total, together	+
Minus, subtracted from, less than, decreased by, difference between,	−
What, how much, how many, a number, Joe's age	x, n, J, etc.

Step 4: Translate the problem into math. Use the appropriate variables when necessary.

Let's look at Step 4 in action. Translate the following English sentence into a mathematical expression:

4. If Frances's mom took $5 away from her normal weekly allowance, then the combined allowance earned by Frances and Gloria this week would be double what Frances's usual allowance would be if it were increased by a half of itself.

Once you have read through the problem, you must identify what type of problem it is. This problem is a Variable Manipulation problem.

Now let's translate this problem into math. First, we will call Frances's and Gloria's allowances F and G, respectively. The problem says that $5 was taken from Frances's allowance. The words *took...away* should indicate subtraction, so this first part means $F - 5$. The problem also says "the combined allowance earned by Frances and Gloria." *Combined* indicates addition (see the translation table above), so this means $F - 5 + G$.

The problem says $F - 5 + G$ would be double what Frances's usual allowance would be if it were increased by a half of itself. Let's deal with that last part first. What would Frances's allowance be if it were increased by a half of itself? Increased by indicates that we need to add. So we need to add a half of Frances's allowance to Frances's allowance. This translates into $F + \frac{1}{2}F$.

We aren't done yet. The problem says that $F - 5 + G$ would be double $F + \frac{1}{2}F$. The word double indicates that we should multiply by 2. So the final expression the problem is looking for is $F - 5 + G = 2(F + \frac{1}{2}F)$.

That's all there is to word problems. Once you understand how to translate from English into math, you can solve the problem just as you would any other problem.

● DRESS REHEARSAL: SAMPLE QUESTIONS AND DETAILED EXPLANATIONS

1. Ms. Holloway is a teacher who is paid by the day. She works 245 days a year and earns $51,940 each year. When she missed a day of work, her substitute earned $140 for that day. How much did the school save by paying the substitute instead of Ms. Holloway that day?

    A. $72
    B. $113
    C. $140
    D. $196
    E. $212

First, identify what you are looking for. You want to know how much money the school saved. You are told that the substitute made $140 for that day, but you have to find how much Ms. Holloway would have earned that day. You are given how much she makes in a year and the number of days she must work to earn that salary. Finding out how much she earned per day is a Rate problem, with the rate being her earnings per day. You need to divide her total salary by the total number of days she works. So her daily earnings are $\frac{\$51,940}{245}$ = $212/day. Notice that this is one of the answer choices. Don't fall for this trap; you're not done yet. The problem asks for the difference between the two salaries, not Ms. Holloway's daily rate. The difference between the two salaries is $212 – $140 = $72. So the school saved $72, and **the answer is A.**

2. In a certain class, the entire grade is based on five 100-point tests. If Erin wants to earn an average of 75 on all five tests and so far she has scored 79, 76, 70, and 52, what must she score on the fifth test?

   F.   69

   G. 70

   H. 71

   J.   98

   K. 100

First, identify what kind of problem this is. It is an Averages problem. The twist here is that you do not know all of the terms, so this is also a Variable Manipulation problem with the fifth term being the variable. Let's call it x. Remember that Average problems can be solved using the three-part average formula:

$$\text{Average} = \frac{\text{sum of terms}}{\text{number of terms}}$$

You are given that the average is 75 and the number of terms is 5. The sum of the terms is $79 + 76 + 70 + 52 + x$. Add all the terms together, and you get $277 + x$. Now plug everything into the average equation and solve for x:

$$75 = \frac{277 + x}{5}$$

Solve this equation for x. The first step is to multiply both sides by 5:

$$277 + x = 375$$

Next, subtract 277 from both sides to get $x = 98$. **The answer is J.**

3. A factory needs to make 6,000 tons of bread today. If 90,000 tons of grain are needed to make 150,000 tons of bread, how many tons of grain does the factory need to meet its quota for the day?

   A.   3,600

   B. 10,000

   C. 25,000

   D. 36,000

   E. 60,000

First, let's identify the type of problem. You have a ratio of how many tons of grain are needed to make a certain amount of bread, and you need to find how many tons of grain are needed to make another amount of bread. This problem involves finding two equal ratios, so it is a Proportions problem. The first proportion is given to you: $\frac{90,000}{150,000}$. You also have the denominator of the second proportion: 6,000. All that is left is to find is the numerator of the second proportion. Remember that to solve proportions, you set the two ratios equal to each other and cross multiply:

$$\frac{90,000}{150,000} \times \frac{x}{6,000}$$

You can simplify the first ratio to $\frac{9}{15}$ to make the problem easier to work with. When you cross multiply, you get $15x = 6,000$. Divide both sides by 15 to get $x = 3,600$. **The answer is A.**

4. Of all the seniors at a college, about $\frac{1}{3}$ are continuing their education, and about $\frac{2}{5}$ of those continuing their education have decided to go to law school. If there are 896 seniors, approximately how many seniors are going to law school?

    F. 120
    G. 180
    H. 240
    J. 299
    K. 360

There are a total of 896 students. You are given two fractions, but here you must be careful. The $\frac{1}{3}$ continuing their education is a fraction of the total number of seniors, but the $\frac{2}{5}$ going to law school is a fraction of those who are continuing their education, not of the total number of seniors. To find how many are going to law school, you must first find how many are continuing their education. The number of students continuing their education is $\frac{1}{3} \times 896 \approx 299$. Of those 299, about $\frac{2}{5}$ are going to law school. So the number of students going to law school is approximately $\frac{2}{5} \times 299 \approx 120$. **The answer is F.** Notice that if you had stopped at the first step, you would have incorrectly picked answer choice J. Also, notice that if you had taken the $\frac{2}{5}$ as a fraction of the total number of seniors, you would have incorrectly chosen answer G.

5. At a certain dance school, 19 students are studying ballet, and 12 are studying tap dance. If the school has a total of 35 students, what is the minimum number of students who are studying both tap dance and ballet?

    A. 0
    B. 7
    C. 9
    D. 12
    E. 31

The maximum number of students who are studying either tap or ballet or both is 12 + 19 = 31. Because a total of 35 students are enrolled in the dance school, this leaves 4 people unaccounted for. This means that the minimum number of students who are studying both tap and ballet is 0. **The answer is A.** Notice that the question asks for the minimum number of students who are studying both tap and ballet, not the total number of students who are studying either. You might have been tempted to pick choice E, but you must read the question carefully to be sure you understand what it is saying.

Now that we've gone through a few problems together, try the quiz on the next page on your own.

● THE FINAL ACT: PRACTICE QUIZ

1. Michael went trick-or-treating for Halloween on Monday and accumulated a bag of candy. On Tuesday, he ate half of the candy. Then on Wednesday, he ate half of what remained from Tuesday. On Thursday, he again ate half of what remained from Wednesday. If he had 6 pieces of candy left on Friday, how much candy did he originally collect?

    A. 18
    B. 24
    C. 36
    D. 48
    E. 96

2. For his phone bill, Jeremy pays $20 plus a fixed rate for every minute of long distance calls. If he used 80 minutes of long distance calls in May and his bill was $28, how much will his bill be in June if he used 20 more long distance minutes than he did in May?

   F. $30.00

   G. $38.20

   H. $39.00

   J. $40.00

   K. $42.50

3. A dance team is selling boxes of chocolate for a fundraiser. They get $7 per box for the first 100 boxes and $10 per box for every box after that. How much will they raise if they sell 350 boxes of chocolate?

   A. $245

   B. $250

   C. $2,450

   D. $2,600

   E. $3,200

4. The price of a sandwich at a local restaurant is $3.99. If the sales tax is 7% and you pay with a five dollar bill, how much change will you receive?

   F. $0.07

   G. $0.27

   H. $0.73

   J. $0.85

   K. $0.93

5. Emily wants to paint her house a certain color. To make the color, she needs to mix 5 parts white paint with 3 parts blue paint. How many quarts of blue paint will she need to make 24 quarts of the color she wants?

   A. 3

   B. 5

   C. 8

   D. 9

   E. 15

6. Anthony can type 3 pages in x minutes. How many minutes will it take him to type 11 pages?

   F. $33x$

   G. $\dfrac{3}{11x}$

   H. $\dfrac{11}{3x}$

   J. $\dfrac{3x}{11}$

   K. $\dfrac{11x}{3}$

7. For every cent decrease in the price of milk, a grocery sells 10 more gallons of milk per day. Right now, the store is selling 65 gallons of milk per day at \$2.25 per gallon. Which of the following expressions represents the number of gallons that will be sold per day if the cost is reduced by c cents?

   A. $65(2.25 - c)$

   B. $2.25(10c + 65)$

   C. $(2.25 - c)(10c + 65)$

   D. $2.25 - c$

   E. $65 + 10c$

8. One hundred eighth-grade students are being divided into 10 teams for intramural sports. Each student draws a token from a bag of tokens numbered 00 through 99. Students whose tokens have the same tens digit will make up a team. Eliza draws first and gets 56. If Alicia is second, what is the probability that she will be on Eliza's team?

   F. $\dfrac{1}{8}$

   G. $\dfrac{1}{9}$

   H. $\dfrac{1}{10}$

   J. $\dfrac{1}{11}$

   K. $\dfrac{1}{99}$

9. A hydroelectric plant has three water pumps that pump 5,000 liters, 10,000 liters, and 15,000 liters of water per day respectively. If all three pumps are operating simultaneously, how many days will it take them to pump 240,000 liters of water?

   A. $2\frac{2}{3}$
   B. 8
   C. 16
   D. 24
   E. 48

10. Amy starts with a full tank of gas and drives 150 miles. She stops to refill and notices that $\frac{1}{4}$ of the gas is gone. If the car averages 25 miles per gallon, approximately how many gallons of gasoline are in a full tank of gas?

   F. 6
   G. 13
   H. 18
   J. 24
   K. 38

• THE FINAL ACT: PRACTICE QUIZ ANSWERS FOR WORD PROBLEMS

1. D. First, identify what the problem is asking. You want to know how many pieces of candy Michael had originally. Let's call that x. Now, that number is reduced by $\frac{1}{2}$ three times. Translating this word problem into math gives: $\frac{1}{2} \times \frac{1}{2} \times \frac{1}{2}x = 6$. This is equal to $\frac{1}{8}x = 6$, or $\frac{x}{8} = 6$. Solving this equation for x gives you $x = 48$.

2. F. This is a very wordy problem, so you have to be careful to pick out the information you need and use it correctly. If 20 more long distance minutes were used in June than in May, then $80 + 20 = 100$ long distance minutes were used in June. Now, you need to know what rate Jeremy is charged per minute. In May, he used 80 minutes, and his bill was $28. Once you subtract the $20 fee from his bill, you are left with $8, which is what he paid for the 80 minutes. So if he paid $8 for 80

---

minutes, he pays $0.10 per minute. In June, he used 100 minutes, so he is charged 100($0.10) = $10 for the minutes he used plus the $20 fee for a total of $30.

3. E.   You want to find the total price, which means you multiply the price per box by the number of boxes. The trick here is that the dance team did not earn the same price for all the boxes, so this problem must be split into two parts. They sold 350 boxes total. These must be separated into two groups: the first 100 and the remaining 250. For the first 100, they earned $7 per box. The total amount they earned for the first 100 boxes is 100 × $7 = $700. Now for the remaining 250 boxes, they earned $10. So they earned a total of 250 × $10 = $2,500 for the remaining 250 boxes. This means that they earned a total of $2,500 + $700 = $3,200.

4. H.   This is a Percents problem. The 7% sales tax means that 7% of the price will be added to get the total, making this a percent increase problem. To tackle a percent increase problem, you must follow the three steps discussed in the Percents lesson:

Step 1: Add the percent to 100: 107%.
Step 2: Convert the percent to a decimal: 1.07.
Step 3: Multiply the decimal by the original whole: $1.07 \times \$3.99 = \$4.269$.

Rounded to the nearest cent, the price for the salad is $4.27. Since you paid with a five dollar bill, your change will be $5.00 − $4.27 = $0.73.

5. D.   This is a Proportions problem. The first ratio of the proportion is given to you as a part-to-part ratio, and you want to turn it into a part-to-whole ratio to find the number of blue quarts of paint needed to make a total of 24 quarts of paint. The part-to-part ratio is 5 parts white to 3 parts blue. Remember to find the whole, you add the parts, so the whole is 8 quarts of paint. Now the part-to-whole ratio is 3 quarts blue:8 quarts paint. Now, the problem tells you that the actual whole is 24 quarts of paint. The proportion is $\frac{3}{8} = \frac{x}{24}$, where x is the number of quarts of blue paint needed. Cross multiplying gives you $8x = 72$. Divide both sides by 8 to get $x = 9$.

6. K.   This is a simple ratio problem with a little twist. Don't let the variable confuse you. Treat x as if it were another number. So if Anthony types 3 pages per x minutes, his rate is $\frac{3}{x}$. Now, let's call the time it takes him to type 11 pages t. So his rate is also $\frac{11}{t}$. The two rates are equal to each other because his typing rate is constant. This gives $\frac{11}{t} = \frac{3}{x}$. Solving this proportion for t gives $t = \frac{11x}{3}$.

7. E. This problem gives you a lot of information. It is up to you to pick out the details that you need. Right now, the store is selling 65 gallons of milk. Every time the price drops by one cent, the store will sell 10 more gallons of milk. So for every cent c that the price drops, the store will sell $10c$ more gallons of milk. Add this to the original price to find that the new number of gallons of milk the store will sell will be $65 + 10c$.

8. J. This is obviously a Probability problem. Remember that the probability of something happening is the number of desired outcomes divided by the number of total possible outcomes. There are 100 tokens total, and 1 has already been pulled, so 99 tokens are left. This is the number of total possible outcomes. Now, Eliza has already drawn 56, and Alicia wants to draw a number that will put her in Eliza's group. This means that Alicia must draw a number with a 5 in the tens digit. She can do this by drawing 50, 51, 52, 53, 54, 55, 57, 58, or 59. So the number of desired outcomes is 9. This means that the chance of Alicia drawing a number that will put her in Eliza's group is $\frac{9}{99}$, or $\frac{1}{11}$.

9. B. If the water pumps operate simultaneously, then in one day, they will pump $5,000 + 10,000 + 15,000 = 30,000$ liters of water. You can set up a proportion to find out how many days it will take them to pump 240,000 liters:

$$\frac{30,000}{1 \text{ day}} = \frac{240,000}{x \text{ days}}$$

Cross multiply to get $30,000x = 240,000$. Divide both sides by 30,000 to get $x = 8$. It takes 8 days to pump 240,000 liters of water.

10. J. This is a multistep Rate problem. Take the problem a step at a time, being sure to use the correct information at the appropriate step. In traveling 150 miles, the car used $\frac{1}{4}$ of a tank. This means that a full tank will take Amy $4 \times 150 = 600$ miles. Because the car averages 25 miles per gallon, the full tank holds 600 miles/25 miles per gallon = 24 gallons of gasoline.

Plane Geometry

DIFFICULTY: ★ ★ ★ ★

FREQUENCY: ★ ★ ★ ★

SURPRISE FACTOR: ★

● INTRODUCTION TO PLANE GEOMETRY QUESTIONS

Plane geometry shows up quite often on the ACT. This topic includes questions about circles and polygons, most often triangles, rectangles, and squares. A picture often accompanies the question, but sometimes you will have to draw your own figure. Plane Geometry questions may involve a single circle or triangle, or they may involve composite or inscribed figures. Composite figures are figures with multiple shapes connected, and inscribed figures are figures with one shape inside of another.

Most Common Types of Plane Geometry Questions

CIRCLES

Many Plane Geometry questions deal with circles. They may ask about the area of a circle, its radius, its circumference, its diameter, arc lengths, or sector areas. Circle questions nearly always center on the radius, because everything about the circle depends on the radius. Here's an example:

1. If a circle has a circumference of 16π, what is the area of the circle?

In a question like this, and in all other questions involving circles, it is necessary to know the basic circle formulas, which will be introduced here and explained more thoroughly later. The circumference, C, of a circle is $C = 2\pi r$, and the area, A, is $A = \pi r^2$. From the formula for area, it is obvious that the radius is needed to find the area. Because the circumference is known, the radius can be found. Based on the circumference formula, the radius in this problem is $r = 8$. Plugging that into the area formula gives us $A = \pi 8^2 = 64\pi$.

TRIANGLES

Triangles also are commonly found in Plane Geometry questions on the ACT. Triangles are a little more difficult to work with than circles because while circles all have the same proportions, triangles vary. Most questions involving triangles ask about the length of one of the sides or the degrees of one of the angles. Many also involve some special triangles that will be explained below. Here's an example of a triangle question:

2. What is the length of the third side of the right triangle below?

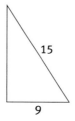

This is a right triangle, so we should use the Pythagorean Theorem. The Pythagorean Theorem is $c^2 = a^2 + b^2$, where c is the length of the hypotenuse (the longest side) and a and b are the lengths of the other two sides. In this case, we have side c and side a, and we want to find side b, so we solve the formula for b:

$$b = \sqrt{c^2 - a^2}$$

Plug in the numbers you have been given, and you will find that $b = 12$. This is also a special right triangle called a **3–4–5 triangle**.

MULTIPLE FIGURES

The last common type of Plane Geometry question is the multiple figures question. Typical multiple figures questions may have a circle inscribed in a square, a triangle within a circle, or a figure that is a composite of triangles and rectangles. Multiple figures problems present no new information and require no special formulas. They simply require you to combine information from different topics in geometry. A square inscribed in a circle is still a square, and all the formulas for a square still apply. The two most common types of multiple figures questions are composite figures and inscribed figures.

COMPOSITE FIGURES

Composite figures connect multiple figures together in succession. For example, a rectangle might have a triangle connected to one end of it, as in the figure below. Composite figures questions usually ask for the area of the entire figure.

INSCRIBED FIGURES

Inscribed figures present one figure inside another. For example, there might be a circle with a square inside of it. These types of questions usually give information about one of the figures and expect you to find information about the other figure. Here's an example of an inscribed figure question:

3. In the square inscribed in the circle below, if the diagonal of the square is 8 inches, what is the circumference of the circle?

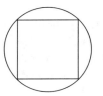

In this case, if the square is inscribed in the circle, then they share a common center. This means that the diagonal of the square runs through the center of the circle and is, therefore, the diameter of the circle. Because the diameter of the circle is 8, the radius of the circle is 4. This means the circumference is 8π.

RULES FOR MULTIPLE FIGURES QUESTIONS

Multiple figures questions can get a lot more complicated than this. They may ask for the area of one of the figures, the entire area in the case of composite figures, the area difference between the figures, or the length of one of the sides. There are a wide variety of approaches to multiple figures and the topic may seem daunting, but some simple rules will help you in approaching these questions.

● THE TRAP DOOR: STEERING CLEAR OF ANSWER TRAPS

In plane geometry, you must be careful when dealing with circles and triangles. Before you start working the problem, make sure you have taken the time to identify all given information. For example, a question might give the diameter instead of the radius.

With multiple figures questions, the most common trap is one that students themselves invent: they make **assumptions.** The test makers will give you all of the information you need to solve a problem. Sometimes you will need to figure out something else with the given information before you can solve the problem. Some students get caught by making assumptions about a picture from looking at it. Sometimes, a problem will tell you that pictures are or are not drawn to scale; do not assume a picture is drawn to scale if it is not explicitly stated. Also, just because two sides of a triangle look equal, don't assume it is an isosceles triangle. The rule of thumb here is to **never assume anything.** If you need a piece of information to solve the problem, there will be a way to figure it out from the information you are given.

Overall, there are no classic traps when it comes to Plane Geometry questions on the ACT. Students often confuse themselves enough that no traps are needed. You can save yourself a lot of trouble and lost points simply by being careful and double-checking your work. Some of the common mistakes students make are

Mistake 1: Misusing information. This most often occurs in circle problems as a result of not paying close attention. Some circle problems give the diameter in the question stem, and students mistakenly use it in formulas that require the radius. When triangle problems do not include a picture, the most common mistake is placing information in the wrong part of the figure.

Mistake 2: Assuming incorrectly. This often happens in multiple figures questions and questions involving triangles. For example, in Question 1 above, the question stem explicitly states that the triangle is a right triangle, but the figure does not make this fact clear. You cannot assume that a triangle is a right triangle based on the figure alone. Such assumptions often lead to wrong answers.

Mistake 3: Incorrectly using formulas. The most common formula that causes students difficulty is that for the area of a triangle: $A = \frac{1}{2}bh$. Most often, students omit the $\frac{1}{2}$ from the formula, yielding a number that is twice as big as the right answer. In questions involving the area of a triangle, the incorrect answer found by omitting the $\frac{1}{2}$ from the area formula will almost always be one of the answer choices. Using the correct formula is especially important in multiple figures questions where you might be working with multiple area formulas and mistakes can compound.

● PERFORMANCE TECHNIQUES: KEY FORMULAS AND RULES

To solve geometry problems, you must first be familiar with the formulas for the components of the problems: triangles, circles, squares, and rectangles.

Circles

The most important thing to remember about circles is that everything depends on the radius. When solving a problem involving circles, always identify all the radii. If no radii are present, then drawing one in will probably help you solve the problem. There are some key formulas for circles that you should commit to memory.

In this circle with radius r, the important formulas to remember are those for area A, circumference C, and diameter d.

$$A = \pi r^2 \qquad C = 2\pi r \qquad d = 2r$$

Circle problems may also include questions about sectors and arcs. In the circle below, the important thing to remember is

$$\frac{x°}{360°} = \frac{\text{arc length}}{\text{circumference}} = \frac{\text{sector area}}{\text{circle area}},$$

where x is the degree measure of the central angle, the arc length is the length of the circle from B to C, and the area is of sector ABC.

These formulas only apply when the central angle is centered at the center of the circle, which means AB and AC are radii. Let's look at an example of a circle question:

4. If the diameter of the circle is 8 inches, what is the length of the arc with a central angle of 60°?

To find the arc length, you need to use the formula:

$$\frac{x°}{360°} = \frac{\text{arc length}}{\text{circumference}}$$

In this case, x is 60°. To find the circumference, you first need the radius. The problem tells you that the diameter is 8 inches. This means that the radius is 4 inches. If the radius is 4 inches, then the circumference is 8π. You can plug all of this into the equation above and find the arc length. Solving the equation for arc length gives:

$$\text{arc length} = \frac{x°}{360°} \times \text{circumference}$$

$$\text{arc length} = \frac{60}{360} \times 8\pi = \frac{4\pi}{3}$$

Triangles

Triangles are a little more complicated than circles because not all triangles are the same. Some things, however, are true about all triangles. In all triangles, the angles add up to 180°. Therefore, if you know any two angles of a triangle, you can find the third. Also, the area of all triangles is $A = \frac{1}{2}bh$, where b is the base of the triangle and h is the height of the triangle.

One type of triangle that might appear on the ACT is an isosceles triangle. An **isosceles triangle** is one in which two of the sides of the triangle are equal in length.

A very special subtype of triangle that comes up often is the right triangle. **Right triangles** have a right (90°) angle as one of their interior angles, as shown in the figure below.

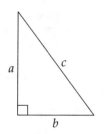

Right triangles follow all the rule of other triangles, but they also have their own special rules. In right triangles, the base and the height are simply the two sides b and a. Also in right triangles, if you know any two of the sides, you can find the third side through the Pythagorean Theorem: $c^2 = a^2 + b^2$

There are some special right triangles. Committing these triangles to memory will save you a lot of time on the ACT. These special triangles, with their dimensions, are shown below.

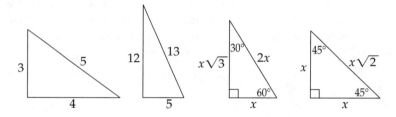

Rectangles and Squares

Rectangles and squares are relatively easy to work with. The area of both is simply their base multiplied by their height. In addition, some problems might ask about the diagonal of a rectangle or a square. For any rectangle or square, the diagonal cuts it into two right triangles. A square is special, however, because its diagonal cuts it into two $45°$–$45°$–$90°$ triangles. These figures show the diagonals of a rectangle and a square.

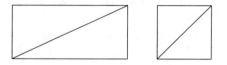

Rectangles and squares are two examples of quadrilaterals (figures with four sides). Some other quadrilaterals that might appear on the ACT Math test are parallelograms and trapezoids. A parallelogram is a quadrilateral in which the opposite sides are parallel and equal. In a trapezoid, the top and bottom sides are parallel, and in an isosceles trapezoid, the left and right sides are also the same length.

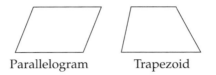

Parallelogram   Trapezoid

Multiple Figures

The formulas and figures above are the basics of what you need to know in dealing with multiple figures. None of the properties of any of these figures changes when the figures are combined. When dealing with multiple figures, however, you might have to draw in extra lines to form complete rectangles, squares, or triangles as in the following example:

5. In the figure below, if angle *CBD* measures 30°, what is the measure of angle *BAD*?

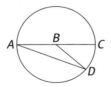

If angle *CBD* measures 30°, then angle *ABD* measures 150° because these two angles together make up a straight line and must add up to 180°. The angles of a triangle must add up to 180° as well, so angles *BAD* and *ADB* must add up to equal 30°. Now, both *AB* and *BD* are radii, so they are equal. Therefore, triangle *ABD* is an isosceles triangle. This means that angles *BAD* and angle *ADB* are equal, and because they add up to 30°, they must each be 15°. That means that angle *BAD* is 15°.

● DRESS REHEARSAL: SAMPLE QUESTIONS AND DETAILED EXPLANATIONS

1. What is the area of the figure below?

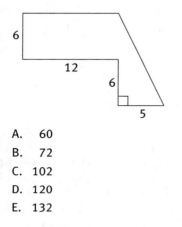

A. 60
B. 72
C. 102
D. 120
E. 132

The first thing to do is to break up this composite figure into simpler figures. Draw a line to turn this composite figure into a rectangle and a triangle. The line is the other side of the rectangle, so it is also 6. That means the total side of the triangle is 12. You are given that the other side of the triangle is 5, so you have the base and height of the triangle. Now let's apply the formulas for the area of a triangle and a rectangle to find the total area. For the rectangle, $A = bh$. The base is 12 and the height is 6, so the area is $12 \times 6 = 72$. Now for the triangle, $A = \frac{1}{2} bh$. The base is 5 and the height is 12, so the area is $\frac{1}{2} \times 5 \times 12 = 30$. Now that you know the areas of the parts of the figure, add them to find the total area. The total area is $72 + 30 = 102$. **The answer is C.**

2. A circle of radius 6 inches is inscribed in a square as shown below. What is the area of the square in square inches?

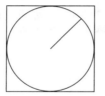

F. 36

G. 42

H. 72

J. 36π

K. 144

When a circle is inscribed inside of the square, its diameter is the same as the length of the side of the square. If the length of each side of the square is 12 (twice the radius), then to find the area of the square, all you have to do is square 12 because the sides are all the same length. The square of 12 is 144, **so the answer is K.**

3. In triangle *XYZ* below, *XS* and *SZ* are 3 and 12 units, respectively. If the area of *XYZ* is 45 square units, what is the area of triangle *SYZ*?

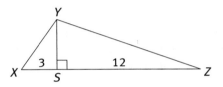

A. 9

B. 36

C. 45

D. 72

E. 108

Let's start with the big triangle, XYZ. It is given that the area of this triangle is 45 square units. You know that $A = \frac{1}{2}bh$. You can find the base by adding 12 and 3 to get 15. Now the only unknown is h. Solving the above equation for h gives $h = \frac{2A}{b}$. Plugging in the known values gives you $h = \frac{2(45)}{15}$, or $h = 6$. Now, the height of triangle XYZ is the same as the height of triangle SYZ. Also, it is given that the base of triangle SYZ is 12 units. Therefore, the area of triangle SYZ is $\frac{1}{2} \times 12 \times 6 = 36$. **The answer is B.** It is important to be careful when working with these formulas. If at either step of the problem the $\frac{1}{2}$ had been left out of the equation, it would have led to a wrong answer.

4. In the figure below, points *A* and *C* of square *ABCD* are on the circumference of the circle centered at *D*. If the area of the square is 16, what is the area of the circle?

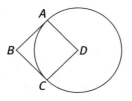

F. 4
G. 4π
H. 8π
J. 32
K. 16π

Take this problem one step at a time. First, you know that the area of the square is 16. This means that each of its sides is 4 units long. Now, you know that *D* is the center of the circle and *A* and *C* are on the circle. This means that *AD* and *CD* are both radii. So the radius of the circle is 4 as well. So the circumference of the circle is $2\pi \times 4 = 8\pi$. **The answer is H.**

5. If a square has a perimeter of 28 units and a triangle has sides of length 6, 8, and 10 units, what is the difference between the area of the square and the area of the triangle?

A. 1
B. 4
C. 24
D. 25
E. 49

Let's start with the square. If the perimeter is 28 units, then each side is 7 units. That means that the area of the square is $7^2 = 49$. Now with the triangle, the sides are 6, 8, and 10 units long. This is a 3–4–5 triangle multiplied by 2, which means that 6 and 8 are the base and the height, respectively. (It may help to draw your own figure, as the question does not provide one. Your figure should look like the one below.)

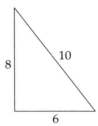

That means that the area of the triangle is $A = \frac{1}{2} \times 6 \times 8 = 24$. Now, it is important that you do not stop until you have found what the problem is asking for. Here the problem is asking for the difference between the two areas. **So the answer is 49 – 24 = 25, which is D.**

Now that you've had some practice with Plane Geometry questions, try a few on your own with the practice quiz on the next page.

● THE FINAL ACT: PRACTICE QUIZ

1. In the figure below, points *A*, *B*, and *C* lie on the circumference of the circle centered at *O*. If angle *OAB* measures 50° and angle *BCO* measures 60°, what is the measure of angle *ABC*?

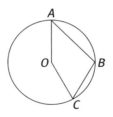

   A. 110°

   B. 120°

   C. 130°

   D. 140°

   E. 150°

2. In the figure below, the circle centered at *R* is tangent to the circle centered at *S*. Point *R* is on the circumference of circle *S*. If the area of circle *R* is 9 square inches, what is the area, in square inches, of circle *S*?

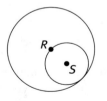

F. 12
G. 24
H. 36
J. 12π
K. 36π

3. In the figure below, *O* is the center of the circle and *P*, *O*, and *Q* are collinear. If angle *ROQ* measures 50°, what is the measure of angle *RPQ*?

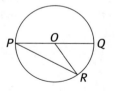

A. 20°
B. 25°
C. 30°
D. 35°
E. 40°

4. A square has a diagonal of length 8 inches. What is the area of the square, in square inches?

F. $4\sqrt{2}$
G. $8\sqrt{2}$
H. 16
J. 32
K. 64

5. The square picture frame has outer dimensions of 6 inches by 6 inches. The inside diagonal of the square picture frame is $4\sqrt{2}$ inches long. What is the width (w), in inches, of the inside of this picture frame?

A. $\dfrac{1}{\sqrt{2}}$

B. 1

C. $\sqrt{2}$

D. 2

E. $2\sqrt{2}$

6. In the triangle below, BD is a perpendicular bisector of AC in triangle ABC. If triangle ABC is an equilateral triangle and BD is $4\sqrt{3}$ units long, how many units long is BC?

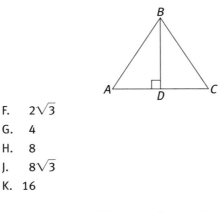

F. $2\sqrt{3}$

G. 4

H. 8

J. $8\sqrt{3}$

K. 16

7. What is the ratio of the area of two circles if the ratio of their radii is 9:16?

A. 3:4

B. 9:16

C. 81:256

D. $9:18\pi$

E. $16:32\pi$

8. In the figure below, the center of the circle is O. If the area of triangle AOB is 18 square units, what is the area of the circle?

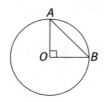

F. 12π

G. 18π

H. 36π

J. 72π

K. 81π

9. In triangle ABC, angle A is a right angle, and angle B is 60°. If BC is 8 inches long, what is the area of triangle ABC?

A. 8

B. $8\sqrt{3}$

C. 16

D. 32

E. $32\sqrt{3}$

10. A rectangle is 3 meters wider than it is long. If its area is 180 square meters, how long is the rectangle?

F. 12

G. 15

H. 20

J. 46.5

K. 60

• THE FINAL ACT: ANSWERS AND EXPLANATIONS FOR PLANE GEOMETRY QUESTIONS

1. A.   Remember that the first step with every circle is to identify all the radii and add any radii if necessary. The figure inscribed inside the circle is a quadrilateral, but by adding a radius from O to B, you can split the figure into two triangles.

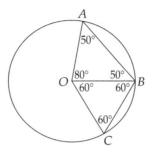

In both the triangles, two of their sides are radii. This means that both triangles are isosceles triangles and their base angles are equal. From here, simply add the two angles that make up angle ABC and you get 110°. **The answer is A.**

2. H.   Whenever you have a multiple figure involving two circles, look at how the two circles relate. Here, the diameter of the smaller circle is the radius of the larger circle. Starting with the smaller circle, you know that its area is 9. Remembering the area formula, this means that $9 = \pi r^2$, which means that the radius r of the smaller circle is $\frac{\sqrt{9}}{\pi}$. Remember, you want to find the area of the larger circle, and to do this, you first need its radius. The radius of the larger circle, R, is equal to the diameter of the smaller circle, which is $2r = \frac{2\sqrt{9}}{\pi}$. Now find the area of the larger circle: $A = \pi R^2 = \pi \times \left(2 \times \frac{\sqrt{9}}{\pi}\right)^2$. Thus, the area of the larger circle is 36. **The answer is H.**

3. B.   All the radii of the circle are the same length, so $OP = OR$ and triangle OPR is isosceles, which means that the two base angles are equal. You are told that angle ROQ is 50°, and angle POR is supplemental to angle ROQ, so angle POR is $180 - 50 = 130°$. Because all angles in any triangle add up to 180°, the sum of the other two angles is 50°. Because the two other angles are equal, they are both $\frac{50}{2} = 25°$. **The answer is B.**

4. J.   Remember that the diagonal of a square divides it into two 45°–45°–90° triangles. The ratio of the sides to the hypotenuse is $x:x:x\sqrt{2}$. Because the diagonal is 8, the sides are $\frac{8}{\sqrt{2}}$, which is $4\sqrt{2}$. The area is the square of the side, so $A = (4 \times \sqrt{2})^2 = 32$ square inches. **The answer is J.**

5. B.   Take this problem step-by-step. First, remember that because the diagonal of a square divides it into two 45°–45°–90° triangles, the relationship between the two sides and the diagonal is $x:x:x\sqrt{2}$. Because the diagonal is $4\sqrt{2}$, that means that $x = 4$. You are told that the total width of the square is 6, so $6 = 4 + 2w$. Solve this equation for w, and you get $w = 1$. **The answer is B.**

6. H.   As with all triangle problems, you always want to be on the lookout for special right triangles. In an equilateral triangle, all of the angles are 60°. This means that angle C is 60°, and because the perpendicular bisector bisects angle B and is perpendicular to segment AC, angle B is $\frac{1}{2}$ of 60, which is 30. The third angle of the new triangle, angle BDC, is a right angle. Thus, the perpendicular bisector creates two 30°–60°–90° triangles. Remember that in a 30°–60°–90° triangle, the sides are in a ratio of $x:x\sqrt{3}:2x$. The side opposite angle C is the side that is $x\sqrt{3}$. Because this side is $4\sqrt{3}$, $x = 4$. So the hypotenuse is $2x = 2(4) = 8$. **The answer is H.**

7. C.   How do you get from the radius to the area? You square the radius. This means that the ratio of the area of the two circles will be the square of the ratio of the radii of the two circles. Because $9^2 = 81$ and $16^2 = 256$, the ratio of their areas is 81:256. **The answer is C.** Notice here that π was not a factor in determining the ratio of the areas, even though it appears in the area equation. This is because it is in the area equations of both circles, so it cancels out.

8. H.   To get the area of the circle, you first need the radii. Both legs of the right triangle AOB are radii, so it is an isosceles right triangle, with both its legs having a length r. This means that the area of triangle AOB is $\frac{1}{2}r^2$. Because we are told that the area of AOB is 18, $18 = \frac{1}{2}r^2$, and $r = \sqrt{36} = 6$. So the radius of the circle is 6. Next, you need to find the area of the circle. Because the radius is 6, the area of the circle is $\pi6^2 = 36\pi$. **The answer is H.**

9. B. This question does not provide a picture, so the first thing to do is draw one. You are told that angle A is a right angle and angle B is 60°. This means that angle C must be 30° because the interior angles of all triangles must add up to 180°. So triangle ABC is a 30°–60°–90° triangle.

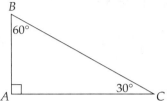

Remember that in a 30°–60°–90° triangle, the sides are in a ratio of x: $x\sqrt{3}$:$2x$. In this case, $2x = 8$, so $x = 4$. Because x is the side opposite the 30° angle, in this case angle C, $AB = x = 4$ and AC is $x\sqrt{3} = 4\sqrt{3}$. AB and AC are the height and base of the triangle respectively, so to get the area, you simply plug them into the area formula for triangles.

$A = \frac{1}{2}(4)(4\sqrt{3}) = 8\sqrt{3}$. **The answer is B.**

10. F. In this problem, you will have to work backwards. First, you know the length is 3 meters more than the width. So if we call the width x, the length will be $x + 3$. Now, you have the area and want to know the length. Because the area of the triangle is equal to length times width, you can create the equation $180 = (x)(x + 3) = x^2 + 3x$. This is a quadratic equation. First, set the equation equal to zero. This can be done by subtracting 180 from both sides:

$x^2 + 3x - 180 = 0$

Now you have to factor the quadratic equation. Doing so gives:

$(x - 12)(x + 15) = 0$

This means that either $x = 12$ or $x = -15$. Because the rectangle cannot have a negative length, x must be equal to 12. **The answer is F.**

Coordinate Geometry and Trigonometry

DIFFICULTY: ★ ★

FREQUENCY: ★ ★ ★

SURPRISE FACTOR: ★

● INTRODUCTION TO COORDINATE GEOMETRY AND TRIGONOMETRY QUESTIONS

Coordinate geometry incorporates some of the principles of plane geometry, but it also has a few rules and formulas of its own. The most prominent of these are the slope-intercept equation for a line, which identifies the slope of a line and its *y*-intercept; the distance formula, which tells you the distance between two points; and the midpoint formula, which allows you to find the midpoint of a line segment. Most coordinate geometry questions involve finding the distance or the midpoint between two points. Some may also ask for the area of a triangle or the radius of a circle inscribed on the coordinate plane.

Trigonometry is a very small component of the ACT Math test. These questions will require you to know the trigonometric sine, cosine, and tangent functions and their inverses, the cosecant, secant, and cotangent functions.

Most Common Types of Coordinate Geometry and Trigonometry Questions

DISTANCE BETWEEN TWO POINTS

One of the most common types of coordinate geometry questions asks you to find the distance between two points. In questions like this, you must use the distance formula. Here's an example:

1. What is the distance between the points (5,2) and (8,4)?

To solve this problem, simply plug the formulas into the distance formula:

$$\sqrt{(x_1 - x_2)^2 + (y_1 - y_2)^2}$$

Thus:

$$\sqrt{(8-5)^2 + (4-2)^2} = \sqrt{3^2 + 2^2} = \sqrt{9+4} = \sqrt{13}$$

TRIANGLE OR CIRCLE ON THE COORDINATE PLANE

Another type of problem will have a triangle or circle on the coordinate plane. In the case of the circle, you may be asked to find an equation for the circle, its radius, its area, or its circumference. All formulas for circles still apply to a circle when it is on the coordinate plane. There is also another formula, the circle equation, which will be explained shortly. With a triangle inscribed on the coordinate plane, you may be asked to find its area, the length of one of the legs, or the midpoint of one of the legs. You can do this using the distance formula and the midpoint formula, respectively.

LINES

Many coordinate geometry problems involve working with lines. For these problems, you need to know the slope-intercept formula. Common questions might ask you to find the equation of a line, find the equation of a line parallel or perpendicular to another line whose equation is known, or solve a system of two line equations.

TRIGONOMETRY

Trigonometry problems most often concern the sine, cosine, and tangent functions, although occasionally the inverse cotangent, secant, and cosecant functions come up as well. Trigonometry problems are limited in scope: they can only be applied to right triangles. Most problems will present a right triangle with one of the angles and the lengths of the legs filled in and ask you to find the tangent, sine, or cosine of the angle. Some problems will not give you a picture, so you will have to draw your own.

• THE TRAP DOOR: STEERING CLEAR OF WRONG ANSWER TRAPS

In coordinate geometry, you must careful when working with the equations. They are somewhat complex and involve the order of operations. It is easy to drop a negative sign here or there. Here are some common mistakes to avoid when dealing with coordinate geometry and trigonometry problems.

DISTANCE FORMULA

When working with the distance formula, be sure that you take the x_1 and y_1 coordinates from the same point. Look back at Question 1 above. The x and y coordinates of the point (8,4) were used as x_1 and y_1 coordinates, respectively. You cannot use 8 as your x_1 coordinate and then use 2 (from [5,2], the other point) as your y_1 coordinate. This would definitely lead to a wrong answer, probably one that will appear among the answer choices.

NEGATIVE NUMBERS

Be careful when working with negative numbers, especially when using the distance formula, the slope-intercept formula, and the circle formula.

For example, the slope-intercept formula is $y = mx + b$. If you have an equation of a line that is $y = 5x - 4$, you must be careful. The $y = u$ intercept is *not* 4. Look at the formula. The formula shows that there is a plus sign in front of the y-intercept. So how can we go from a plus sign to a minus sign? If you are adding a *negative* number, the plus sign turns into a *minus* sign. So the real y-intercept is -4.

PARALLEL AND PERPENDICULAR LINES

When working with lines and systems of equations, remember that parallel lines have equal slopes and perpendicular lines have negative, reciprocal slopes. Some students remember the reciprocal but forget the negative. This lapse always leads to a wrong answer. Again, you must be careful with negative signs.

DRAWING A PICTURE

When working with problems that don't give you a picture, be very careful when you draw your own. Read the problem thoroughly and be sure you are putting the information in the right spot. Here's an example:

2. A ladder is placed against a 12-foot wall with its base 9 feet from the wall. How long is the ladder?

The first thing you have to do is draw a picture with the ladder.

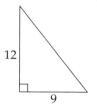

The wall is 12 feet high, so your triangle is 12 feet high. Secondly, the base of the ladder is 9 feet from the wall, so the base of your triangle is 9 feet. Finally, you want to know the length of the ladder, which is the hypotenuse of the triangle. If you look carefully, you will notice that this is a 3–4–5 triangle multiplied by 3, so the hypotenuse is 5 × 3 = 15. In problems that do not have an accompanying picture, you will have to draw your own. You must be careful when drawing pictures to make sure that you label them correctly. To be sure you are labeling the picture correctly, you must first read the problem carefully.

• PERFORMANCE TECHNIQUES: KEY FORMULAS AND RULES

Coordinate Geometry

In coordinate geometry, there are three basic formulas that you need to know.

Distance Formula: To find the distance between two points, (x_1, y_1) and (x_2, y_2), use the distance formula:

$$\sqrt{(x_1 - x_2)^2 + (y_1 - y_2)^2}$$

Midpoint Formula: To find the midpoints between the same two points use the midpoint formula:

$$\frac{(x_1 - x_2)^2}{2}, \frac{(y_1 - y_2)^2}{2}$$

Slope-Intercept Formula: The last formula is the slope-intercept formula. It gives the equation of a line:

$$y = mx + b$$

where x and y can represent a point on the line, m is the slope of the line, and b is its y-intercept.

These are the three basic equations you will need to use with Coordinate Geometry problems. Typical problems involving these formulas will ask you to fit an equation to a line on the coordinate plane.

Other problems might ask about circles and triangles on a coordinate plane. **Triangles** on a coordinate plane are the same as triangles in plane geometry. **Circles** on the coordinate plane are treated a little differently. All the rules and formulas of plane geometry still apply, but you need to know an additional formula to work with these types of problems.

Circle on the Coordinate Plane Formula: The algebraic formula for a circle on the coordinate plane is

$$(x - h)^2 + (y - k)^2 = r^2,$$

where h and k are the coordinates of the center point of the circle and r is the radius. To graph a circle on the coordinate plane, all you need to know is its center (h, k) and its radius, r.

Here's an example of a Coordinate Geometry circle problem:

3. A circle of radius 5 is placed on the coordinate plane so that it is centered at the point (3,4). What is the equation of the circle?

Remember, all you need to find the equation of the circle is its center and its radius. You have both, so this should be easy. In this problem, $h = 3$ and $k = 4$, and the radius is 5. Therefore, the formula for this circle is $(x - 3)^2 + (y - 4)^2 = 25$. That's all there is to working with the circle equation.

Still other questions might ask you about a system of equations. The important thing to remember about systems of equations involving lines is that **parallel lines** have equal slopes and **perpendicular lines** have negative reciprocal slopes.

Trigonometry

These questions make up a very small portion of the ACT Math test, but to get the most points, it is still important to know how to handle them. To deal with these questions, you need to know how to work with the sine, cosine, and tangent functions:

$$\text{sine} = \frac{\text{opposite}}{\text{hypotenuse}} \qquad \text{cosine} = \frac{\text{adjacent}}{\text{hypotenuse}} \qquad \text{tangent} = \frac{\text{opposite}}{\text{adjacent}}$$

These can be remembered by the acronym SOHCAHTOA. In the case of the triangle below, for example, the sine of the angle θ is equal to $\frac{4}{5}$.

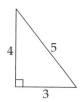

Some trigonometry problems may also require you to know the inverse trig functions:

$$\text{secant} = \frac{1}{\text{cosine}} = \frac{\text{hypotenuse}}{\text{adjacent}}$$

$$\text{cosecant} = \frac{1}{\text{sine}} = \frac{\text{hypotenuse}}{\text{opposite}}$$

$$\text{cotangent} = \frac{1}{\text{tangent}} = \frac{\text{adjacent}}{\text{opposite}}$$

Let's look at an example of a Trigonometry question:

4. **What is the cosecant of the angle θ in the triangle above?**

As with most Trigonometry problems, finding the answer is simply a matter of knowing the different trig functions. In this case, you need to know that the cosecant is the inverse sine function, which means that $\text{cosecant } \theta = \frac{\text{hypotenuse}}{\text{opposite}} = \frac{5}{4}$.

Although all trigonometry problems are not this straightforward, they all come down to knowing the formulas.

• DRESS REHEARSAL: SAMPLE QUESTIONS AND DETAILED EXPLANATIONS

1. What are the coordinates of the point of intersection of *AB* and its perpendicular bisector?

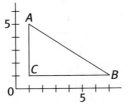

A. (1,1)

B. (4,3)

C. (3,4)

D. (3,1)

E. (1,4)

The first step is to define perpendicular bisector. The *perpendicular bisector* of *AB* will split it into two equal halves. This means that the perpendicular bisector will intersect *AB* at its midpoint. So the midpoint is the point of intersection. Remember that to find the midpoint coordinates, you average the coordinates of the two endpoints. So the *x* coordinate of the midpoint is $\frac{1+7}{2} = \frac{8}{2} = 4$, and the *y* coordinate of the midpoint is $\frac{5+1}{2} = \frac{6}{2} = 3$. Therefore, the coordinates of the midpoint are (4,3). **The answer is B.**

2. In the figure below, if $\sin \theta = \frac{4}{5}$, what is $\sin \theta$?

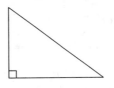

F. $\frac{3}{4}$

G. $\frac{3}{5}$

H. $\frac{4}{5}$

J. $\dfrac{5}{4}$

K. $\dfrac{4}{3}$

The first step is to fill in everything you know. If $\sin \theta = \dfrac{4}{5}$, then this is a 3–4–5 triangle. Therefore, $\sin \theta = \dfrac{3}{5}$. **The answer is B.**

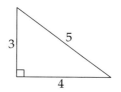

Notice how knowing the special right triangles rule saves time and work. You could have found the third side using the Pythagorean Theorem, but this method is easier.

3. What is the x coordinate of the point in the standard (x,y) plane at which the two lines $y = 4x + 10$ and $y = 5x + 7$ intersect?

   A.   2
   B.   3
   C.   7
   D.   10
   E.   22

The first thing to do here is to figure out what exactly the question is asking. You need to find where the two lines intersect. Remember that when two lines intersect, their x and y values are the same. This problem can be attacked in multiple ways. The easiest way is to set the two equations equal to each other, because the y value is the same, and solve for x:

$$
\begin{array}{r}
4x + 10 = 5x + 7 \\
\underline{-4x \qquad\quad -x} \\
10 = x + 7 \\
\underline{-7 \qquad -7} \\
3 = x
\end{array}
$$

The answer is B.

4. If $\cos A = \frac{15}{17}$ and $0 \leq A \leq 90$, what is the value of cotangent A?

F. $\dfrac{8}{17}$

G. $\dfrac{8}{15}$

H. $\dfrac{17}{15}$

J. $\dfrac{15}{8}$

K. $\dfrac{17}{8}$

This question does not give you a picture, so the first step is to draw one. Because the trig functions are being used, we know that this is a right triangle. In addition, it is a special right triangle. With a hypotenuse of 17 and one leg that is 15 units long, the other leg must be 8 units long. This is a special 8–15–17 triangle. Recognizing this fact will save you a lot of time.

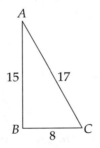

From the figure above, you can see that $\tan A = \frac{8}{15}$. Remember that $\tan A = \frac{\text{opposite}}{\text{adjacent}}$. Now, this is not the end of the problem. If you stopped here and chose answer choice G, you would have fallen for a distracter. The problem asks for the cotangent A, which is the inverse of the tangent. So cotangent $A = \frac{15}{8}$. **The answer is J.**

5. The secant of angle A is $\frac{5}{4}$. The hypotenuse of triangle ABC is 18 feet long. How many feet long is AC?

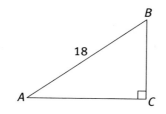

A. 5.0

B. 14.4

C. 18.0

D. 22.5

E. 24.8

This problem simply tests your knowledge of the trig functions. The cosine of an angle is equal to $\frac{\text{adjacent}}{\text{hypotenuse}}$. This means that the $\cos A = \frac{AC}{BA}$. The problem tells you that $\cos A = \frac{4}{5}$. This means that the ratio of AC to AB is $\frac{4}{5}$. To solve this problem, you need to set up a proportion: $\frac{4}{5} = \frac{AC}{AB}$. You already know that $AB = 18$, so plug that into your proportion and cross multiply:

$$\frac{4}{5} = \frac{AC}{18}$$
$$5AC = 72$$
$$AC = 14.4$$

The answer is B.

● THE FINAL ACT: PRACTICE QUIZ

1. Alana wants to determine the height of a flagpole. She stands 100 feet from the base of the flagpole and measures the angle of elevation, which is 40°. Which of the following is the best approximation of the height of the flagpole, in feet?

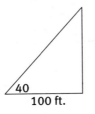

100 ft.

   A. 40
   B. 50
   C. 64
   D. 77
   E. 84

2. The triangles below share one side. Given that sin $(a + b)$ = (sin$a$ cos$b$) + (sin$b$ cos$a$) for all a and b, what is the value of sin $(x + y)$?

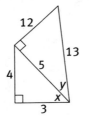

   F. $\dfrac{46}{65}$

   G. $\dfrac{48}{65}$

   H. $\dfrac{51}{65}$

   J. $\dfrac{56}{65}$

   K. $\dfrac{65}{56}$

3. Line m has a y-intercept of -3 and is parallel to the line having the equation $3x - 5 = 4$. Which of the following is an equation for line m?

   A. $y = -\dfrac{3}{5}x + 3$

   B. $y = -\dfrac{5}{3}x - 3$

   C. $y = \dfrac{3}{5}x + 3$

   D. $y = \dfrac{5}{3}x + 3$

   E. $y = \dfrac{3}{5}x - 3$

4. Line l is perpendicular to the line containing the points $(5,6)$ and $(6,10)$. What is the slope of line l?

   F. -4

   G. $-\dfrac{1}{4}$

   H. $\dfrac{1}{4}$

   J. 4

   K. 8

5. In the standard (x,y) coordinate plane, if the distance between $(a,2)$ and $(16,a)$ is 10 units, which of the following could be the value of a?

   A. -10

   B. -8

   C. 6

   D. 8

   E. 10

6. A circle is tangent to the y-axis at 4 and to the x-axis at 4. What is an equation of the circle?

   F. $x^2 + y^2 = 4$

   G. $x^2 + y^2 = 16$

   H. $(x - 4)^2 + (y - 4)^2 = 4$

   J. $(x - 4)^2 + (y - 4)^2 = 16$

   K. $(x + 4)^2 + (y + 4)^2 = 16$

7. *RS* is a line segment in the standard coordinate plane. If point R has coordinates (5,−4) and the midpoint of *RS* has coordinates (−2,4), what are the coordinates of point *S*?

   A. (−9,12)
   B. (−3,−16)
   C. (3,−16)
   D. (3,−1)
   E. (9,12)

8. The equation of line *l* below is $y = x$. Line *m* is perpendicular to *l* and intercepts the *x*-axis at (3,0). Which of the following is an equation for *m*?

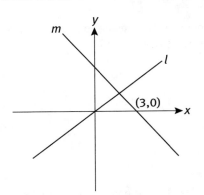

   F. $y = x + 3\sqrt{2}$
   G. $y = x + 3$
   H. $y = -x + 3$
   J. $y = -x + 3\sqrt{2}$
   K. $y = -3x + 3$

9. If θ is between 0° and 90° and $\cos\theta = \dfrac{5\sqrt{2}}{8}$, what is the value of $\tan\theta$?

   A. $\dfrac{5}{\sqrt{7}}$

   B. $\dfrac{\sqrt{7}}{5}$

   C. $\dfrac{\sqrt{14}}{8}$

D. $\dfrac{8}{\sqrt{14}}$

E. $\dfrac{8}{5\sqrt{2}}$

10. A system of two linear equations has no solution. One of the equations is below. What could be an equation of the other line?

F. $y = x + 1$

G. $y = -x - 1$

H. $y = x + 2$

J. $y = -x + 2$

K. $y = 1$

- **THE FINAL ACT: ANSWERS AND EXPLANATIONS FOR COORDINATE GEOMETRY AND TRIGONOMETRY QUESTIONS**

1. E. From the picture, you know an angle and the side adjacent to it. You want to know the side opposite the angle. What trig function will you use to relate an angle to its adjacent and opposite sides? The tangent function is $\tan \theta = \dfrac{\text{opposite}}{\text{adjacent}}$. Now you want to solve this equation for the opposite side, so multiply both sides by adj. to get opp. = adj. $\tan \theta$, where adj. is 100 and $\theta = 40°$. So the height of the flagpole is 100 $\tan 40$, which is ≈ 83.9.

2. J. You have all the sides, so all you have to do is plug the values into the appropriate formulas. Just be sure to remember the trig functions. $\sin x = \dfrac{4}{5}$, $\cos y = \dfrac{5}{13}$, $\sin y = \dfrac{12}{13}$, and $\cos x = \dfrac{3}{5}$. So:

$$\sin (x + y) = \left(\dfrac{4}{5}\right)\left(\dfrac{5}{13}\right) + \left(\dfrac{12}{13}\right)\left(\dfrac{3}{5}\right) = \dfrac{20}{65} + \dfrac{36}{65} = \dfrac{56}{65}$$

3. E. Let's take this problem step-by-step. The first thing to note is that the line has a y-intercept of -3. This means that you can automatically eliminate A, C, and D because their y-intercepts are not -3. That leaves B and E. To find the correct answer, you must find the slope of the line. You are given that it is parallel to the line $3x - 5y = 4$. Put this equation into slope-intercept form, and you get $y = \dfrac{3}{5}x - \dfrac{4}{5}$, so the slope of the line is $\dfrac{3}{5}$. Therefore, the equation of the line is $y = \dfrac{3}{5}x - 3$.

4. G. This is a very straightforward problem. The slopes of perpendicular lines are negative reciprocals. Find the slope of the line with points (5,6) and (6,10). Remember that slope is $\frac{\text{rise}}{\text{run}} = \frac{10-6}{6-5} = \frac{4}{1} = 4$. Don't stop here! This is not the end of the problem. You want to find the slope of the line that is *perpendicular* to this line. That means you need the negative reciprocal of this slope: $-\frac{1}{4}$.

5. E. Don't let the variables scare you. When you have a problem involving the distance between two points, you need to use the distance formula. With points (a,2) and (16,a), the distance between them is $\sqrt{(a-2)^2 + (16-a)^2} = 10$. Now you need to solve this equation for a. The first thing is to square both sides.

This gives you $(a-2)^2 + (16-a)^2 = 100$. Now you need to FOIL both of the quadratic equations. (Remember that FOIL stands for First, Outer, Inner, Last and refers to the order in which you multiply the terms.) This gives you $(a^2 - 4a + 4) + (256 - 32a + a^2) = 100$. Combine like terms and simplify to $2a^2 - 36a + 260 = 100$. To solve for a, you must get one side of the equation equal to 0. To do this, subtract 100 from both sides. This gives you $2a^2 - 36a + 160 = 0$. You can simplify this equation by dividing both sides by 2: $a^2 - 18a + 80 = 0$.

Now you need to factor the equation. Factoring the equation gives $(a-8)(a-10) = 0$.

This means that either $a - 8 = 0$ or $a - 10 = 0$, so $a = 8$ or $a = 10$. Because 10 is the only answer choice available of these two, the answer is E.

6. J. The first step is to draw a diagram.

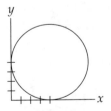

The circle is tangent to the y-axis and the x-axis at 4. From your diagram, you should be able to see that the circle is centered at (4,4) and has a radius of 4. Remember that these are the only things you need to find the equation of a circle. Plug what you know into the circle equation formula. H, k, and r are all 4, giving you $(x-4)^2 + (y-4)^2 = 16$.

7. A. This problem involves the midpoint formula, but you have to be sure to solve it for an endpoint, because you already know the midpoint. First, let's find the x coordinate of S. Remember that the x coordinate of the midpoint is just the average of the x coordinates of the two endpoints: $\frac{5 + x_s}{2} = -2$. Solve this equation for x_s: $x_s = -9$.

Now let's take a look at our answer choices. The only choice that has an x coordinate of -9 is A, so there is no need to find the y coordinate. Look for shortcuts like this on the test. They will save you time and extra work.

8. H. Remember that perpendicular lines have negative reciprocal slopes. The slope of line l is 1. Therefore, the slope of line m is -1 (1 is its own reciprocal). Only H and J have slopes of -1, so the correct answer choice is one of the two. To distinguish between them, you need to find the y-intercept. You can do this by plugging the point $(3,0)$ into the slope-intercept form of the equation of line m: $y = -x + b$, where $x = 3$ and $y = 0$. Plug those values into the equation, and you get $0 = -3 + b$. Solving this equation for b gets $b = 3$. So the y-intercept is 3, and the equation of line m is $y = -x + 3$.

9. B. This problem does not give you a picture so the first step is to draw one.

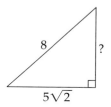

To get the tan θ, you need to find the opposite side. This is not a special right triangle, so you must use the Pythagorean Theorem:

$$8^2 = (5\sqrt{2})^2 + b^2$$

Solve this equation for b, and you get $b = \sqrt{64 - 50} = \sqrt{14}$. Now you have the missing side. The tangent is equal to the opposite divided by the adjacent side, in this case $\frac{\sqrt{14}}{5\sqrt{2}}$. However, you will see that this not one of the answer choices. This means you have to simplify the answer. When you divide the square roots, this simplifies to $\frac{\sqrt{7}}{5}$, which is one of the answer choices.

10. J. When a system of equations has no solution, the two lines do not intersect. When two lines do not intersect, they are parallel. Parallel lines have equal slopes. They also cannot have the same y-intercept because this would make them the same line. The exact slope of the line graphed is not known, but it is obviously negative. This eliminates H, F, and K. Of the two remaining answer choices, G has the same y-intercept as the line that is already graphed. Therefore G cannot be the equation of a parallel line.

READING

READING BASICS

The ACT Reading test is 35 minutes long and includes 40 questions—4 passages, each followed by 10 questions. You will see one passage in each of these four categories: Social Studies, Natural Sciences, Humanities, and Prose Fiction. The passages are about 1,000 words long and are written at a college textbook difficulty level.

Each essay has a specific theme. The questions that follow expect you to recognize this theme, to comprehend specific facts contained in the passage, and to understand the structure of the essay. Prose Fiction passages require you to understand the thoughts, feelings, and motivations of fictional characters.

There are six specific types of ACT Reading questions: Writer's View questions, Detail questions, Inference questions, Generalization questions, Function questions, and Vocab-in-Context questions. This section of the book will go into detail for each.

Reading Comprehension questions are not arranged by difficulty. That means easy, medium, and hard questions can appear in any order. Anytime you find yourself spending too much time on a question, skip it and return to it later.

● AN OVERVIEW OF READING WRONG ANSWER TRAPS

Throughout the Reading section of this book, we will refer to the typical wrong answer traps that the test makers use again and again to lure you into making wrong choices on Test Day. If you remain on the lookout for these traps, you'll soon realize that the same "wrong answer" themes repeat throughout the ACT. Here are the definitions of these common traps.

The **misused detail** answer refers to a detail that you remember from reading the passage but that does not correctly answer the given question stem. A misused detail can be a particularly tempting trap when it uses the exact wording present in the passage. However, if an answer choice doesn't answer the question posed in the stem of the question you're working with, it can't be the best choice.

The **distortion** is an answer choice that you can think of as half-right and half-wrong. A distortion contains a reference to a detail from the passage, and it may be on the right track to answering the question correctly. However, the distortion answer choice adds inappropriate information or uses a phrase that twists the meaning of the words as they are used in the passage.

The **opposite** answer choice contradicts something that is stated in the passage. Opposites can be tempting because they refer to something that you remember reading in the passage. However, they're worded in such a way that they turn the statement around, leading to a meaning that's the opposite of what the passage actually says.

The **out-of-scope** answer choice has the wrong focus for the question. An out-of-scope choice may be too broad, covering more information than needed to answer the question, or be too narrow, being too specific and limited to answer the question. Some out-of-scope traps introduce topics or details that the passage doesn't even mention.

The **extreme** answer choice uses language, such as *always, best, certainly, greatest, least, most, never,* or *without a doubt,* that makes the statement true only under specific conditions. Sometimes an extreme trap goes beyond what is stated in the passage. For example, suppose a passage says, "Some people can catch a cold from being in a crowded theater with others who are sick." It would be an extreme interpretation of this statement to say, "People *always* catch colds from being in a crowded theater with others who are sick." Some extreme traps use language that is emotionally charged to an inappropriate degree. If the passage says, "The model's features in this painting are interesting for several reasons," it would be too extreme to conclude that "the artist portrays the model's features in a most fascinating manner."

Extreme answers can be easy to avoid if you train yourself to watch for language that limits a statement or goes beyond what is said in the passage. For example, suppose a passage states, "Abraham Lincoln, author of the famous Gettysburg Address, is known for being a powerful orator." Based on this statement, an answer choice describing Lincoln as "America's best orator" would be considered an extreme. It *is* possible for an answer choice that includes extreme language, such as *best* or *never,* to be correct if the passage explicitly uses the extreme language. More often than not, though, an answer choice that contains extreme language is a trap answer. You can use this knowledge to help you eliminate incorrect answers quickly.

LESSON 14

Mapping the Passage and Writer's View Questions

DIFFICULTY: ★ ★

FREQUENCY: ★

SURPRISE FACTOR: ★ ★

Please note that the above ratings refer to Writer's View questions only. Mapping the Passage is a crucial strategy that should be used on all ACT Reading passages.

● INTRODUCTION TO MAPPING THE PASSAGE

Answering 40 passage-based questions in 35 minutes is definitely a challenge. That's why you need to approach reading on the ACT differently than reading in everyday life. The Kaplan Method for ACT Reading will help you use your time efficiently, giving you a strategic approach for reading the passage and handling the questions that follow.

The first thing you should know about the ACT Reading section is that the questions about the passage **do not necessarily appear in chronological order.** In other words, the first question may ask you about a detail in the last paragraph of the passage, while one of the middle questions may ask you about the first paragraph of the passage. Because questions appear in a random order, you'll find yourself moving around in the passage as you look back to find the answer to each question. Focusing on the main ideas of each paragraph as you read through the passage the first time will save you time later when you answer the questions. You should read actively, asking questions as you quickly go through the passage

Practice active reading by keeping these questions in mind as you read:

- Why did the author write this passage?
- Is the author attempting to persuade the reader?
- What—generally speaking—is this passage about?
- How does the author feel about the topic: opinionated or detached?
- What is the purpose of each individual paragraph?

You should try to complete your first read-through of the passage in less than three minutes. Yes, that seems like a short amount of time to get through a whole page of text. You can do it, though, because you're looking only for main ideas at this point. Pause briefly after each paragraph to jot a short note in the margin describing the paragraph's purpose or main idea. Your notes should resemble newspaper headlines—you want to express the main point in as few words as possible. We call this strategy Mapping the Passage. Make a passage map for every passage as you read it for the first time. This practice might take some getting used to, but you'll find these margin notes invaluable when referring back to the passage to answer individual questions.

You may be wondering why you should map the passage when time is so tight in the Reading section. Remember, the test maker presents the questions in random order. The order of questions on the ACT gives you no clue about where in the passage to find the information you need. Your passage map, with notes about main ideas, is a crucial guide that will save you time when you research answers to the questions.

For the question type discussed in this lesson, **Writer's View**, there's a good chance that you may not even have to look for answers in the text itself. Your passage map notes may be enough to let you answer Writer's View questions.

Characteristics of Writer's View Questions

Different question types in the Reading section of the ACT are usually easily identified because they contain certain wording in the question stems. Writer's View questions ask you about the writer's attitude, opinion, or point of view. You can spot a Writer's View question because it uses the following phrasing in the question stem:

- How does **the writer view** the changes made in the performance?
- **The author would most likely agree** that...
- **The writer sees** her early years as...
- **In the author's opinion,** the results of the 2006 study were...

Note, however, that not every question referring to "the author" is a Writer's View question. A question beginning "According to the author" is a Detail question, asking you about something directly stated in the passage rather than about the author's view. (You can read about Detail questions in Lesson 15.)

Most Common Types of Writer's View Questions

The most common type of Writer's View question asks in some way about the writer's attitude toward the subject at hand. Often the answer choices include two words, such as an adverb modifying an adjective—for example, "stubbornly committed."

A less common type of Writer's View question asks you to choose the statement with which the author would be most likely to agree or in which the author might be most likely to believe. Here's an example of this question type:

1. Based on the passage, the author would most likely agree that:

    A. The research done on women and heart disease has been inadequate.

    B. All women should meet with a cardiologist by the time they turn 50.

    C. Heart disease is a concern for women in some populations.

    D. Heart disease is the most pressing health issue for elderly women.

For a question like this, you need to pay attention to clues in the passage that indicate what the author thinks about a topic. Sometimes, simply being alert for language that indicates the author is expressing an opinion is enough. At other times, you may have to make an inference based on several different statements in the passage.

• THE TRAP DOOR: STEERING CLEAR OF ANSWER TRAPS

While any of the answer traps described in the Reading Basics section could appear among the choices for Writer's View questions, the ones that occur most frequently are distortion, out-of-scope, and opposite.

Types of Writer's View Question Answer Traps

DISTORTIONS

For a Writer's View question, the test maker is likely to include answer choices that are distortions, that is, choices in which one part may be correct but the overall choice is incorrect.

Suppose you see the following question:

2. The writer's tone in this passage can best be described as

    F. remarkably disgruntled.

    G. mildly annoyed.

    H. seemingly unconcerned.

    J. playfully involved.

For one of these answer choices to be correct, both words used must be true. In the text of the passage, let's say you find the phrases "regrettably shortsighted" and "woefully inadequate." Both phrases are quite negative. Further, suppose this negative attitude is consistent throughout the whole passage. Then you can narrow the answer choices down to choices F and G. While choice G does include the word "annoyed," which addresses the negative tone you find in the passage, the modifier "mildly" inappropriately qualifies the negativity. The words "regrettably" and "woefully" that are used in the passage indicate that choice F, "remarkably disgruntled," is a better fit than choice G, "mildly annoyed." Choice G is a distortion because it's only half right. On the ACT, if an answer choice is only half right, then it's not the best answer.

OUT-OF-SCOPE ANSWERS

Note that because the question above doesn't refer to any specific part of the passage, it is asking for an answer that applies to the passage as a whole. Other Writer's View questions may ask about the writer's attitude toward a small part of the passage. For example, in a prose fiction passage, you may be asked to determine the narrator's view of one of the characters. For questions such as these, pay attention to answer choices that may be out of scope. Make sure you read the question carefully and base your response on the appropriate range of text, whether it's the whole passage or only part of it.

OPPOSITES

A third trap the test maker frequently uses for Writer's View questions is the **opposite** trap. Many Writer's View questions test your ability to determine if the author uses a detached or an opinionated tone. If the tone is detached, then any answer choice involving a strongly stated opinion must be considered an opposite trap. (For an example, see Question 3 in the Dress Rehearsal, in which choice C constitutes an opposite.)

Techniques for Avoiding Writer's View Question Answer Traps

Avoiding trap answers for Writer's View questions starts even before you tackle the questions. As you read actively and map the passage, you should note any words that indicate the author's opinion or attitude. Watch for words and phrases that express agreement or approval, such as *fortunately* and *as the well-planned study shows*. One of the most important questions to keep in mind as you do your first (quick) reading of the passages is, "How does the author feel about what she's writing about here?" Also be on the lookout for words that indicate the author wants to persuade the reader. Wordings such as *we can conclude* and *the evidence shows that* indicate that the author is taking a position on the topic and wants to lead the reader to agree.

Sometimes in an ACT passage, the author isn't trying to persuade but merely to describe or explain. For a passage like this, a question asking about the author's tone would be answered with a word like *disinterested, impartial,* or even *detached.* To avoid a trap, you should always **read the passage first with the goal of determining the writer's purpose and attitude.** If you quickly underline words that indicate a clear statement of the author's opinion, the author's attitude, and any phrases that show an attempt to persuade the reader, you'll be much better able to answer a Writer's View question. If the writer takes an impartial or detached tone, an answer choice that conveys strong emotional content should be considered an **opposite** trap.

● PERFORMANCE TECHNIQUES: KEY STEPS

Here's the Kaplan Method for ACT Reading:

Step 1: Read the passage, taking notes as you go.

Step 2: Examine the question stem, looking for clues.

Step 3: Predict the answer and **select** the choice that matches your prediction.

You should follow this method for all four passages in the ACT Reading section. Let's look at how you can apply the Kaplan Method for Writer's View questions.

STEP 1: READ THE PASSAGE, TAKING NOTES AS YOU GO.

Step 1 describes Mapping the Passage, discussed in the introduction to this lesson. You may be wondering just how much you should use your pencil during this step. Your primary note taking should be the brief notes you make in the margin after you read a paragraph and determine its purpose or main idea. However, you can keep your pencil in hand as you read and occasionally do some limited underlining in the text. If you underline words that indicate opinion, such as *fortunately, regrettably, with remarkable skill, an astounding accomplishment, severely lacking,* or other similar words that convey opinion or assessment, you'll be more prepared to answer a Writer's View question.

STEP 2: EXAMINE THE QUESTION STEM, LOOKING FOR CLUES.

Don't move to Step 2 until you've read the passage and made your passage map. Steps 2 and 3 describe how you should approach each question. "Examine the question stem" means look only at the part of the question that introduces the answer choices. You shouldn't read the choices yet!

"Clues" in the question stem are words that help you determine what kind of question you're dealing with. Sometimes the stem offers a location, such as paragraph or line numbers, to which the question refers. However, most ACT Reading questions don't contain such references to parts of the text. Without your passage map, you'd have to skim through the entire passage again to know where in the passage to find the answer. With a passage map, you can usually find pretty quickly where you need to go.

Again, remember at this step to read *only* the question stem and not the answer choices. Not peeking ahead at the answer choices is a crucial part of the Kaplan Method. It will make more sense to you as you learn more about how the test maker tries to distract you with trap answer choices. Especially at the beginning of your practice, it's actually a good idea to cover the answer choices with your hand so you're not tempted to read them before you should.

STEP 3: PREDICT THE ANSWER AND SELECT THE MATCHING CHOICE.

In Step 3, "Predict the answer" means go back to your passage map (and look in the passage itself if necessary) to put the answer to the question into your own words. Mentally say the answer in your own words before you read the answer choices. To help you remember this, think, "Predict before you peek." For Writer's View questions, you may be able to state your prediction based on the work you did making your passage map. (For other kinds of questions, referring back to the passage is usually essential.) Very occasionally, you'll find a question that you can't make a prediction for, but 90 percent of the time, you can and should predict. If you've made an effective prediction, you'll usually find that the best answer is easy to spot when you read through the choices. Again, predicting before you peek does take a little practice to get used to, but it saves time in the long run because it helps you avoid falling for trap answers that the test maker includes to distract you.

● DRESS REHEARSAL: SAMPLE QUESTIONS AND DETAILED EXPLANATIONS

Though reading passages on the ACT are usually about a page long, these sample questions present some shorter passages so you can start to recognize the specific words in a passage that can help you identify a writer's goals and views.

Writer's View: Fluoride

The question is based on the paragraph below. Because this first passage is brief, your passage map should simply state the purpose of the paragraph.

Many communities have added fluoride to their municipal water supplies for decades. The thinking has been that fluoride is crucial
to the development of healthy teeth in babies and children. However,
excessive amounts of fluoride can be toxic. It is unwise to add a poten-
(5) tially dangerous chemical to the water supply when there is inadequate
evidence about its effectiveness in preventing tooth decay. The greatest danger from overexposure to fluoride is dental fluorosis, a condition
in which the teeth can yellow, develop white spots, and exhibit pitting
of the tooth's enamel surface.

1. The writer's primary goal in this passage is to:

    A. describe the effectiveness of fluoride in preventing tooth decay.

    B. argue against the practice of adding fluoride to water supplies.

    C. discuss the causes of tooth decay.

    D. refute the idea that fluoride is toxic.

Select your answer after following all three steps of the Kaplan
Method.

Step 1: Read. Even though this isn't a test-length passage, pause after
reading it to note briefly the main idea of the paragraph. You should
come up with something like:

Overexposure to fluoride is harmful; it shouldn't be added to water.

Step 2: Examine. In the question stem, the words "writer's primary
goal" give you a clue that this is a global question that asks about the
passage as a whole.

Step 3: Predict and select. Your statement of the paragraph's purpose
in Step 1 may be enough to let you predict *the author doesn't think fluoride should be added to water supplies because it can cause fluorosis*. Let's
look at what words in the passage lead to this. The word "however"
in line 3 signals a contrast. The words that follow it present an objection to the idea that fluoride is necessary for healthy teeth. In the next
sentence, the words "it is unwise to add" are a clear statement of the
author's opinion. Knowing that the author is making an argument,
you can narrow the choices down to choices B and D. (Choices A and
C are out of scope.) Choice D is an opposite, because it's contradicted
in the passage. **Choice B nicely matches the prediction; the correct
answer is B.**

Writer's View: J. M. Synge

The questions are based on the passage below. Though it's not as long as the passages you'll see on Test Day, you should still map the passage. Remember to jot down the main idea or purpose after you read each paragraph.

Irish writer J. M. Synge is not nearly as well-known as his contemporaries. Perhaps because his literary output was small, he has received less attention than more prolific authors such as James Joyce and W. B. Yeats. Indeed, Synge's work consists primarily of six plays, including
(5) several one-act plays. Some of the plays, including *Playboy of the Western World*, were performed at Dublin's Abbey Theatre.

Most people who have heard of Synge associate his name with the riots that occurred during the opening run of *Playboy*. The play was controversial because, in 1907 when it was first produced, it was thought to
(10) include material that was morally questionable and offensive to Ireland.

Those who know only this one play and the uproar surrounding it are missing out on Synge's literary achievements. Even more impressive than the uproar Synge's play caused in the theater world are his lyrical language and stunning imagery based on the natural
(15) world. As a young man, Synge had trained to be a musician, and his strong musical sense is evident in the poetic language of his plays. He spent time living among the Irish-speaking people of the Aran Islands. The language of Synge's characters reflects his intimacy with the Irish language; some of his phrasings are English translations of
(20) the wording used in Irish phrases. This linkage to the rhythms of the Irish syntax also contributes to the beauty of Synge's language.

2. The writer of this passage primarily wants to:

   F. describe the riots surrounding the production of *Playboy of the Western World*.

   G. compare J. M. Synge to James Joyce and W. B. Yeats.

   H. suggest that J. M. Synge's literary achievement has been underrated.

   J. discuss the sources of J. M. Synge's plays.

Step 1: Read. Did you jot down your notes in the margin as you read? Your passage map should look something like this:

Paragraph 1: J. M. Synge—author of plays, not well-known

Paragraph 2: Riots after *Playboy*

Paragraph 3: Synge's language: music, related to Irish

Step 2: Examine. The phrasing "writer of this passage primarily wants" tells you that this is a Writer's View question.

Step 3: Predict and select. Paragraph 1 states that Synge is not well-known compared to two other Irish writers. Paragraph 2 describes the one reason most people have heard of Synge. Paragraph 3 praises Synge's use of language. Putting these ideas all together, we can predict that the writer's purpose is *to call attention to the beauty of Synge's language.* **This prediction matches choice H.** Choice F is out of scope. It's too narrow, because it applies only to Paragraph 2. Choice G is also too narrow. Though Joyce and Yeats are mentioned in the first paragraph, comparing them to Synge is not the writer's main purpose. Choice J is also out of scope. While Paragraph 3 mentions Synge's experience with the Irish people, Synge's sources aren't the author's primary concern.

3. The author's attitude toward J. M. Synge's work is one of:

    A. unbiased reporting.

    B. wholehearted admiration.

    C. mild criticism.

    D. moderate respect.

Step 1: Read. There's nothing to do here because you only make the passage map once for each passage.

Step 2: Examine. The words "author's attitude toward" in the question stem give a clue that this is a Writer's View question.

Step 3: Predict and select. It's likely that you picked up on the author's positive tone in your first reading. Look specifically at the first and last sentences of Paragraph 3, including the phrases "missing out on Synge's literary achievement" and "contributes to the beauty of Synge's language." Your prediction should be that *the author has a high opinion of Synge.* **Choice B is the best match.** Choice A is incorrect because "unbiased" means "not opinionated." Choice C is an opposite, because the author never criticizes Synge. Choice D might be tempting because it includes the word "respect," but the choice is a distortion because the author's enthusiastic praise of Synge makes "moderate" an inappropriate qualifier for "respect."

Writer's View: William Shakespeare

Remember to make your passage map as you read. Questions 4 and 5 are based on the following passage:

For most people, the name William Shakespeare brings to mind the familiar image of a balding man in elaborate Elizabethan dress and a list of plays they may have read in school. For literary scholars, however, the name Shakespeare does not include these familiar certainties.
(5) Many experts question whether all the plays conventionally attributed to Shakespeare were actually written by "the bard of Avon" from Stratford, England. Even among these "anti-Stratfordians," as they call themselves, there is disagreement about who actually authored the plays. Various groups attribute authorship to different people, includ-
(10) ing Francis Bacon, the Earl of Oxford, and Christopher Marlowe.

The conventional view of Shakespeare's authorship is that William Shakespeare, who was born in Stratford-upon-Avon and later moved to London, is the author of the plays. This person, according to the available records, was not only a playwright but also an actor and
(15) shareholder in the group that owned the Globe Theatre. While opponents of the conventional view argue that there is simply not enough information available about William Shakespeare's life to support his authorship, those who hold this conventional view maintain that records about the lives of the Elizabethan middle class are sparse in all
(20) cases. Therefore, they aren't surprised that documentation of Shakespeare's life is similiarly meager.

4.   The writer's goal in this passage is to:

   F.   argue that William Shakespeare is not the author of the plays commonly attributed to him.

   G.   describe the life of William Shakespeare.

   H.   encourage greater appreciation for Shakespeare's plays.

   J.   discuss the conflicting viewpoints about who wrote the plays that are associated with Shakespeare's name.

Step 1: Read. Your passage map should look something like this:

Paragraph 1: Controversy—who wrote Shakespeare's plays? anti-Stratfordian view

Paragraph 2: Conventional view

Step 2: Examine. The words "writer's goal" tell you this is a Writer's View question.

Step 3: Predict and select. Use your passage map here. The author's purpose in writing is *to introduce the controversy surrounding the authorship of Shakespeare's plays and point out some differences between the conventional view and the anti-Stratfordian view.* **This prediction nicely matches choice J.** Choice F is incorrect because the author doesn't agree with one view or the other. The passage merely describes both views. Choice G is out of scope. While a few details of Shakespeare's life are mentioned, they aren't the main point of the passage. Choice H is also out of scope. The passage doesn't address the topic of appreciating Shakespeare's plays.

5. The author's tone in this passage is one of:

    A. frustration at the lack of certainty about the issue discussed.

    B. detached description.

    C. bias toward the anti-Stratfordians.

    D. untempered admiration of Shakespeare.

Step 1: Read. Your passage map is already made!

Step 2: Examine. The words "author's tone" in the question stem tell you this is a Writer's View question.

Step 3: Predict and select. While the topic of the passage is a controversy, the author simply describes the controversy without taking sides. *The author doesn't reveal a personal viewpoint on the controversy.* **This prediction leads to choice B.** All the other choices are wrong because they include an opinion or emotional content. Choice A is wrong because the author doesn't express frustration. Choice C doesn't work because "bias" means "leaning toward one side or the other." Choice D doesn't work because the writer doesn't voice an opinion about Shakespeare.

● THE FINAL ACT: PRACTICE QUIZ

Because it's difficult to draw several Writer's View questions from a single passage, the questions in this Final Practice are based on individual paragraphs. You will encounter these passages again in expanded form in the other Reading lessons. Remember as you read the paragraphs to pay special attention to words that indicate the author's attitude and opinion.

Kathleen Yardley Lonsdale (1903–1971), a British X-ray crystallographer, strongly influenced the direction of organic chemistry with her findings about the compound benzene. After graduating with a degree in physics, she went to work in the labs of Nobel Prize winners Law-
(5) rence Bragg and William Bragg, where she discovered the planar structure of benzene. Benzene, also known as benzol, is an organic compound that had been previously investigated by other scientists. While the German inorganic chemist Friedrich August Kekulé had earlier suggested that benzene has a ring structure, this structure was not
(10) confirmed until Kathleen Lonsdale demonstrated it experimentally.

1. The author's tone in this paragraph is one of:

A. critical judgment.

B. detached description.

C. enthusiastic involvement.

D. exaggerated praise.

Galileo extensively investigated the geologic diversity of Jupiter's four largest moons: Ganymede, Callisto, Io, and Europa. Stunning images revealed the contrasting and changing surfaces of these moons. Io has extensive volcanic activity, which is continually modifying the sur-
(5) face. The heat and the frequency of eruption can be 100 times more than that of Earth, something reminiscent of Earth's early days. The similarities make Io an ideal laboratory for the study of what Earth was like more than 3 billion years ago.

2. In this paragraph, the author describes Jupiter's moons with:

F. commentary.

G. a purely speculative tone.

H. an idealistic tone that does not take the facts into account.

J. a critical attitude toward previous studies.

The moon Europa, Galileo unveiled, could be hiding a salty ocean up to 100 kilometers (62 miles) deep underneath its frozen surface. Images also revealed ice "rafts" the size of cities that have broken and drifted apart to create a scalloped and broken surface. There are also indica-
(5) tions of volcanic ice flows, with liquid water flowing across the surface. These discoveries are particularly intriguing since liquid water is a key ingredient in the process that may lead to the formation of life.

3. In the above paragraph, the author's attitude regarding the presence of water on Europa appears to be one of:

   A. certainty and conviction.

   B. cautious openness.

   C. general indifference.

   D. unreserved fascination.

Some experts, however, remain skeptical. These scientists are not convinced that water is responsible for the changes on the surface of Mars. It is possible, they say, that the features imaged by the Global Surveyor are caused by substances other than water. They assert that
(5) sand and dust can move in a flowing pattern and could be responsible for the geological changes that others attribute to water.

4. In this paragraph, the author writes from a perspective of:

   F. skeptical judgment.

   G. personal conviction.

   H. detached analysis.

   J. exaggerated enthusiasm.

Modern scholars, however, take a different view of the historic battle. Professor Anne Curry, who has thoroughly researched and analyzed chronicles of the battle, has been able to reconstruct the conflict from the views of both sides. In *Agincourt: A New History,* Curry asserts that
(5) the traditional view of Agincourt as a dramatic and unlikely victory for the British has been vastly overstated. Though Curry's work does not discount the view of Henry V as a powerful military leader, she does claim that the Battle of Agincourt was built up by Henry's contempo-raries as a more dramatic and significant victory than it actually was,
(10) largely for the purposes of enhancing his reputation as a king.

Thus, Curry cautions that historical documents should be read with a questioning mind and a certain degree of skepticism, understanding that the contemporary chroniclers may have had other purposes in mind than simply recording events as clearly and as accurately as pos-
(15) sible. Curry's work illustrates how the modern concept of "spin," referring to factors that promote a biased interpretation, may be applied not only to the modern media but to historical writings as well.

5. In the above paragraphs, the author's view of Anne Curry's work appears to be one of:

   A. unreserved praise and appreciation.
   B. sincere respect.
   C. skepticism about Curry's purposes.
   D. criticism for applying the modern term "spin" to historical works.

6. From the above paragraphs, it appears that the author sees the "traditional view of Agincourt" (line 5) as:

   F. based on faulty assumptions.
   G. conflicting in some respects with the modern view.
   H. the only interpretation supported by historical facts.
   J. holding more validity than Anne Curry's interpretation.

Mrs. Gardiner about this time reminded Elizabeth of her promise concerning Mr. Wickham, and required information. Elizabeth had such to send as might rather give contentment to her aunt than to herself. Mr. Wickham's apparent partiality had subsided, his attentions were over,
(5) he was the admirer of someone else. Elizabeth was watchful enough to see it all, but she could see it and write of it without material pain. Her heart had been but slightly touched, and her vanity was satisfied with believing that she would have been his only choice, had fortune permitted it. The sudden acquisition of ten thousand pounds was the
(10) most remarkable charm of the young lady to whom he was now rendering himself agreeable, but Elizabeth did not quarrel with him for his wish of independence. Nothing, on the contrary, could be more natural, and while able to suppose that it cost him a few struggles to relinquish her, she was ready to allow it a wise and desirable measure
(15) for both, and could very sincerely wish him happy.

7. In the above paragraph, the narrator wishes to portray Elizabeth as one who is:

   A. capable of rational analysis.

   B. uniquely partial to Mr. Wickham.

   C. influenced primarily by her emotions.

   D. too cautious to enjoy life.

Another factor pointing to an optimistic outlook for classical music is a spate of recent research that indicates that music education, including lessons in performance as well as classes in music appreci-ation, has a profoundly positive effect on young people's academic
(5) performance. While Don Campbell's book *The Mozart Effect* extols the benefits of classical music for the health of body, mind, and soul, educational researchers have conducted studies that show strong correlations between musical training and high standardized test scores. Even parents of very young children, some still in the womb,
(10) have taken to using classical music to create educational advantages for their children. Recordings with titles such as *Beethoven to Build Baby's Brain* have joined phonics books and early math games on the shelves of parents who want the best for their children.

8. In the above paragraph, the author's attitude can best be described as:

   F. an unopinionated analysis of a situation.

   G. uncertain speculation about the future of classical music.

   H. praise for Don Campbell's *The Mozart Effect*.

   J. a positive outlook backed up by evidence.

"Here is a new companion for you, to shake hands with, Tulliver," said that gentleman on entering the study, "Master Philip Wakem. I shall leave you to make acquaintance by yourselves. You already know something of each other, I imagine, for you are neighbors at home."
(5)   Tom looked confused and awkward while Philip rose and glanced at him timidly. Tom did not like to go up and put out his hand, and he was not prepared to say, "How do you do?" on so short a notice. Mr. Stelling wisely turned away and closed the door behind him: boys' shyness only wears off in the absence of their elders.

9. In the above paragraphs, the narrator appears to view Mr. Stelling as one who is:

    A. lacking in understanding of young people.

    B. interested in controlling others.

    C. confused about the relationship between Tom and Philip.

    D. experienced and confident in dealing with young people.

The primary distinctions between damselflies and dragonflies relate to the wings. In damselflies, the hindwing is similar to the forewing while in dragonflies the hindwing is broader at the base. In addition, damselflies and dragonflies differ in the position of the wings at
(5) rest. While most dragonflies hold the wings open horizontally when not flying, most damsel flies rest with the wings held together along the long axis of the body. Damselflies tend to be weaker fliers than dragonflies. One other difference between the two is that the eyes of most damselflies are separated whereas the eyes of most dragon-
(10) flies touch.

10. In the paragraph above, the author's tone can best be described as creating:

    F. a critical judgment of scientists who have studied damselflies and dragonflies.

    G. an analytical presentation of facts.

    H. a detached description of a new hypothesis.

    J. a conflicted statement about two groups of insects.

● THE FINAL ACT: ANSWERS AND EXPLANATIONS FOR WRITER'S VIEW QUESTIONS

1. B. The paragraph describes without presenting any opinion. Choice A is an opposite because the author is not critical of anything. Choice C is an opposite because the author is merely reporting and indicates no personal involvement with the topic. Choice D is an extreme. While the author does state that Lonsdale "strongly influenced the direction of organic chemistry," which could be understood as "praise," the word "exaggerated" is not justified by the passage.

2. F. This paragraph is mainly descriptive, but the last sentence goes beyond description, to commentary or speculation. Choice G combines the extreme and distortion traps. The paragraph is partially, but not "purely," speculative. Choice H is a distortion. The author uses the phrase "an ideal laboratory," but the author's tone is not idealistic. Choice J is out of scope because this paragraph doesn't mention "previous studies."

3. B. When speaking of water, the author uses the phrases "could be" and "indications of." This word choice expresses speculation rather than certainty, so choice B works well while choice A is an opposite. Choice C is an opposite because the author views the discoveries suggesting that water may be present as "particularly intriguing." Choice D is extreme in using the word "unreserved."

4. H. In this paragraph, the author discusses the ideas of "some experts" without revealing a personal opinion. Choice F is a distortion; the author describes the "experts" in question as "skeptical." Choice J is an opposite; the author is analytical and detached rather than enthusiastic here.

5. B. The only time the author directly states an opinion of Curry's work is in the phrase "thoroughly researched and analyzed." This indicates respect. Choice A is extreme because, while the author does seem to be praising Curry's work, the word "unreserved" is an extreme qualifier that isn't justified by the passage. Choice C is a distortion. The author says that Curry recommends "skepticism," but this doesn't indicate that the author feels skeptical about Curry's work. Choice D combines the opposite and distortion traps. While "spin" is mentioned in the passage, the author is not critical of Curry for applying the concept to historical works.

6. G. The author mentions the "traditional view" only to contrast it with the view of "modern scholars," of which Anne Curry is mentioned as an example. Thus, the author clearly sees the modern and traditional views as opposing each other in some ways. The author, however, doesn't weigh in directly with a personal opinion about the "traditional view." Choice F is out of scope: no "assumption" is mentioned here. Choice H is an opposite, because the author views Curry's interpretation as having at least some credibility. Choice J is an opposite; if anything, the author seems to support Curry's view.

7. A. This paragraph shows Elizabeth's rational side more than her emotional side. The words "Her heart had been but lightly touched," "on the contrary," and "ready to allow it a wise and desirable measure" characterize Elizabeth as being analytical and in control of her emotions. Thus, choice C is an opposite. Choice B is a distortion. The paragraph refers to Mr. Wickham's "partiality," not Elizabeth's. Choice D combines the distortion and out-of-scope traps. Though the paragraph describes Elizabeth as "watchful," it is going too far to say that she can't "enjoy life."

8. J. The author does reveal an opinion, that there is "an optimistic outlook for classical music." The paragraph gives reasons the author holds this opinion. Choice F is an opposite because the author's analysis is in service of supporting an opinion. Choice G is an opposite because the author's opinion is confident, not "uncertain." Choice H is a distortion; the author states that Campbell "extols [praises] the benefits of classical music," but the author is not expressing praise for Campbell's book here.

9. D. The narrator's use of "wisely" to describe Mr. Stelling's behavior expresses a positive view of Mr. Stelling. Choice D is the only choice that is positive. Choice A is a an opposite. Choice B is out of scope. Nothing in the passage suggests that Mr. Stelling wants to control Tom and Philip. Choice C is an opposite; the passage states that Mr. Stelling knows that Tom and Philip have some familiarity with each other but are shy with each other.

10. G. The tone in this paragraph is descriptive. The author states and analyzes facts without presenting any opinions. Choice F is out of scope because the author doesn't mention any "scientists" here. Choice H is out of scope because the passage doesn't mention a hypothesis. Choice J is a distortion. While the paragraph describes some differences between damselflies and dragonflies, the tone is confident and certain, not "conflicted."

LESSON 15

Detail Questions

DIFFICULTY: ★ ★

FREQUENCY: ★ ★ ★

SURPRISE FACTOR: ★ ★

• INTRODUCTION TO DETAIL QUESTIONS

Detail questions ask you about material that is directly stated in the passage. In fact, the correct answer to a Detail question sometimes features the exact wording used in the passage. More often, however, it paraphrases the text of the passage. Detail questions should be some of the easiest on the ACT because they're the most straightforward. You don't need to interpret information as you do with the other question types. If you know exactly where to go in the passage to find the answer, you're certain to get a Detail question right.

But Detail questions can be challenging if you don't know where to look to find the answer. That's one reason your passage map is so important! Remember—on your first reading of the passage, don't focus on details; just pay attention to main ideas. You won't be able to answer a Detail question without referring to the appropriate lines in the passage, but if you've made a passage map, you'll know exactly which paragraph to turn to after reading your question stem. Sometimes, you may need to skim the whole passage for key words used in the question stem; other times you can use your passage map to help you zero in on the appropriate part of the text to research a Detail question. In either case, the details of the passage are "researchable." **Don't try to remember details** on your first reading of the passage. You won't need to recall or understand every detail in a passage. Don't waste your time and energy! Focus on details only when you need to in order to answer the questions.

Characteristics of Detail Questions

You can easily recognize Detail questions by the wording of the question stem. Here are some phrases that typically appear in Detail question stems:

- According to the author...
- According to the passage...
- As stated in the passage...
- The passage indicates that...

Most Common Types of Detail Questions

Most Detail questions focus strictly on verbal skills. You read the question, refer back to the passage, predict an answer in your own words, and select the answer that matches your prediction. Knowing the main idea of each paragraph helps you determine where to search in the text. Being able to paraphrase what you read helps you make your prediction and find the answer choice that corresponds to it. All Detail questions require you to recognize something that is clearly and directly stated in the passage.

There are, however, two less common types of Detail questions that are presented in a more challenging way. The first type uses **Roman numerals** to offer choices within the question stem, as in this example:

1. According to the passage, it is possible that a salt water ocean is present on:

    I. Callisto
    II. Europa
    III. Ganymede
    IV. Io

  A. I, II, III, and IV
  B. I, II, and III
  C. I, III, and IV
  D. II, III, and IV

It's easy to recognize these questions, but it sometimes takes a little longer to work through them. You can use logic as well as your reading skills to help you rule out incorrect answer choices. Roman numeral questions tend to be more time consuming than other Detail questions because they encompass more than one detail—perhaps a list or a sequence—and require more time to research and predict for. (See Rule 3 in Performance Techniques for help with this question type.)

The second, less common type of Detail question is one that **uses the word EXCEPT** in the question stem. As with NOT questions in the English section, it's a good idea to circle the word EXCEPT in the question stem. It's important to read the question stem carefully and understand what it's asking to avoid getting confused by the reverse logic of this question type. Question 1 in the Dress Rehearsal section is an example of this type.

• THE TRAP DOOR: STEERING CLEAR OF ANSWER TRAPS

Any of the five traps described in the Reading Basics section may appear among the answer choices for a Detail question. However, three are likely to show up more frequently in Detail questions. All of these traps can be avoided by following the Kaplan Method for ACT Reading. Remember, for Detail questions, the answer is right there somewhere in the passage. The ACT Reading section is like an open-book test, and the passage is your "book." The Kaplan Method helps you make the most of this "book."

Types of Detail Question Answer Traps

The three answer traps seen most often in Detail questions are the misused detail, distortion, and opposite traps. The misused detail trap is easy to fall for if you don't take the time to understand precisely what the question is asking and from which section of the passage you should find your answer. The distortion trap is one you might fall for if you don't read the relevant words in the passage carefully enough. The opposite answer trap is an answer choice that contradicts something that is stated in the passage. Opposites can be tempting because they refer to something that you remember reading in the passage, but they're worded in such a way that they actually contradict the passage. A simple little word like *not* or *no* in the answer choice can make the difference between a correct answer and an opposite trap.

Techniques for Avoiding Detail Question Answer Traps

Following the Kaplan Method and training yourself to become aware of how the test maker creates challenging answer choices are your best strategies for avoiding the answer traps. Taking the time to verbalize your prediction in your own words is key. Here are some additional pointers to help you steer clear of the most common Detail question traps.

MISUSED DETAIL

Read the question stem carefully! If the question is at all complicated, it may help for you to put the question in your own words, starting with one of the question words: *how, what, when, where,* or *why.* The misused detail answer trap is most tempting when you haven't taken the necessary time to understand exactly what the question is asking. Always remember: The correct choice must answer the question posed in the question stem. Sometimes a misused detail trap answer choice contains a true statement that is made in the passage, but just because a statement is true and you can find it in the passage doesn't means it answers this particular question.

DISTORTION

To avoid the distortion answer trap, carefully re-read the appropriate part of the passage. You're more likely to fall for a distortion if you're trying to answer a question from memory instead of looking back at the passage.

OPPOSITE

The opposite trap is tempting because it treats an issue that is indeed in the passage so the detail mentioned in the trap answer may be familiar to you. Do not choose an answer simply because you remember that the phrase or detail was used in the passage. Go back to the part of the passage where the detail is discussed and read it carefully to understand exactly what's being said.

● PERFORMANCE TECHNIQUES: KEY RULES

The Kaplan Method for ACT Reading introduced in the last lesson gives you a strategic approach that's key for tackling all Reading question types. Here are some other rules to help you score points on Detail questions.

RULE 1: READ THE QUESTION STEM CAREFULLY.

Though this rule seems obvious, it's easy to become overwhelmed and not take a few seconds to think about what the question is asking, putting it into your own words if necessary.

RULE 2: USE YOUR PASSAGE MAP.

Understanding the structure of the passage can guide you to the location of the detail in the passage. Most Detail questions can be answered correctly by referring to a single sentence in the passage. The difficulty lies in determining where that sentence is. While you will sometimes have to skim the passage for words relating to the question stem, frequently your understanding of how the passage is structured, based on your passage map, will save you time by letting you locate the appropriate spot in the passage quickly.

RULE 3: LET LOGIC HELP YOU WITH ROMAN NUMERAL QUESTIONS.

Suppose a passage describes the following events in the life of a person named Josephine Schnell: 1945—published first novel; 1947—married to Kenneth Schnell; 1953—moved from Germany to New York. A Roman numeral question for such a passage might look like this:

2. Which sequence correctly orders the events in Josephine Snell's life?
   I. Published first novel
   II. Married to Kenneth Schnell
   III. Moved from Germany to New York

   F. III, II, I
   G. II, I, III
   H. II, III, I
   J. I, II, III

You can reduce the amount of time you spend on a Roman numeral question by using common sense and logic. Suppose you research the passage and find the date of the first novel (1945) and the date of marriage (1947). Even if you can't quickly locate the date of Schnell's move, you know that event I occurred before event II. Thus you can eliminate choices F, G, and H because they all place event II before event I. Because of the way this question and the answer choices are constructed, you can find the answer through logic without locating every last detail in the passage.

● DRESS REHEARSAL: SAMPLE QUESTIONS AND DETAILED EXPLANATIONS

The sample questions are based on the following passage. Remember to make your passage map—jot down brief notes describing the purpose of each paragraph as you read.

NATURAL SCIENCE: This passage is taken from a collection of biographical sketches of women in science.

Kathleen Yardley Lonsdale (1903–1971), a British X-ray crystallographer, strongly influenced the direction of organic chemistry with her discovery of the planar structure of benzene. After graduating with a degree in physics, she went to work in the labs of Nobel prize winners
(5) Lawrence Bragg and William Bragg. Benzene, also known as benzol, is an organic compound that had been previously investigated by other scientists. While it was the German inorganic chemist Friedrich August Kekulé who had earlier suggested that benzene has a ring structure, this structure was not confirmed until Kathleen Lonsdale demonstrated
(10) it experimentally.

The benzene molecule can be represented as a regular hexagon with carbon atoms at the vertices and a hydrogen atom attached to each carbon atom. Lonsdale showed that the bonds between the carbon atoms were all the same length and that the internal angles between these
(15) bonds were all 120 degrees, thus confirming the hexagonal shape and planar structure of benzene.

In addition to determining the precise molecular structure of benzene, Lonsdale did other work that had a significant impact on the field of X-ray crystallography. In 1945, she became one of the first two
(20) female Fellows of the Royal Society, Britain's most prestigious scientific organization. Far from isolating herself in the laboratory, however, she also became involved in political issues
of her time. In 1935, she became a Quaker and a devoted pacifist. Her beliefs led her to protest against World War II by refusing to partici-
(25) pate in civil defense duties. Because of this lack of participation and Lonsdale's failure to pay the resulting fine, she spent a month in jail. Following her release, she became a prison visitor, using her own experience to relate to others. She became active in the penal reform movement, advocating for improved conditions for prisoners.

(30)   In a time when it was uncommon for a woman to have a lifetime career in science, Lonsdale managed to balance carrying out her research, acting on her political beliefs, and raising her three children. She had the support and encouragement of her husband, Thomas Jackson Lonsdale, in an age when few men were known for promoting the careers of their wives.

Detail Question: "EXCEPT"

1. According to the passage, all of the following were scientists EXCEPT:
    A. Kathleen Lonsdale.
    B. William Bragg.
    C. Friedrich August Kekulé.
    D. Thomas Jackson Lonsdale.

Before you attempt to answer any questions, you should always have a good idea of how the passage is structured. What notes did you jot down in the margin? Your passage map should be something along these lines:

Paragraph 1: Lonsdale confirmed structure of benzene.

Paragraph 2: Description of benzene molecule

Paragraph 3: Lonsdale's nonscience concerns

Paragraph 4: Family life

Because Question 1 is an "except" question, the correct answer will be the choice that doesn't fit the criteria in the question stem. Use a combination of margin notes, memory, and scanning the text of the passage to eliminate answer choices quickly. Even the most basic understanding of the passage tells you that choice A can be eliminated. Because you should focus on *why*, not *what*, during your first reading of the passage, you may not recall anything about choice B. Scan the passage quickly for the name "William Bragg." In Paragraph 1, you see that Lonsdale worked in Bragg's lab, so Bragg was a scientist. Similarly, you may need to scan the passage for the name "Kekulé." Because Paragraph 1 states that he was an organic chemist, you can also rule out choice C. By process of elimination, you can see that choice D is correct. If you confidently eliminate three answer choices, logic tells you that the fourth choice must be the correct answer. The passage does not state that Thomas Lonsdale was or was not a scientist. You must answer all reading questions based only on the information provided in the passage, not on any outside knowledge you may bring to the topic.

Detail Question: Benzene

2. The passage indicates that the structure of benzene:

    F. consists of six carbon atoms with attached hydrogen atoms.

    G. was confirmed by Friedrich August Kekulé.

    H. was completely unknown until Kathleen Lonsdale discovered it.

    J. plays a minor role in the field of organic chemistry.

Using your passage map, you can tell that Paragraphs 1 and 2 are the parts of the text most likely to provide the answer to this question. Quickly reviewing Paragraph 1, you might predict that *the structure of benzene was confirmed by Kathleen Lonsdale.* (Note that choice G is a distortion; although it uses the word "confirmed," it attributes the confirmation to Kekulé instead of to Lonsdale.) Because this prediction doesn't match any of the answer choices, go back and re-read Paragraph 2. Using the first sentence here, you can predict that the structure of benzene is *represented as a regular hexagon with carbon atoms at the vertices.* **This prediction matches well with choice F.** Note that choice H is an opposite because Paragraph 1 contradicts it. Choice J is an opposite; if Lonsdale "strongly influenced the direction of organic chemistry with her discovery," then we can infer that benzene is important to organic chemistry.

Detail Question: Thomas Lonsdale

3. The last paragraph states that Thomas Jackson Lonsdale:

    A. was an early supporter of women's rights.

    B. was a member of the Royal Society.

    C. did research that earned him a Nobel Prize.

    D. encouraged his wife in her scientific endeavors.

Quickly reviewing the last paragraph, you can predict that Thomas Lonsdale supported and encouraged his wife's career. **This prediction corresponds nicely with choice D.** Note that choice A is out of scope. It goes too far beyond what is stated in the passage. Choice B is a misused detail: it was Kathleen, not Thomas, Lonsdale who was a member of the Royal Society. Likewise, choice C is a misused detail. The only Nobel Prize winners mentioned in the passage are Lawrence and William Bragg.

Detail Question: Kathleen Lonsdale

4. According to the passage, Kathleen Lonsdale spent a month in jail because she

    F. did chemical research in a controversial area.
    G. wanted to improve the conditions of prisoners.
    H. protested World War II.
    J. was found guilty of fraud.

Because the reference to "jail" in this passage is a detail and not a main idea, there's a good chance you don't remember noticing it on your first reading. Good margin notes are essential for a question like this. With the passage map described above, you know immediately that you should look in Paragraph 3. Scanning Paragraph 3 for the word "jail" and reading the sentence where it appears, as well as the previous sentence, you might predict that Lonsdale went to jail because she refused to participate in civil defense during World War II. **This prediction leads you to choice H, the correct answer.** Choice F is completely out of scope of the passage because there is no indication that Lonsdale's research was in a controversial area. Choice G is a distortion because, although the passage does state that Lonsdale advocated "improved conditions for prisoners," that is not the reason that she herself served a jail sentence. Choice J is out of scope because the passage never mentions "fraud."

Detail Question: Carbon Atoms

5. The passage states that the carbon atoms in benzene:

    A. are joined together with bonds at 120-degree angles from one another.
    B. are each bonded to two hydrogen atoms.
    C. do not form part of its crystallographic structure.
    D. are attached to a hexagon made up of hydrogen atoms.

Once again, a good passage map is crucial to answering this question efficiently. Because the question stem refers to atoms, you can be pretty sure that the answer will be in Paragraph 2, which describes the benzene molecule. This paragraph includes some technical details, and you may not fully understand all the scientific jargon. That doesn't matter, so don't panic! Your margin notes lead you directly to this paragraph, which is fairly short. You should have time to re-read it, paying careful attention to what is stated about the carbon atoms. Your prediction might include several components: they are the vertices of a hexagon, or they each have a hydrogen atom attached, or they involve equal bond lengths and 120-degree angles. Even with this prediction, the correct answer may not immediately jump out at you. However, you should be able to rule out choice C as an out-of-scope trap.

As you consider other choices, you must be very careful of how the details are used. Carefully reading the first sentence of the paragraph, you can see that the carbon atoms in benzene form the vertices of a regular hexagon and that each has an attached hydrogen atom. This fact lets you eliminate choice D as a distortion because the hexagon is not formed by hydrogen atoms. Choice B is also a distortion because each carbon atom is bonded to a single hydrogen atom. This is a challenging Detail question, but working with the passage map, a prediction, and the process of elimination, **you can arrive at choice A as the only acceptable answer.**

● THE FINAL ACT: PRACTICE QUIZ

Remember to read for main ideas and jot your passage map notes in the margin. A sample passage map appears before the answers at the end of the quiz.

NATURAL SCIENCE: This passage is taken from a NASA report on the Galileo mission and its investigation of the solar system.

In 1994, the spacecraft Galileo was in the right place at the right time and made the only direct observation of a comet impacting a planet. It took images of fragments of comet Shoemaker-Levy 9 crashing into Jupiter. Images of the impact, which was not visible from earth, helped
(5)   scientists better understand this type of event.

Galileo began its tour of the Jovian system in December 1995. Carefully designed orbits allowed the spacecraft to observe Jupiter's atmosphere, revealing numerous large thunderstorms many times larger than those on Earth, with lightning strikes up to 1,000 times
(10)   more powerful than terrestrial lightning. Data collected by the descent probe made the first in-place studies of the planet's clouds and winds, and it furthered scientists' understanding of how Jupiter evolved. The probe also made measurements designed to assess the degree of

evolution of Jupiter compared to the Sun. As the first spacecraft in long-
(15) term residence in Jovian orbit, Galileo also successfully studied the
global structure and dynamics of Jupiter's magnetic field. Galileo determined that Jupiter's ring system is formed by dust kicked up as
interplanetary meteoroids smash into the planet's four small inner
moons. Data also showed that Jupiter's outermost ring is actually made
(20) up of two rings, one embedded within another.

Galileo extensively investigated the geologic diversity of Jupiter's
four largest moons: Ganymede, Callisto, Io, and Europa. Stunning
images revealed the contrasting and changing surfaces of these
moons. Io has extensive volcanic activity, which is continually modi-
(25) fying the surface. The heat and the frequency of eruption can be 100
times more than that of Earth, something reminiscent of Earth's early
days. The similarities make Io an ideal laboratory for the study of what
Earth was like more than 3 billion years ago.

The moon Europa, Galileo unveiled, could be hiding a salty ocean
(30) up to 100 kilometers (62 miles) deep underneath its frozen surface.
Images also revealed ice "rafts" the size of cities that have broken and
drifted apart to create a scalloped and broken surface. There are also
indications of volcanic ice flows, with liquid water flowing across the
surface. These discoveries are particularly intriguing since liquid water
(35) is a key ingredient in the process that may lead to the formation of life.

The biggest discovery surrounding Ganymede was the presence
of a magnetic field, the first moon of any planet known to have one.
Images of this moon featured a faulted and fractured surface that demonstrated high tectonic activity. Like Europa and Io, Ganymede has a
(40) metallic core. Galileo's magnetic data also provided evidence that Ganymede might have a liquid-saltwater layer as well.

Galileo determined that, while Callisto doesn't have a metallic core,
its surface shows evidence of extensive erosion. Data collected raise the
question of whether Callisto's surface may also hide an ocean.

1. As indicated by the passage, the following are moons of Jupiter:

   A. Galileo and Ganymede.

   B. Levy and Io.

   C. Shoemaker and Io.

   D. Europa and Callisto.

2. According to the author, the volcanic activity on Io:

   F. has a heat and frequency that is consistently 100 times greater than that of earth.

   G. cannot be compared with earth's volcanic activity.

   H. can have a heat and frequency of up to 100 times more than that of Earth.

   J. is not strong enough to modify Io's surface.

3. According to the passage, it is possible that a saltwater ocean is present on:

   I. Callisto

   II. Europa

   III. Ganymede

   IV. Io

   A. I, II, III, and IV

   B. I, II, and III

   C. I, III, and IV

   D. II, III, and IV

4. According to the second paragraph, data from the Galileo mission:

   F. showed that Jupiter is more evolved than the sun.

   G. did not provide any new information about Europa.

   H. focused primarily on Jupiter's thunderstorms.

   J. indicated that the outermost ring of Jupiter is made up one ring embedded within another.

5. The author of the passage indicates that large ice rafts have affected the surface of:

   A. Callisto.

   B. Europa.

   C. Ganymede.

   D. Io.

6. The author states that further study of Io could help scientists learn more about Earth's early days because:

   F. The volcanic activity on Io is similar to that present on Earth more than 3 billion years ago.

   G. Io is one of Jupiter's largest moons.

   H. Io is the first moon known to have a magnetic field.

   J. The volcanic activity on Io causes its surface to change frequently.

7. According to the passage, the moon that lacks a metallic core is:

   A. Callisto.

   B. Europa.

   C. Ganymede.

   D. Io.

8. The author states that the water flowing across the surface of Europa's volcanic ice flows is of interest because:

   F. The ice flows have given Europa a scalloped surface.

   G. The presence of water is a clear indication that there was life on Europa.

   H. The ice flows are the size of cities.

   J. Liquid water is key factor necessary for the formation of life.

9. According to the passage, the first spacecraft to spend a significant amount of time orbiting Jupiter was:

   A. Shoemaker-Levy 9.

   B. Challenger.

   C. Galileo.

   D. Apollo 13.

10. According to the author, the ring system of Jupiter:

    F. is formed by meteoroids smashing into Jupiter's inner moons.

    G. is not as extensive as it was once thought to be.

    H. is influenced by the magnetic field of Ganymede.

    J. is expected to disintegrate over the next 3 billion years.

● THE FINAL ACT: ANSWERS AND EXPLANATIONS FOR DETAIL QUESTIONS

Here's a suggested passage map:

Paragraph 1: Galileo gets pictures of comet crashing into planet.

Paragraph 2: Aspects of Jupiter explored by Galileo

Paragraph 3: Study of Jupiter's four moons; detail about Io

Paragraph 4: Details about Europa

Paragraph 5: Details about Ganymede

Paragraph 6: Details about Callisto

1. D. Your passage map should tell you to research Paragraph 3. Choices A, B, and C are all distortions because each answer includes a moon of Jupiter but pairs the name of the moon with an irrelevant detail from the passage.

2. H. Your passage map should tell you to research paragraph 3. Predict something like *changes the surface and is greater than on earth.* Choice F is an extreme because of the word "consistently." Choices G and J are opposites.

3. B. This question could take a lot of time because you need to research in Paragraphs 3–6. It might be wise to guess on this question unless you can skim to get to the answer quickly. Even a little research can help you eliminate incorrect answers and increase your odds of guessing correctly. Lines 44–45 state that Callisto may have an ocean. Thus, the correct answer must include I, so you can eliminate choice D. Line 29 states that Europa may have an ocean. Because the correct answer must also include II, you can eliminate choice C. Line 42 states that Ganymede may have "a liquid-saltwater layer," so the correct answer must also include III. Because of the way this particular question is written, you still need to research the paragraph on Io to choose between choices A and B. Choice B is correct because the passage doesn't mention the possibility of salt water on Io.

4. J. Researching the second paragraph should lead to a good prediction: *Galileo returned information about Jupiter's thunderstorms, evolution, magnetic core, and rings.* Though choice F might be tempting, the word "more" makes it an extreme choice because this word is not used in the passage. Choice G should strike you as an obvious opposite. Because your prediction includes much more than thunderstorms, choice H is out of scope. Choice J is an accurate detail (lines 19–20) consistent with your prediction.

5. B.   Your passage map may not be helpful here. Scan the passage for the phrase "ice rafts." If you spot it in line 31, you'll have your answer. If not, skip this question the first time around and come back if you have time.

6. F.   Your passage map should tell you that the third paragraph, about Io, is the best place to research, allowing you to make a prediction: *studying Io could help scientists learn more about earth's early days because the heat and frequency of Io's volcanic eruptions are "something reminiscent of earth's early days."* (lines 26–27) This prediction points to choice F. Choice G is a misused detail. Choice H is an opposite (Ganymede, not Io, was the first known moon to have a magnetic field.), and in any case, it doesn't relate to the question. Choice J is a misused detail: it's true but doesn't address the question.

7. A.   Your passage map should direct you to one of the last four paragraphs. Scanning for "metallic core," you can find the answer in Paragraph 6. All the other choices are opposites.

8. J.   Go to Paragraph 4. The last two sentences lead to choice J. Choice F is a distortion. Choice G is extreme. Choice H is a misused detail.

9. C.   This detail can be found in Paragraph 2, lines 14–15: "As the first spacecraft in long-term residence in Jovian orbit, Galileo...." All other choices are opposites. Additionally, choices B and D can be considered out of scope because neither is mentioned in the passage. Choice A can be considered a misused detail: it is mentioned in the passage, but it's the name of a comet, not a spacecraft.

10. F.   Scanning the passage for "ring system," you should then read Paragraph 2. Lines 17–19 let you make a prediction that matches choice F. Choice G is out of scope. Choices H and J are distortions.

LESSON 16

Inference Questions

DIFFICULTY: ★ ★ ★

FREQUENCY: ★ ★ ★

SURPRISE FACTOR: ★

• INTRODUCTION TO INFERENCE QUESTIONS

Inference questions require you to draw a conclusion based on what is stated in the passage. The author implies—that is hints at or suggests—something that's not directly spelled out in the text. When the author implies something, you, the reader, make an inference. While you can think of making an inference as "putting two and two together" or "reading between the lines," it's important to remember that the answer to an Inference question will not stray too far from the passage. Yes, you have to apply your reasoning skills and go a little beyond what's stated, but you shouldn't go too far beyond this. Even for the toughest Inference questions, the best answer choice is always strongly grounded in the passage. When making your predictions for Inference questions, read the relevant lines carefully and don't get too creative in your interpretation.

Characteristics of Inference Questions

You can recognize Inference questions by the wording used in the question stem. Some typical phrasings that signal an Inference question are shown in bold face in these question stems:

- The description of Carla in the second paragraph **implies that...**
- From the narrator's recollection about her mother, **it can most reasonably be inferred that**...
- Regarding Chekhov's contribution to world literature, **the author suggests that**...

- From Angel's response to Tess's confession in the fourth paragraph, **it is most reasonable to conclude that**…

You should note that the above question stems refer to specific parts of the passage. In this sense, Inference questions are similar to Detail questions: You can put your finger on the part of the passage that you need to read to predict the answer. This fact is what sets Inference questions apart from other question types that ask you to make inferences. You can read in Lesson 17 about Generalization questions, which also require you to make an inference based on the passage. The difference is that, with Inference questions, the question stem will point you to a specific part of the passage whereas with Generalization questions, you have to make a broad inference that takes into account the passage as a whole. For the Inference questions discussed in this lesson, you need to make small-scale ("little picture") inferences instead of broad inferences.

It's important to understand that inferences are neither facts nor opinions. Rather, an **inference** is a conclusion that a careful reader can draw from the facts or opinions that are presented in the passage. The best answer choice for an Inference question will be firmly based on the words of the passage; it will *never* introduce material that wasn't brought up in the passage.

Most Common Types of Inference Questions

Inference questions are associated with all four kinds of ACT Reading passages: prose fiction, social studies, humanities, and natural science. However, Inference questions are more likely to appear with the prose fiction passage, which you must read a little differently than the nonfiction passages. You can expect each nonfiction selection to have a recognizable organizational structure. Each paragraph will have one main idea, and the author will use transition words (such as *however, whereas, despite, on the other hand, for example, in addition, indeed, because, consequently,* and *as a result of*) that serve as a kind of shorthand to help you understand the logical flow of the passage. In your active reading of nonfiction passages, you should pay close attention to the key transition words to help you determine the author's purpose and the structure of the passage.

Unlike the three nonfiction passages, however, **prose fiction passages** don't follow a particular or precise logical flow. It's not that prose passages are completely without logic or structure; it's that a fiction passage expresses meaning that's more psychological than logical. In your active reading of the fiction passage, you need to pay close attention to **characters**: their moods, motivations, and behaviors. An ACT fiction passage may have one or more major characters. Keep the following questions in mind for each:

- Who is this person?
- What is this person feeling and thinking?
- How can I understand this person's behavior?
- What is this person's relationship to other characters?

Because novelists and short story writers tend to "show, not tell," you must make inferences as you read fiction if you want to understand and enjoy the story. For example, instead of writing, "Melinda came home from work irritable and exhausted," a novelist might write:

Melinda walked into the house slowly and dropped her coat and briefcase onto the floor. She practically fell onto the couch and turned her head toward the wall. "Are you okay?" David asked. "Just leave me alone!" Melinda screamed at him.

Here, instead of making explicit statements, the author describes Melinda's behavior in a way that lets the reader conclude that Melinda is tired and irritable.

THE TRAP DOOR: STEERING CLEAR OF ANSWER TRAPS

While any of the classic answer traps might appear among the choices for Inference questions, three tend to turn up more often than the others: the out-of-scope trap, the distortion trap, and the opposite trap.

Types of Inference Question Answer Traps

The most common answer trap for Inference questions is the out-of-scope trap. Because you must draw a conclusion to answer an Inference question, it's tempting to get carried away and go too far beyond what's in the passage. Remember that the conclusion you draw must be based firmly on the words of the passage. An answer choice that mentions details not related to the passage is likely to be out of scope for an Inference question. The distortion trap also occurs fairly often. A distortion answer choice includes material from the passage, but in this trap, the material may be misinterpreted or inappropriately combined with another detail. The opposite trap may also occur for Inference questions. Failing to notice a particular phrase in the passage may cause you to fall for an opposite trap.

For an example of an Inference question with typical trap answer choices, consider the question based on the following paragraph:

> Scholars have recently discovered that medieval Islamic artists were far more mathematically advanced than had previously been supposed. These artists created intricate abstract patterns that were based on mathematical techniques that Western mathematicians did not fully
> (5) understand until the 20th century. Peter Lu and Paul Steinhardt have shown that the medieval patterns, widely used in the decoration of mosques and palaces, were created with a set of just five geometric shapes, or templates: a decagon, a pentagon, a hexagon, a rhombus, and a bowtie shape. The ornate geometric designs are based on compli-
> (10) cated mathematical principles involving rotational symmetry. Amazingly, these patterns can cover a surface infinitely without repetition. The math behind such infinitely extendable, nonrepeating patterns, now called quasicrystalline geometry, was thought to have been discovered by British mathematician Roger Penrose in the 1970s. However, the discovery
> (15) made by Lu and Steinhardt that the complex medieval Islamic designs can be created from a limited set of five shapes is an indication that the artists had at least an intuitive understanding of highly complex mathematical principles.

1. The phrase "at least an intuitive understanding of highly complex mathematical principles" suggests that:

    A. Roger Penrose's discovery of quasicrystalline geometry was not based on intuition.
    B. scholars have traditionally underestimated the cultural contributions made by Islamic artists.
    C. the Islamic designs, because they were created by only five shapes used repeatedly, are rather simplistic.
    D. the precise nature of the Islamic designers' mathematical understanding has not been determined.

Here, choice A is a distortion. Roger Penrose is mentioned in the passage, but nothing suggests that his discovery of quasiqrystalline geometry lacked an intuitive element. Choice B is out of scope because it's too broad. The passage discusses only Islamic geometric designs, not "cultural contributions" in general. Choice C is an opposite. The passage indicates that the designs, despite being created with only five shapes, are actually quite complex. Only choice D makes an appropriate interpretation of the quoted phrase. Note that the proper interpretation here hinges on the quoted words "at least."

Techniques for Avoiding Inference Question Answer Traps

One of the best techniques for avoiding Inference question traps is to read the question stem carefully, focusing on the part of the passage the stem directs you to in order to make your prediction. Remember, your prediction must be grounded in the words of the passage, even though this question type requires you to apply your reasoning skills. It's always important to predict before you peek for all question types, but taking a shortcut by skipping the prediction step is especially dangerous for Inference questions. By making a prediction when your eyes are on the words in the passage (and never after only reading answer choices), the prediction step keeps you focused on the passage and makes you less likely to fall for out-of-scope answer choices and distortions.

● PERFORMANCE TECHNIQUES: KEY STEPS AND RULES

As with other question types, reading actively, taking good notes for your passage map, and following the Kaplan Method for ACT Reading will help you score points on Inference questions.

To review, here's the Kaplan Method for ACT Reading:

Step 1: Read the passage, taking notes as you go.

Step 2: Examine the question stem, looking for clues.

Step 3: Predict the answer and **select** the choice that matches your prediction.

In addition, you should keep in mind two important guidelines that relate especially to Inference questions.

RULE 1: *WHY* IS MORE IMPORTANT THAN *WHAT*.

When you do your first reading of the passage focusing on *why* (the purpose) instead of *what* (the details), you form an understanding of the passage as a whole. While your primary strategy for Inference questions is to read the referenced part of the passage carefully and predict, you may at times also work by process of elimination. Even though an Inference question is based on a limited part of the passage, keeping the purpose of the passage as a whole in mind as you consider each choice can often help you effectively eliminate incorrect answer choices.

RULE 2: KEEP STRAIGHT WHO SAID WHAT.

This rule is important for all four ACT Reading passage types, but it applies especially to the prose fiction passages. Because these center on characters rather than ideas, it's important to know which character is which. In your active reading of prose passages, you should expand this rule to "Keep straight who said what, who did what, and who felt what." This applies to the one or two major characters that will appear in an ACT prose passage. Putting this rule together with Rule 1 will help you keep the big picture in mind. In prose passages, minor characters may appear as details. Focus on the major characters, and worry about the minor ones only if a particular question asks you to.

• DRESS REHEARSAL: SAMPLE QUESTIONS AND DETAILED EXPLANATIONS

The passage on which the questions in this Dress Rehearsal are based is somewhat shorter than a passage you would see on Test Day.

PROSE FICTION: This passage is adapted from George Eliot's novel *The Mill on the Floss*, originally published in 1860.

It was a cold, wet January day on which Tom [Tulliver] went back to school: a day quite in keeping with this severe phase of his destiny.... "Well, Tulliver, we're glad to see you again," said Mr. Stelling heartily. "Take off your wrappings and come into the study till dinner. You'll find
(5) a bright fire there and a new companion."

Tom felt in an uncomfortable flutter as he took off his woolen comforter and other wrappings. He had seen Philip Wakem at St. Ogg's, but had always turned his eyes away from him as quickly as possible.

He would have disliked having a deformed boy for his companion
(10) even if Philip had not been the son of a bad man. And Tom did not see how a bad man's son could be very good. His own father was a good man, and he would readily have fought anyone who said the contrary.

He was in a state of mingled embarrassment and defiance as he followed Mr. Stelling to the study.

(15)   "Here is a new companion for you, to shake hands with, Tulliver,"
said that gentleman on entering the study, "Master Philip Wakem. I
shall leave you to make acquaintance by yourselves. You already know
something of each other, I imagine, for you are neighbors at home."

Tom looked confused and awkward while Philip rose and glanced at
(20) him timidly. Tom did not like to go up and put out his hand, and he was
not prepared to say, "How do you do?" on so short a notice. Mr. Stelling wisely turned away and closed the door behind him: boys' shyness
only wears off in the absence of their elders.

1. It can be inferred from lines 21–23 ("Mr. Stelling...their elders") that
    Mr. Stelling:

    A. thinks it would be wise for him to remain and listen to the boys.
    B. leaves the boys because he is in a hurry.
    C. trusts that the boys will interact more easily if he leaves them
        alone.
    D. does not like spending time with people younger than he is.

Step 1: Read. Your passage map might look something like this:

Paragraph 1: Tom returns to school.

Paragraph 2: Tom's previous knowledge of Philip

Paragraph 3: Mr. Stelling introduces Tom and Philip.

Paragraph 4: Tom's discomfort with Philip

Step 2: Examine. The words "it can be inferred from" tell us this is an
Inference question. The stem provides a line reference.

Step 3: Predict and select. Pay attention to the punctuation in the last
sentence. The colon after the words "closed the door behind him" indicates that an explanation of Mr. Stelling's behavior follows. Predict
something like *Mr. Stelling knows that the boys will remain shy in his presence.* **This lines up nicely with choice C.** Choice A is an opposite because
Mr. Stelling thinks it is wiser for him to leave the boys alone. Choice B
is out of scope of the passage. There's nothing here to suggest that Mr.
Stelling is in a hurry. Choice D is a distortion that may be tempting if
you focus too heavily on the word "elders." Though the passage indicates that Mr. Stelling is indeed older than Tom and Philip, the passage
doesn't say anything about Mr. Stelling's not enjoying younger people.

2. In the second paragraph, Tom's thoughts suggest that his attitude toward his father is:

    F. characterized by loyalty and devotion.

    G. embarrassment because of his father's belligerence.

    H. resentment that Tom cannot live up to his father's standards.

    J. gratitude that his father is sending him away to school.

Step 1: Read. You've already made your passage map!

Step 2: Examine. The word "suggest" in the question stem tells us this is an Inference question. The question stem directs us to focus on Tom's feelings about his father in Paragraph 2.

Step 3: Predict and select. Paragraph 2 is written from Tom's perspective. When the narrator writes, "his own father was a good man, and he would readily have fought anyone who said the contrary," we know that these words express Tom's opinion. Thus, we can predict something like, *Tom admired his father and was willing to fight to defend him.* **This matches nicely with choice F.** Choice G is a distortion. The "embarrassment" mentioned in the second paragraph reflects Tom's current state of mind, not his attitude toward his father. Choice C is out of scope of the passage. There is nothing to indicate that Tom feels "resentment" toward his father. Choice D is out of scope of the passage. Though Tom admires his father, there is no specific reference to "gratitude."

3. It is reasonable to conclude that Tom feels "an uncomfortable flutter" (line 6) because:

    A. the fire in the study is bright but not warm enough.

    B. he is nervous in Mr. Stelling's presence.

    C. he does not want to be in the room with Philip Wakem.

    D. he is hungry after his long journey back to school.

Step 1: Read. Done.

Step 2 : Examine. The words "it is reasonable to conclude" in the question stem tell us this is an Inference question. The question stem provides a line reference.

Step 3: Predict and select. Go to the specified sentence and look at the context. The previous paragraph gives no indication that Tom is uncomfortable with Mr. Stelling, so we can conclude that the "uncomfortable flutter" that he feels is associated with the person mentioned in the following sentence, Philip. Use your passage map note to predict something like *Tom already knows some things about Philip and doesn't like him.* **This prediction works well with choice C.** Choice A is out of scope. There is no indication that the fire is not warm enough for Tom. Choice B is an opposite. From the first paragraph, every indication is that Mr. Stelling is aiming to make Tom comfortable. The words "glad to see you," "heartily," "come into the study," and "bright fire' illustrate that Mr. Stelling is trying to create a welcoming atmosphere for Tom. Choice D is a distortion. Though "dinner" is mentioned in the first paragraph, nothing indicates that Tom is uncomfortable because is hungry.

4. From the second paragraph, it can be inferred that Philip Wakem:
   F. has few friends at St. Ogg's because of his deformity.
   G. disapproves of his father's behavior.
   H. feels shy at the prospect of conversing with Tom.
   J. is the son of a man whom Tom dislikes.

Step 1: Read. Done.

Step 2: Examine. The words "it can be inferred" indicate that this in an Inference question. Research the second paragraph, as the question stem directs, for information about Philip.

Step 3: Predict and select. Although the question stem points us to the second paragraph, there is not a lot of information there about Philip Wakem. Recall from the passage map that the paragraph describes Philip from Tom's perspective. A prediction might be, *Tom doesn't want to be friendly with Philip both because Philip is deformed and because Philip's father is not a good man.* **Choice J works well with this prediction.** Choice F is out of scope of the passage. While the passage states that Tom is not inclined to be friendly toward Philip, no information is given about how others feel about Philip. Choice G is a distortion. Tom, not Philip, disapproves of Philip's father. Choice H is a misused detail. Paragraph 4 describes Philip as timid, but the question stem asks for an inference based on Paragraph 2.

5. It is most likely that Tom looks "confused and awkward" (line 19) because:

 A. he fears Mr. Stelling's departure.

 B. he is recalling a fight he had with Philip Wakem in their home neighborhood.

 C. he uncertain how he should behave around Philip.

 D. Mr. Stelling has noticed Philip's shyness.

Step 1: Read. Done.

Step 2: Examine. The wording "it is most likely that" in the question stem is a clue that this is an Inference question. A specific line reference is provided.

Step 3: Predict and select. Use the passage map to recall that the fourth paragraph treats Tom's discomfort with Philip. Thus, we can predict that the reason Tom looks "confused and awkward" has something to do with Philip. With this prediction, we must consider choices B and C. Choice B is out of scope of the passage. While the passage mentions that Tom is not disposed to like Philip, it doesn't refer to a fight the two had had. **By process of elimination, choice C is the best answer.** Choice A is out of scope. There's nothing to suggest that Tom fears Mr. Stelling's departure from the room. Choice D is a distortion. Though Philip's shyness is alluded to in the paragraph, Mr. Stelling's observation of Philip's shyness has nothing to do with Tom's looking "confused and awkward."

• THE FINAL ACT: PRACTICE QUIZ

The first five questions here are based on a natural science passage that is shorter than the passages you'll see on Test Day. The second five questions are based on a test-length prose fiction passage. Don't forget to jot down brief headline notes as you read. A suggested passage map for each passage is provided in the Answers and Explanations section.

NATURAL SCIENCE: This passage is taken from a discussion of classification of animal species.

The order Odonata is a group of insects. In these insects, the head is large and rounded, with much of its surface covered by large, faceted eyes. The segmented thorax includes three pairs of flexible legs on

(5) on the lower surface and two pairs of wings on the upper surface. The long transparent wings move independently. The abdomen is elongated. Members of the order range in length from 1.8 to 15 centimeters. The wingspan is between 18 and 19.3 centimeters.

The order Odonata now includes two suborders. One, Epiproctor, is further broken down into the infraorder Anisoptera, also known as (10) true dragonflies. Members of the second suborder, Zygoptera, are known as damselflies. At one time, the order Odonata also included a third suborder, Anisozygoptera. This is no longer considered a suborder because it has been shown that these insects, mostly extinct, are offshoots of dragonfly evolution rather than a separate order.

(15) Damselflies are quite similar to the true dragonflies. Both are considered aquatic insects. Many adults are found near either freshwater or saltwater because eggs must be laid either directly in water or on plants near water. When the egg hatches, it produces a nymph, which later develops into an adult. The nymph stage is entirely aquatic. Odo-(20) nata in the nymph stage prey on other aquatic life, including insects, small fish, and even snails. While adults of some species remain near water, others fly away from their hatching ground, moving to open fields or hilltops. Regardless of locale, the adult feeds on smaller insects, which it is able to catch in midflight thanks to its flexible legs.

(25) The primary distinctions between damselflies and dragonflies relate to the wings. In damselflies, the hindwing is similar to the forewing while in dragonflies the hindwing is broader at the base. In addition, damselflies and dragonflies differ in the position of the wings at rest. While most dragonflies hold the wings open horizon-(30) tally when not flying, most damsel flies rest with the wings held together along the long axis of the body. Damselflies tend to be weaker fliers than dragonflies. One other difference between the two is that the eyes of most damselflies are separated whereas the eyes of most dragonflies touch.

1. The description of the suborders of Odonata in lines 8–12 implies that:

    A. damsel flies and dragonflies are so similar that it is difficult to tell them apart by looking at them.

    B. classification of insects may change to reflect new scientific understandings.

    C. all members of the suborder Anisozygoptera are now extinct.

    D. historically, the order Odonata included two suborders.

2. The information in lines 21–25 suggests that a variation among different species of the Odonata order is that:

    F. the wings have a different texture.

    G. some adults are able to survive at a distance from where they hatched.

    H. in some Odonata species, the nymphs remain in water while in others, the nymphs can survive in trees.

    J. some species have faceted eyes while others do not.

3. Lines 28–32 imply that a dragonfly in a stationary position:

    A. sacrifices some of the flexibility of its legs.

    B. is likely to look similar to a damselfly at rest.

    C. usually holds the wings open horizontally.

    D. usually holds the wings closed along the body's lengthwise axis.

4. The description in lines 1–3 suggest that, in insects of the Odonata order, the head:

    F. has very little space not taken up by the eyes.

    G. almost always bears antennae.

    H. may be very close to the forewing.

    J. is elongated when compared with the hindwing.

5. Which of the following statements may be inferred regarding the feeding habits of damselflies and dragonflies?

    A. The larger hindwing of the dragonfly makes it a more capable predator than the damselfly.

    B. Only damselflies eat snails while dragonflies eat snails and insects.

    C. Both the damselfly and the dragonfly have the ability to capture food while moving.

    D. All adult damselflies and dragonflies remain near water to prey on aquatic life.

PROSE FICTION: The following passage is adapted from Charlotte Bronte's *Jane Eyre,* published in 1847.

The more I knew of the inmates of Moor House, the better I liked them. In a few days I had so far recovered my health that I could sit up all day, and walk out sometimes. I could join with Diana and Mary in all their occupations, converse with them as much as they wished, and
(5) aid them when and where they would allow me. There was a reviving pleasure in this intercourse, of a kind now tasted by me for the first time—the pleasure arising from perfect congeniality of tastes, sentiments, and principles.

I liked to read what they liked to read: what they enjoyed, delighted
(10) me; what they approved, I reverenced. They loved their sequestered home. I, too, in the grey, small, antique structure, with its low roof, its latticed casements, its mouldering walls, its avenue of aged firs—all grown aslant under the stress of mountain winds; its garden, dark with yew and holly—and where no flowers but of the hardiest species
(15) would bloom—found a charm both potent and permanent....

They were both more accomplished and better read than I was, but with eagerness I followed in the path of knowledge they had trodden before me. I devoured the books they lent me; then it was full satisfaction to discuss with them in the evening what I had perused
(20) during the day. Thought fitted thought; opinion met opinion: we coincided, in short, perfectly.

If in our trio there was a superior and a leader, it was Diana. Physically, she far excelled me: she was handsome; she was vigorous. In her animal spirits there was an affluence of life and certainty
(25) of flow, such as excited my wonder, while it baffled my comprehension. I could talk a while when the evening commenced, but with the first gush of vivacity and fluency gone, I was fain to sit on a stool at Diana's feet, to rest my head on her knee, and listen alternately to her and Mary, while they sounded thoroughly the
(30) topic on which I had but touched. Diana offered to teach me German. I liked to learn of her: I saw the part of instructress pleased and suited her; that of scholar pleased and suited me no less. Our natures dovetailed: mutual affection—of the strongest kind—was the result. They discovered I could draw: their pencils and color-boxes were imme-
(35) diately at my service. My skill, greater in this one point than theirs, surprised and charmed them. Mary would sit and watch me by the hour together. Then she would take lessons, and a docile, intelligent,

assiduous pupil she made. Thus occupied, and mutually entertained, days passed like hours, and weeks like days.

(40)   As to Mr. St. John, the intimacy which had arisen so naturally and rapidly between me and his sisters did not extend to him. One reason of the distance yet observed between us was that he was comparatively seldom at home. A large proportion of his time appeared devoted to visiting the sick and poor among the scattered population of his parish.

6. It can be inferred from the narrator's description of Diana's "animal spirits" (line 24) that:

    F. Diana's wildness makes her difficult to get along with at times.

    G. this temperament adds to the narrator's understanding of Diana.

    H. Diana's exuberance reminds the narrator of a wild horse.

    J. this aspect of Diana's personality fascinates the narrator.

7. In lines 5–8 ("There was a reviving pleasure...and principles"), the narrator suggests that:

    A. the congenial socializing she enjoys with Diana and Mary reminds her of her relationship with her sisters.

    B. her enjoyment of Diana and Mary arises from her hosts' professional activities.

    C. she has never before experienced the comfort and understanding that Diana and Mary offer her.

    D. close relationships can be formed only by sharing tastes, feelings, and beliefs.

8. The pleasure the narrator feels when Diana "offered to teach me German" (line 30) suggests that:

    F. the narrator is comfortable in the role of Diana's student.

    G. Diana is on leave from her job as a teacher while the narrator is visiting.

    H. Mary has never studied German.

    J. Diana is the most intelligent of the three women.

9. In lines 36–37 ("Mary would sit and watch me by the hour"), Mary's patience with watching the narrator draw most likely indicates that:

   A. Mary herself has never been able to draw.
   B. the narrator's drawing ability is shocking to Diana and Mary.
   C. Mary is interested in improving her drawing skills.
   D. Mary is surprised by the colors the narrator chooses.

10. In lines 18–20 ("I devoured...during the day."), it can be inferred that the books Diana and Mary loan to the narrator:

    F. challenge the narrator's long-held beliefs.
    G. strengthen the bond between the narrator and her hosts.
    H. fail to generate any fully satisfying discussions.
    J. cause the narrator to feel inferior to the other two women.

● THE FINAL ACT: ANSWERS AND EXPLANATIONS FOR INFERENCE QUESTIONS

Here is a suggested passage map for the Natural Science passage:

Paragraph 1: Describes physical appearance of Odonata insects

Paragraph 2: Subcategories of Odonata

Paragraph 3: Similarities between damselflies and dragonflies

Paragraph 4: Differences between damselflies and dragonflies

1. B. This choice reflects an appropriate conclusion that can be drawn from lines 8–12. Choice A is a misused detail. These differences are addressed in Paragraph 4, not Paragraph 2. Choice C is extreme in its use of "all." (Line 13 says "mostly extinct.") Choice D is an opposite. (The order historically included three, not two, suborders.)

2. G. Focus on the sentence in lines 21–23 "While some...others" to locate differences. Choice G paraphrases this sentence. Choice F is out of scope. Choice H is an opposite ("The nymph stage is entirely aquatic.") Choice J is a misused detail. (Eyes are mentioned in Paragraph 1.)

3. C. Predict, *dragonflies at rest hold wings open horizontally*. Choice A is a misused detail. Leg flexibility is not mentioned in this paragraph. Choice B is an opposite. Choice D is an opposite (this statement describes damselflies, not dragonflies).

4. F. Predict, *the surface of the head is covered mostly by eyes.* Choice G is out of scope (antennae aren't mentioned here). Choice H is a misused detail because the "forewing" isn't mentioned in Paragraph 1. Choice J is a distortion. The abdomen, not the head, is described as "elongated."

5. C. Only Paragraph 3 discusses the feeding habits of dragonflies and damselflies. From lines 23–25, predict, *both can catch food in flight.* Choice A is a distortion. Choice B is an opposite (both eat snails at the nymph stage). Choice D is extreme because of the word "all."

Here is a suggested passage map for the Prose Fiction passage:

Paragraph 1: Narrator's relationship with hosts Diana and Mary: positive, appreciative

Paragraph 2: Common interest in reading; description of house

Paragraph 3: Narrator learns from hosts.

Paragraph 4: Dominance of Diana's personality; activities the three engaged in

Paragraph 5: Contrast between narrator's relationship w/the women & their brother, St. John

6. J. Choice F is out of scope (the passage never says Diana is hard to get along with). Choice G is an opposite (notice lines 25–26, "baffled my comprehension"). Choice H is out of scope of the passage. Nothing in the passage suggests that Diana "reminds the narrator of a wild horse."

7. C. Choice A is out of scope of the passage (it never says the narrator has sisters). Choice B is a distortion of the word "occupation." Choice D is an extreme because it uses the word "only."

8. F. This is justified by lines 31–32 ("the part...of scholar...pleased me.") Choice G is out of scope (there is no indication that Diana has been employed as a teacher). Choice H is an extreme and an out-of-scope trap (that Diana teaches the narrator German does not necessarily indicate that Mary has *never* studied German). Choice J uses an extreme word, "most," that is not justified by the passage. Though Diana is described as "superior" (line 22) in some ways, nothing in the passage suggests that she is the "most intelligent."

9. C. The sentence describing Mary watching the narrator draw concludes with the statement that Mary also took lessons and was a hardworking ("assiduous") student. Choice A is an extreme (it uses the word "never"). Choice B is an extreme (that the narrator's drawing skill "surprises" her hosts doesn't necessarily imply that it is "shocking"). Choice D inappropriately combines and distorts two details—the "surprise" and the art materials—in this paragraph.

10. G. This is justified by "devoured the books they lent me" (line 18) and "full satisfaction to discuss" and "we coincided perfectly" (lines 18–21). Choice F is out of scope (there is no mention of "the narrator's long-held beliefs"). Choice H is an opposite. Choice J is a distortion (the narrator recognizes Diana as "superior" to both herself and Mary).

Generalization Questions

DIFFICULTY: ★ ★ ★

FREQUENCY: ★ ★

SURPRISE FACTOR: ★

INTRODUCTION TO GENERALIZATION QUESTIONS

Generalization questions are similar to Inference questions. Like Inference questions, they require you to draw a conclusion based on the author's statements. The difference lies in how much of the passage you need to consider. Whereas Inference questions refer to a smaller part of the passage, such as a particular phrase, Generalization questions ask about broad themes in the passage. A Generalization question may ask about the purpose of the whole passage or the purpose of a specific paragraph. Your active reading skills and passage map notes are crucial in selecting the best answer.

Characteristics of Generalization Questions

Generalization questions use the same language as Inference questions. The difference is that the question stem of a Generalization question directs you to take a broader focus It usually doesn't include a reference to a localized part of the passage. Instead, the wording in the stem references a larger part of the passage, such as a particular paragraph or simply "the passage." Here are some examples of phrasings you might see in a Generalization question stem:

- The passage **suggests**…
- The **main idea** of the passage is…

- **It may be inferred from the passage** that the author...
- A **view shared** by all the scholars mentioned in the passage is...
- The **main purpose of the passage** can best be described as...
- The first paragraph **suggests**...
- The information in the second and third paragraphs **implies** that...
- The **assumption underlying the argument** in lines 28–45 is...

Most Common Types of Generalization Questions

As you can tell from the phrasings above, the big difference among Generalization questions is that some test your understanding of the passage as a whole while others test your understanding of a specific paragraph or set of paragraphs. You can think of the first type as a **global question.** As their name suggests, global questions must be answered based on your big-picture understanding of the passage. The first five question stems listed in the Characteristics section above illustrate wordings used in global questions.

The second group of question stems listed above is associated with the second type of Generalization question. You can think of this type as the **local generalization question.** This question type is based on a segment of the passage, such as a paragraph or two, but is not based on a minute part of the passage, such as a phrase or a single sentence, as the Inference question would be.

If keeping track of the distinctions among Inference questions and two types of Generalization questions seems too tedious to think about, don't worry. Remember, on Test Day, you score points for answering questions correctly, not for being able to discriminate subtle differences in question types. The bottom line is that you need to read the question stem carefully to determine how much of the passage to consider as you draw your inference. If a question stem refers only to *the passage,* the answer must be based on the passage as a whole, not on a single paragraph. If a question stem asks about the *second and third paragraphs,* you may need to combine information from both paragraphs in your answer.

• THE TRAP DOOR: STEERING CLEAR OF ANSWER TRAPS

Reading the question stem carefully and making a prediction based on your passage map or the part of the passage referred to in the question stem will help you avoid the answer traps for Generalization questions.

Types of Generalization Question Answer Traps

The most common type of Generalization trap is the out-of-scope answer choice. For global questions (The primary purpose of the passage is...), out-of-scope answers are likely to introduce material that isn't addressed in the passage or to describe the purpose too broadly. For example, if the purpose of a passage is to describe American voting habits, an answer choice that says "to describe the various ways Americans engage in civic participation" is too broad. Global questions usually include at least one answer choice that is too narrow in scope. For example, an answer choice that adequately describes the purpose of a single paragraph in the passage can never be the correct answer to a global question, because the answer to a global question must be based on the entire passage. For global questions, focus on broad themes.

The answer choices for local generalization questions also include **out-of-scope** trap answers. In addition, **distortions** and **misused details** appear frequently and are often tempting choices. For local generalization questions, you'll probably need to go back to the passage to research your prediction. **Check the question stem carefully to make sure you're focusing on the right part of the text to make your prediction.**

For both global and local generalization questions, you can expect to find the **opposite** answer trap. Remember that an opposite answer choice is tempting because part of its phrasing refers to something that is indeed in the passage. However, with an opposite, the answer is turned around so that the statement is not true.

Techniques for Avoiding Generalization Question Answer Traps

Your best defense against these answer traps is to keep the big picture in mind on your first reading. Remember to practice active reading! Read through enough of each paragraph to get a rough sense of what it's about and jot down your understanding in the passage map. Sometimes, your passage map notes alone will be enough to let you make an effective prediction for a global or local generalization question. Be ready, however, to research the text of the passage if necessary.

For global questions, the answer choices will always include some out-of-scope traps. You can avoid these traps by considering each answer choice in light of your big-picture understanding of the passage. Remember, global generalization questions don't refer to a specific part of the passage. Rather they refer to the passage as a whole. Suppose you read a passage that describes how Beethoven composed his symphonies in general. Suppose this passage includes one detailed paragraph about the composition of the Fifth Symphony. Here's a global question you might see:

1. The main purpose of this passage is to:

   A. describe the composing process Beethoven used for the Fifth Symphony.

   B. discuss the way modern orchestras perform Beethoven's symphonies.

   C. outline the history of the Romantic period in music.

   D. explain how Beethoven composed his symphonies.

Choice A is out of scope because it's too narrow. If only one paragraph is concerned with the Fifth Symphony, then this can't be the right answer for a global question. Choice C is also out of scope but because it is too broad. Though the passage mentions that Beethoven was a Romantic composer, the purpose of the passage is not to discuss Romantic composers in general. Choice B is out of scope because modern orchestras have nothing to do with Beethoven's composing process. Only choice D is both general enough and specific enough to be appropriate.

● PERFORMANCE TECHNIQUES: KEY GUIDELINES

The simple act of making your passage map will usually give you a good understanding of the passage's big picture. Remember to do your first reading of the passage following the principle that *why* is **more important than** *what*. This guideline is meant to help you avoid getting bogged down in details as you read, and it's particularly helpful when answering global questions. Also, don't forget that the short introduction to the passage sometimes offers a clue about the purpose and main idea of the passage. In the case of the sample passage below, the introductory blurb doesn't give you the main idea but does provide context that will help you understand the passage. You can't always count on this introductory blurb to be helpful, but just in case, skim it quickly before you start the passage.

For local generalization questions, remember that **the answer is in the passage.** While it's true that for some Generalization questions, simply reviewing your passage map and working with your big-picture understanding of the passage will help you get to the right answer choice, you may sometimes need to research the passage itself to check on a detail.

● DRESS REHEARSAL: SAMPLE QUESTIONS AND DETAILED EXPLANATIONS

All five questions in this Dress Rehearsal are based on the following passage:

PROSE FICTION: This passage is adapted from the novel *Pride and Prejudice* by Jane Austin, published in 1813. The passage begins with a description of Elizabeth's reaction to a letter from her sister Jane.

This letter gave Elizabeth some pain, but her spirits returned as she considered that Jane would no longer be duped. All expectation from Mr. Bingley was now absolutely over. She would not even wish for a
(5) renewal of his attentions. His character sunk on every review of it. As a punishment for him, as well as a possible advantage to Jane, Elizabeth seriously hoped he might really soon marry Mr. Darcy's sister, as by Wickham's account, she would make him abundantly regret what he had thrown away.

(10)   Mrs. Gardiner about this time reminded Elizabeth of her promise concerning Mr. Wickham, and required information. Elizabeth had such to send as might rather give contentment to her aunt than to herself. Mr. Wickham's apparent partiality had subsided, his attentions were over, he was the admirer of someone else. Elizabeth was
(15) watchful enough to see it all, but she could see it and write of it without material pain. Her heart had been but slightly touched, and her vanity was satisfied with believing that she would have been his only choice, had fortune permitted it. The sudden acquisition of ten thousand pounds was the most remarkable charm of the young lady

(20) to whom he was now rendering himself agreeable, but Elizabeth did not quarrel with him for his wish of independence. Nothing, on the contrary, could be more natural, and while able to suppose that it cost him a few struggles to relinquish her, she was ready to allow it a wise and desirable measure for both, and could very sincerely wish him happy.

(25) All this was acknowledged to Mrs. Gardiner, and after relating the circumstances, Elizabeth thus went on, "I am now convinced, my dear aunt, that I have never been much in love, for had I really experienced that pure and elevating passion, I should at present detest his very name, and wish him all manner of evil. However, my feelings are not

(30) only cordial towards *him,* they are even impartial towards *her.* I cannot find that I hate her at all, or that I am in the least unwilling to think her a very good sort of girl. There can be no love in all this. My watchfulness has been effectual, and though I certainly should be a more interesting object to all my acquaintances were I distractedly in love with him, I

(35) cannot say that I regret my comparative insignificance. Importance may sometimes be purchased too dearly. My sisters take his defection much more to heart than I do. They are young in the ways of the world and not yet open to the conviction that handsome young men must have something to live on as well as the plain."

1. The third paragraph suggests that Elizabeth:

   A. is angry at the woman who has replaced her as Mr. Wickham's romantic interest.

   B. is having second thoughts about whether she had been in love with Mr. Wickham.

   C. agrees with her sisters in being upset about Mr. Wickham's change of heart.

   D. is angry with Mr. Bingley for not returning her sister's interest.

Step 1: Read. Your passage map should look something like this:

Paragraph 1: Elizabeth is disappointed that Mr. Bingley is not interested in Jane; Elizabeth hopes he will marry Mr. Darcy's sister and regret not marrying Jane.

Paragraph 2: Elizabeth has learned that Mr. Wickham is not interested in her; she understands it is only because she is not rich enough, but she doesn't hold this against him.

Paragraph 3: After explaining the situation to her aunt, Mrs. Gardiner, Elizabeth decides that she must not really have been in love with Mr. Wickham.

Step 2: Examine. The word "suggests" and the paragraph reference indicate that this is a local generalization question.

Step 3: Predict and select. Start with your passage map. It's likely you noted that *Elizabeth now doubts whether she had truly loved Wickham.* This works as a prediction and **nicely matches choice B.** Choice A is an opposite because Elizabeth describes her feeling toward her replacement as "I cannot find that I hate her at all" and says she finds her "a very good sort of girl." Choice C is also an opposite. Elizabeth states she is not upset about Mr. Wickham's rejection of her. Choice D is a misused detail. It contains a true statement, but the detail comes from the first paragraph and so does not address this question, which asks for an answer based on the third paragraph.

2. An attitude expressed in the first paragraph is:

    F. Elizabeth's understanding of Mr. Wickham's decision.

    G. Jane's anger at Mr. Bingley for rejecting her.

    H. Elizabeth's sisterly concern for Jane's feelings.

    J. Elizabeth's hope that Mr. Wickham will eventually be interested in Jane again.

Step 1: Read. Your passage map is done.

Step 2: Examine. The question stem directs you to a specific paragraph but asks a general question, so this is a local generalization question.

Step 3: Predict and select. The passage map is a good place to start in making your prediction. The purpose of the paragraph is *to convey Elizabeth's reaction to the news that Mr. Bingley has rejected Jane.* **Choice H accurately describes Elizabeth's reaction.** Refer to the passage if necessary to eliminate wrong answer choices. Choice F is a misused detail. This detail is included in Paragraph 3, not Paragraph 1. Choice G is a distortion. Paragraph 1 describes Elizabeth's reaction, not Jane's reaction. Choice J is an opposite. Paragraph 1 states that Elizabeth hopes that Wickham will marry someone else and regret his rejection of Jane. Thus, choice H is the best answer here.

3. The second paragraph suggests that Mr. Wickham's "wish of independence" (line 20) refers to:

    A. his desire not to be tied down by marriage.

    B. his inclination to avoid controlling women.

    C. the need to ensure financial comfort by choosing a wife who has money.

    D. the fear that Elizabeth would not allow him the freedom he craves.

Step 1: Read. Done.

Step 2: Examine. The question stem refers to a specific phrase but indicates that its meaning should be inferred from the context of the whole paragraph. This is a local generalization question.

Step 3: Predict and select. You must refer to your passage map or to the passage itself here. Remember, the answer is in the passage, so you can't answer this question based on what *you* think the word "independence" means. You may have noted in your passage map that Wickham's rejection of Elizabeth is based on financial concerns. If this in not included in your passage map for Paragraph 2, refer to lines 16–17, which conveys Elizabeth's belief that she herself "would have been his only choice, had fortune [chance] permitted it." In addition, lines 17–18 indicate that Wickham's attraction to Elizabeth's replacement is based primarily on the new woman's financial situation, her "sudden acquisition of ten thousand pounds." Putting this information together, you can identify **choice C as the best answer.** Choices A, B, and D are all out of scope; none of these reasons is mentioned in or justified by the passage.

4. The passage implies that Mrs. Gardiner:

    F. is a significant presence in Elizabeth's life.

    G. harshly judges Mr. Bingley for rejecting Jane.

    H. is absolutely convinced that Mr. Wickham would not have made a good husband for Elizabeth.

    J. maintains a detached attitude toward Elizabeth's life.

Step 1: Read. Done.

Step 2: Examine. The word "implies" and the general reference to "the passage" indicate that this is a global generalization question.

Step 3: Predict and select. You may have to skim the passage looking for references to "Mrs. Gardiner." Mrs. Gardiner, Elizabeth's aunt, is mentioned in Paragraphs 2 and 3. Lines 9–10 state that Mrs. Gardiner "reminded Elizabeth of her promise concerning Mr. Wickham, and required information." In addition, most of Paragraph 3 is Elizabeth's commentary about her situation addressed to Mrs. Gardner. Synthesizing the information in Paragraphs 2 and 3, you can infer that *Mrs. Gardiner cares about Elizabeth and is involved in her life, and Elizabeth communicates readily with her aunt.* **This prediction works well with choice F.** Choice G is out of scope; the passage doesn't describe Mrs. Gardiner's opinion of Jane's situation with Mr. Bingley. Choice H is an extreme because of the word "absolutely." Choice J is an opposite. Mrs. Gardiner is anything but detached.

5. Based on the passage, Elizabeth's attitude toward her circumstances appears to be one of:

   A. marked resentment that her financial situation limits her prospects for marriage.

   B. keen longing to increase her social standing.

   C. relative acceptance of her situation and the constraints it imposes on her.

   D. outright rebellion against a social structure in which money can be more important than love.

Step 1: Read. Done.

Step 2: Examine. The words "based on the passage" in the question stem tell you that this is a global generalization question. Look for a broad theme and keep the big picture in mind.

Step 3: Predict and select. Your overall understanding of the passage may lead you to predict that Elizabeth is fairly accepting of her circumstances. If you're not sure, work through the answer choices eliminating traps. Choice A is an opposite. Elizabeth does not show resentment. Though she understands that her financial situation is not strong enough for Mr. Wickham to want to marry her, she is accepting of her circumstances and does not hold Wickham's decision against him. Choice B is out of scope. Nothing in the passage suggests that Elizabeth wishes to elevate her position in society. **Choice C works well and is the best choice.** Choice D is out of scope. Recall that the question asks about Elizabeth's attitude toward her situation, and nothing in the passage indicates that she wants to rebel.

● THE FINAL ACT: PRACTICE QUIZ

HUMANITIES: The following passage is taken from a collection of essays about the future of the arts in America.

In recent years, a number of professional musicians and cultural critics have expressed growing concern about the future of the symphony orchestra. Public interest is waning, and, moreover, when orchestras do attract an audience, it is likely to be made up of senior
(5) citizens. Young people, according to these doomsayers, are more interested in downloading pop music than in playing or listening to symphonic music. Norman Lebrecht, music critic and author of *Who Killed Classical Music?*, points also to the competitive economic climate and the poor management of symphony orchestras as another
(10) reason to be pessimistic about the orchestra's prospects.

These gloomy prophets fail to notice signs that are encouraging. Advances in technology, far from pushing listeners away from symphonic music, have actually opened new vistas. Whereas orchestral music was, not many generations ago, primarily known and valued
(15) by the upper middle classes, the availability and popularity of movie soundtracks on compact disc has in fact expanded the audience for orchestral music. Now at outdoor performances at city parks, multitudes of children gather enthusiastically to hear orchestras play music from the *Star Wars* and *Harry Potter* movies.

(20) Another factor pointing to an optimistic outlook for classical music is a spate of recent research that indicates that music education, including lessons in performance as well as classes in music appreciation, has a profoundly positive effect on young people's academic performance. While Don Campbell's book *The Mozart Effect*
(25) extols the benefits of classical music for the health of body, mind, and soul, educational researchers have conducted studies that show strong correlations between musical training and high standardized test scores. Even parents of very young children, some still in the womb, have taken to using classical music to create educational
(30) advantages for their children. Recordings with titles such as *Beethoven to Build Baby's Brain* have joined phonics books and early math games on the shelves of parents who want the best for their children.

With the booming interest in orchestral music's role in blockbuster movies, its potential to add to psychological and perhaps even physical (35) health, and its role in promoting brain development and improving academic performance, it is ridiculous to think that classical music is dead. The fact is that people are more interested in classical and symphonic music than ever. Indeed, it may be argued that classical music today appeals to an even wider variety of people than it did in the past.

(40)   It is true that not everyone who is interested in classical music is a regular patron of symphony orchestra concerts. However, nearly every urban orchestra in America has some kind of educational outreach program, encouraging people who might not otherwise attend a symphony concert to do so. Once a new listener arrives in the concert hall, (45) the magic begins. The energy and the immediacy of the live concert can be matched by nothing else. Even today, when the avenues for taking in recorded music are wider than ever, sitting quietly in a darkened auditorium as the orchestra plays is still a vital experience. It is precisely because humans need the sense of immediacy and living in (50) the moment that I can confidently assert that classical music and the symphony orchestra are not dead.

1. The primary purpose of this passage is to:

    A. argue against the view that classical music is dead.

    B. describe the research about the correlations between music and academic performance.

    C. summarize recent writings about classical music.

    D. provide evidence that the symphony orchestra has a dreary future.

2. The passage suggests that:

    F. studying music always leads to improved academic performance.

    G. the outlook for classical music in the future is gloomy.

    H. there is some disagreement among cultural commentators about the state of classical music.

    J. the audience for classical music is made up primarily of older people.

3. The main purpose of the first paragraph is to:

   A. express the author's belief that classical music is dead.
   B. introduce a point of view that the author will later refute.
   C. indicate that downloading popular music is a major pastime of young people.
   D. state that financial concerns will be the downfall of the symphony orchestra.

4. The author most likely views classical recordings for infants and young children as:

   F. a harmful influence pushed onto children by overly ambitious parents.
   G. an indication that many people value classical music.
   H. a watering down of musical sophistication that Norman Lebrecht would disapprove of.
   J. absolutely crucial for their later academic success.

5. The author believes that outreach and education programs offered by symphony orchestras:

   A. can do little to spur society's waning interest in classical music performance.
   B. do not go far enough in trying to reach a wide audience.
   C. have the potential to increase interest in classical music by offering new concert goers a meaningful experience.
   D. would be more effective if they attempted to draw in very young children and their parents.

6. The passage suggests that technology affects interest in orchestral music by:

   F. overwhelming listeners with too many choices.
   G. reducing interest in orchestral music by making other types of music more accessible.
   H. creating an unhealthy competition between recorded music and live music.
   J. broadening the kinds of orchestral music available to listeners beyond the traditional symphonic works.

7. The primary purpose of the second paragraph is to:

   A. introduce several reasons for the author's belief that classical music is not dead.

   B. express the author's agreement with "gloomy prophets" such as Norman Lebrecht.

   C. provide evidence that music education is beneficial for students.

   D. indicate that many young people enjoy the orchestral music from *Star Wars*.

8. The third paragraph suggests that:

   F. the author has experienced health benefits from listening to the music of Mozart.

   G. *The Mozart Effect* is an example of new ways that classical music is being valued.

   H. Don Campbell is single-handedly responsible for promoting a resurgence of interest in Mozart's music.

   J. students will perform better on standardized tests if they listen to Mozart the night before a test.

9. A central assumption underlying this passage is that:

   A. infants and children who are not exposed to classical music at a young age are deprived.

   B. economic reality is the bottom line regarding the future of the symphony orchestra.

   C. the increasing awareness of music's effect on listeners is likely to strengthen rather than weaken the symphony orchestra.

   D. the doomsayers mentioned in the first paragraph should support more comprehensive music education in schools.

10. The author of this passage would most likely support:

   F. further research into the value of various educational products for preschoolers.

   G. attempts by orchestra managers to limit their marketing efforts to those who have been adequately trained to appreciate classical music.

   H. policies in schools that ban the use of personal music players.

   J. increased outreach efforts to bring live orchestra concerts to those who haven't previously attended the symphony.

● THE FINAL ACT: ANSWERS AND EXPLANATIONS FOR GENERALIZATION QUESTIONS

Suggested passage map notes:

Paragraph 1: Views of critics who think classical music is dead

Paragraph 2: Author's belief that orchestral music is alive and well

Paragraph 3: Evidence for optimistic outlook: awareness that classical music is beneficial in several ways

Paragraph 4: Classical music appeals to more people than ever.

Paragraph 5: Urban orchestra outreach promotes vital experience of symphony attendance.

1. A. Passage map notes for Paragraphs 1 and 2 indicate that *the author is refuting the view that interest in classical music is declining.* Indeed, this is the purpose of the passage, as the last sentence of the passage states. The prediction matches choice A. Choice B is a misused detail. Choice C is out of scope (too broad). Choice D is an opposite.

2. H. This question is so broad that it's hard to make a prediction. Use your passage map and your understanding of the big picture to help you eliminate answers. Choice F is an extreme because it uses the word "always." Choice G is contradicted by Paragraph 2. Choice H is nicely sums up the main idea of the passage, so it works well. Choice J is contradicted by Paragraph 4.

3. B. Read the first paragraph carefully to make a prediction. Note that the ideas in this paragraph are attributed to "a number of professional musicians and cultural critics and to the writer Norman Lebrecht." The author of the passage is describing the opinions of others here, not stating her own. The first sentence of Paragraph 2 is the first time the author reveals her own opinion. Thus, you can predict that in the first paragraph the author *describes a view she disagrees with.* This prediction matches choice B. Choice A is an opposite. Choice C is a misused detail because it's not mentioned in the first paragraph. Choice D is distortion of the detail "competitive economic climate" in the first paragraph.

4. G. Research in Paragraph 3 to predict, keeping the purpose of the paragraph in mind. The detail about parents using classical music to create an educational advantage for young children appears in the context of the author's argument in favor of "an optimistic outlook for classical music," so the author must view recordings for young children as a good thing. This prediction leads to choice G. Choices F and H are out of scope. Choice J is extreme ("absolutely").

5. C. Your passage map sends you to Paragraph 5 to research this question. Predict something like, *the author views urban orchestras' educational outreach programs in a positive light and believes they're effective in generating interest in classical music.* Choice C fits well with this prediction. Choices A and B are opposites, and choice D is out of scope.

6. J. Research in Paragraph 2 to predict, *the author believes that technology has spurred wider interest than ever in orchestral music.* This prediction points to choice J. Choices F, G, and H are out of scope, introducing details that aren't mentioned in the passage.

7. A. Your passage map should help you predict something along the lines of *the second paragraph asserts the author's view that interest in orchestral music is not declining.* Choice B is an opposite. Choice C is a misused detail. While Paragraph 3 mentions music's benefits for students, this detail doesn't answer the question about Paragraph 2. Choice D can be considered out of scope, because it's too narrow. Paragraph 2 does mention children enjoying the music from *Star Wars,* but this is a detail that supports the purpose of the paragraph, not a description of the paragraph's purpose.

8. G. Use your passage map: The paragraph *describes new reasons people are valuing music, especially classical music.* Choice G is a good match. Choice F is a distortion. Although *The Mozart Effect* discusses health benefits, the author of the passage doesn't claim to have personally experienced them. Choice H is an extreme ("single-handedly"). Choice J is a distortion. While the paragraph does mention "standardized tests," it doesn't say anything about what students should do the night before taking them.

9. C. For a question as general as this, it's tough to predict. Instead, keep in mind the overall purpose of the passage (describing ways in which classical music is flourishing) and work through the answer choices using elimination. Choice A is out of scope. Deprivation is not mentioned in the passage, and the well-being of children is not the focus of the passage. Choice B is a distortion. In Paragraph 1, the author refers to Lebrecht's concern with the financial management of orchestras, but this issue isn't central to the passage. Choice C fits well with the purpose of the passage. Choice D is out of scope. Though "doomsayers" and "music education" are both mentioned in the passage, the author doesn't link the two.

10. J. Again, it's difficult to predict for this question, so use elimination. Choice F is out of scope because the passage focuses on music, not preschool education. Choice G is an opposite. The author suggests that orchestras should try to attract listeners who may have limited experience of orchestral music. Choice H is out of scope. The author doesn't state or even suggest that personal music players should be banned in schools. Choice J is justified by Paragraph 5, in which the author suggests that a "new listener" is easily convinced that a "live concert" offers a "vital experience."

Function Questions

DIFFICULTY: ★ ★

FREQUENCY: ★ ★

SURPRISE FACTOR: ★

● INTRODUCTION TO FUNCTION QUESTIONS

Function questions ask about how a specific part of the passage, such as a phrase or paragraph, works ("functions") in the context of the passage. Because the question stem directs you to a specific part of the passage, you always know exactly where you should look to make your prediction. You can find the answer to a Function question in the text surrounding the part of the passage referred to in the question stem. For example, to answer a Function question asking about a specific phrase, you need to read the sentence containing that phrase and maybe a sentence before or after it. On the other hand, a Function question that asks about the purpose of a specific paragraph requires you to take a big-picture view. You need to think about the passage as a whole to determine the function of the given paragraph.

Characteristics of Function Questions

Function questions are easy to recognize because of the wording they use. Here are some phrasings you might see in Function question stems:

- In Lines 14–18, the author describes Newton's education **in order to...**
- The phrase "even though some data had been falsified" **serves to...**
- The fourth paragraph **serves to...**

- The author **uses** quotation marks around the word "original" **in order to**...
- The description of Serkin's performing career in Lines 24–28 **functions as**...

Most Common Types of Function Questions

All Function questions demand that you think about the author's purpose in writing certain parts of the passage. Function questions differ only in which aspect of the writing they ask about. A Function question can ask about

- why the author uses a specific word or phrase;
- why the author uses specific punctuation marks, either quotation marks or question marks;
- how a given sentence works in the paragraph; or
- how a given paragraph works in the overall structure of the passage.

The first type of Function question, which asks about word choice or phrasing, tends to appear more frequently than others on the ACT.

● THE TRAP DOOR: STEERING CLEAR OF ANSWER TRAPS

Any of the answer traps described in the Reading Basics section may be associated with Function questions. However, several appear more frequently with Function questions.

Types of Function Question Answer Traps

The traps that the test maker uses most frequently with Function questions are misused details, distortions, and out-of-scope answers. The out-of-scope trap is particularly tempting because the question stem of a Function question always includes a clue about much of the passage to consider when you answer the question. For example, a question that asks about the purpose of the third paragraph may include out-of-scope traps that describe the purpose of a paragraph other than the third paragraph.

Techniques for Avoiding Function Question Answer Traps

Two techniques that will help you steer clear of Function question answer traps are to **read the question stem carefully** and **always research before making your prediction**. Function questions are particularly dependent on context. If you want to determine how or why a writer uses a particular detail, don't answer from memory! Instead, go back to the part of the passage where it's used and determine what the author is trying to do in that specific part of the passage. If the Function question asks about how a phrase is used, look at that phrase in the context of the sentence it appears in. Remember, sometimes you have to refer to the context a little before and after the line number references that a Function question stem provides. To answer a question about how a phrase functions, you may need to be familiar with the context of whole paragraph that surrounds it.

To answer a question about how a paragraph functions within the passage, you need to have a good sense of the overall structure and purpose of the passage. (Remember, this is one of the reasons you make a passage map!) For a question asking about a paragraph, your passage map alone is probably all you need; if your passage map is good, you won't need to spend time delving into the text of the passage.

● PERFORMANCE TECHNIQUES: KEY RULES

Rule 1: Pay attention to context. Direct your attention to the specific part of the passage the question asks about. The great thing about Function questions is that the question stem lets you know how much context is important, and it gives you line or paragraph numbers that let you research quickly. Function questions are challenging if you don't recognize what they're asking or if you don't take the time to go back to your passage map or the text itself to predict. With practice, however, you should become very comfortable with Function questions.

Rule 2: Be ready to adapt your prediction. Your prediction may not exactly match an answer choice. Some Function questions have answer choices that are worded abstractly instead of concretely. After making your prediction and moving on to read the answer choices, you may find that your prediction—even though it's a good one—doesn't appear to correspond to any of the answer choices. When this occurs, it's usually because your prediction is expressed in concrete language—as it should be, because you base it on words in the passage. However, the answer choices might be phrased in a more generalized, abstract way.

For example, suppose a passage gives a brief overview of the works of the painter El Greco. Let's say Paragraph 2 discusses the sources of the artist's inspiration, while Paragraphs 3, 4, and 5 address the use of color that El Greco is famous for. A Function question about this passage might say, "The function of Paragraph 3 within the passage is to…" Your prediction for this question might be something like *Paragraph 3 discusses El Greco's use of dark colors in his landscapes.* Suppose the answer choices are worded in this way:

A. argue that one source for the El Greco's paintings is his childhood home.

B. state that the El Greco is famous for his use of color.

C. shift the discussion to a treatment of El Greco's use of color in the paintings.

D. persuade the reader that El Greco's use of dark colors was proof that he was depressed.

None of these answer choices offers an immediate match for your prediction. If you have a good passage map, however, indicating that Paragraphs 3, 4, and 5 are all concerned with color, it should be easier for you to realize that your prediction actually harmonizes well with choice C. Each answer choice begins with an abstract rhetorical term: "argue," "state," "shift," and "persuade." Because your prediction is concretely grounded in the language of the passage, you need to be able to recognize abstract language in the answer choices and adapt your prediction to find a match if necessary.

● DRESS REHEARSAL: SAMPLE QUESTIONS AND DETAILED EXPLANATIONS

Remember to focus on main ideas for your first reading and make a brief note for each paragraph to create your passage map in the margin.

NATURAL SCIENCE: This passage discusses NASA's investigation of Mars using the Mars Global Surveyor.

The Mars Global Surveyor, a spacecraft launched in 1996, has had the longest and most fruitful run of any mission sent to Mars. This space-

craft was the first to use a technique called "aerobraking," allowing dips into the atmosphere to give the craft a nearly circular path around
(5) Mars. Global Surveyor's orbit of the red planet began in 1997, with the primary mapping phase of the mission beginning in 1999. Initially, NASA's plan was to allow the craft to orbit Mars for one full Mars year, approximately two earth years. Because of the valuable data returned, much of it in images, NASA prolonged the length of Global Surveyor's
(10) mission. Tom Thorpe, project manager for the mission, states, "It is an extraordinary machine that has done things the designers never envisioned, despite a broken wing, a failed gyro, and a worn-out traction wheel. The builders and operating staff can be proud of their legacy of scientific discoveries."
(15)   Among the discoveries made by Global Surveyor is the presence of gullies on the surface of Mars. These gullies appear to be cut into many slopes that show few, if any, impact craters. The lack of craters indicates that the gullies are relatively young, geologically speaking. Scientists interpret these gullies as evidence that liquid water flowed
(20) on Mars as recently as a few years ago and perhaps continues to do so. The presence of water on Mars is tremendously exciting because it holds open the possibility of life. Water is almost certainly required if an environment is to be capable of supporting life.
        Some experts, however, remain skeptical. These scientists are not
(25) convinced that water is responsible for the changes on the surface of Mars. It is possible, they say, that the features imaged by the Global Surveyor are caused by substances other than water. They assert that sand and dust can move in a flowing pattern and could be responsible for the geological changes that others attribute to water.

1. The author refers to the gullies that "appear to be cut into many slopes" (lines 16–17) in order to

    A. demonstrate conclusively that water is present on Mars.
    B. describe surface features that suggest water may have flowed on Mars.
    C. provide justification for prolonging the mission of the Global Surveyor.
    D. reveal one of the problems the spacecraft encountered.

Step 1: Read. Your passage map should be along these lines:

Paragraph 1: M.G.S. took pictures & made maps of Mars.

Paragraph 2: Gullies associated with water

Paragraph 3: Experts disagree; presence of water not certain.

Step 2: Examine. The phrasing "the author...in order to" is a clue that this is a Function question.

Step 3: Predict and select. To predict, you should make sure you understand fully what Paragraph 2 is saying: *the gullies, because they lack craters, are relatively young, suggesting that water may have flowed on Mars.* **Choice B is the best match.** Choice A, because it uses the word "conclusively," is extreme. Choice C is a misused detail, bringing in the lengthening of the Surveyor's mission. That's mentioned in Paragraph 1 but doesn't relate to this question. Choice D, mentioning problems with the spacecraft, is also a misused detail.

2. The author uses the words "sand and dust" (line 28) to

   F. describe factors that reduced the usefulness of images made by the Global Surveyor.

   G. explain the reasons that some scientists are skeptical about whether water flows on Mars.

   H. promote the idea that further explorations of Mars are justified.

   J. indicate the need for aerobraking when orbiting Mars.

Step 1: Read. Your passage map is done.

Step 2: Examine. You should recognize this as a function question because of the phrasing "the author uses the words...to."

Step 3: Predict and select: Make sure you understand the immediate context of the quoted words. The previous sentence says that some experts believe substances other than water may have affected the surface features of Mars. The phrase "sand and dust" is provided as an example of what, instead of water, these experts believe may have affected the surface of Mars. **Choice G is the best match.** Choice F is out of scope. The passage doesn't include any statement that the images made by the Surveyor were less than useful. Choice H is a misused detail. While Paragraph 1 mentions that the length of the surveyor's original mission was increased, this information is too far away from the quoted words "sand and dust" to be applied to this question. Choice J is a misused detail. Aerobraking is mentioned in the passage but has nothing to do with this question.

3. The author quotes Tom Thorpe's words (lines 11–14) to:

   A. give an example of an expert who doesn't believe water exists on Mars.

   B. convey the enthusiasm that NASA scientists associate with the Global Surveyor's mission.

   C. express regret that several parts of the spacecraft malfunctioned during its mission.

   D. specifically describe the valuable data returned by the Global Surveyor.

Step 1: Read. Done.

Step 2: Examine. The phrasing "The author quotes…to" is a clue that this is a Function question.

Step 3: Predict and select. Because this quotation is more than a few words, you should read carefully. In this case, the quoted words, more than the context in which the quotation appears, are most useful for making a prediction. Certain words in this quotation express an attitude of optimism and enthusiasm: "extraordinary," "done things the designers never envisioned," and "proud of their legacy of scientific discoveries." The word "despite" lessens the emphasis on the problems with the spacecraft and makes the overall tone very positive. **Choice B is the best match.** Choice A combines the distortion and misused detail traps. While elsewhere the passage mentions experts who don't believe there's water on Mars, Tom Thorpe is never included in this group, and his quotation doesn't place him in the group of skeptics. Choice C is an opposite. The quoted words express pride, not regret. Choice D is a distortion. While Thorpe's quotation indicates that the mission produced significant results, no specific descriptions of discoveries are included in the quotation.

4. The first sentence of the passage serves to:

   F. state that life exists on Mars.

   G. indicate a chronology that will be revised later in the passage.

   H. introduce the topic of the passage.

   J. indicate that the gullies on Mars are thought to house plant life.

Step 1: Read. Done.

Step 2: Examine. The phrase "serves to" in the question stem tells us this is a Function question.

Step 3: Predict and select. The first sentence of a passage either introduces the topic or discusses background information that leads up to the topic. Because the Global Surveyor is mentioned in every paragraph, it's reasonable to conclude that it is the main topic. **This prediction matches nicely with choice H.** Here, as in some cases, making your prediction can feel like stating the obvious. Do it anyway, because it will help you recognize wrong answers. Choice F combines the distortion and out-of-scope traps. The passage states that some scientists believe there is water on Mars and that water is associated with life, but the first sentence doesn't state that there is life on Mars. (In fact, nowhere in the passage is this directly stated.) Choice G is a distortion. It may be tempting because the first sentence includes a date, but the passage never revises a chronology. Choice J combines the distortion and the misused detail traps. The passage does mention "gullies," but not in the first sentence. The first sentence does include the word "fruitful," but it isn't used to indicate that gullies on Mars contain plant life.

5. The word "however" is used in line 24 for the purpose of:
   A. indicating the continuity between this paragraph and the previous one.
   B. expressing a contradiction between the goals of the Global Surveyor's mission and the actual outcome.
   C. conveying the contrast between the opinions of two groups of scientists.
   D. illustrating how the findings of the Global Surveyor conflict with previous expectations about the geological features of Mars.

Step 1: Read. Done.

Step 2: Examine. The question stem contains the phrasing "is used… for the purpose of," indicating that this is a Function question.

Step 3: Predict and select. In general, the word "however" is used to express contrast. Read the sentence and pay attention to its context to determine what two things are being contrasted here. The second paragraph describes the views of scientists who believe gullies indicate the presence of water. The first sentence of the third paragraph introduces a different group of experts who aren't convinced. Thus, the contrast is between experts who hold conflicting opinions. **This prediction matches choice C.** Choice A is an opposite: the word "however" indicates a contrast, not continuity. Choice B is out of scope. The sentence in question does not indicate that the Global Surveyor failed to meet its goals. Choice D is also out of scope. The immediate context of this sentence has nothing to do with previous expectations.

● THE FINAL ACT: PRACTICE QUIZ

Remember to focus on *why* not *what* as you do a quick first reading of this passage. Jot down notes in the margin for your passage map.

SOCIAL SCIENCE: This passage is taken from a modern discussion of the Hundred Years' War, a late-medieval conflict between England and France.

The battle of Agincourt, which took place on October 25, 1415, was a decisive battle in the Hundred Years' War. England's King Henry V led his army into northern France in August of that year to attack the port of Harfleur. This attack took much longer than expected. Henry's army,
(5) suffering from exhaustion, hunger, and disease, retreated to Calais, an English stronghold, where Henry hoped they could spend the winter regaining their strength.

Though Henry had hoped to avoid another conflict during the fall, he was forced to confront the French army, led by Charles d'Albret,
(10) at Agincourt. The battle has long been regarded as a surprising victory for the English, whose forces were severely outnumbered by the French. This view of the Battle of Agincourt as an unlikely victory was promoted in part by Shakespeare's fictionalized treatment of the event in his play *Henry V.* Shakespeare enhanced the perception of
(15) the English army as the weaker group at Agincourt. Though information about the relative number of casualties does conflict in various primary sources, it is known that Shakespeare exaggerated the number of French casualties while understating the number of British deaths. With details such as this, Shakespeare's play uses the Battle
(20) of Agincourt to enhance Henry's reputation as a legendary leader.

Modern scholars, however, take a different view of the historic battle. Professor Anne Curry, who has thoroughly researched and analyzed chronicles of the battle, has been able to reconstruct the conflict from the views of both sides. In *Agincourt: A New History,*

(25) Curry asserts that the traditional view of Agincourt as a dramatic and unlikely victory for the British has been vastly overstated. Though Curry's work does not discount the view of Henry V as a powerful military leader, she does claim that the Battle of Agincourt was built up by Henry's contemporaries as a more dramatic and significant victory (30) than it actually was, largely for the purpose of enhancing his reputation as a king.

Thus, Curry cautions that historical documents should be read with a questioning mind and a certain degree of skepticism, understanding that contemporary chroniclers may have had other purposes (35) in mind than simply recording events as clearly and as accurately as possible. Curry's work illustrates how the modern concept of "spin," referring to factors that promote a biased interpretation, may be applied not only to modern media but to historical writings as well.

1. The author uses quotation marks around the word "spin" (line 36) in order to

   A. show that it is part of a quotation from Anne Curry's book.

   B. call attention to a particular meaning of the word.

   C. indicate that the word is being used derisively.

   D. suggest that Shakespeare used this word in *Henry V.*

2. Within the passage, the first paragraph functions as:

   F. an introduction to the topic of the passage.

   G. a detailed description of King Henry's attack on Harfleur.

   H. a refutation of an outmoded view.

   J. an initial presentation of the evidence.

3. The first sentence of the third paragraph serves to:

   A. question whether the battle actually took place.

   B. signal a shift in the author's focus.

   C. question the accuracy of modern scholarship.

   D. provide a specific description of Anne Curry's view.

4. The phrase "suffering from exhaustion, hunger, and disease" (line 5) serves to:

   F. offer a reason that the British victory at Agincourt was considered surprising.

   G. describe what conditions were like for soldiers who fought in the Hundred Years' War.

   H. provide an explanation for why Henry's army retreated to Calais.

   J. diminish Henry's reputation as a leader.

5. The author uses the phrase "vastly overstated" (line 26) to:

   A. criticize Anne Curry's analysis of the Battle of Agincourt.

   B. point out a difference between a traditional view and modern view.

   C. support the belief that British forces were outnumbered at Agincourt.

   D. indicate that Anne Curry's scholarly expertise has been exaggerated.

6. In Paragraph 2, the author mentions Shakespeare's play to:

   F. illustrate that Shakespeare's work supported a particular view of the battle.

   G. promote greater interest in Shakespeare's history plays.

   H. cite a primary source relating to the Battle of Agincourt.

   J. enhance Henry's reputation as skilled leader.

7. The first sentence of Paragraph 2 serves to:

   A. show a discrepancy between what Henry initially hoped for and what actually occurred.

   B. suggest that Charles d'Albret had a confrontational personality.

   C. illustrate a contrast between the French army and the British army.

   D. provide evidence that Henry was a weak leader.

8. The author uses the phrase "the traditional view of Agincourt as a dramatic and unlikely victory" (lines 25–26) to:

   F. provide a detailed description of Anne Curry's viewpoint as expressed in her book.

   G. reveal the author's own opinion.

   H. describe aspects of the traditional view that Anne Curry disagrees with.

   J. support the view that Henry V was incompetent.

9. The phrase "a certain degree of skepticism" (line 33) is used to:

   A. describe an approach recommended by Anne Curry.

   B. indicate the author's view of Henry's reputation as a leader.

   C. illustrate Anne Curry's attitude toward Shakespeare.

   D. explain why historical events are not always recorded accurately.

10. The mention of "Henry's contemporaries" (line 29) is used to refer to:

   F. modern historians such as Anne Curry.

   G. historians of Henry's day who supported him politically.

   H. other monarchs ruling in Europe at the time.

   J. everyone living in England during Henry's reign.

● THE FINAL ACT: ANSWERS AND EXPLANATIONS FOR FUNCTION QUESTIONS

Your passage map should look something like this:

Paragraph 1: Background info about battle

Paragraph 2: Henry forced to battle: view promoted by Shakespeare

Paragraph 3: Modern view—Curry—different view of Henry

Paragraph 4: Curry's view includes idea of spin, bias.

1. B. Predict *describe the modern concept of bias*. The answer choices are worded abstractly, but your prediction describes a particular meaning. Choice A is opposite; this is not true. Choice C is out of scope; there is no evidence for it in the passage. Choice D is also out of scope. Shakespeare is not even mentioned in this paragraph.

2. F. It's a good bet that the first paragraph offers an introduction. Note that the other choices are traps. Choice G is a distortion (the description is not detailed.) Choice H is out of scope. Nothing in the first paragraph is refuted. Choice J is a distortion (the paragraph merely describes; it does not offer the description as evidence).

3. B. The words "however" and "different" certainly indicate a break or a change. Choices A and C are out of scope; they're not mentioned in the passage. Choice D is a misused detail because, while it addresses the main idea of the paragraph, it doesn't address the first sentence of the paragraph.

4. H. A prediction of *explains the retreat* leads to the correct answer. Choice F is a misused detail; it addresses the second paragraph, not the first. Choice G is out of scope; these details are not generalized to the whole war. Choice J is a misused detail. Henry's reputation as a leader is mentioned elsewhere in the passage, but it is not relevant here.

5. B. This fits the prediction *to point out the difference between the traditional view and Curry's view*. Choice A is a distortion; the phrase is not applied to Curry's view. Choice C is out of scope; the author is more descriptive than persuasive. Choice D is out of scope because the author of the passage doesn't criticize Curry's scholarship.

6. F. Keep the big picture in mind in making your prediction: the passage as a whole is about different views of the battle, so it makes sense that Shakespeare is mentioned in connection with one view or the other. Choice G is out of scope of the passage. Choice H is an opposite. Choice J is a distortion: it was Shakespeare, not the passage author, enhancing Henry's reputation.

7. A. Paying attention to the word "though," you can predict that this has something to do with a contrast between Henry's hopes and reality. Choice B is out of scope because the passage doesn't describe d'Albret's personality. Choice C is a distortion that erroneously equates the words "conflict" and "confront" used in the passage with "contrast" in the answer choice. Choice D is out of scope. The condition of Henry's army doesn't necessarily indicate that he was a weak leader.

8. H.   Looking at the context of the sentence in which the phrase appears, you can see that the word "assert" is associated with Curry's argument. This understanding leads to choices F and H. Choice H is better because it is more limited and specific. Choice F is out of scope (too narrow). Choice G is a distortion (it's not the author's opinion). Choice J is extreme. Though the passage describes Shakespeare and Henry's contemporaries as trying to enhance Henry's reputation as king, the passage never suggests that Henry was "incompetent."

9. A.   Reading the phrase in its context, you might predict *suggest keeping a questioning mind about the goals of chroniclers*. This prediction might seem to support choices A and D. Choice A is better because it's more limited and specific; choice D actually goes beyond the scope of the passage. Choice B is a distortion. Though Henry's reputation is mentioned in the passage, it's not relevant to this question. Choice C is out of scope (too narrow) because in Paragraph 4, Curry is talking about historical documents, not Shakespeare's play.

10. G.   Looking at the context, predict *those who wrote history in favor of Henry*. Choice F is a distortion, confusing the words "contemporaries" and "modern." Choice H is out of scope because no other European monarchs are mentioned in the passage. Choice J is extreme. It uses the word "everyone" and misses the point that "contemporaries" here refers to those were shaping the history of the battle in a way that would enhance Henry's reputation.

Vocab-in-Context Questions and Pacing

DIFFICULTY: ★
FREQUENCY: ★
SURPRISE FACTOR: ★

Please note that the above ratings refer to Vocab-in-Context questions only. The issue of pacing is important throughout the Reading section.

● INTRODUCTION TO PACING

If you're like most people, you find the prospect of running out of time to be the biggest challenge on the ACT Reading section. You probably think, "If I had just 10 extra minutes, I could answer more questions correctly." Although we can't give you more than 35 minutes to work on the Reading section, we can give you some advice about managing your time effectively so that you can maximize the number of questions you answer correctly.

In fact, the strategies you've already been practicing in previous lessons, mapping the passage, following the Kaplan Method for ACT Reading, and predicting the answer in your own words before reading the answer choices, are the foundations of managing your time well in ACT Reading.

This lesson will give you some additional pointers to keep in mind to help you pace yourself and get the best reading score possible. This lesson features **Vocab-in-Context questions** because they're particularly easy to answer correctly in a short amount of time. No matter how rushed you feel, you should always find the Vocab-in-Context questions and quickly research the sentence context to answer them.

Because the key to success with Vocab-in-Context questions lies more in taking the right approach to answering them than in spotting a variety of traps, the Performance Techniques section of this lesson focuses on Vocab-in-Context questions, but the Traps section focuses on pacing issues in general.

Characteristics of Vocab-in-Context Questions

Vocab-in-Context questions are easy to identify. The question stem always includes an italicized word and a line number reference. In addition, the question stem uses phrasing very similar to the following: **"As used in the passage** (line 15), **primitive most nearly means…"**

Most Common Types of Vocab-in-Context Questions

There's only slight variety among Vocab-in-Context questions. Most test your understanding of how a single word is used in its immediate context in the passage. (Once in a while, however, a Vocab-in-Context question does asks about a phrase.) The word tested is likely to be either a common word that has multiple meanings or a more challenging word whose meaning you may not be familiar with. In either case, you must infer the appropriate meaning from the context.

Vocab-in-Context questions don't make use of the all the typical answer traps that may be associated with other question types. Instead, Vocab-in-Context answer choices almost always offer a common definition of the word in question when the common definition does not fit the context. Such an answer choice can be considered **out of scope**. For example, when you see the word *bias,* you might immediately think of the meaning "prejudice or favoritism." However, in the context "the garment was cut on the *bias,*" the word has a different meaning ("the diagonal line of a woven fabric"). A typical answer trap that appears occasionally for Vocab-in-Context questions is **distortion**. For example, in the sentence, "The students' drawings showed a *marked* improvement after they had spent only a semester in studio art," the word *marked* means "significant" or "noticeable." Choosing "having an identifying mark" as the meaning of "marked" here is a distortion that might result from overfocusing on the words "drawings" and "art" in this sentence. In the case of Vocab-in-Context questions, a distortion is an answer choice that focuses on part of the sentence in too limited a way.

● THE TRAP DOOR: STEERING CLEAR OF PACING TRAPS

In this section, we use the word trap a little differently than it's used above and in the other lessons. So far, you've been thinking of a trap as particular kind of wrong answer choice that the test maker includes to distract you from the right answer. In this sense, a trap answer is tempting for one reason or another. It may even be half right, but it's not the best answer choice. (On the ACT, if an answer is only "half right," it can't be the correct answer.) In this section, the traps discussed aren't particular incorrect answer choices. Instead, pacing traps are less-than-effective ways of approaching the Reading section. Thinking carefully about the advice in this lesson and putting it together with what you know from previous lessons about the best way to handle each question type will boost your Reading score.

Pacing Traps in the Reading Section

Trap 1: Not working through the section in the best order for you. Most people have passage types or topics that they absolutely hate. While you have to be open-minded and not expect to be fascinated by everything you read on the ACT, you don't need to work through the four passages in the order in which they appear on the test.

Trap 2: Reading the questions before reading the passage. You may be tempted to think you can save time by looking at the questions first. In fact, doing so is likely to cost you time instead of saving time.

Trap 3: Underlining too much as you read the passage. You may think that underlining in the text as you read will help you know where to refer back to in the passage when answering the questions. To some extent this is true, but don't get carried away. Underlining takes time, and if you do too much of it, the material you want to stand out visually will get lost in a trail of underlining.

Trap 4: Spending too long reading the passage. You may feel that you have to understand everything about the passage before you look at the questions. You don't! Remember that your only purpose for reading the passage is to answer 10 questions about it correctly. You don't need to know every detail or understand every statement in the passage to answer all 10 questions correctly.

Trap 5: Spending too much time on a single question. Every question is worth the same number of points. You don't get extra points for answering a question that's harder, so you shouldn't spend too much time on any one question.

Techniques for Avoiding Pacing Traps

TRAP 1

Avoid Trap 1 by quickly scanning through the passages to decide if tackling them in a different order than they're presented will help you. Start with passages you feel you'll do well on. Here, you should think not only about the particular test booklet you're holding but also about your own strengths and weaknesses. If you know you tend to hate humanities passages and this one looks especially boring, save it for last. If you know that prose passages are always more difficult for you than the three nonfiction passages, you should automatically save the prose passage for last. Don't spend more than half a minute deciding on the order you'll work the passages. Take this time leading up to Test day to assess your own strengths and weaknesses.

TRAP 2

Avoid Trap 2 by reading the passage, not the questions, first. It's true that if you skim the question stems first, you might remember the topics brought up by some of the question stems and be able to mark the answers on your first reading of the passage. You're highly unlikely to remember more than half the question topics, however. In addition, reading the passage while looking for specific details will probably prevent you from getting that important big-picture understanding of the passage on your first time through. Remember, the purpose of your first reading is to get a good general sense of why the author wrote the passage and to make your passage map, noting briefly the main point of each paragraph.

TRAP 3

Avoid Trap 3 by using your pencil primarily to jot down notes for your passage map. Underlining a few words may be helpful, but don't underline too many. Words showing a logical flow (such as *however, in contrast, on the other hand, because, consequently, as the evidence shows*) and words that convey opinion or emotion (such as *regrettably, unfor-*

tunately, the opinion of, thankfully, successfully) are examples of words it can be helpful to underline. Some people like to underline proper names, while others feel no need because the upper case letters help names stand out when you're researching the passage. Experiment as you practice and see what, if any, kinds of information you find it helpful to underline. If you do underline, stick to words or phrases only, not whole sentences, and remember that underlining shouldn't replace the process of making your passage map.

You might wonder why we recommend writing down notes for your passage map instead of simply underlining topic sentences in the paragraphs. The reason is that writing the notes down—and keeping them short—makes you process the paragraph in your own mind. Doing so forces you to separate the main idea from the details. There's value in this thought process that would be lost if you simply underlined words in the passage instead of jotting down your own quick notes.

TRAP 4

Trap 4, spending too long reading the passage, can be a tough one to avoid. If you ordinarily think of yourself as a slow reader (and some of the best readers do!), you may have to practice harder to get the right approach for an ACT Reading passage. **Start by mentally letting go of the details.** The purpose of your first reading is limited: all you need to do is get a general idea of why the author wrote (for example, to describe and explain or to argue and persuade) and get a sense of the author's attitude toward the topic.

Take a few notes to create your passage map in the margin, keeping in mind that *why* **is more important than** *what.* Suppose the passage is a biographical sketch about Abraham Lincoln and contains a paragraph about his childhood. As you read, notice, *This paragraph describes Lincoln's childhood and education.* Don't focus on the details. Where Lincoln grew up or what he studied aren't the issue at this point. On your first reading, you should simply note in the margin *childhood, education.* As you move on to the next paragraph, try to get a sense of why the author is writing about Lincoln and how each paragraph might contribute to that purpose. Remember that in ACT Reading, **a specific detail matters only if the test includes a question about it.** The passage map is meant to help you go back and find a detail if you need it to answer a question.

Keep your eye on the clock, both during your practice and on Test Day. If you plan to get through all four passages, you have only about 8.75 minutes per passage. You should aim to spend no more than 3 minutes on your first reading of the passage, so you leave enough time to answer the passage's 10 questions, then move on to the next passage.

TRAP 5

To avoid Trap 5, remember that the point value is the same for all questions. This means you should do the easier questions first! Rack up those points as quickly as you can by tackling the questions with which you're most comfortable. For a single passage, answer questions in the order that makes the most sense to you. Just be careful with your answer grid! In the Reading section, it's smart to work through the questions, circling your answer choices in the test booklet and waiting to grid in all the answers after you finish all questions for the passage. This way, you don't waste time switching gears between question-answering mode and gridding mode; you can give your whole attention to the passage and the questions before you think about gridding.

Remember that Vocab-in-Context questions always come with a line reference, and you can answer them by taking a methodical approach (described below). Although they aren't the most common question type, you'll probably see two or three of them on Test Day. If you're feeling pressed for time, Vocab-in-Context questions are your friends. Even if you have only a minute or so left for the Reading section and you're just turning to your fourth passage, you should be able to get Vocab-in-Context questions correct by referring to the sentence containing the line number in the question stem. If you have to, make blind guesses on other question types, but always think about Vocab-in-Context questions. Because you can answer them quickly, there's no need to guess.

● PERFORMANCE TECHNIQUES: KEY STEPS

One quick way to help you avoid Trap 5 is by learning to recognize Vocab-in-Context questions quickly. You can easily answer these questions correctly even if you have no idea what the whole passage is about. Follow this method for Vocab-in-Context questions:

Step 1: Using the line number reference, go to the passage and find the word identified in the question stem. Draw a light line through it.

Step 2: Read the whole sentence that contains the word, looking for clues to the meaning of the "blank" you created by crossing out the word you need to define. Use these clues to predict, in your own words, the meaning of blank in the context of this sentence.

Step 3: Read the answer choices and select the one that best fits your prediction.

Occasionally in Step 2, you won't find any helpful clues in the sentence containing the word. If this is the case, quickly read the sentence before and, if necessary, the sentence after to locate clues. Keep in mind that every question on a standardized test must have a clearly justifiable best answer choice. In the case of a Vocab-in-Context question, you can count on the justification for the best answer to be in the sentence referenced by the question stem or only one sentence away from it.

Recall the important point about Vocab-in-Context questions that was mentioned earlier: frequently, the word you're asked about is a word with multiple meanings. **Generally, the most common meaning of the word is *not* the correct one for the given context.** This means you can't just read a Vocab-in-Context question and use your previous knowledge to guess what the word means. Instead, you must locate the word in the passage and predict its meaning **based on how the word is used in the passage.** Fortunately, doing so takes little time and doesn't require you to read or understand very much of the passage. So always answer Vocab-in-Context questions, but do so by referring to the passage, not by guessing.

Another trap you may see among the answer choices for a Vocab-in-Context question is **a word that "sounds like" another word.** The correct answer is always based on meaning, not sound. For example, suppose you're asked about the meaning of the word "glacial" in this sentence: "The committee was so resistant to new ideas that its work progressed at a *glacial* pace." As used here, "glacial" means "slow." An answer choice like "palatial" may be tempting because it sounds similar to "glacial." It's not the right answer, however, because "palatial" means either "stately" or "relating to a palace," depending on context.

● DRESS REHEARSAL: SAMPLE QUESTIONS AND DETAILED EXPLANATIONS

To give you practice recognizing and answering Vocab-in-Context questions, this dress rehearsal presents five questions. Each question here is based on one or two sentences rather than a whole passage to emphasize that the immediate context, not the big picture of the passage, is all you need to answer Vocab-in-Context questions.

> (line 11) After reading through the latest research studies, the physician qualified her statement that all adults over the age of 45 should take a cholesterol-lowering medication. She is now recommending that only her patients whose cholesterol level is significantly above normal take the medication.

1. As used in line 11, the word the word *qualified* most nearly means:

   A. capable.
   B. competent.
   C. restricted.
   D. classified.

Follow the method for Vocab-in-Context questions:

Step 1: Draw a line through *"qualified."*

Step 2: The first part of the sentence, "after reading through...latest research," is a clue that the word in question is something a physician would do as a result of knowing the latest research. The following sentence uses the words "now" and "only," which indicate some kind of change. This understanding leads to a prediction of something like *changed* or *limited.*

Step 3: Choice C is the best match. Note that choices A and B are traps: They are common meanings of the word "qualified." In addition, because they're close in meaning, neither can be correct, because the correct answer to a standardized test question must be unique. Choice D sounds like "qualified" but doesn't express the meaning we predicted.

(line 48) Though it took years for habituation to develop, Frieda eventually became accustomed to many of the differences between rural Germany and urban America.

2. The word *habituation,* as used in line 48, can most nearly be understood to mean:

    F. residential complex.
    G. routine.
    H. acclimation.
    J. conflict.

Step 1: Draw a line through *"habituation."*

Step 2: The phrases "became accustomed to" and "the many differences between" indicate that habituation has something to do with *getting used to a new environment.* This phrase works well as our prediction.

Step 3: Our prediction matches choice H perfectly. Choice F is a trap you might fall into if you thought of the word *habitat,* which means "place to live." Choice G is a trap based on the meaning of the word *habit.* Choice J is a distortion, focusing too narrowly on the word "differences."

(line 26) When he was inspecting the equipment, the technician noticed that the metal counter, which was supposed to be perfectly smooth, actually had several lines scored across the surface.

3. As used in line 26, the word *scored* most nearly means:

    A. grouped in units of twenty.
    B. earned points.
    C. made glossy.
    D. cut.

Step 1: Draw a line through *"scored."*

Step 2: The first part of the sentence, "while…inspecting the equipment the technician noticed," is a clue that scoring is something that can be observed or seen. The word "actually" indicates contrast. In this sentence, "the counter…was supposed to be…smooth," but that was not the case. So scoring is something that would prevent a surface from being smooth. Predict something like *made not smooth.* Keep in mind that **your prediction doesn't have to sound elegant;** it doesn't need to be a word or phrase that you can plug into the "blank" to create a well-worded sentence. The only requirement of your prediction is that it expresses a meaning that is based on the clues you identify from the context of the sentence.

Step 3: Our prediction best matches choice D. Choice A is a trap based on a definition of "score" that means "twenty." Choice B is also a trap based on a common meaning. Choice C is tempting if you focus on the words "perfectly smooth" and "surface," but a careful reading of the sentence indicates that "made glossy" is actually the opposite of what we're looking for here.

> (line 5) Members of the advocacy group worked tirelessly to promote the passage of the bill because they believed that significant improvements in the school system would issue from their work.

4. The phrase *issue from*, as it is used in line 5, most nearly means:

   F. become a topic in.
   G. cause difficulty with.
   H. be a result of.
   J. emphasize.

Step 1: Draw a line through the phrase *"issue from."*

Step 2: The phrases "worked tirelessly" and "because they believed" indicate motivation and a cause-and-effect relationship. Therefore, ask yourself, "What would motivate the advocacy group to work hard?" The answer is something along the lines of *something that would have a beneficial effect.* This leads to a prediction that includes a word like *effect* or *result.*

Step 3: ChoiceH is a good match for our prediction. Choice F is a trap. "Topic" is a common meaning of the word "issue," but it doesn't fit this context. Choice G is also a common meaning trap, caused by associating the word "issue" with another common meaning—"problem or complaint." Choice J may be a tempting answer, but it doesn't line up with our prediction, and it is not as logical as choice H.

(line 49) If the integrity of the fence becomes compromised, it is possible that the animals will be able to wander into dangerous territory.

5. As it is used in line 49, the word *integrity* most nearly means:

   A. honor.

   B. working order.

   C. respectability.

   D. surface finish.

Step 1: Draw a line through *"integrity."*

Step 2: The context tells us that "integrity" is something that, if it is interfered with, will possibly have a dangerous consequence. Thinking in a different way about the sentence as a whole, consider the relationship between a "fence" and "territory." Fences mark borders between different territories. If one territory is dangerous, a fence can separate it from another territory, but the separation will be effective only if the fence is in *good repair*. This is a good prediction.

Step 3: Our prediction matches well with choice B. Both choices A and C are traps based on a common meaning of "integrity." Choice D mentions one aspect of a fence, but "surface finish" is not relevant in the context of the sentence.

● THE FINAL ACT: PRACTICE QUIZ

To help you put everything together for pacing, this quiz is based on a single passage that is testlike in every way, including length. You have worked with this passage before, in Lesson 18, Function Questions. Here, instead of being restricted to a single question type like the previous Final Act Practice Quizzes, this quiz includes a variety of question types, just like each passage on the actual ACT. Use this quiz to apply everything you've learned about the best approach for different question types and answering questions in the most sensible order.

SOCIAL SCIENCE: This passage is taken from a modern discussion of the Hundred Years' War, a late-medieval conflict between England and France.

   The battle of Agincourt, which took place on October 25, 1415, was a decisive battle in the Hundred Years' War. England's King Henry V

led his army into northern France in August of that year to attack the port of Harfleur. This attack took much longer than expected. Henry's
(5) army, suffering from exhaustion, hunger, and disease, retreated to Calais, an English stronghold, where Henry hoped they could spend the winter regaining their strength.

Though Henry had hoped to avoid another conflict during the fall, he was forced to confront the French army, led by Charles d'Albret, at
(10) Agincourt. The battle has long been regarded as a surprising victory for the English, whose forces were severely outnumbered by the French. This view of the Battle of Agincourt as an unlikely victory was promoted in part by Shakespeare's fictionalized treatment of the event in his play *Henry V.* Shakespeare enhanced the perception of
(15) the English army as the weaker group at Agincourt. Though information about the relative number of casualties does conflict in various primary sources, it is known that Shakespeare exaggerated the number of French casualties while understating the number of British deaths. With details such as this, Shakespeare's play uses the Battle
(20) of Agincourt to enhance Henry's reputation as a legendary leader.

Modern scholars, however, take a different view of the historic battle. Professor Anne Curry, who has thoroughly researched and analyzed chronicles of the battle, has been able to reconstruct the conflict from the views of both sides. In *Agincourt: A New History,*
(25) Curry asserts that the traditional view of Agincourt as a dramatic and unlikely victory for the British has been vastly overstated. Though

Curry's work does not discount the view of Henry V as a powerful military leader, she does claim that the Battle of Agincourt was built up by Henry's contemporaries as a more dramatic and significant
(30) victory than it actually was, largely for the purpose of enhancing his reputation as a king.

Thus, Curry cautions that historical documents should be read with a questioning mind and a certain degree of skepticism, understanding that contemporary chroniclers may have had other purposes in mind
(35) than simply recording events as clearly and as accurately as possible. Curry's work illustrates how the modern concept of "spin," referring to factors that promote a biased interpretation, may be applied not only to the modern media but to historical writings as well.

1. In the second paragraph, the author refers to *Henry V* in order to:

    A. prove that Shakespeare had met King Henry V.
    B. illustrate a traditional view of the Battle of Agincourt.
    C. contrast King Henry's behavior with that of Charles d'Albret.
    D. emphasize King Henry's reputation as a powerful monarch.

2. In line 5, the word *retreated* most nearly means:

    F. relaxed.
    G. wasted away.
    H. moved back.
    J. strengthened.

3. The description of Curry as one who has "thoroughly researched and analyzed the chronicles of the battle" (lines 22–23) most likely indicates that:

    A. Curry is a recognized leader in her field.
    B. there is little primary source material available relating to the Battle of Agincourt.
    C. historical records of the Battle of Agincourt confirm King Henry V's power.
    D. the author respects Curry's scholarship.

4. The primary purpose of this passage is to:

    F. present a revision of the traditional view of the Battle of Agincourt.
    G. weaken the reputation of King Henry V.
    H. encourage the reader to become more familiar with Shakespeare's plays.
    J. explain Anne Curry's use of the concept of "spin."

5. According to the author, the Battle of Agincourt:

    A. has been described most accurately by Anne Curry.
    B. was won by the French, led by Charles D'Albret.
    C. took place when King Henry V's army was already weakened from previous fighting.
    D. has been the source of contentious disagreement among scholars.

6. The author refers to "skepticism" (line 33) to:

   F. state a personal opinion about Anne Curry's work.

   G. indicate Anne Curry's willingness to view historical records from a fresh perspective.

   H. prove that the traditional view of the Battle of Agincourt is incorrect.

   J. illustrate the bias of traditional historians.

7. The third paragraph functions within the passage as:

   A. evidence supporting the traditional view.

   B. a turning point in the discussion, shifting from the traditional view to a modern view.

   C. an appreciation of modern historical research methods.

   D. a summary of the book *Agincourt: A New History*.

8. The author's tone in this passage is one of:

   F. sharp criticism of earlier historical interpretations.

   G. strong bias in favor of the modern viewpoint about Agincourt.

   H. casual flippancy.

   J. largely objective assessment.

9. As stated in the passage, Charles d'Albret is:

   A. a character in Shakespeare's play Henry V.

   B. a lifelong archenemy of Henry V.

   C. the subject of Anne Curry's book *Agincourt: A New History*.

   D. the leader of the French forces at the Battle of Agincourt.

10. In the second paragraph, the author mentions the relative numbers of French and British casualties to:

    F. make a point about Shakespeare's fictionalization of the battle.

    G. contradict Anne Curry's report of the death toll.

    H. indicate the dangerous terrain near the port of Harfleur.

    J. argue that the numbers have been incorrectly reported.

- **THE FINAL ACT: ANSWERS AND EXPLANATIONS FOR VOCAB-IN-CONTEXT AND PACING STRATEGIES**

1. B. Predict *to show view of Battle of Agincourt as unlikely victory.* Choice A is out of scope. Nothing in the passage indicates that Shakespeare met King Henry V. Choice C is a misused detail. Though Charles d'Albret is mentioned in the first paragraph, he is not mentioned in connection with Shakespeare's play, *Henry V.* Choice D is a particularly tempting distortion. While Henry's reputation is mentioned in connection with the play, choice B is better because it fits better with the overall purpose of the passage. .

2. H. In context, "retreated" must make sense as something done relative to a particular place. Choice F is wrong because it uses a different meaning. The context doesn't justify choices G and J.

3. D. Predict *"thoroughly" used in the quoted phrase indicates respect.* Choice A is extreme/out of scope; it's not justified by the passage. Choice B is out of scope of the passage (the amount of available material isn't mentioned). Choice C is a distortion. While the passage does discuss King Henry's reputation in light of the Battle of Agincourt, it doesn't suggest that "historical records" in general testify to Henry's power.

4. F. Your passage map (a suggested one is on page 314 of Lesson 18 on Function questions) leads to a prediction of *present two views of Battle of Agincourt.* Choice G is a distortion (the passage doesn't attempt this). Choice H is out of scope (this isn't mentioned in the passage). Choice J is also out of scope for this question (the concept is a detail in the passage, not the main purpose).

5. C. This broadly based Detail question is one of the few question types you can't make a prediction for. Review your passage map and keep the big picture in mind as you read through the answer choices. Choice A seems extreme in its use of the word "most." Choice B is an opposite. The passage states that the Battle of Agincourt has been seen as "a surprising victory for the English." Although the passage describes different interpretations of the battle, the idea that it was an English victory is never denied. Choice C is true based on wording in Paragraph 1. Choice D is extreme because of the modifier "contentious."

6. G. Predict *to show the cautious perspective Curry recommends.* Choice F is a distortion. The author of the passage doesn't explicitly reveal an opinion of Anne Curry's work but does hint at a high opinion of Curry's work in lins 22–23 ("thoroughly researched and anlayzed"). Choice H is a distortion (the author is describing more than attempting to prove anything). Choice J is out of scope (this choice is stated too broadly).

7. B. For questions about the purpose of a paragraph, use your passage map to predict. Choice A is an opposite. Choice C is out of scope (the paragraph describes Curry's approach, not that of "modern historical research methods" in general). Choice D is out of scope for the question. While the paragraph does summarize Curry's book, its function in the passage is broader than that.

8. J. Predict *the author is mostly neutral, making one comment that sounds mildly admiring of Curry's work.* Choice F is an extreme. The author discusses and evaluates historical interpretations, but "sharp criticism" is too strong a term to describe the tone here accurately. Choice G is an extreme. It's true that the author seems respectful of Anne Curry's ("modern") viewpoint, but nothing in the passage justifies the words "strong bias in favor of." Choice H is an opposite (the passage is a serious analysis; "flippancy" means "lack of seriousness").

9. D. Skim the passage for "Charles d'Albret" to predict *he opposed Henry V at the Battle of Agincourt.* Choice A is a misused detail. Charles d'Albret isn't mentioned as being in Shakespeare's play. Choice B is an extreme. The passage states only that d'Albret and Henry opposed each other at the Battle of Agincourt. It's possible, in fact, that they were "lifelong archenemies," but the passage doesn't support such dramatic language. Choice C is a distortion. Charles d'Albret is presumably mentioned in Curry's book on Agincourt, but this is a Detail question and so must be answered based only on information that is spelled out in the passage.

10. F. Predict *to indicate that Shakespeare wanted to advance Henry's reputation.* This prediction is more specific than any of the answer choices, but elimination helps you see that it matches choice F. Choice B is an opposite (the author doesn't contradict Curry). Choice H is out of scope. The passage doesn't mention "dangerous terrain." Choice J is out of scope (the author is not making an argument about specific details of the battle).

SCIENCE

SCIENCE BASICS

The ACT Science Test is 35 minutes long and includes 40 questions. It has seven passages, each with five to seven questions. Factoring in the amount of time you'll spend reading each passage gives you something over 30 seconds for each question.

No, you don't have to be a scientist to succeed on the ACT Science Test. You don't have to know the atomic number of cadmium or the preferred mating habits of the monarch butterfly. All that's required is common sense (though familiarity with a standard scientific experiment does help). You'll be given passages containing various kinds of scientific information—drawn from the fields of biology, chemistry, physics, geology, astronomy, and meteorology—which you'll have to understand and use as a basis for inferences. All the information you need to know to answer the questions is always in the passage and figures given to you.

On most Science Reasoning subtests, there are six passages that present scientific data, often based on specific experiments. Also, there's usually one passage in which two scientists state opposing views on the same issue. Each passage will generate between five and seven questions. A warning: Some passages will be very difficult to understand, but they'll usually make up for that fact by having many easy questions attached to them. The test makers do show some mercy once in a while.

ACT SCIENCE QUESTION BREAKDOWN

The ACT Science Test covers biology, chemistry, earth/space sciences, and physics. It includes:

3 Data Representation passages with 5 questions each

3 Experiment passages with 6 questions each

1 Conflicting Viewpoint passage with 7 questions

● REMAINING CALM FOR ACT SCIENCE

The ACT Science Test causes a lot of unnecessary anxiety among ACT takers. Many people get so overwhelmed by the terminology and technicality of the passages that they just give up. What they fail to realize is that Science is a little like the reverse of Math. In Math, many of the questions are difficult problems based on simple concepts. In Science, on the other hand, many of the questions are simple concepts based on difficult material. So it's important not to panic if you don't understand the passage in Science Reasoning. You can often get many of the questions right on a passage, even if you find it virtually incomprehensible!

Many ACT takers also tend to rely too heavily on what they've learned in school when approaching the Science Reasoning subject test. But "remembering" is not the mind-set the ACT rewards. You couldn't possibly know the answers to ACT Science Reasoning questions in advance: You have to pull them out of the passages. All the information you need to answer the questions is right on the page.

ACT Science also requires many of the same skills as ACT Reading. The strategies discussed in the Reading section of this book will therefore also work well for many Science passages. The most important difference between Reading and Science is that the "details" you have to find in the Science passages almost all relate to numbers or scientific processes, and they are often contained in graphs and tables rather than in paragraph form.

- **Reading graphs, tables, and research summaries.** Many questions involve accurately retrieving data from a single graph or table. Others involve combining knowledge from two different graphs or tables. Still others involve understanding experimental methods well enough to evaluate information contained in summaries of experiments.

- **Looking for patterns in the numbers.** Do the numbers get bigger or smaller? Where are the highest numbers? The lowest? At what point do the numbers change? A little calculation is sometimes required, but not much. In Science, you won't be computing with numbers so much as thinking about what they mean.

In Science, as in Reading, it's crucial to consider the questions and at least try to answer them before looking at the answer choices. Refer to the passage to find the answer and try to match wording or data in the passage with one of the choices. Use the process of elimination as a fallback strategy for hard questions—but don't make it your main approach.

Turn the page to begin your exploration of ACT Science questions.

Figure Interpretation

DIFFICULTY: ★ ★

FREQUENCY: ★ ★ ★

SURPRISE FACTOR: ★

- ## INTRODUCTION TO FIGURE INTERPRETATION QUESTIONS

The best thing about the ACT Science Test is that all the information you need is right there in the test booklet in front of you. You don't need a background in chemistry, physics, biology, or any other branch of science. You simply have to be able to comprehend the information you are given in the passage and the figures.

Figure Interpretation questions are the most common type of questions on the ACT Science Test. Knowing the different types of Figure Interpretation questions and how to deal with them will save you a lot of time on Test Day and will ensure you earn all the points you can.

Characteristics of Figure Interpretation Questions

Figures accompany almost all ACT Science passages, so knowing how to interpret all the different figures you might encounter is vital to doing well on the test. Different figures that may appear include charts, graphs, tables, and diagrams. For example, in a passage about gravitational force, you might see a table comparing the gravitational force on earth at different heights above sea level. Understanding figures is essential to understanding the passages they accompany and then answering the questions that follow. Although no two passages, and consequently no two figures, are exactly the same, there are some common Figure Interpretation question types with which you can become familiar.

Most Common Types of Figure Interpretation Questions

Many Figure Interpretation questions will ask you to interpret a graph or a table. In a graph-related question, the test maker may give you a value on the x-axis and ask you to find the corresponding value on the y-axis, or vice versa. When a table is involved, questions may ask you to simply find a specific value on the table. These are the simplest types of Figure Interpretation questions—they just require that you read the graph or table carefully and correctly. Take a look at the graph below to get an idea of one kind of graph you might encounter on Test Day.

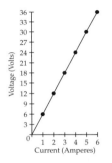

Other Figure Interpretation questions might ask you to interpret a diagram or a flowchart. These types of figures are not as common as graphs or tables, but at least one will most likely appear. Diagrams and flowcharts are a little more complicated than graphs, as the information you need is not always stated explicitly. For these questions, you will usually be asked about the role of one particular step in a process or about what would happen to an entire process if a particular step was inhibited or removed. Take a look at the flowchart below describing the nitrogen cycle.

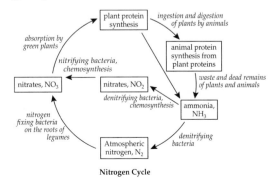

Nitrogen Cycle

Some passages are accompanied by multiple figures that all correspond to variations of the same experiment. In this case, you might be asked to integrate information from more than one figure to determine an answer. The question might require you to use the information you find on one figure to find your final answer from another figure. These questions are more complicated because they involve multiple steps. Still, getting to the correct answer on these question types simply involves understanding how the figure presents information and reading that information correctly.

● THE TRAP DOOR: STEERING CLEAR OF ANSWER TRAPS

Despite the fact that the answers are right there in the given figures, many students still are intimidated by ACT Science questions. You should know that most questions missed on the ACT Science Test are missed as a result of mistakes that students commit time and time again.

Many ACT Science passages include **more than one figure**. Most often, these figures are very similar but show different aspects of the same experiment. These passages give students trouble because they require careful interpretation and analysis. In many cases, the only difference between two figures might be which variable is being manipulated or which element is being studied, or something similar.

Other Figure Interpretation questions might ask you about something that, at first glance, seems to be impossible to answer from the information in the figure. These **not-enough-information questions** usually require you to incorporate information from the passage *and* the figure. For example, in a passage about Beer's law, what is written out as words in the passage as the "extinction coefficient" might be referenced in a figure simply as the symbol for the extinction coefficient, ε. In cases like these, you must make the connection between the passage and the figure.

Sometimes, a question might ask about a figure, such as a graph or a table, that includes units but give the answer choices in **a different unit**. These questions are twofold traps. First, you must recognize the difference between the units of the figure and the units in the questions. Second, you must correctly convert the units you have into the units you need to get to the correct answer.

The typical traps that students fall into when working with Figure Interpretation questions are the result of not being thorough when reading the passage and looking over the figure(s). For example, in passages with very similar figures, a student might look at the wrong figure for the answer. The test makers know this and will incorporate these little nuances to test whether or not you can read and comprehend all the details of the passage and the figures. The simplest way to avoid the subtleties that often steer students towards the wrong answer types is to follow the techniques outlined in the following section.

● PERFORMANCE TECHNIQUES: KEY GUIDELINES AND STEPS

The most obvious and most important way to avoid wrong answers is to make sure you completely understand what each figure is showing, the significance of each figure, and, if more than one figure accompanies the passage, the differences between the figures.

In passages that have **similar-but-different figures,** you should circle or put a star next to the parts that are different. That way you know exactly where to look when you need to decide which figure contains the information you are looking for.

In passages where you feel as if **the figure does not provide enough information** to answer the question, the first thing you should do is go back to the text of the passage. Many times, the passage will explain the figures or explain one of the variables in the figures. This extra information will almost always be enough to understand the question. Remember, all the information you need to answer an ACT Science question is in either the passage, the figure, or both. You do not need to have any prior knowledge of the scientific concepts presented.

In general, you can avoid a wrong answer on Figure Interpretation questions by following some simple steps:

Step 1: Read the passage carefully. Do not be afraid to make marks, underline things you think are important, or write in little notes.

Step 2: Examine each figure carefully. Be sure you know what each figure shows and, in the case of multiple figures, the differences between them.

Step 3: Read the questions carefully. Be sure you look for the answer in the correct figure.

Once again, always remember that with Figure Interpretation questions, all the information you need is in the passage. You simply have to determine where and how to look.

Now that you have the tools you need, go through the sample passage on the next page to get some practice applying these Figure Interpretation question techniques.

● DRESS REHEARSAL: SAMPLE QUESTIONS AND DETAILED EXPLANATIONS

Directions: Read each passage and select the best answer to each question. You may refer to the passages while answering the questions. You may NOT use a calculator on this test.

Passage 1

Each cell in our body contains many different proteins. Often scientists want to separate just one or a few of these proteins to study them apart from all the others. There are many ways of doing this, but one very powerful way is two-dimensional gel electrophoresis. This technique separates proteins on the basis of their mass and their isoelectric point, the point at which the net charge on the protein is zero. A protein's net charge is positive below its isoelectric point and negative above it. Because they each have a unique composition, proteins each have their own isoelectric points. The more acidic the protein, the lower its isoelectric point. The first step is isoelectric focusing, which separates the proteins on the basis of their isoelectric point. The separated proteins are then subjected to SDS-PAGE, which separates the proteins on the basis of their molecular weights. The resulting combination separates the proteins more efficiently than either of the two methods alone.

EXPERIMENT

A scientist, hoping to isolate a particular protein found only in the lysozyme, an organelle in the cell, performed two-dimensional gel electrophoresis on the protein contents of the lysozyme. The results are shown below.

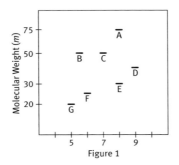

Figure 1

1. According to the figure, what two proteins have the same mass but different isoelectric points?

   A. A and E
   B. B and C
   C. B and F
   D. F and G

To answer this problem correctly, you must examine the figure very carefully. The question asks for two proteins with the same mass, or molecular weight. You can tell by looking at the labels that the molecular weight of the proteins is shown on the y-axis. So find a molecular weight along the y-axis at which two proteins have the same value. You should be able to see that two proteins have a molecular weight of 50. These two proteins are B and C. **The correct answer is B.**

2. Physiological pH, the pH of the cellular environment, is around 7. What protein would have a net charge of 0 at this pH?

   F. A
   G. B
   H. C
   J. E

There are a couple of steps here. First, the problem asks about net charge. From reading the passage, you should know that a protein has a net charge of zero at its isoelectric point. Next, you want to know what protein has a net charge of zero at pH 7. A net charge of zero at pH 7 means that this protein has an isoelectric point of 7. Now, look at the figure. Isoelectric point is along the x-axis. Looking along the x-axis, what protein has an isoelectric point of 7? The only protein that fits the description is protein H. **The answer is H.**

3. What protein is most acidic?

    A. A

    B. B

    C. D

    D. G

The figure neither says nor shows anything about acidity. Therefore, you must find where in the passage acidity is mentioned. The passage says that the more acidic the protein, the lower its isoelectric point. This means that the protein with the lowest pH will be the most acidic. Looking at the figure, the protein with the lowest pH is protein G. So protein G is the most acidic and **the correct answer is D.**

4. At pH 7, what can be said about the net charge of protein E?

    F. It is negative.

    G. It is positive.

    H. Its net charge depends on its molecular weight.

    J. There is not enough information to determine.

This problem asks about the net charge of protein E at a pH other than its isoelectric point. To answer this question, you need to go back to the passage. The passage said that below its isoelectric point, a protein is positive, and above it, it's negative. The isoelectric point of protein E is about 8.5. This means that at pH 7, which is below its isoelectric point, protein E will have a net positive charge. **The correct answer is B.** Notice that just from looking at the figure, you might have been tempted to choose J. However, you must remember that the information in the passage is there to supplement the figure—you have to take it into account, as well.

5. The protein a scientist wants to study has a molecular weight of 50 kDa and is positive at pH 6. Which one of the proteins does the scientist want to study?

   A. A
   B. B
   C. C
   D. G

This problem should be approached two parts. First, you know that the protein of interest has a molecular weight of 50 kDa. If you recall from Question 1, two proteins fit this description, B and C. The next step is to determine which of these proteins will be positive at pH 6. This depends on their isoelectric points. The isoelectric point of protein B is about 5.5, and that of protein C is 7. The problem wants the protein that will be positive at pH 6. Remember that a protein is positive when the pH is below its isoelectric point. Therefore only protein C will be positive. **The answer is C.**

Now that you have gone through some practice problems, try the quiz on the next page on your own.

● THE FINAL ACT: PRACTICE QUIZ

Directions: Read each passage and select the best answer to each question. You may refer to the passages while answering the questions. You may NOT use a calculator on this test.

Passage 2

The motion of an object in the two-dimensional plane can be described by measuring its displacement, its velocity, and its acceleration. All three of these properties are vectors, meaning that their directions matter. Displacement is the measure of an object's change in position. If an object moves from point A to point B and back again, its displacement is 0—the total change in position is 0 since the starting and ending place are the same. Velocity is a measure of an object's change in position divided by the change in time, or displacement divided by time. If an object starts at rest and accelerates forward to move 4 meters per second in 2 seconds, then its velocity is 2 m/sec. Because it is a vector, velocity also depends on direction. If an object starts out going in one direction and then reverses to the opposite direction, its sign changes as well. Acceleration is the change in velocity divided by the change in time. Just as with displacement and velocity, acceleration is a vector, which means it is dependent on direction. If the acceleration of an object switches direction, so does its sign. To demonstrate the relationship between velocity and acceleration, a scientist measured these vectors for a car in motion. The resulting velocity and acceleration graphs are shown below.

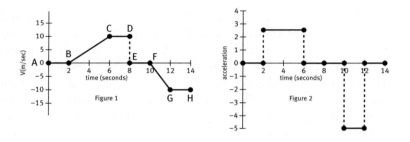

1. During which intervals is the car at rest?

    A. A to B and B to C

    B. B to C and E to F

    C. G to H and C to D

    D. A to B and E to F

2. During which interval does the velocity change, but the acceleration does not?

    F. C to D

    G. G to H

    H. A to C

    J. F to G

3. What is the longest interval during which the car is accelerating?

    A. B to C

    B. F to G

    C. C to F

    D. A to B

4. At what point does the car begin to travel in the reverse direction?

    F. A

    G. B

    H. D

    J. F

5. What can be said about the relationship between acceleration and velocity?

    A. When velocity is constant, acceleration is zero.

    B. When acceleration is constant, velocity is zero.

    C. Velocity depends on time.

    D. Velocity and acceleration have nothing to do with each other.

Passage 3

Nitrogen is necessary for human life. It is an essential component of amino acids and nucleic acids, which are the building blocks for every living thing on earth. A finite amount of nitrogen is available here on earth, so it must be continually recovered, reused, and recycled. This is accomplished by the nitrogen cycle. This all-important cycle is shown below.

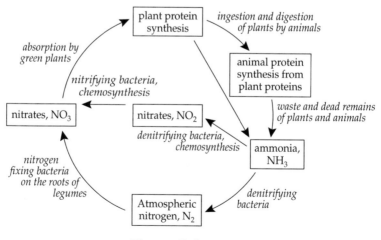

Nitrogen Cycle

6. What is the source of nitrogen for animals?

    F. nitrifying bacteria
    G. denitrifying bacteria
    H. plants
    J. nitrogen-fixing bacteria

7. What is the source of atmospheric nitrogen?

    A. nitrifying bacteria
    B. waste and dead remains of plants and animals
    C. nitrogen fixing bacteria on the roots of legumes
    D. denitrifying bacteria

8. Which of the following, if eliminated, would not stop the nitrogen cycle?

    F. plant protein synthesis
    G. synthesis of nitrates
    H. ammonia
    J. nitrifying bacteria

9. What role do green plants play in the nitrogen cycle?

    A. They turn nitrates into ammonia.
    B. They turn ammonia into nitrites.
    C. They turn ammonia into nitrates.
    D. They turn atmospheric nitrogen into nitrates.

10. What organisms participate in the most steps in the nitrogen cycle?

    F. plants
    G. bacteria
    H. animals
    J. They all participate to the same degree.

● THE FINAL ACT: ANSWERS AND EXPLANATIONS FOR FIGURE INTERPRETATION QUESTIONS

1. D. To answer this question, you should have looked at Figure 1. The car is at rest when the velocity is zero. In other words, as the time progresses, there is no motion or displacement. This happens only at the intervals A to B and E to F. The car moves in one direction or the other between the other values. **The answer is D.**

2. J. A constant acceleration produces an increasing velocity. (Even if a car moves at the same speed for a long time, it is still moving forward or backward in a certain direction.) Therefore, velocity is changing and acceleration is not when the velocity moves up or down and the acceleration is at a constant, nonzero value. This is true from B to C and from F to G. The only one of the two of those present in the answer choices is F to G. **The answer is J.**

3. A. For this question, look at Figure 2, the acceleration graph. This figure shows two intervals at which the acceleration is *not* zero: B to C and F to G. Of the two intervals, B to C is the longest. The answer is A.

4. J. Remember from the passage that velocity is a vector and depends on direction. When the car reverses direction, the sign of velocity will also reverse. This happens at point F, when velocity goes negative. **The answer is choice J.**

5. A. Let's go through what is known. According to the passage, the speed a car is traveling, its velocity, depends on its acceleration. This eliminates D. The relationship between velocity and time has nothing to do with acceleration. Choice C does not answer the question, so it is incorrect. If you recall from Question 2, a car can have a constant acceleration and a changing velocity, so B is wrong. The only answer choice left is A. If an object is not moving at all in any direction, then it is obviously not accelerating, either.

6. H. This is a simple case of following the arrows. Locate animals in the chart, and you will see that they get their nitrogen from plants. Nitrifying bacteria, denitrifying bacteria, and nitrogen-fixing bacteria are not directly connected to plants in any way, and ammonia is a product of plant and animal waste.

7. D. Locate atmospheric nitrogen on the graph. The only arrow pointing to it is denitrifying bacteria. Nitrifying bacteria create nitrites, plant and animal waste leads to ammonia, and nitrogen-fixing bacteria create nitrates. Plant protein synthesis leads to ammonia and animal protein synthesis. The only thing that leads to the production of atmospheric nitrogen is denitrifying bacteria.

8. J. For this question, you must ask yourself what, if eliminated, would not break the continuity of the circle. The only thing in the chart that would not break the continuity of the cycle is nitrifying bacteria. You can eliminate the middle of the circle and still have a complete cycle through the outside of the circle. However, if you eliminate any of the other answer choices, this will create a break in the cycle that cannot be recovered by anything else in the cycle.

9. A. To answer this question, ask yourself: what do plants use, and what do they produce? Follow the arrows going to and from plants. You will see that plants use nitrates, which they can convert into ammonia. Plants are not directly connected to atmospheric nitrogen or nitrites, so B and D can be eliminated. Finally, C says the exact opposite of the correct answer. Watch out for answer traps like this on Test Day.

10. G. Look at all of the organisms involved in the cycle. The organisms that are the most numerous are the bacteria. There are four different kinds of bacteria involved in the cycle.

LESSON 21

Pattern Analysis

DIFFICULTY: ★ ★ ★

FREQUENCY: ★ ★ ★

SURPRISE FACTOR: ★

● INTRODUCTION TO PATTERN ANALYSIS QUESTIONS

Pattern Analysis questions, the second most common question type on the ACT Science test, can range in difficulty from very easy questions that require one step to more complicated questions that require multiple steps or require you to go beyond the scope of the data presented. There are a few basic different types of Pattern Analysis questions with which you can familiarize yourself. They often accompany Data Representation passages, which summarize the results of one or multiple related experiments. Knowing how to recognize and deal with these different types of questions will save you a lot of time on Test Day. Remember, don't get intimidated if a passage talks about a concept with which you are not familiar. All the information you need to answer these questions will be right there in the passage.

Characteristics of Pattern Analysis Questions

Like Figure Interpretation questions, Pattern Analysis questions deal with figures. Often, these questions will be found right along with Figure Interpretation questions—you might sometimes find it hard to distinguish between the two. However, unlike Figure Interpretation questions, Pattern Analysis questions require you not only to be able to find information in the figures but to understand the patterns and trends in that information. Also, Pattern Analysis questions might extend beyond the actual scope of the figure. This means that you might be asked for information that goes beyond the information that is actually present in the figure. For example, If the x-axis of a graph measures time and only goes up to 10 seconds, you might be asked what goes on at $t = 15$ seconds.

Most Common Types of Pattern Analysis Questions

IDENTIFY TRENDS

Some Pattern Analysis questions simply require you to be able to analyze the data to identify general trends. This may include describing a curve; deciding which of five given graphs correctly plots the data from a table; or describing the relationship between two variables on a graph, chart, or table. For example, you might be expected to determine whether two variables are directly or inversely related:

1. The relationship between resistance and current is

   A. a linear relationship.
   B. a direct relationship.
   C. an inverse relationship.
   D. There is no relationship.

EXTRAPOLATE

Other Pattern Analysis questions require you to extrapolate beyond the information shown on a figure. For example, a question relating to a graph of velocity versus time for a car whose acceleration is constant may ask you to estimate the velocity at a time of 20 seconds, even though the graph only shows the time through 15 seconds. In cases like these, you must analyze the pattern in the information you are given to decide how that pattern will project off the graph.

PREDICT

Still other questions give you a new variable, element, substance, compound, etc., and ask you to **predict** how it will respond when put through the same experiment based on the data you have for other variables, elements, substances, etc., that are similar.

Example:

2. If a fluorophor of absorbance 535–555 was found, what could be said about its interaction with the fluorophors in Table 1?

 F. It would interact with fluorophor B only.

 G. It would interact with fluorophor C only.

 H. It would interact with all the fluorophors except for fluorophor A.

 J. It would only interact with fluorophors B and C.

DESCRIBES VARIABLE RELATIONSHIPS

Sometimes, but not very often, Pattern Analysis questions ask you to describe the relationship between variables based on the data and come up with an equation for the relationship. These types of questions are not very specific. For example, they may require you to determine whether or not the two variables vary directly or inversely and to choose an equation that reflects your choice.

● THE TRAP DOOR: STEERING CLEAR OF ANSWER TRAPS

Many of the same answer traps that students fall into for Figure Interpretation questions also apply for Pattern Analysis questions. Because they often accompany the same types of passages as Figure Interpretation questions (namely Data Representation passages) Pattern Analysis questions also often involve more than one figure. In dealing with questions that deal with identifying trends in the data, you absolutely must be sure you are looking at the correct figure. Often, figures look very similar, and it is easy to get confused.

Other times, figures will show related data but will show different aspects of the problem. In these cases you must **be sure of what the question is asking** and choose the answer that actually answers the question.

For the subset of Pattern Analysis questions that ask you to extrapolate beyond the scope of the information presented, **be sure that you understand the general trends in that information** before you attempt to answer the question. For questions of this type, although usually no classic "trap" is involved, students usually get these questions wrong simply because they read the graph or figure or table incorrectly.

When questions introduce a new variable, it will be similar to one of the variables already in the passage. Be sure that you read the question carefully to **be sure which variable the new variable imitates.** Sometimes, different variables will behave differently under the experimental conditions.

When Pattern Analysis questions ask you to describe the relationship between variables, either in a sentence or mathematically, a common answer trap is to have the variables in a relationship that is **the exact opposite** of the correct relationship. These traps work when students get confused by a set of very similar mathematical equations. A good way to avoid falling into answer traps of this type is to attempt to describe the relationship between the variables on your own, *then* look at the answer choices and see which one matches your answer.

● PERFORMANCE TECHNIQUES: KEY STEPS

As with Figure Interpretation questions, Pattern Analysis question traps work mostly because students do not read the passage, the questions, or the answer choices thoroughly. To avoid this, you should approach all Pattern Analysis questions with a plan of attack.

STEP 1: READ CAREFULLY.

Read the passage text carefully. In Research Summary passages, which Pattern Analysis questions sometimes accompany, this will amount to reading the introductory text carefully. Underline the important points in the text so that they will be easier to pick out when you refer back to it.

STEP 2: LOOK AT THE FIGURES.

Examine and understand all of the figures that accompany the passage. In the case of a Data Representation passage, this step will involve simply looking at the figures. However, if the Pattern Analysis question is part of a Research Summary passage, you will need to read each experiment and examine its accompanying figures separately. This will help to avoid confusing the experiments and the results.

STEP 3: ATTACK EACH QUESTION INDEPENDENTLY.

For each question, read both the question and the answer choices carefully and thoroughly. Once you are sure you know what the question is asking, ask yourself where you need to look to find the answer. Sometimes the question will give you a hint as to where to look. If a particular figure is mentioned in the question stem, then you probably want to start with that figure when you are looking for the answer.

STEP 4: IDENTIFY GENERAL TRENDS IN THE DATA.

For those Pattern Analysis questions that ask you to extrapolate beyond the information presented in the passage, there are two important points to remember. First, you must understand the general trend in the data presented along with the passages. Second, when trying to predict what will happen beyond the graph, always remember that data beyond the graph will follow the general trend already apparent in the data. If a line is going straight, it will continue to go straight; if it is curving it will continue to curve, and so on.

If you follow these simple guidelines, the common traps of Pattern Analysis questions should be no problem for you. Put what you've learned to the test by trying the sample passage in the Dress Rehearsal.

● DRESS REHEARSAL: SAMPLE QUESTIONS AND DETAILED EXPLANATIONS

Directions: Read each passage and select the best answer to each question. You may refer to the passages while answering the questions. You may NOT use a calculator on this test.

Passage 1

When scientists want to study the interactions between different proteins in vivo, they use a technique called Fluorescence Resonance Energy Transfer, or FRET. FRET takes advantage of fluorophors, molecules that absorb light at one wavelength and emit light at another, lower energy wavelength. If two fluorophors are within 10 nm of each other, then energy can be transferred between them. One fluorophor is attached to the molecule of interest, and another is attached to the molecule thought to interact with it. The sample is then illuminated at the absorbance peak of the first, and fluorescence is measured at the emission peak of the second. FRET detects interaction because the first fluorophor will absorb light at the incident wavelength and then emit it at a lower energy wavelength. This emitted light is then automatically absorbed by the second fluorophor, which emits the final light product. The emission of the first fluorophor must overlap with the absorbance peak of the second fluorophor to transfer energy. So if a FRET signal is observed, the two molecules interact; and if it is not observed, then they do not interact. Table 1 below is a list of the absorbance and emission ranges of some fluorophors.

Table 1

Fluorophor	Absorbance Range	Emission Range
Fluorophor A	465–495	515–525
Fluorophor B	495–515	525–545
Fluorophor C	515–525	545–565
Fluorophor D	525–545	565–585

A scientist found a new cell adhesion molecule and wanted to see which cell adhesion junction it was a part of. To do this, the scientist tested the molecule for interaction with proteins that were specifically a part of the different cell junctions via FRET. The results can be seen below in Table 2.

Table 2

Cell Junction	Cell Junction Protein	FRET Signal Detected?
Adheren	E-Cadherin	NO
Tight	Claudin	NO
Tight	Occludin	YES
Desmosome	Desmoglein	NO

1. Which junction is the new cell adhesion protein a part of?

    A. adheren
    B. tight
    C. desmosome
    D. both adheren and desmosome

The first thing to ask yourself is where to find the information you need. Table 2 shows the results of the experiment with the new protein, so look there. Remember, according to the passage, if there is a FRET signal, that means the new protein did interact with that protein. From the last column of Table 2, the only protein our protein interacted with was occludin. Now looking at the first two columns of Table 2, you will see that occludin is located only in Tight junctions. Therefore, this new protein must also be in tight junctions. **The answer is B.** The other answers are wrong because these junctions do not include occludin.

2. What two fluorophors could the scientist have used for this experiment?

F. A and C

G. A and B

H. D and A

J. B and C

To answer this question, you will have to go back to the passage text. Remember that in the text, it was explicitly stated that for two proteins to interact, the emission range of one must overlap with the absorption range of the other. You must carefully examine Table 1, which has the absorption and emission data. By examining this data, you should be able to see that only A and C overlap. The emission of A is 515–525, which is the same as the absorbance of C. **The answer is F.**

3. If the second fluorophor used in a FRET experiment is fluorophor B, at what emission range should the detector be set to record?

A. 565–585

B. 545–565

C. 525–545

D. 515–525

Remember that to detect a FRET signal, you must record in the emission range of the second fluorophor. The question tells you that the second fluorophor is fluorophor B. Looking at Table 1, you can see that the emission range of fluorophor B is 525–545. **The answer is C.**

4. What fluorophor(s) can be used with one that has an absorbance range of 545–565 and an emission range of 615–625?

F. A

G. B

H. C

J. D

The question doesn't specify whether this fluorophor is meant to be the first or second fluorophor, so you must look at it from both perspectives. First, if it is to be used as the first fluorophor, then it must be used with a fluorophor that has an absorbance range of 615–625. Looking at the fluorophors in Table 1, none of them has that absorbance range. That means this new fluorophor must be used as the second one in the FRET experiment. Therefore, it must be coupled to a first fluorophor that has an emission range of 545–565. The only fluorophor with this emission range is fluorophor C. **The answer is H.**

5. If a fluorophor of absorbance 535–555 was found, what could be said about its interaction with the fluorophors in Table 1?

    A. It would interact with fluorophor B only.

    B. It would interact with fluorophor C only.

    C. It would interact with all the fluorophors except for fluorophor A.

    D. It would only interact with fluorophors B and C.

You only have information about the absorbance of this fluorophor, so you can only give information about it as a second fluorophor. This means that it would have to be used with a first fluorophor that has an emission range that coincides with its absorption range. Looking at the fluorophors in Table 1, the absorbance range of this new fluorophor coincides with the emission ranges of both B and C. You might want to say that it would work with fluorophor D as well, but remember that for two fluorophors to interact, the absorbance of one must coincide with the emission of the other. Fluorophor D's absorbance coincides with the absorbance of the new fluorophor, so they will not work together in a FRET experiment. **The correct answer is D.** This was a pretty tough question, but just like every other question on the ACT Science test, all the information you needed was right there in the passage and the question.

Now that you have finished with the sample questions, test yourself by completing the quiz on the following page.

● THE FINAL ACT: PRACTICE QUIZ

Directions: Read each passage and select the best answer to each question. You may refer to the passages while answering the questions. You may NOT use a calculator on this test.

Passage 2

The human nervous system is a principle system of the body. It is responsible for all the sensations that we feel and every movement we make. The nervous system accomplishes these daunting tasks through the use of special cells called neurons. Neurons are abundant throughout the human body. They communicate with each other through the release of special molecules called neurotransmitters. Neurotransmitters released at the axon terminal of one neuron will diffuse to the dendrites of another neuron in what is known as the synaptic cleft. There are multiple neurotransmitters, and each can have different effects once it is released. Neurotransmitters can either excite or inhibit; some may do both. Scientists wanted to determine the properties of these different neurotransmitters and their distribution throughout the body.

EXPERIMENT 1

Scientists wanted to determine the effects that the different neurotransmitters exerted. To do this, they injected the different neurotransmitters into a synaptic cleft and monitored their effects the postsynaptic membrane. The results can be seen in Table 1.

Table 1

Neurotransmitter	Effect
Acetylcholine (ACh)	excitatory
GABA	inhibitory
Glycine	inhibitory
Glutamate	excitatory
Nitric oxide	excitatory and inhibitory

EXPERIMENT 2

To test the distribution of these neurotransmitters throughout the body, scientists excited different neurons in the body and tested their synaptic clefts to see which neurotransmitters were released. The results can be seen below in Table 2.

Table 2

Neuron	Neurotransmitter Used
Muscle sudo-motor neuron	ACh
Pyramidal neurons in cerebral cortex	Glutamate
Interneuron in dorsal column of spinal cord	GABA
Parallel fibers in cerebellum	Nitric oxide

1. A neuron is exclusively excitatory if it contains which of the following neurotransmitters?

   A. acetylcholine
   B. GABA
   C. glycine
   D. nitric oxide

2. Interneurons in the dorsal column of the spinal cord are mostly

   F. excitatory.
   G. inhibitory.
   H. both excitatory and inhibitory.
   J. There is not enough information in the passage to determine.

3. What two types of neurons will always have the same effect?

   A. sudo-motor neurons and spinal cord interneurons
   B. parallel fibers in the cerebellum and spinal cord interneurons
   C. pyramidal neurons in the cerebral cortex and muscle-motor neurons
   D. parallel fibers in the cerebellum and pyramidal neurons in the cerebral cortex

4. Another type of nerve cell was found to always be excitatory. What type of neurotransmitter could it possibly use?

   F. glycine

   G. nitric oxide

   H. GABA

   J. glutamate

5. If both glycine and glutamate were released by a neuron, what could be said about that neuron's effect?

   A. It would be excitatory.

   B. It would be inhibitory.

   C. It would behave like a neuron that released nitric oxide.

   D. The neuron would behave like a neuron that released acetylcholine.

Passage 3

When a light switch is flipped on, the light comes on because the switch closes the circuit. A complete circuit consists of a battery and a continuous wire connected to either end of the battery. The battery has a potential difference, meaning that one end is positive and the other is negative. The potential difference across a battery is known as voltage. When wires are connected to the ends of the battery, positive charge begins to flow from the positive end of the battery, through the wire, to the negative end of the battery. This flow of positive charge is called a current. Because the wire is made up of matter, as the current flows through it, some electrical friction is created. The electrical friction is called resistance. A study was performed to determine the relationship between voltage, current, and resistance.

EXPERIMENT 1

To determine the relationship between resistance and current, a circuit was created with a battery of 24 volts, and the resistance was varied by changing the resistors in the circuit. At each resistance level, the current was measured. The results can be seen in Figure 1 below.

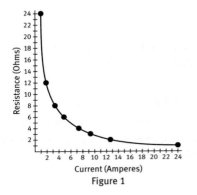

Current (Amperes)

Figure 1

EXPERIMENT 2

To measure the relationship between voltage and current, the same circuit was used, but this time the resistance was kept constant by using a resistor of 6 ohms, and the voltage was varied by changing the battery in the circuit. At each different voltage, the current was measured. The result can be seen in Figure 2 below.

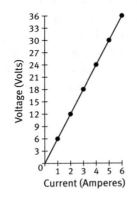

Current (Amperes)

6. The purpose of Experiment 1 was to

    F. determine the relationship between current and voltage.

    G. build a circuit that worked.

    H. vary the resistance of a circuit.

    J. determine the relationship between current and resistance.

7. Experiment 2 differed from Experiment 1 in that Experiment 2

    A. measured current.

    B. varied resistance.

    C. varied voltage.

    D. used a circuit.

8. The relationship between resistance and current is

    F. a linear relationship.

    G. a direct relationship.

    H. an inverse relationship.

    J. There is no relationship.

9. What would be the current in a circuit with a resistance of 6 ohms and a voltage of 45 volts?

    A. 3.5

    B. 5

    C. 5.5

    D. 7.5

10. What is the relationship between voltage (V), current (I), and resistance (R)?

    F. $V = IR$

    G. $V = I + R$

    H. $V = \dfrac{I}{R}$

    J. $V = \dfrac{R}{I}$

• THE FINAL ACT: ANSWERS AND EXPLANATIONS FOR PATTERN ANALYSIS

1. A. Do not spend a lot of time on easy questions. This question wants to know which of the neurotransmitters was exclusively excitatory. Look back at Table 1 and you will see that of those listed, only acetylcholine is exclusively excitatory. The answer is A.

2. G. For this question, you need to know if interneurons are excitatory, inhibitory, or both. To answer this question, you first need to look at Table 2 and see which neurotransmitter the interneurons use. Looking at Table 2, you will see that they use GABA. Take this information to Table 1, which tells you that GABA is inhibitory. Therefore, you know that the interneurons are inhibitory. The answer is G.

3. C. The question asks which neurons will always have the same effect. Right away, you know that any question with parallel fibers in the answer is incorrect because they can be either excitatory or inhibitory. This rules out B and D. Of the two choices left, only C lists two kinds of neurons that are always excitatory. Choice A lists neurons that have the completely opposite effect. The answer is C.

4. J. Looking at those neurotransmitters, you need to ask yourself which one is always excitatory. This information is in Table 1. From Table 1, the only neurotransmitter in the answer choices that is always excitatory is glutamate. You might have been tempted to choose nitric oxide, but remember to read the question stem carefully. It says that the neurotransmitter is always excitatory. A neuron that uses nitric oxide as a neurotransmitter can be both excitatory and inhibitory. The answer is J.

5. C. What effects do glycine and glutamate have? They have opposing effects. Glycine is inhibitory; glutamate is excitatory. So if a neuron released both of these, it would be both excitatory and inhibitory. This eliminates A and B. Now, if it is both excitatory and inhibitory, then its effects would be just like any other neuron that releases nitric oxide, which is also excitatory and inhibitory. The answer is C.

6. J. In Experiment 1, the scientists varied the resistance and measured the current to see how it changed as resistance changed. This is a Simple Purpose question. You should have underlined the purpose while reading through the passage.

7. C.   Both experiments measured current and used a circuit. Experiment 2 varied voltage. You should have marked that as part of the method. Be careful not to confuse the experiments. This question asks about Experiment 2, not Experiment 1, which varied resistance.

8. H.   To answer this question, you need to look at Figure 1. You should be able to see that as resistance increases, the current decreases. This is an inverse relationship.

It would be a linear relationship if the graph was a straight line and a direct relationship if the current increased as the resistance increased. It is important that you understand these concepts because it might be assumed on the ACT Science Test that you know them.

9. D.   For this question, you should have used Figure 2, which already fulfilled one of the question's requirements because the experiment was performed at a resistance of 6 ohms. Next, you should have realized that you would need to extend the graph. Extend the line as straight as you can, while being sure to continue along the same path. You should see that at a voltage of 45, there is a current of about 7.5.

10. F.   Because you know how both resistance and voltage vary with current, it would be easier for you to consider the equation in terms of current first. You already determined in Question 8 that current varies inversely with resistance. Next, look at Figure 2 to discern that as voltage increases, current also increases, so these vary directly. Therefore, for an equation of the current, you should have $I = \frac{V}{R}$. As current goes up, voltage goes up and resistance goes down. You can pick a number to plug in for the variables to see a clearer picture of this. One final step—all the answer choices have the equation in terms of V, so solve the equation for V by multiplying both sides by R, and you get $V = IR$.

LESSON 22

Scientific Method

DIFFICULTY: ★ ★ ★

FREQUENCY: ★ ★

SURPRISE FACTOR: ★

● INTRODUCTION TO SCIENTIFIC METHOD QUESTIONS

The scientific method is a systematic approach that scientists from all disciplines use to answer questions and test hypotheses. On the ACT Science test, passages that deal with the Scientific Method will present a complete experiment and ask you questions about what, why, and how the scientists did something. This boils down to understanding the purpose, method, and results of the experiment. As with every other type of question on the ACT Science test, you are not required to know any scientific facts. These questions will accompany passages that lay out, step by step, exactly what the scientists did, how they did it, and what their conclusions were.

Characteristics of Scientific Method Questions

Scientific Method questions require you to understand the why of an experiment. You will need to analyze the thought process behind the experimental design with specific questions: What did the experimenter do? How did he or she do it? Why? What were the variables? What was held constant? What was measured? What was manipulated? Unlike Figure Interpretation and Pattern Analysis experiments, which focus on the results of experiments, Scientific Method questions focus on the experimental process itself. These types of questions most often accompany Research Summary passages—passages that give descriptions of experiments and summarize their results.

Types of Scientific Method Questions

EXPERIMENTAL PURPOSE

One type of Scientific Method question asks about the purpose of the experiment. These types of questions are usually very straightforward, because the purpose is usually stated directly somewhere in the text of the passage. Here's an example:

1. What was the purpose of Experiment 1?

EXPERIMENTAL METHOD

Another type of Scientific Method question asks about the method of the experiment. The method of an experiment is the procedure by which the scientists seek to find an answer to their hypothesis. Questions that ask about the method of the experiment might be a little more complicated than those that ask about the purpose, because the method is not always as clearly identifiable in the text of the passage. Finding the answer might require interpreting how the data from a figure was collected.

A third type of Scientific Method question asks **why something was done.** These are often among the most difficult questions included on the ACT Science Test. These questions require you to think like the scientist—you must examine the experimental design and determine why the experimenter set it up in a certain way. These questions are difficult because the answer is not often written explicitly in the passage. Following is an example:

2. Why did the scientist measure alkenes and alkadienes separately?

COMPARING EXPERIMENTS

In Research Summary passages that summarize multiple experiments, you might run into Scientific Method questions that ask you about the differences between the several experiments presented. You might be asked how their methods are different, what the different measured variables are, how their results differed, or what variables were changed throughout the experiment and which ones were constant. For example:

3. Experiment 1 differed from Experiment 2 in that Experiment 1...

• THE TRAP DOOR: STEERING CLEAR OF ANSWER TRAPS

Because there are many types of Scientific Method questions, it is possible to get caught up in several common answer traps.

First, Research Summary passages include quite a lot of material. Some material is more important while some might be irrelevant, depending on the question. When working with Scientific Method questions, you must know how to distinguish between information that is relevant to the question and information that is irrelevant.

Determining what is relevant is key if **multiple answer choices appear correct** based on what's in the passage. For example, a question may ask about a particular measurement or result from one experiment. Among the answer choices, one may be correct based on one figure or experiment while another is correct based on another figure or experiment. However, only one of these answer choices will be correct based on what the question asks. You must steer clear of these traps by focusing on the answer choice that is *most* relevant and is the *best* answer for the question being asked. If a question specifically asks about the results of Experiment 3 and an answer choice is based on the results of Experiment 1, you should automatically cross out this answer choice, even if it is correct! Be aware of what the question is asking. Most Research Summary passages include multiple experiments, and the Scientific Method questions that accompany them may address any one of these experiments or all of them.

In questions that ask about the results of an experiment, **be sure you are looking at the actual results,** *not* at what the scientist or researcher predicted would happen. Sometimes, in the passage text, the viewpoint of the researcher is expressed before the actual experiments are described. Remember that this viewpoint is a *prediction* of what the results will be, not the actual results. **Usually when a question is asking about the results of an experiment, you will need to look in the figure.**

Overall, the traps on Scientific Method questions work when students do not read the question and the passage carefully enough. The key to avoiding many of these traps is simply to be thorough when you are first reading the passage and when you read each question. This approach will ensure that you do not fall for any of the trap answers commonly found in Scientific Method questions.

• PERFORMANCE TECHNIQUES: KEY STEPS

When dealing with Scientific Method questions on the ACT Science test, the basic approach is the same as when dealing with any question on the ACT Science test:

Step 1: Read the passage carefully. Do not be afraid to make marks, underline things you think are important, or write notations in the margins of your test book.

Step 2: Examine each figure carefully. Be sure you know exactly what each figure shows and what the differences are among figures if there are more than one.

Step 3: Read the questions carefully. Be sure you look for the answer in the correct place.

In Scientific Method questions, Step 1 is extremely important. Because Scientific Method questions, especially, deal with the experimental design and setup, you must take extra care when reading the text of the passage.

Remember, for the purpose of ACT Scientific Method questions, you can think of the scientific method as having only three parts: the **purpose,** the **method,** and the **results.** It is important that you identify all three of these components while reading through the passage whenever possible. Make a different notation for each one so that you can easily identify them when you need to refer back to the passage. For example, you might put a *P* next to the purpose, an *M* next to the method, and an *R* next to the results.

Step 3 of the process is also very important. You've learned that in Research Summary passages that include multiple experiments, it is important that you look at the correct figure for the experiments. You must be especially careful of this when the experiments differ by only one factor and if their figures are very similar. Many times, the question itself will provide clues as to where you should look for the answer. For example, some questions may start off saying, "According to Figure 2…" This question makes it obvious that you should look at Figure 2, and *only* Figure 2, to find your answer!

Scientific Method questions quickly become manageable as long as you **read both the passage and the questions carefully.** We cannot stress this point enough. ACT Science questions do not test how well you can design an experiment or how much you know about the particular phenomenon being tested. They simply test how well you can read, understand, and interpret experimental procedure and data.

Now that we've gone through some key formulas and rules for you to follow, let's put them to the test by working on a sample passage.

• DRESS REHEARSAL: SAMPLE QUESTIONS AND DETAILED EXPLANATIONS

Directions: Read each passage and select the best answer to each question. You may refer to the passages while answering the questions. You may NOT use a calculator on this test.

Passage 1

In any reaction, the rate of the reaction depends on the amount of reactants and products present. In a reaction catalyzed by an enzyme, the reaction looks like:

$$E + S \qquad ES \qquad E + P$$

E is the enzyme, S is its substrate, P is the product, and ES is the enzyme-substrate complex. The measure of how quickly or slowly a reaction proceeds is a measure of that reaction's kinetics. A theory for enzyme kinetics is the steady state hypothesis. This says that after an initial period, the concentration of ES remains constant because it is turned into product just as rapidly as it is formed from the enzyme and the substrate.

EXPERIMENT 1

Experiment 1 tested how the concentration of the substrate affects the pre-steady state rate of an enzymatic reaction. The initial rates were measured at various substrate concentrations. The results can be seen in Figures 1 and 2 below.

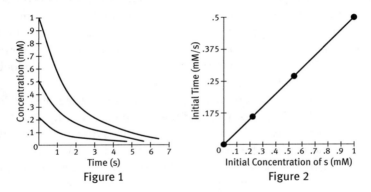

Figure 1 Figure 2

EXPERIMENT 2

Experiment 2 determined how the concentrations of the enzyme, substrate, product, and the enzyme-substrate complex varied with time. All of these factors were measured from the initiation of the reaction until its completion. The results can be seen as Figure 3 below.

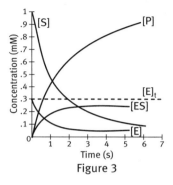

Figure 3

1. What was the purpose of Experiment 1?

   A. To determine the initial rate of the reaction

   B. To see how the enzyme-substrate complex was formed

   C. To see how substrate concentration affected the initial rate of the reaction

   D. To measure the substrate concentration

The purpose of Experiment 1 was stated in the first sentence. You should have underlined or marked it somehow as you were reading through the passage. The purpose was to determine how initial substrate concentration affected the initial rate. **The answer is C.**

2. What is the relationship between initial substrate concentration and initial rate?

   F. As the initial substrate concentration increases, the initial rate increases.

   G. As the initial substrate concentration increases, the initial rate decreases.

   H. As the initial substrate concentration decreases, the initial rate stays the same.

   J. Both the initial substrate concentration and the initial rate depend on time.

To answer this question, you can look at either Figure 1 or Figure 2. Figure 2 is a little easier to work with. Look at the labels of both axes— the values questioned are both right there. From this figure, you can see that there is a straight line with a positive slope. This means that as the initial substrate concentration gets higher, so does the initial rate. **The answer is F.** Alternatively, if you want to get the answer from Figure 1, you must understand that the initial rate is the initial slope of the concentration lines. As the initial concentration increases, the initial slope gets steeper, meaning the initial rate gets bigger.

3. Experiment 1 differed from Experiment 2 in that Experiment 1

   A. measured only product concentration.

   B. measured only substrate concentration.

   C. measured concentrations for the entire reaction.

   D. measured the concentration of the enzyme-substrate complex.

To answer this question, you can look at the figures or read the text. In Figure 1, you only see the substrate concentration, whereas in Figure 3, you can see the concentration of the substrate, product, enzyme, and enzyme-substrate complex. Therefore, Experiment 1 differed in that it only measured substrate concentration. **The answer is B.**

4. The steady state hypothesis states that:

   F. A substrate's concentration will remain the same.

   G. An enzyme's concentration will remain the same.

   H. After a brief initial period, the enzyme-substrate complex concentration remains the same.

   J. The enzyme-substrate complex concentration varies with time.

To find the answer to this question, you need to go back and read the introductory text. You should have taken special note of the "steady state hypothesis" on your initial read through the passage and marked it somehow. This will save you time when going back to look for its definition. **The answer is H.**

5. As the reaction goes forward in time,

A. the enzyme concentration decreases.

B. the substrate concentration decreases.

C. the product concentration decreases.

D. the enzyme-substrate complex concentration decreases.

The best figure to look at for this question is Figure 3 because it shows the concentrations for everything involved in the reaction. Let's look at each answer choice independently. First, choice A says that the enzyme concentration decreases, but from the dotted line, you can see that the total enzyme concentration stays the same. Choice B says that substrate concentration decreases. Look at the line representing substrate concentration, and you will see that it goes down, so substrate concentration does decrease. This makes sense because as the reaction goes forward in time, the substrate is turned into product. Choice C is wrong because from looking at Figure 3, it is clear that the product concentration increases as the reaction goes forward. Finally, choice D says that the enzyme-substrate complex concentration decreases, but looking at Figure 3, the enzyme-substrate complex concentration first increases, then remains the same. **The correct answer is B.**

● THE FINAL ACT: PRACTICE QUESTIONS

Directions: Read each passage and select the best answer to each question. You may refer to the passages while answering the questions. You may NOT use a calculator on this test.

Passage 2

Water is often called the universal solvent, but in reality this is not true. Water dissolves a great number of things because of its special properties and its polarity. However, a better statement would be to say that "like dissolves like." This means that because water is polar, it will dissolve other polar molecules, but it is not a very good solvent for nonpolar molecules. One very big class of nonpolar molecules is hydrocarbons. Hydrocarbons are just what their name indicates: long chains of carbons with hydrogens attached. Hydrocarbons can be saturated or unsaturated. Saturated hydrocarbons have as many hydrogens as they can possibly have and no double bonds. Hence they are saturated with hydrogens. Unsaturated hydrocarbons are missing some hydrogens and instead have some double bonds. A hydrocarbon with a single double bond is an alkene; one with two double bonds is called an alkadiene. These hydrocarbons are very hydrophobic, meaning they do not like to be in water. To put them into water therefore takes a certain amount of energy. Scientists want to measure the relationship between hydrocarbon structure and the amount of energy it takes to transfer a hydrocarbon into water.

EXPERIMENT 1

A scientist wanted to measure the standard free energies for transferring hydrocarbons from a water solution to pure liquid hydrocarbon. To do this, he measured the solubility of the different hydrocarbons at 25°C. He then plotted the standard free energy of transfer as a function of chain length and saturation state. The results can be seen below in Figure 1.

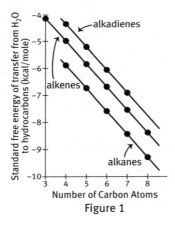

Figure 1

EXPERIMENT 2

Next, to determine the unitary free energy for transferring hydrocarbons from pure liquid hydrocarbon to a water solution, the solubility of the different hydrocarbons was measured at 25°C. The unitary free energy was plotted as a function of the relative surface area of the hydrocarbons, and a line of best fit was determined. The results can be seen in Figure 2 below.

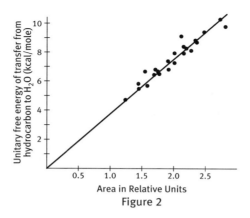

Figure 2

1. How much energy does it take to transfer a hydrocarbon with a relative surface area of 1 from a hydrocarbon solution to an aqueous solution?

    A. 1
    B. 3
    C. 4
    D. 5

2. Experiment 1 differed from Experiment 2 in that Experiment 1

    F. took solubility measurements.
    G. plotted energy as a function of area.
    H. measured unitary free energy.
    J. measured standard free energy.

3. The purpose of Experiment 2 was to

    A. determine the unitary free energy of transfer of hydrocarbons as a function of their area.
    B. determine the standard free energy of transfer of hydrocarbons as a function of the number of carbon atoms.
    C. measure the area of hydrocarbons.
    D. measure the lengths of different hydrocarbons.

4. Why did the scientist measure alkenes and alkadienes separately?

    F. Alkenes have two double bonds, so they have different properties than alkadienes.
    G. Alkadienes have two double bonds, so they have different properties than alkenes.
    H. Alkadienes have a single double bond, so they have different properties than alkenes.
    J. Alkenes are saturated, so they have different properties than alkadienes.

5. Both Experiment 1 and Experiment 2 show that:

    A. As the hydrocarbons get bigger, they are harder to dissolve in water.
    B. Hydrocarbons are easily dissolved in water.
    C. Water is a universal solvent.
    D. Water is an ideal solvent for hydrocarbons.

Passage 3

The human eye is extraordinarily flexible and adaptive. With a single glance at an object, its shape, color, size, location, and mobility can all be determined. This is especially remarkable because the eye can perform these tasks no matter what time of day it is or what kind of light is available. Even in a dark room, your eyes adjust so that you can see where you are going. The eye accomplishes this task through the use of special cells called photoreceptors. These photoreceptors are located in the back of the eye on the retina, and they transform the light that goes into our eye into electrical impulses for our brain, allowing it to determine what we see when we look at something. There are two types of photoreceptors: rods and cones. Rods allow us to see black and white, and cones allow us to see color. There are three special types of cones: one for long wavelengths, or red; one for medium wavelengths, or green; and one for short wavelengths, or blue. Together, these three types of cones allow us to see a range of colors extending through the full spectrum.

EXPERIMENT 1

A scientist wants to determine how rods and cones were distributed in our retina. To do this, he measured the number of rods and cones at angles from the center of the retina. The results can be seen in Figure 1 below.

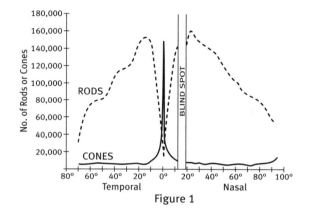

Figure 1

EXPERIMENT 2

The scientist then wanted to determine how we use these different photoreceptors in different intensities of light. To do this, he measured the activation of the different photoreceptors at different luminances (light intensities). The results can be seen below in Figure 2.

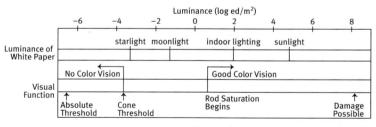

Figure 2

6. What was the purpose of Experiment 2?

   F. To determine where rods and cones are located
   G. To determine how rods and cones are used at different light intensities
   H. To determine the difference between rods and cones
   J. To see where the blind spot is

7. How did the scientist determine the distribution of photoreceptors in Experiment 1?

   A. He looked with a microscope.
   B. He counted the number of rods and cones.
   C. He measured color vision.
   D. He determined the number of rods and cones at angles from the center of the retina.

8. According to Figure 2, in starlight we can mostly see

   F. black and white.
   G. color.
   H. the same way we see during the day.
   J. everything.

9. Figure 1 shows that:

   A. There are more cones than rods.
   B. There are more rods than cones.
   C. There is an equal number of rods and cones.
   D. Rods and cones are in the same positions on the retina.

10. The majority of cones are located

    F. on the pupil.
    G. in the center of the retina.
    H. on the cornea.
    J. They are everywhere in the eye.

• THE FINAL ACT: ANSWERS AND EXPLANATIONS FOR SCIENTIFIC METHOD QUESTIONS

1. C. Where in the text was relative surface area discussed? Experiment 2 measured relative surface area, so you should have looked at Figure 2 for the answer to this question. This is a very simple problem. All you have to do is read the graph correctly, and you will see that for a relative surface area of 1, the energy change is 4 kcal/mole.

2. J. When comparing the experiments, you should have noticed that their methods differed, with Experiment 1 measuring *standard* free energy and Experiment 2 measuring *unitary* free energy. Be careful: Make sure you read the question stem carefully so as not to confuse the experiments. Choice F is incorrect because both experiments took solubility measurements, so they did not differ in this aspect. Choices G and H are wrong because they state methods that were used in Experiment 2, whereas the question asks about Experiment 1. These answer choices represent classic traps where an answer choice states a fact that is correct but does not answer the question being asked.

3. A. This is a simple question that asks about the experiment's purpose, which you should have underlined while reading through the passage. The first sentence in Experiment 2 tells you that the experimenter wanted to determine the unitary free energy.

4. G. To answer this question correctly, you need to go back to the introductory text of the passage. It states that alkadienes have two double bonds while alkenes only have one. Thus, the correct answer will state that alkadienes are different from alkenes because they have two double bonds. The only answer that correctly identifies this difference is G.

5. A. This question can be answered by process of elimination. Recall from reading the text that water is not a universal solvent, nor is it ideal for dissolving hydrocarbons because they are nonpolar and do not dissolve easily. This eliminates all of the answer choices except for A. It makes sense that bigger hydrocarbons are harder to dissolve because there is more of them.

6. G. You should have underlined the purpose when you were reading through the passage, making this problem straightforward. The very first sentence of Experiment 2 states its purpose. Don't be trapped by choice F, which is the purpose of Experiment 1.

7. D. This is a method question. Again, you should have underlined the method while you were reading through the passage initially. It explicitly states that to perform the experiment, the scientist measured the distribution of rods and cones at different angles. Choice A is wrong because there the passage did not mention a microscope being used. Remember that everything you need is in the passage, so a question asking about a detail that isn't in the passage is probably wrong. Choice B is wrong because the scientist did not count individual photoreceptors, and choice C is wrong because color vision was not measured in Experiment 1.

8. F. Looking at Figure 2, you should see that starlight is very near the lower threshold for cones. This means that not many cones are active. If cones aren't active, then we can't see color very well, making choices G and J wrong. Choice H is wrong because our vision varies with the intensity of light and is, therefore, the same at night as it is during the day. If cones aren't very active, then rods account for most of our vision, and we mostly have black-and-white vision. This makes choice F the correct answer.

9. B. Looking at Figure 1, you should see that the rods are more widely spread along the retina than the cones. Choice A is incorrect because the cones are virtually absent everywhere but right in the center of the retina at 0°. Choice C is incorrect because more rods are distributed at different points throughout the retina, and choice D is wrong because when there is a higher concentration of rods, there is a lower concentration of cones and vice versa.

10. G. Again, to find where cones are located, you should be looking at Figure 1. Here you will see that a large number of cones is located at just about 0°, which corresponds to the center of the retina. Elsewhere, the number of cones drops off rapidly.

Scientific Reasoning

DIFFICULTY: ★ ★

FREQUENCY: ★

SURPRISE FACTOR: ★

● INTRODUCTION TO SCIENTIFIC REASONING QUESTIONS

Of all the question types on the ACT Science Test, Scientific Reasoning questions are the least common. They are usually only found with a type of passage called a Conflicting Viewpoints passage, where two different viewpoints, theories, or explanations are presented for some phenomenon. On the ACT Science test, you will most likely see one Conflicting Viewpoints passage accompanied by seven questions. Some of these questions have similarities to other question types, so understanding the question types we've already covered will certainly aid you in attacking Conflicting Viewpoints questions. However, some slight nuances pertain only to Conflicting Viewpoints passages and Scientific Reasoning questions. Understanding the subtle differences among Scientific Reasoning questions will leave you better equipped to earn quick and easy points on Test Day.

Types of Scientific Reasoning Questions

There are four main types of Scientific Reasoning questions. They each require you to understand, evaluate, and compare the different theories presented in the passage.

Type 1: Why did a scientist offer a certain piece of evidence? In just about all Conflicting Viewpoints passages, each scientist will offer evidence that supports his or her claim. The evidence may show that the scientist's own viewpoint has support, or it may disprove the validity of the other scientist's viewpoint.

Type 2: Details of the passage. These questions simply require you to know and understand what is in the passage. The majority of these questions will have an answer that comes directly from the passage text. This type of Scientific Reasoning question should be the easiest to answer.

Type 3: What information would support or refute one of the hypotheses given? These questions are probably among the most difficult on the ACT Science test. Before you can begin to answer them, you must thoroughly understand the scientists' viewpoints and the evidence that is already given in the passage. Then you must decide what evidence would make that viewpoint either stronger or weaker. Like some types of Pattern Analysis questions, these questions may ask you to go beyond the information presented in the passage.

Type 4: Identify or differentiate hypotheses. Some questions will ask you either to identify the hypothesis of one of the scientists or to determine how the two hypotheses are the same or different. These questions simply require you to understand both scientists' viewpoints and to decide whether or not they agree or disagree on certain points.

• THE TRAP DOOR: STEERING CLEAR OF ANSWER TRAPS

On Scientific Reasoning questions, some common trap answer choices appear quite often. Being able to recognize and eliminate these trap answer choices will save you from picking the wrong answer choice, letting you earn more points on Test Day.

MISUSED DETAILS

One common type of answer trap involves misused details. These answer traps usually feature an answer that is from the wrong scientist's viewpoint in a Conflicting Viewpoint passage. These traps work when students do not read the question carefully enough or zoom in on one part of the question and forget to incorporate the rest of it. Students fall into this trap because the wrong answer choices contain information that is actually true. For example, if a question asks about the viewpoint of Scientist 2, one of the answer choices might give Scientist 1's viewpoint. It would be a correct viewpoint but from the wrong scientist. Something correct can, therefore, still be a wrong answer.

PARTIALLY RIGHT ANSWERS

Another common type of answer trap that commonly appears is an answer choice that is half right and half wrong. For example, if a question asks what Scientist 1 believes and why, a trap answer choice might include what Scientist 1 believes but give reasons that would actually support Scientist 2's viewpoint. Students most often fall into this answer trap when they do not read the entire answer; once they see that the first part of the answer choice is correct, they stop reading.

OPPOSITE ANSWER CHOICES

Yet another common type of answer trap is a choice that gives the exact opposite of the answer you want. These answer traps are tricky because often the trap differs from the correct answer choice by only one word. For example, the trap answer and the correct answer may differ in that one says that a certain quantity increases while the other says that it decreases.

ANSWER OUTSIDE THE SCOPE

The last type of Scientific Reasoning answer trap you might see is one that is outside the scope of what is in the passage. These answer choice types often give details that cannot be verified based on what's in the passage. These answer traps are among the easiest to eliminate because they include details, terms, or ideas that were not mentioned in the passage. Remember, only use the passage in front of you as a reference. You will never have to bring in outside information to answer an ACT Science question correctly. If you find yourself doing so, the answer is probably wrong!

● PERFORMANCE TECHNIQUES: KEY STEPS

So how exactly should you approach Conflicting Viewpoints passages and Scientific Reasoning questions to avoid those answer traps and get to the correct answer? Because these passages and questions are a little different from those you've seen before, the method for approaching these questions are different as well.

STEP 1: READ THE INTRODUCTORY MATERIAL FIRST.

This will give all the background information you will need about the passages to acome. The information contained here will usually be relevant to the viewpoints of both scientists. You should underline or mark anything in this section that you think is important, which will help when you move on to the actual viewpoints of the scientists.

STEP 2: READ THE FIRST SCIENTIST'S VIEWPOINT.

When reading through this part of the passage, you want to focus on the scientist's viewpoint and any evidence given in support of that viewpoint. Do not be afraid to mark up this part of the passage as well, noting any information you think might be important.

STEP 3: READ THE SECOND SCIENTIST'S VIEWPOINT.

As you read through the second passage, you again want to take note of the scientist's viewpoint and the details given to support that viewpoint. In addition as you read, you will want to take note of how the viewpoint of the second scientist is the same and how it is different from the viewpoint of the first scientist.

STEP 4: FOCUS ON THE QUESTIONS.

Once you have read through and marked up the passage, it is time to focus your attention on the questions. When reading the questions and answer choices, there are some general rules that you should follow to make sure you get all of the points you can.

- **Read the entire question very carefully**. Being thorough will ensure you won't fall into any of the question traps. You may even want to underline words or phrases if you think they are especially important. This way, when you start on the answer choices, you will already have a good idea of what type of answer you are looking for.

- **Read each answer choice carefully.** Eliminate any answer choices that you know are wrong. If the answer choices are very similar, you might want to underline the word(s) that make them different to make sure you can easily identify how they vary. For example, if two answer choices differ only in that one says a quantity increases and the other says it decreases, as in the example given above, then you might want to underline or put a star next to these two words so you won't lose track of how the answer choices are different.

Overall, if you read the passage and the questions carefully and understand what they ask and what you are looking for, you should do very well on Scientific Reasoning questions and on the ACT Science test in general. Take some time now to put everything you've learned to the test by trying the practice passage on the next page.

• DRESS REHEARSAL: SAMPLE QUESTIONS AND DETAILED EXPLANATIONS

Directions: Read each passage and select the best answer to each question. You may refer to the passages while answering the questions. You may NOT use a calculator on this test.

Passage 1

The human body carries out many different reactions. These reactions are accelerated by enzymes. Enzymes are specialized proteins that act as catalysts in many of the reactions completed in our bodies. Without enzymes, many of the chemical reactions necessary to sustain life would not happen fast enough, and some might not even happen at all. Enzymes upped some reactions by a factor of 106, which is one million times faster than without enzymes! Enzymes work by bringing together the reactants in such a way as to make it easier to turn them into the desired products. Each enzyme has a specific turnover rate, which is the number of molecules that enzymes can turn into product every second. The molecules that enzymes react with are called substrates. There are two prevailing theories for how an enzyme interacts with its substrate.

THEORY 1

The active site of each enzyme is unique. The three-dimensional conformation of each enzyme is structured so that it can interact with its specific substrate. In its active site, each enzyme is specifically shaped so that its substrate will fit directly into the site. This lock-and-key model of enzyme-substrate interaction ensures enzyme specificity by ensuring that a substrate will not fit into the active site of an enzyme unless it has the correct shape.

THEORY 2

The active site of each particular enzyme has a three-dimensional conformation that changes to fit its specific substrate during enzyme-substrate interaction. The enzyme-substrate interaction begins when complementary parts of the enzyme and substrate interact. As the substrate continues on and enters the active site, it induces a conformational change in the enzyme until both enzyme and substrate finally become exact matches for each other. This induced-fit model ensures enzyme specificity by ensuring that a substrate will not fit into the enzyme active site unless it has all the correct, complementary parts that will interact with the active site and induce the correct conformational change so that the enzyme is active.

1. According to Theory 1:

   A. Each enzyme can interact with many substrates.

   B. An enzyme's turnover rate depends on its substrate.

   C. An enzyme has a definitive conformation that does not change.

   D. An enzyme's conformation changes when it interacts with its substrate.

What does Theory 1 say about an enzyme and its substrate? Theory 1 is the lock-and-key model, so an enzyme does not change conformation and it does not interact with many substrates. Both A and D are wrong. Nothing was said in Theory 1 about an enzyme's turnover rate, so choice B is wrong as well. **The only answer choice left is C.**

2. Both theories agree that:

   F. Each enzyme has a certain specificity.

   G. Each enzyme has a constant shape.

   H. An enzyme's active site is variable.

   J. An enzyme can interact with any substrate.

Both theories are trying to explain why an enzyme is specific for its particular substrate and how it interacts with it. Therefore, both of these theories take it as a given that an enzyme has a certain specificity. **The answer is F.**

3. According to Theory 2:

   A. An enzyme can have multiple active sites.

   B. An enzyme is shaped so that its substrate fits perfectly into its active site.

   C. An enzyme's conformation blocks its active site.

   D. An enzyme's active site can change conformation when interacting with a substrate.

Again, recall that Theory 2 is the induced-fit theory. The only answer that would coincide with the induced-fit theory is D. Choices A and C are irrelevant because there is no mention of multiple active sites or of active sites being blocked in Theory 2. Choice B is just the opposite of what Theory 2 says. **The only answer choice that correctly describes Theory 2 is D.**

4. Theory 1 would be supported by evidence that

   F. proved an enzyme had multiple active sites.

   G. showed an enzyme's conformation changed upon interaction with a substrate.

   H. showed an enzyme's conformation did not change upon interaction with a substrate.

   J. showed an enzyme had an active site.

Theory 1 is the lock-and-key model. Which one of the answer choices would support the theory that each enzyme is a fixed lock with a particular key? This theory would be supported if the enzyme did not change conformation when the substrate was introduced. This would imply that the enzyme was already in its correct conformation to interact with the substrate, supporting the theory of a lock-and-key model. **The correct answer is H.**

5. Suppose it was determined that an enzyme interacted with multiple substrates? This would support

   A. Theory 1.

   B. Theory 2.

   C. neither theory.

   D. both theories.

Both theories focus on enzyme specificity, giving reasons for how their particular model ensures enzyme specificity. If an enzyme was found to interact with multiple substrates, then it has no specificity. This would be evidence against both theories. **The answer is C.**

Now that you have tried this sample passage, go through the problems on the next page to get some more practice.

● THE FINAL ACT: PRACTICE QUIZ

Directions: Read each passage and select the best answer to each question. You may refer to the passages while answering the questions. You may NOT use a calculator on this test.

Passage 2

Abnormal psychology deals with the psychological disorders that plague our society. These disorders include bipolar disorder, anxiety, obsessive-compulsive disorders, schizophrenia, sexual dysfunctions, eating disorders, and sleeping disorders. These disorders affect a fair amount of the population, and the ultimate goal of abnormal psychology is to determine the causes of these disorders so that treatments and medicines can be prepared to help deal with them. In abnormal psychology, however, there are conflicting viewpoints as to the causal factors of disease and how to go about determining the best course of treatment.

VIEWPOINT 1

Psychological disorders are caused by biological factors. These include biochemical imbalances, hormonal imbalances, and genetic vulnerabilities. Many of the medications used to treat psychological disorders have a biochemical basis, acting either on neurotransmitters or hormones. The hypothalamic-pituitary-adrenal-cortical axis is one example of how hormonal imbalances promote psychological disorders, as imbalances in this area have been linked to various mood and anxiety disorders. To advance our knowledge of psychological disorders, we must do research on the biochemical, hormonal, and genetic abnormalities in these disorders and seek to find psychotropic medications that will correct them.

VIEWPOINT 2

Psychological disorders are impacted in large part by culture and other features in one's social environment. Many of these disorders can be a result of low socioeconomic status; unemployment problems; discrimination and prejudice based on gender, race, or ethnicity; social change and uncertainty; and urban stressors such as violence. The social environment is a major source of both vulnerability and resistance to mental disorders. The differences in psychological disorders among people raised in different societies and cultures demonstrates that these factors play a key role in the development of these disorders. Research into the cultural and societal influences on abnormal behavior can answer many of our question about the origin, course, and treatment of these disorders.

1. A researcher who supports Viewpoint 1 believes:

   A. Urban violence causes psychological disorders.

   B. Psychological disorders have a biological basis.

   C. Abnormal psychology is not a legitimate field of study.

   D. A person of high socioeconomic status will not have mental disorders.

2. Both viewpoints agree that:

   F. There is a biological basis to abnormal psychology.

   G. There are social causes of abnormal behavior.

   H. Before treatments can be developed, causes must be understood.

   J. Psychotropic medications should be prescribed for people with mental disorders.

3. A psychologist who supports Viewpoint 2 would be most likely to

   A. analyze a person's childhood environment to determine causes of the disorder.

   B. do a genetic screening to identify any abnormalities.

   C. give a prescription for an antidepressive medication to a person who was depressed.

   D. refer a bipolar person to a brain specialist.

4. According to Viewpoint 2, a person who grew up amidst violence would

    F. be a normal, productive member of society.
    G. become a gang member.
    H. live in the same neighborhood where he or she grew up.
    J. be more likely to develop a psychological disorder.

5. It has been found that general paresis, a psychological disorder, is caused by syphilis, a bacteria-caused disease. This would support

    A. Viewpoint 1.
    B. Viewpoint 2.
    C. both viewpoints.
    D. neither viewpoint.

Passage 3

Blood enables a body to transport nutrients, hormones, and other things to sites in our bodies where they are needed. One of the most important things that is transported by our blood is oxygen. Oxygen allows our muscles to function properly and is necessary to maintain enough energy to carry out all the reactions in the body. The molecule that is responsible for oxygen transport in the body is hemoglobin (Hb). Hemoglobin is a protein that is made up of four subunits, two alpha subunits and two beta subunits. Each of these subunits carries one molecule of oxygen. Hemoglobin works by binding oxygen in the oxygen-rich lungs and releasing it into the oxygen-deficient tissues in the legs, arms, etc. Hemoglobin can bind and release oxygen because it can exist in two different states, or conformations: the T state, which has a low affinity for oxygen, and the R state, which has a high affinity for oxygen. Two scientists have different theories about how the molecule alternates between these two conformations.

SCIENTIST 1

Hemoglobin can exist with all of its subunits in either the T state or in the R state. When a single oxygen molecule binds to a subunit of hemoglobin whose subunits are all in the T state, that subunit can remain in the T state, or it can change conformation into the R state. If that subunit does change into the R state, all of the other subunits will subsequently change into the R state as well. This concerted model of hemoglobin shows that the binding of one molecule of oxygen to a single subunit can make it easier for subsequent molecules of oxygen to bind to the other subunits by transforming them from a T to an R state.

SCIENTIST 2

Hemoglobin can exist in a multitude of conformations. Each subunit can be in either the T or the R state independently of the other subunits. When a molecule of oxygen binds to a subunit in the T state, that subunit alone will change conformation to its R state. This change in conformation is independent, although it can make the R state more favorable for the other subunits. This stepwise model shows how the binding of a molecule of oxygen to a single subunit can make it easier for other oxygen molecules to bind to other subunits by showing how the binding of a single oxygen molecule can make the R state more favorable for the other subunits, thereby making it easier for oxygen to bind.

6. Both scientists would agree that after a single oxygen molecule binds to a subunit:

   F. It dissociates from the other subunits.

   G. It is easier for other oxygen molecules to bind.

   H. It will remain in the tense state.

   J. All the subunits will change to the R state.

7. Scientist 1 believes that:

   A. The subunits of hemoglobin must all be in the same state.

   B. The subunits of hemoglobin are independent.

   C. Hemoglobin subunits can exist in different states simultaneously.

   D. Hemoglobin subunits can change states in a stepwise fashion.

8. If a molecule of hemoglobin was examined and two of its subunits were in a T state while the other two were in an R state, this evidence would support

   F. both scientists.

   G. neither scientist.

   H. Scientist 1.

   J. Scientist 2.

9. Hemoglobin can bind

   A. one oxygen molecule at a time.

   B. two oxygen molecules.

   C. up to four oxygen molecules.

   D. an unlimited number of oxygen molecules.

10. If Scientist 1 is correct, then hemoglobin can exist

   F. in many different conformations.

   G. only in the T state.

   H. only in the R state.

   J. only in either the all-T state or the all-R state.

• THE FINAL ACT: ANSWERS AND EXPLANATIONS FOR SCIENTIFIC REASONING QUESTIONS

1. B. Viewpoint 1 expresses the importance of biological factors, so a researcher who supports this viewpoint believes that psychological disorders have a biological basis. Choices A and D are wrong because they focus on environmental factors and would, therefore, be more supportive of Viewpoint 2. C is wrong because it is not in agreement with Viewpoint 1.

2. H. Both Viewpoint 1 and Viewpoint 2 are attempting to explain the causes of psychological disorders so that they can figure out how to treat them. Thus, both viewpoints agree that the causes must be known before the treatments can be created. Choice F would be true only for Viewpoint 1 and choice G only for Viewpoint 2, so they are wrong.

3. A. Viewpoint 2 stresses the social and environmental influences on abnormal behavior. Therefore, a psychologist who believes in this viewpoint would want to determine what environments the person had been exposed to. All the other answer choices are things that a person who supported Viewpoint 1 would do.

4. J. Viewpoint 2 emphasizes the influence of environment, so if a person grew up in a negative environment, it would negatively affect and make them more likely to develop some kind of adverse behavior. This makes choice F wrong. Choice G is wrong because it is too specific a detail and is never explicitly stated in the passage. Finally, choice H is wrong because the passage says nothing about how violence would influence where a person would live.

5. A. A virus caused by bacteria would be a biological cause of a psychological disorder. This evidence supports Viewpoint 1. Choice B is wrong because it would be consistent with Viewpoint 2, and choices C and D are wrong because the viewpoints are different and thus cannot be supported by the same facts.

6. G. At the end of both passages, it is explained how that particular viewpoint shows how one oxygen molecule's binding makes it easier for others to bind. You should have made note of this when you were reading through the second scientist's hypothesis and comparing it to the first one. Choice F is wrong because neither scientist states that the subunits dissociate. Choices H and J are wrong because they are details that would support one or the other of the scientists' viewpoints but not both.

7. A. This is a simple question about Scientist 1's viewpoint, which you should have made a note of when you were reading through the passage. This scientist believes that the subunits can be either all T or all R. The correct answer is A. Choice D is scientist 2's viewpoint. Choice C is wrong because the scientist believes they must all be in the same state, and choice B is wrong because both believe that the subunits work together.

8. J. If a molecule of hemoglobin has its subunits in different states, that would mean they do not all have to be in the same state at the same time. This evidence would refute Scientist 1's viewpoint and support Scientist 2's viewpoint.

9. C. To answer this question, you need to recall what you read in the introductory text. There it stated that hemoglobin has four subunits and each one can bind a molecule of oxygen. This means that hemoglobin can bind up to four oxygen molecules at one time. Thus, choices A, B, and D are incorrect; the only answer choice left is C.

10. J. This question is sort of a twist on the classic question about a scientist's hypothesis. Scientist 1 states that all the hemoglobin subunits must be in the same state, but the passage does not say that the state cannot change. Therefore, choices G and H are wrong. There are only two states; this makes choice F wrong. Choice J is correct.

WRITING BASICS

●

● SHOULD YOU TAKE THE OPTIONAL WRITING TEST?

You should decide whether to take the ACT Writing Test based on the admissions policies of the schools to which you will apply and on the advice of your high school guidance counselors. A list of colleges requiring the test is maintained on the ACT website, www.act.org/aap/writing/. If you are unsure about what schools you will apply to, you should plan to take the Writing Test. However, testing will be available later if you decide not to take the Writing Test and discover later that you need it.

How Will Schools Use the Optional Writing Test?

The ACT Writing Test may be used for either admissions or course placement purposes, or both. About one third of the schools using the ACT will require the Writing Test, and another 20 percent will recommend but not require it. Many schools already had their own writing assessment tests, and many will continue to use those; but as the Writing Test becomes better known, we can assume that some of those schools will also elect to rely on the ACT essay.

Students who take the Writing Test will receive an English score, a Writing subscore, and a combined English-Writing score on a 1–36 scale. Copies of the essay (with the graders' comments) will also be available online for downloading. Schools that do not require the Writing Test will also receive the Combined English-Writing score for students who have taken the Writing Test, unless the school specifically asks *not* to receive those results.

● FORMAT

The Writing Test is 30 minutes long and includes one essay. You'll be given a topic or issue and be expected to take a position on it, supporting your point of view with examples and evidence.

You don't have to be a great creative writer to succeed on the ACT Writing Test. Instead, you have to show that you can focus on an issue and argue your point of view in a coherent, direct way with concrete examples. Furthermore, the essay graders are not primarily concerned with your grammar and punctuation skills. In terms of writing, clarity is what they are looking for. You are being tested on your ability to get an idea across in writing.

One of the biggest challenges of the Writing Test is the time frame. With only 30 minutes to read about the issue, plan your response, draft the essay, and proofread it, you have to work quickly and efficiently. Coming up with a plan and sticking to it are key to succeeding on the Writing Test.

• WHAT DO GRADERS LOOK FOR?

The Writing Test consists of one prompt that lays out the issue and gives directions for your response. There is no choice of topic; you must respond to the topic that's there. Don't worry too much about not knowing anything about the issue you have to write about. Test makers try to craft topics that will be relevant to high school students.

The readers realize you're writing under time pressure and expect you to make some mistakes. The content of your essay is not relevant; readers are not checking your facts. Nor will they judge you on your opinions. What they want to see is how well you can communicate a relevant, coherent point of view.

The test makers identify the following as the skills tested by the Writing Test:

- **Stating a clear perspective on an issue**. This means answering the question in the prompt.
- **Providing supporting evidence and logical reasoning.** This means offering relevant support for your opinion, building an argument based on concrete details and examples.
- **Maintaining focus and organizing ideas logically.** You've got to be organized, avoid digressions, and tie all your ideas together in a sensible way.
- **Writing clearly**. This is the only skill addressing your ability to write directly, and it's limited to clarity.

The Writing Test is not principally a test of your grammar and punctuation (which are tested in the English Test). Rather, colleges want to see your reasoning and communication skills.

Essay Organization

INTRODUCTION TO ESSAY ORGANIZATION

The ACT demands a specific kind of writing: a persuasive essay. You need to read the essay prompt, choose a definitive position that addresses the question in the prompt, and write a well-organized response that presents evidence and logical reasoning to support your position. You have 30 minutes to accomplish this, so you must plan your time carefully.

Before you panic and protest that you can't possibly finish the task in only 30 minutes, stop and take a deep breath. You *can* succeed on the essay. Here's why. Before you even open your test booklet, you know exactly what's expected of you. The ACT essay always raises an issue that's relevant to high school students. The prompt briefly presents some context for the issue and then poses a question for you to answer. You can use the question as a starting point for developing your thesis, that is, the position you will argue in favor of. Though the issue varies from test to test, the assignment is always the same: Choose a position and support it.

The Kaplan Method for essay writing will help you manage your time effectively once you know your topic. Here are the steps in the method, along with timing suggestions:

Step 1: Prompt (2 minutes). Read the prompt to identify the issue.

Step 2: Plan (3–5 minutes). Decide on your position and write a short list of examples to support it.

Step 3: Produce (15–20 minutes). Write your essay.

Step 4: Proofread (5–6 minutes). Review your work to look for any corrections or clarifications you can make quickly.

Because the first two steps, Prompt and Plan, are essential to writing a strong essay in a short amount of time, much of this lesson focuses on those steps. Though you'll only spend about five to seven minutes on them, the Prompt and Plan steps lay the groundwork for a well-organized essay. You must be more disciplined in writing your ACT essay than when working on an assignment such as a paper for school. When you work on a paper over several days, you can try out different ideas and approaches and revise along the way. Because you must complete your ACT essay in 30 minutes, however, you need to know where your essay is going before you start writing it. In the Prompt and Plan steps, you decide where you're going.

Characteristics of Essay Organization

You may be familiar with a format called the five-paragraph essay. The first paragraph serves as an introduction, the next three present three examples or pieces of evidence, and the fifth paragraph sums up and concludes the essay. The ACT does not require you to use this format or any other specific format. If you're comfortable working with the five-paragraph structure, however, it can be a useful tool to help you organize your thoughts quickly. Whatever the format, top-scoring essays share several characteristics. An organized response to an ACT essay prompt:

- opens with a strong **introduction.**
- takes a clear **position** on the issue addressed by the prompt.
- is broken down into separate **paragraphs.**
- maintains a consistent **focus** on the topic.
- uses **transitions** effectively.
- finishes with a strong **conclusion.**

Examples of Essay Organization

Let's look at how you can include these important features in your essay.

INTRODUCTION

Your first sentence need not necessarily be your thesis statement. It's often a good idea to take a few sentences to discuss the context of the issue you're addressing. You can do this by using some key words from the prompt, but you shouldn't simply copy the prompt. Your essay should show that you understand the issue and can bring your own ideas, knowledge, and experience to your discussion. You might find that it makes sense to set the stage first and build up to stating your position. On the other hand, it's also possible to start with your position and then explain the context of the issue.

You might want to describe briefly each piece of evidence that you'll use to support your thesis, but you don't necessarily have to offer your reader this preview of your arguments. Remember that you're not limited to one particular organizational format. Your main goal in the introduction is to make it clear that you've read the prompt and thought carefully about the issue.

Here's an approach you can take to give your essay a more sophisticated tone: word your introduction in such a way that it makes sense standing on its own. In other words, don't refer directly to the prompt or the question. Avoid a sentence such as "I agree with the second position in the prompt," or "As stated in the prompt, parents are concerned that…" Write your introduction so that it makes sense to a general reader who hasn't seen the prompt.

POSITION

Your thesis statement should be clear and should lead into your presentation of evidence. "I believe that sports programs should be allotted more generous funding than arts programs," is a good thesis statement because it clearly states a position that can be argued. "I don't like sports," isn't a good thesis statement because, while it does present an opinion, it doesn't state a position on an issue. Another example of an inadequate thesis statement is "It's not fair that sports programs receive more funding than other programs." A statement that something isn't fair, if backed up by a reason, may be part of your evidence, but this statement by itself isn't a good thesis on which to build your argument. A better thesis statement is "Sports programs should not receive more funding than other activities."

PARAGRAPHS

Because the essay requires you to present a well-reasoned argument, you'll need to provide more than one example or describe more than one aspect of a single larger example. You can't do justice to the assignment in one paragraph, so plan on having several paragraphs. If you choose the five-paragraph essay format, you'll know exactly how many paragraphs to use. If you choose a different format, simply remember that each paragraph should focus on a single topic. When you move on to a new topic, start a new paragraph. While this may seem obvious to you, many people forget to do this on test day because they feel unprepared and get stressed by the essay's time limit. This won't happen to you!

FOCUS

If you haven't planned your essay carefully, it's easy to get carried away by the flow of your own ideas while you're writing. You may start discussing an example and find yourself getting sidetracked by bringing up material related to the example but not strongly related to your argument, or thesis statement. Actually writing out your thesis statement as part of your plan and referring frequently to your plan as you write the essay (certainly at least between paragraphs) will help you stay focused.

TRANSITIONS

"Transitions" refers to two different things: connecting words and phrases, such as because and therefore, and transitions between paragraphs. Both are important to your essay. You can find an extensive list of connecting words and phrases in the Performance Techniques section of the next lesson, Idea Development. You should become familiar with these words and phrases and the logical relationships they express. Practice by using them in the writing you do for school as well as in your ACT practice essays. Contrast, cause and effect, similarity, and emphasis are relationships that you need to express clearly when you make your argument in the Produce step.

In the Plan step, you should determine how many paragraphs you'll use, what the topic of each will be, and how they relate to one another. Consider these questions: Is one piece of evidence much stronger than the others? If so, does it make sense to discuss it first or build up to it and use it at the end? Does one piece of evidence lead to another? Thinking about these issues, if only briefly, before you start writing the essay will make it easier for you to create effective transition sentences between paragraphs when you move on to the Produce step.

CONCLUSION

The conclusion is important because it's the final impression your reader is left with. Having enough time to write a good conclusion (more than a single sentence) is an indication that you understood the issue and planned your time well. A strong conclusion restates your position and summarizes your reasoning.

● THE TRAP DOOR: STEERING CLEAR OF PITFALLS

By allowing adequate time for planning, doing some hard, clear thinking before you start writing, and jotting down notes to remind you of your evidence and examples, you can easily avoid the pitfalls that plague many students' essays.

Types of Essay Organization Pitfalls

Your essay will be poorly organized if you

- Do not develop a clearly stated thesis that addresses the question in the prompt.
- Start providing evidence for one position and later shift to supporting a different position.
- Center your essay on your own opinions and emotions instead of on a logical flow of ideas.

Techniques for Avoiding Essay Organization Pitfalls

You can avoid the common pitfalls by following these suggestions.

TAKE A CLEAR POSITION BEFORE YOU START WRITING.

Do not begin writing the essay itself until you're clear about what position you will take and have several examples or pieces of evidence you can use to support your position. Your writing may exhibit an impressive command of grammar and usage, sophisticated sentence structure, and a precise and expressive vocabulary, but if you don't take a position and support it, you fail to do what the essay question asks, and your score will reflect that. You can be creative in generating a thesis statement; the question in the prompt may be worded as a yes-or-no question, but you needn't limit yourself to one side or the other. You may combine aspects of each position presented in the prompt, or you may offer a completely different answer to the question. The key thing is to address the issue presented by stating your position, whatever it is, clearly and unambiguously and by supporting that position consistently throughout the essay.

DO NOT SWITCH SIDES IN THE MIDDLE OF THE ESSAY.

To help you avoid this trap, briefly consider alternative positions while you're still in the Plan stage. You may notice that, using different examples and evidence, you could easily support opposite sides of the question. Feeling that two different positions are equally valid, you could panic under pressure and worry about how to choose the "right" one. Do not panic. On the essay question, there is no "right" answer. Your score is not affected by the position you choose to support. The questions are in fact chosen precisely because they treat issues on which reasonable people could legitimately hold differing opinions. What matters is that you choose a position and stick with it throughout the essay.

SUPPORT YOUR OPINION; DON'T JUST DESCRIBE IT.

Your opinion does have a place in the essay, but it's a limited place. The thesis statement reflects an opinion. It's perfectly okay to use the word "I" in stating your position, as in, "I believe that public schools should offer bilingual classes for those students who would benefit from them." You don't need to use phrases such as "I believe" or "in my opinion" frequently, however, because the essay implicitly expresses your opinion through your choice of which position to argue.

● PERFORMANCE TECHNIQUES: KEY RULES

RULE 1: NAIL DOWN A POSITION FIRST.

Decide on your position and identify several examples or pieces of supporting evidence before you begin writing. In other words, do not skip the Prompt and Plan steps! If you start to write before you know where you want your essay to go, it's highly unlikely that your essay will present a strong argument backed by a logical progression of ideas. It is possible to write an organized essay in 30 minutes, but it won't happen unless you plan before you start writing.

RULE 2: GENERATE EXAMPLES FOR THE OTHER POSITION.

If you're stuck in the Plan step because you can't think of several different points to support your position, try generating examples to support the opposite position. You may find it easier to argue a different position. It's okay to switch sides very early in the Plan step. However, you should not start writing the essay in support of one position and then, partway through, decide you really want to change your thesis. You must maintain a consistent focus on supporting one position throughout the essay. Remember that it doesn't matter what position your support. You earn a good score by presenting a strong, organized argument.

RULE 3: DON'T DIGRESS.

Make sure that each paragraph has a central focus: don't digress! You lay the groundwork for a strong focus in the Plan stage and then carry out your plan in the Produce stage. Paragraph focus is especially important in the middle paragraphs. You know what you need to do for the introductory and concluding paragraphs: set the stage for your argument and wrap up your argument. Digressions are more likely to occur in the middle of the essay. It may be helpful to start each of your middle paragraphs intentionally with a topic sentence, that is, a statement of the paragraph's main idea. Also, remember to keep your position in mind as you write each paragraph. Every sentence in the paragraph should relate in some way to the topic of the paragraph and contribute to the point you're making to support your argument.

• DRESS REHEARSAL: SAMPLE ESSAYS AND SCORING EXPLANATIONS

> Currently, the law in your state allows 16-year-olds who have taken a driver education course to obtain a license. A group of concerned citizens is working to change the law so that no one under 18 will be allowed to drive. Supporters believe the change would promote highway safety. Opponents feel the change is unnecessary and would do nothing to improve safety. In your opinion, should people under 18 be able to get a driver's license?
>
> In your essay, take a position on this question. You may write about either one of the two points of view given, or you may present a different point of view on this question. Use specific reasons and examples to support your position.

Sample Essay Response 1

It would be incredibly unfair to not let kids who are 16 and 17 drive just because some kids aren't very good drivers. I can't believe they would even consider that! I'm 16, I've had my license for three months now, and I haven't had an accident. I'm a good driver! If those people change the law, I'll be really mad if they try to take my license away from me. I been through 15 hours of driver training and lots of road practice before I could even take the test. I can't believe anyone would think I'm not a good driver.

Look at my friend. I have this friend who crashed her mother's car the first week she had her license. Her mom was really mad, and now my friend is going to have to pay even more for her share of the car insurance. What's worse, now my parents won't even let me ride to the mall with this girl when she's driving. In some ways, I can't blame them, because I know they worry about my safety. They can be hard to get along with sometimes, but at least I know they really love me. I love them too, most of the time anyway. I can see that parents would want to protect their kids. Most parents do anyway. What about kids whose parents don't care? That's probably why those people want to change the law. Well, when you really think about it, they do have a point. My parents won't let me ride with kids who've already crashed a car. But if your parents don't try to protect you, then maybe it's good to have laws that protect you. I guess I can see why some people don't want 16-years to drive. But I don't want to have to give up my license til I'm 18.

Comments on Essay Response 1

This is a very weak essay that is not well organized. There's no evidence that this writer spent any time planning. Here are some particular weaknesses. This essay:

- isn't divided into paragraphs.
- doesn't clearly state a position.
- starts out appearing to support one side but eventually wavers.
- centers on the writer's feelings instead of presenting an argument that's supported by logic and evidence.
- veers off-topic in discussing the writer's relationship with her parents.

The essay is confusing in part because the writer jumps right into the discussion without providing any context. The second sentence uses the word "they" without indicating to whom the word refers. Briefly giving some background information about the issue presented in the prompt would be helpful here.

In addition, this essay exhibits some problems with usage and word choice. "Kids" is slang. "They" is used several times without a noun to refer to. "Those people" is used without clearly referring to anything. "I been through" should be "I've been through."

Essay Response 2

(1) The safety record of teenage drivers has been a concern for generations. Young, inexperienced drivers have always had accidents. It's understandable, therefore, that a group of concerned citizens is working to change our state law to raise the driving age to 18. Safety is a huge concern for everyone. There are, however, other issues to consider as well. The competitive environment in which today's high school students are growing up means that they're involved in many activities, which makes having a driver's license a practical advantage for families. Most parents are busy and can't meet all of a high school student's transportation needs. Finally, driving is a responsibility, and it makes sense for young people to take on adult responsibilities gradually. For these reasons, I believe that our state should maintain the right of competent, well-trained 16- and 17-year olds to drive.

(2) Because today's teens live an environment that's more competitive than ever, they have many activities on their schedule. Most high school students feel they need to have a well-rounded background for their college applications. A lot of the activities teens are involved in take place away from home or school. Sports practices, music lessons, play rehearsals, service projects, even church activities—all these activities require teens to be in different places. It's a great convenience for parents and teens alike that some high school juniors and seniors can drive themselves to some activities.

(3) While the competitive college admissions environment leads students to take on many activities that make driving privileges beneficial, still another factor to consider is how busy and stressed parents are. Most parents today work long hours, and they're not always available to drive teenagers to their various activities. Even if parents are home, they may be tired. If I have to leave for drama practice at 7:30 pm and my mother didn't get home from work until 7:00 and is exhausted from staying up late for a week to meet a work deadline, it would be safer for everyone—other people on the road included—if my mom could stay home and rest and let me drive myself to drama practice. Adults have stress, deadlines, and pressures that can make them just as likely to have a car accident as an inexperienced teen driver.

(4) In addition to parents who are stressed and tired, another factor points toward the benefits of letting 16- and 17-year-olds get licenses. It makes sense for young people to take on adult responsibilities gradually. Any student who's gone through driver's education knows very well about

the potential dangers of driving. Most teens associate driving with independence and are therefore highly motivated to earn a license. They know it's a privilege, and most try to prove themselves worthy of the responsibility. It makes sense to let them start driving before they have to worry about a lot of other adult responsibilities as well.

(5) Thus, several reasons point to the wisdom of our state's continuing to allow well-prepared 16- and 17-year-olds to drive. The high level of involvement in activities of most teens makes it a practical necessity for some high school students to drive. The reality of parents' lives means that they can not always be refreshed and available to drive safely themselves. Finally, teens under 18 who drive understand that they're being trusted with a privilege and will work hard to prove themselves worthy of it. Raising the driving age to 18 won't necessarily make our roads safer.

Comments on Essay Response 2

This is a strong essay that's well-organized. It follows the five-paragraph format, with an introduction, three paragraphs each treating one piece of evidence, and a conclusion that restates the position and summarizes the evidence. The writer's position is clearly articulated in the words, "our state should maintain the right of competent, well-trained 16- and 17-year-olds to drive." Topic sentences are used in paragraphs 2–4:

Paragraph 2: "Because today's teens live [in—a small mistake that does not detract from readability] an environment that's more competitive than ever, they have many activities on their schedule[s]."

Paragraph 3: "another factor to consider is how busy and stressed parents are."

Paragraph 4: "It makes sense for young people to take on adult responsibilities gradually.

This essay reflects a valuable investment of a few minutes in planning. The writer clearly knew what he wanted to accomplish in the essay before he started writing. Notice that the progression of ideas is structured and logical. The writer makes good use of connecting words and phrases, such as "therefore," "however," "as well," "for these reasons," "because," "while," "in addition," and "thus." Paragraphs 3 and 4 each begin with a transitional comment that moves the discussion smoothly to the next topic. Paragraph 5 is an effective conclusion, restating the position and briefly reviewing each of the essay's main points.

• THE FINAL ACT: PRACTICE QUIZ

> Your school has computers for educational use in many classrooms, not just the technology rooms. In an effort to make students take schoolwork more seriously, your school has instituted a policy regarding student computer use: A student who is found by a teacher to be doing anything on a computer other than work strictly related to a specific academic assignment will receive a failing grade in that class for the quarter. Some people believe this policy is necessary to promote a disciplined academic focus in the classroom, while others believe that the policy is overly rigid and does not improve students' learning. In your opinion, should this policy be maintained or changed?
>
> In your essay, take a position on this question. You may write about either one of the two points of view given, or you may present a different point of view on this question. Use specific reasons and examples to support your position.

• THE FINAL ACT: SAMPLE ESSAY RESPONSE

Plan: Policy too rigid—should be not exactly abolished but made more flexible—give students a 2nd chance

    evidence: existing policy:

        not fair; some will get caught, some won't

        pits students against teachers

        not reasonable—adults use computers at work for personal stuff

Produce:

    (1) Computers in the classroom are a double-edged sword. On one hand, they provide expanded opportunities for learning. On the other hand, the Internet offers many possibilities for distraction. Given this concern, some restrictions must be placed on how students can use computers at school. The current policy, however, which assigns a failing grade for a whole quarter when a student is caught doing anything other than schoolwork on the computer, should be revised to be less restrictive. It's not reasonable to expect students to completely avoid using school computers for anything other than schoolwork, within reason, of course. The current policy is not fair, because some students will get caught while others won't. Secondly, the policy pits teachers and students against each other and limits trust. Finally, it's common knowledge that adults

use the Internet at work for personal purposes, and it isn't reasonable to hold teens to a higher standard.

(2) Because the current policy penalizes a student for a single infraction of the rule, it simply isn't fair. Teachers can't supervise a large group of students who are using computers. For example, I could be caught taking a few minutes to check out MySpace at the end of the class period after I've spent almost the entire class working diligently on research for my history paper. A classmate may have spent 15 minutes of the class reading reviews of the weekend's new movies, but she won't be penalized if the teacher doesn't catch her. The policy isn't effective because it's impossible to enforce fairly.

(3) A second reason the policy is bad is that it creates a bad climate in the classroom. It makes students and teachers into enemies by fostering distrust on both sides. I learn best in classes when the teacher seems to be on the same side as the students. I like to have a teacher who's encouraging and motivating and acts like he's on the same team with me. The current policy makes teachers and students too suspicious of each other and so is damaging to the learning environment.

(4) In addition to creating a suspicious atmosphere in the classroom, the current policy is unreasonable because it forces students to live with restrictions that even adults in the workplace don't have to deal with. It's true that most companies have some policies about personal use of computers, but I doubt they're as rigid as our school's current policy. Computers are simply part of our lives now. If managers in the workforce don't dock the pay of an employee who's been caught once sending a personal email on work time, then teachers shouldn't penalize a student's quarter grade for one instance of non-school-related computer use.

(5) Therefore, while I acknowledge that some consequences are necessary when students use school computers excessively for personal reasons or mere entertainment, I believe that the current policy is inappropriately harsh. The existing rules should be revised to be somewhat more lenient. Reducing the severity of the consequences would establish reasonably appropriate computer use in the classroom without creating a climate of suspicion among teachers and students.

Comments

This essay reflects a discernable plan and is well organized. It consistently supports the position that the current policy is inappropriate. Each paragraph maintains its focus on a single topic. Connecting words and phrases are used throughout to indicate the relationships between ideas. Examples of connecting words here are "on one hand/ on the other hand," "however," "because," "for example," "in addition," "if…then," "therefore," and "while." There are good paragraph transitions, especially at the beginnings of paragraphs 3 and 4. The first paragraph sets the stage for a presentation of evidence by providing background to the issue, while the final paragraph sums up the writer's position effectively.

Idea Development

● INTRODUCTION TO IDEA DEVELOPMENT

Recall the steps of the Kaplan Method for essay writing presented in the previous lesson:

Step 1: Prompt (2 minutes). Read the prompt to identify the issue.

Step 2: Plan (3–5 minutes). Decide on your position and write a short list of examples to support it.

Step 3: Produce (15–20 minutes). Write your essay.

Step 4: Proofread (5–6 minutes). Review your work to look for any corrections or clarifications you can make quickly.

This lesson addresses the third and fourth steps of the method. In the Plan step you generate and organize your examples and evidence, but not until the Produce step do you actually develop your ideas.

Managing your time is crucial. Though the actual writing of the essay takes the most time, the few minutes you spend thinking about the Prompt and making a short written Plan allow you to work efficiently as you Produce your essay. If you spend the recommended times on the first two steps, you'll still have 15–20 minutes to write the essay, leaving several minutes to Proofread.

This lesson will help you learn to develop your ideas appropriately and to proofread effectively. Given the time constraints of the essay, the Proofread step obviously doesn't involve major revisions. Your goal in proofreading is to make small corrections that can have a big impact on the quality of your writing. Though you may find and correct errors in mechanics (grammar, spelling, punctuation, and usage), don't feel pressured to make your essay perfect. The graders know that you have only 30 minutes to write the essay; even a top-scoring essay will have some minor flaws and weaknesses. The most important thing to think about as you proofread is how well your ideas are developed and how easily a reader can follow your argument. Quick adjustments, such as inserting a key word you accidentally left out and adding an appropriate connecting (transition) word, can go a long way toward making your essay easy to read and understand.

Characteristics of Idea Development

One key to developing your ideas is to choose good examples and pieces of evidence to support your thesis. Your goal is to demonstrate clear, logical, and mature reflection on the issue in the prompt. Here are some indications that your ideas are well developed:

- You use specific, concrete examples and evidence.
- You clearly show how each paragraph relates to your position.
- You use connecting words and phrases effectively.
- You address a possible objection to your argument.

Examples of Idea Development

Let's look at how these characteristics might be displayed in a top-scoring essay.

CONCRETE EXAMPLES AND EVIDENCE

Although the essay prompt presents a specific question, it doesn't dictate exactly what you must discuss to answer the question. It's up to you to choose your approach. One approach might be to use part of your first paragraph to define a term introduced by the prompt.

Suppose the prompt uses the term *a good education*. Here are some questions you could consider to help yourself write: What is a good education? Does it focus purely on academics, or does it include social and emotional components? What are the goals and results of a good education? The more precisely you define key concepts from the prompt in your introductory paragraph, the more specific your examples and evidence will be.

Suppose an essay prompt addresses the issue of junk food in the school cafeteria. Think about how you want to define *junk food*. Does it refer only to chips, candy, and sugary beverages? Does it refer to anything other than organic fruits and vegetables and free-range meat products? Or does junk food occupy an area somewhere between these two extremes?

You can define terms used in the prompt in a way that works for you, as long as you do so appropriately and reasonably. Specifying the meanings of words for the purpose of your essay can help you develop your ideas more precisely.

EXAMPLES RELATE TO POSITION

The goal of your ACT essay is to persuade your reader, so each example or piece of evidence you use should tie explicitly to your position. You can't assume that your reader will automatically understand your thinking and agree with you. You must thoughtfully explain why your examples are relevant to your argument.

CONNECTING WORDS AND PHRASES

You'll find a list of transitions in the Performance Techniques section. These connecting words and phrases are crucial in helping your reader understand your logic. They serve several functions. They can enable you to qualify your statements and avoid overgeneralizations. Connecting words and phrases also present the relationships between various parts of your essay. Contrast, cause and effect, similarity, and emphasis are important relationships to develop as you make your argument. You should become familiar with connecting words and phrases and the logical relationships they express and practice using them in the writing you do for yourself and for school. You can refer to "Organization" (Lesson 6) in the English section for practice with connecting words and phrases.

ADDRESSING OBJECTIONS

Because your essay should demonstrate that you've thought carefully about the issue, you should acknowledge—however briefly—at least one objection that might be made by someone who disagrees with your position. You can't discuss every possible counterargument, but you should address at least one concern that might be raised and explain why the benefits of your position outweigh the possible objection to it.

● THE TRAP DOOR: STEERING CLEAR OF PITFALLS

By choosing your words carefully as you Produce your essay, you can avoid some common pitfalls.

Types of Idea Development Pitfalls

Here are some specific pitfalls you should avoid in the Produce step of the essay:

- Don't simply restate the prompt.
- Don't use description instead of persuasion.
- Don't make generalizations and unsupported assertions.

Techniques for Avoiding Idea Development Pitfalls

USE KEY WORDS FROM THE PROMPT APPROPRIATELY.

When using statements from the prompt, you need to put the ideas in your own words and expand upon them. A strong essay will include several different examples that aren't mentioned at all in the prompt.

KEEP IN MIND THAT YOUR GOAL IS TO PERSUADE THE READER.

Think about the differences between descriptive writing and persuasive writing. Any description you include should help advance your argument. Your essay must be a persuasive piece of writing that is based on a logical progression of ideas.

QUALIFY YOUR STATEMENTS TO AVOID GENERALIZATIONS AND UNSUPPORTED ASSERTIONS.

A generalization is a broad, sweeping statement. Generalizations often use words such as *all, always, ever, every, never, no,* and *none.* If you focus on writing about specific, concrete examples and don't assume that your reader will automatically agree with you, your essay is likely to be free of overgeneralizations. In the following sentences, notice how the italicized words either generalize or assume that the reader agrees with the writer:

> *Obviously, everyone* should be required to speak English.

> It *has* to be the case that *all* schools have an honor roll.

> *Everyone knows* that teenagers are irresponsible.

An adequately developed essay uses evidence and logic to support assertions. You may need to temper a strong assertion or qualify it so that you're able to support it. In qualifying a statement, you show a more nuanced understanding of the issue. While the examples above attempt to bludgeon the reader into agreeing with you, notice how the alternatives below gently invite the reader to understand your thinking and go along with you:

> *Because* English is the *primary* language of business, government, and education, all students in the United States *who are able to* should learn English.

> *While some* schools have eliminated the honor roll, it is, in fact, a *time-honored* tradition that *still* serves *several* functions.

> Teenagers *can be* irresponsible *at times, especially* in situations when they're trying to show off and impress their friends.

The revisions above use the connecting words "because" and "while," and the qualifications "can be" and "at times," to avoid making overgeneralizations and extreme statements.

● PERFORMANCE TECHNIQUES: KEY RULES

RULE 1: AVOID BROAD, SWEEPING STATEMENTS THAT ARE DIFFICULT TO SUPPORT.

Refer to the box below for extreme language that may signal a broad statement or overgeneralization. You don't need to eliminate such words entirely; simply be aware that using them too much or in an unqualified way will weaken your essay. A second box lists phrasings that can help you qualify your statements to make your argument more precise. The idea is to make specific statements that you justify with concrete evidence and examples.

EXAMPLES OF EXTREME LANGUAGE		
all	entirely	never
always	every	no
certainly	everyone	none
completely		

EXAMPLES OF PHRASINGS THAT QUALIFY STATEMENTS

at such a time	in this situation
can	may
especially when	might
if...then	particularly
in the case of	when...then
in these circumstances	

RULE 2: PAY SPECIAL ATTENTION TO HOW YOU USE PRONOUNS.

A pronoun is used to take the place of a noun or another pronoun, and a pronoun should have a clearly understood antecedent, that is, a word that it refers to. Using pronouns carefully and consistently throughout your essay indicates precise thinking. Be particularly careful with the pronouns *they, you, it, this,* and *that.* See if you can spot some pronoun problems in this example:

> Junk food should be eliminated from the school cafeteria because it is bad for *you. They* don't want students to be coming to classes without a good meal. If *they* do *that, they* won't be able to concentrate on the schoolwork. If *you*'re allowed to buy junk food in the cafeteria, of course *students* will choose to do so.

Because your essay should make sense to a general reader, rather than a specific audience such as administrators, parents, or other students, it's best to avoid using the pronoun *you.* The pronoun *they* should be used only to refer to a plural noun. In the revisions below, notice how simply adjusting the use of nouns and pronouns improves the readability of the paragraph:

> Junk food should be eliminated from the school cafeteria because it is bad for *people. Teachers* don't want students to be coming to classes without a good meal. If *students aren't well-nourished,* they won't be able to concentrate on the schoolwork. If *one* is allowed to buy junk food in the cafeteria, of course *the average student* will choose to do so.

Because you must write quickly, you're likely to fall into some carelessness with pronouns in the Produce step. Train yourself during your writing for school and for yourself to pay careful attention to pronouns and make quick revisions as needed in the Proofread step.

RULE 3: USE CONNECTING WORDS AND PHRASES EFFECTIVELY.

In the box below, you'll find connecting words listed in five categories. You certainly won't use all of these words in a single essay; you probably won't even use words from each category. Do remember to include connecting words and phrases where appropriate, however. They help you develop your topic more fully by expressing how an idea relates to what follows it.

CONNECTING WORDS AND PHRASES

Cause and Effect	**Contrast**	**Emphasis**
as a result	although	indeed
because	at one time...now	in fact
causes	but	of course
consequently	conversely	
for this reason	despite	**Illustration**
if...then	even though	demonstrates
leading to	however	for example
resulting in	in the past...	for instance
results from	currently	illustrates
so	in spite of	in this way
therefore	instead	shows
thus	nonetheless	
when *x* happens, *y* occurs	on the other hand	**Similarity or Continuity**
	originally...now	additionally
	surprisingly	furthermore
	though	in addition
	whereas	like
	while	likewise
	yet	moreover
		similar to
		similarly

RULE 4: DON'T USE TOO MANY RHETORICAL QUESTIONS.

Use a rhetorical question to introduce an idea and set up an explanation. Don't use questions that are meant to serve as evidence. Here's an example that illustrates the difference:

> Why does homework contribute to student stress? Students spend most of their school day concentrating on academic material. After school, most students have sports and extracurricular activities, and many students even have part-time jobs and family responsibilities to worry about. Students' brains are taxed during the day, and their lives outside of school are jam-packed. *Why should students be given excessive amounts of homework when it only adds to their stress and doesn't improve their learning?*

The above paragraph opens with a well-placed rhetorical question that introduces the connection between homework and stress in students' lives. However, it would be more effective to end this paragraph with a statement: *Students shouldn't be given excessive amounts of homework, because doing so will create additional stress in their lives without enhancing their learning.*

● DRESS REHEARSAL: SAMPLE ESSAYS AND SCORING EXPLANATIONS

> Your state mandates specific course requirements for high school graduation: four years of English, three years of science, three years of math, three years of social studies, and three years of a foreign language. Some people believe that these requirements are the bare minimum needed to prepare students adequately for higher education or on-the-job training. Others believe that these requirements are too rigid and don't allow students the opportunity to explore fully their individual interests. In your opinion, should these state requirements be maintained or eliminated?
>
> In your essay, take a position on this question. You may write about either one of the two points of view given, or you may present a different point of view on this question. Use specific reasons and examples to support your position.

Sample Essay Response 1

(1) Our state requires students to take specific courses for high school graduation. These are four years of English, three years of science, three years of math, three years of social studies, and three years of a foreign language. In my opinion, these requirements are what you need to prepare you for your future, whether that is higher education or on-the-job training. These state requirements should be maintained.

(2) My first reason for my opinion is that using good English is important for success in life, so obviously everyone needs to take four years of English classes. If you can't read and write, how can you communicate with other people? If you have a job, you will need to read memos and manuals, and you may need to write letters or stuff for your company's website. If you go on to higher education, you will have to write more papers, so four years of English is the necessary preparation.

(3) My second reason for why they should maintain the current requirements is kids can't be trusted to pick their own courses. Some people think that kids should have the opportunity to fully explore their individual interests in school. Let's face it, how many kids do you know who are truly interested in taking all those hard courses? Wouldn't most kids rather sign up for technology courses and hope that they can surf the Web when the teacher isn't looking over their shoulder? State requirements are needed to make sure that every kid gets at least some real education.

(4) The last reason I think the requirements should be maintained is that everyone needs to know a little bit about everything. Some English, some science, some math, some social studies, even a foreign language—it's all important in today's society.

(5) In conclusion, I agree with the people who believe that state requirements for high school graduation are truly necessary. You need good communication skills, most kids wouldn't choose hard courses, and being well-rounded is important. This is why you need to keep state requirements in place for us.

Comments on Essay Response 1

The writer does a good job of taking a position and organizing ideas. The last sentence of paragraph 1 clearly states a position, and the essay doesn't waver from this position. The essay is appropriately organized in paragraphs. The organizational structure is somewhat rigid, because paragraphs 2, 3, 4, and 5 begin rather predictably with "My first reason,"

"My second reason," "The last reason," and "In conclusion." However, it's clear that the writer has made an effort to organize ideas logically.

The essay's main weakness lies in its shallow development of ideas. (Some sloppiness with language, especially inconsistency in the use of pronouns, also reflects a lack of clear thinking.) Paragraph 1 uses a lot of direct quotation from the prompt instead of defining the terms in the writer's own words and setting the stage for a presentation of evidence. Your introductory paragraph should provide some background information, beyond what's given in the prompt, to establish a context for the discussion and lead the reader directly to the first example you use as evidence to support your position.

Paragraph 2 introduces a concept not mentioned in the prompt, "success in life," but fails to explain what it means. This paragraph uses pronouns in a way that's not followed consistently throughout the essay. The writer uses "you," apparently addressing students, but then in paragraph 3 refers to "kids" in the third person. (Eliminate the word *kids* because it's slang and replace it with a more formal term such as *teens, young people,* or *high school students*.) In addition, the rhetorical questions in paragraph 2 are used ineffectively. Evidence sounds stronger if it's worded as a statement instead of a question.

Paragraph 3 uses the pronoun "they" without a noun for it to refer to and, again, ineffectively uses rhetorical questions instead of statements to make points. Paragraph 3 also ends with an undefined general term, "real education." Explaining what is meant by this phrase would contribute to the development of this essay.

Paragraph 4, with only two sentences, is not long enough to develop its topic adequately. In addition, it uses the generalization "everyone needs to know a little bit about everything" without explaining or supporting it. Likewise, the phrase "today's society" is not explained. The ideas in this paragraph could be developed by elaborating on what about "today's society" makes being well-rounded necessary.

Paragraph 5 is more developed than the others. The author restates the position clearly and summarizes the main idea of each paragraph. However, the last sentence is confusing because of the pronoun inconsistency. "You" is used here, apparently to address teachers or administrators, and "us" apparently refers to students. Recall that earlier in the essay, "you" is used to address students. Correcting the pronoun inconsistencies in this essay would improve the logical flow of ideas and allow the reader to follow the writer's meaning more easily.

Sample Essay Response 2

(1) The requirements for high school graduation imposed by our state were originally intended to serve some valuable purposes. They were meant to prepare students for college or successful job performance and ensure that all students receive a well-rounded education. While these are indeed worthwhile goals, I believe that the negative aspects of the state requirements currently outweigh the benefits. Students would receive a better education, more suited to their interests and personal goals, if the state requirements were restructured to be less demanding.

(2) How would changing the state requirements help students? First, the change would give students who are interested in the arts more time to take courses that foster their artistic development. With the current requirements, many students can't take all the electives they'd like to, as my experience shows. I hope to have a career as an illustrator, so some aspects of science are important to me, especially perspective and anatomy. Thus, some topics in my biology and physics classes have been helpful to me as an artist, but I'm struggling through my chemistry course this year. I can't find a way to relate it to my passion for drawing. I could spend my school time more productively by doing a fine arts independent study instead of slogging through chemistry to fulfill a state requirement.

(3) Minimizing state requirements would help students by allowing more time for internships and off-campus experiences. Not every student in my school plans to go to college immediately, and some haven't yet chosen a career field. High school is a good time to explore and actually see what people in different professions do. If state graduation requirements were reduced, then schools could offer courses in career exploration. Giving students real-life experience would help them more than academic work in fields they don't care a lot about.

(4) Finally, reducing state requirements would let each student have more input into designing his or her schedule. Experts frequently state that students learn best when they have a personal motivation to learn. Letting the individual, instead of a state law, determine the content of a student's education will help students learn more in the long run. It's true that minimizing the state requirements would result in some students having an academic program that's not as well-rounded as others. I think, however, that the benefit of letting students study what they care most about would outweigh the drawbacks.

(5) Curtailing state graduation requirements—not eliminating them entirely but reducing the number of years that a student must take a course in each field—can have several positive effects. First, students would have more time to take courses that interest them, whether as electives or independent studies. Next, students would have more time to explore various career fields in high school, leading them to make more appropriate decisions about their futures. Ultimately, however, the best reason to reduce mandated course requirements is to allow each individual to have a say in what he or she will study. People learn best when they're excited about what they're learning.

Comments on Essay Response 2

This essay is well organized and makes good use of specific examples, evidence, and connecting words to develop the topic. Paragraph 2 focuses on an example from the writer's personal experience. Paragraph 3 describes a benefit of the writer's position: Reduced academic requirements would allow more time for learning outside the classroom. Paragraph 4 describes another specific benefit of the writer's position: Reducing the state requirements would allow the individual student to follow a more tailored academic program that is aligned with his or her own interests. This paragraph also acknowledges an objection to the writer's position, specifically, that reducing state requirements would result in some students having less well-rounded academic programs. The essay presents this drawback as secondary to the benefit of individual choice. Paragraph 5 restates the position and briefly summarizes the evidence.

Here are some points to notice about how the writer develops her ideas in this essay. First, she takes a position that is not either/or (either maintain the state requirements or eliminate them). Instead, she suggests a middle ground, expressed most clearly in paragraph 5 with the words "not eliminating them entirely but reducing the number of years that a student must take a course in each field." No specific replacement is offered for the list of current requirements that is included in the prompt. This is acceptable because the specific content of new requirements is not as important to the writer's argument as the benefit of individual choice. The writer centers her essay around the value of students being able to spend time studying in areas they care about. Each piece of evidence is clearly and explicitly tied to the writer's stated position, and connecting words and phrases are appropriately used throughout to show the relationships between ideas. (Connecting words used here include "originally," "currently," "because," "instead," "if…then," and "result in.")

● THE FINAL ACT: PRACTICE QUIZ

Your school currently allows students to be in any part of the school building during their free periods. Administrators, concerned about the school's declining academic performance over the past several years, are considering instituting mandatory study halls for all students during free periods. Some people believe this change will make students take their work more seriously. Others believe that it will hinder academic performance by forcing students to concentrate all day without any breaks. In your opinion, should the school institute mandatory study halls?

In your essay, take a position on this question. You may write about either one of the two points of view given, or you may present a different point of view on this question. Use specific reasons and examples to support your position.

● THE FINAL ACT: SAMPLE ESSAY RESPONSE

(1) The purpose of school is to prepare students for their futures. For those of us who will be going to college, much of this preparation is necessarily academic. Therefore, it's important for the school to promote a culture of academic excellence. With this in mind, I support the administration's proposal to make study halls mandatory during students' free periods.

(2) One reason mandatory study halls are valuable is that they give students greater access to teachers. For example, if I needed some extra help in math and my study hall were monitored by a math teacher, I would be able to approach the teacher and ask for some guidance about how to tackle a challenging homework problem. If study halls weren't mandatory, I might spend my free period socializing in the cafeteria. In that case, I wouldn't even know that I needed help with a problem until after the end of the school day, when it would be too late to ask a teacher for help. If

I had access to a helpful teacher during a mandatory study hall, I would get more out of that particular homework assignment.

(3) While my first reason for supporting mandatory study halls is a practical one, my second reason is more psychological. Mandatory study hall sends the school community—students, teachers, and even parents—a message that a high value is placed on academics. When this message is clearly conveyed to students, it may motivate students who don't necessarily find that academic work comes naturally to them. Mandatory study halls remind all students that attending to academic work is the primary reason for being in school. When the administration allows students to socialize during free periods, it sends a destructive message that they don't really expect every student to take academic work seriously.

(4) Those who disagree with me will argue that the lives of most high school students are filled with stress from academic pressures, family problems, and social relationships. It is true that everyone needs a chance to relax, and being allowed go to the gym to play basketball or even nap on the gym mats could be a good thing. However, if a student really needs a break, she could find a way to get it even in a mandatory study hall. A student who is truly exhausted could put his head on the table and rest. Someone who needs a break from concentrating could choose to read a magazine or sketch cartoons in a notebook once in a while in study hall. However, usually students should be doing schoolwork during school time, and mandatory study halls hold up the expectation that students will use their free periods to enhance their academic goals.

(5) Therefore, for reasons both practical and philosophical, I believe that our school's administration should institute mandatory study halls. Implementing this policy would benefit students in several ways. Most importantly, the mandatory study hall policy would give students the clear message that they should give a high priority to their academic work.

Comments

This essay is well organized. The first paragraph briefly sets the stage for the discussion, elaborating on the prompt by asserting that school should prepare students for the future and that doing so involves promoting academic excellence. The position—favoring mandatory study halls—is clearly stated. Paragraphs 2 and 3 present examples and evidence. Paragraph 4 addresses an objection in detail and uses the discussion of the objection to emphasize the point that academic endeavors should receive priority in school. Paragraph 5 restates the position and briefly summarizes the reasoning presented in the essay.

Consider paragraph 2 in terms of idea development. Whereas sometimes a writer might present an example drawn from actual personal experience, in this case, the writer draws on imagined personal experience. To do this, the writer assumes that his suggestion—making study halls mandatory—has been implemented and describes a benefit that would follow. This description of imagined experience works well to develop the topic of the paragraph because it shows the writer has considered the implications of his argument.

Note that paragraph 4 focuses on addressing a possible objection. While this writer spends a lot of time addressing the objection, it's not necessary for you to devote a whole paragraph to objections. Even a brief mention that you've considered the views of those who might disagree with you lends depth to your argument. Note also that, while this essay doesn't make excessive use of transition words and phrases, the writer uses them appropriately to show logical relationships between ideas.

That's not all, folks.

Don't forget to access more practice online for *Spotlight ACT*!

kaptest.com/booksonline